IMPACT OF TERRORISM ON JAMMU AND KASHMIR TOURISM

Dedicated to All Security Forces Personnel Who Sacrificed Their Life for Preserving Peace and Prosperity in Jammu and Kashmir

IMPACT OF TERRORISM ON JAMMU AND KASHMIR TOURISM

Dr. R. Soundararajan
Major P. Rajan

Publications

KALPAZ PUBLICATIONS
DELHI-110 052

Impact of Terrorism on Jammu and Kashmir Tourism

Rs. 750

ISBN : 81-7835-474-8

Published in 2006 in India by
Kalpaz Publications,
C-30, Satyawati Nagar,
Delhi-110 052
E-mail : kalpaz@hotmail.com

Lasertype Setting by: Tact Computer Graphics, Delhi
Printed at: Salasar Imaging System, Delhi

Contents

	Preface	7
	Acknowledgement	11
1.	**Introduction**	**13**
2.	**Historical Survey of Jammu and Kashmir**	**23**
3.	**Scenario of Global Terrorism**	**50**
4.	**Terrorism in Jammu and Kashmir**	**76**
5.	**Tourism in Jammu and Kashmir**	**112**
6.	**Impact of Terrorism on J&K Tourism**	**163**
7.	**Review of Current Situation in Jammu and Kashmir**	**242**
8.	**Conclusion**	**306**

Appendices

1.	*Geneological Tree of Dogra Rulers in Jammu and Kashmir*	310
2.	*Rice Varieties Cultivated in J&K*	311
3.	*Monuments in Srinagar and Its Vicinity*	312
4.	*Route Chart: Amarnath Ji Yatra*	315
5.	*Srinagar-Leh Route Chart*	316
6.	*Trekking Routes in Ladakh Region*	317
7.	*Mountaineering in Ladakh Region*	322
8.	*Organisational Chart of Tourism*	324
9.	*J&K Feel Good Factor: Tourism*	325
10.	*Road to Peace between India and Pakistan*	326
11.	*PM's Kashmir Visit*	328
12.	*Questionnaire*	330

Annexures–Map

1.	*Sketch of J & K Showing Actual Positions*	337
2.	*Map of J & K Showing International Boundary*	338

3. *State of J & K with Communal Groupings* 339
4. *State of J & K Sourced by JKLF* 340
5. *Tourist Places in Jammu* 341
6. *Tourist Plalces in Kashmir* 342
7. *Major Infiltration Routes* 343

Tables

1.1. *Area and Population: J & K State* 344
1.2. *Yatries Visiting Amarnathji and Vaishno Deviji Holy Caves* 346
1.3. *Tourists Visiting Kashmir Valley* 348
1.4. *Country-wise Number of Foreign Tourists Visiting Kashmir Valley* 349
1.5. *No. of Tourists Visiting to Ladakh Region* 350

Graphs

1. *Terrorist Incidents in J & K 1988-2004* 351
2. *Militants Killed in J & K 1990-2004* 352
3. *Attack on Security Forces* 353
4. *Indian Forces Killed* 354
5. *Attack on Civilians* 355
6. *Civilians Killed* 356
7. *Terrorists Killed* 357
8. *Surge in Infiltration–2004* 358
9. *Yatries Visiting Vaishno Deviji Holy Cave* 360
10. *Tourists Visiting Kashmir Valley: Indian Tourists* 361
11. *Tourists Visiting Kashmir Valley: Non-Indian Tourists* 362
12. *Yatries Visiting Amar Nathji Holy Cave* 363
13. *Tourist Inflow to Ladakh Region* 364

Bibliography 365
Index 371

Preface

International terrorism has emerged as a global threat jeopardizing countries across the continents. This has assumed an alarming proportion breeding gravious situations, where terrorism is sponsored by National States across frontiers against the adjacent neighbours in quest for unjustifiable territorial aggrandizement. The pestering peril of terrorism is no longer confined to a particular country or a region, but transcends international boundaries threatening even the so-called super-powers too. Terrorists use ultramodern, sophisticated gadgets to organize their subversive inhuman atrocities. The terrorist outfits have access to enormous funds from disgruntled quarters, including money raised through the so-called charitable organizations. They enjoy foreign sanctuaries and are answerable to none. They violate the international code of human rights, and humanitarian law, with impunity. The involvement of Pakistan in fomenting insurgency and encouraging terrorism in the Border States of India, especially Jammu and Kashmir, has been well documented, accepted and endorsed by all impartial observers. Thus, Pakistan sponsored terrorism in Jammu and Kashmir is a lethal instrument of destruction of sovereignty, unity and integrity of our country especially the State of Jammu and Kashmir.

While *Terrorism* fuels insurgent animosity and militancy escalates confrontation and spells catastrophe, *Tourism*, on the other hand, promotes amity and understanding, friendship and an universal sense of fraternity. While terrorism is an adverse instrument of destruction, tourism has been instrumental to promote international peace and order. Tourism brings people together to cherish the beauty of the nature, explore the cultural legacy of others and share the experiences of every society.

Internationally, tourism occupies a predominant place in the economics of several world countries. It has today achieved the status of an industry. Governments across the world are competing with each other in marketing *"tourism and travel"* concept, its history, culture, heritage, the green landscape, sunshine, snow and sands to people all over the world. As the world's largest industry, it is forecasted to grow at 4 percent annually till 2010. At present it generates 4,494 billion dollars in economic activity and contributes about 11.6% to the global GDP and employs about 9.4% of the global labour force. There has been phenomenal growth in tourism all over the world. International tourist arrival reached 699 million in 2000, almost 50 million more than in 1999.

What is heartening about this industry is the fact despite innumerous conflicts and confrontations all over the world, in last fifty years, it has never seen a single year of decline. However, in India, the industry has largely remained dormant, performing far below its rich potential, despite the fact that India has a unique and unparallel heritage with a vibrant kaleidoscopic culture and a wide gamut of tourism attractions. Tourism economy in India accounts for 5.6 % of the GDP, supports 5.8% of the total employment in the country and generates 10.8% of the total exports from the country. With just 2.4 million arrivals, India accounts for only 0.4% of the world tourists arrivals in the year 2000. In spite of the fact, which India can boost of some of the most exquisite and exotic sites and locales and of the best and rare monuments, it ranks only a poor 43rd position in the world. Smaller countries like France, Spain, Hungary and Poland are way ahead of India. Even a tiny small island like Sri Lanka despite ethnic strife torn her asunder for the last twelve years, it is ahead of India with about 4 million international arrivals.

Of late welcome signs are visible in the tourism and travel industry in India. The tourist inflow from the UK – one of its biggest markets – has gone up by 35 percent. Goa, the hottest destination is sold out. The surge in demand has pushed to ramp up chartered flights into the Seaside State from 350 flights last season to over 550 in 2005. The corresponding rise in the number of passengers will be around 34,000. Hotels across the country are nearly full. The Union Tourism Ministry forecasts that the country will have over two million visitors between November 2004 and March 2005, a quantum jump of 30 percent from an year ago. This year's upsurge follows a growth rate of over 11 percent from 2.7 million tourists in 2002-2003 to around three million in 2003-2004. Even outbound travel is expected to grow by about 25 percent to touch 5.5 million tourists against four million in 2003-2004, driven by rising incomes, changing lifestyle and aggressive marketing by various travel operators.

With an upbeat trend, while the tourism has been flourishing in the entire world despite ethnic, religious, and political disturbances besides natural calamities like tsunami in the recent past, the quest for travelling has been increasing among the masses. One of the most celebrated and much sought after tourism destination in our country is the State of Jammu and Kashmir. Recent events and developments have once again generated curiosity and interest in the issue of terrorism and tourism. Jammu and Kashmir lacking in other natural resources is heavily dependent upon tourism for its development, which of late, contributing considerable revenue to the Government.

The demand for independence in the Valley is not going to vanish overnight, but it should not discourage the policy makers from working out a constitutional formula, which would meet the day-to-day requirements of travelling and exploring the nature's bounty of the Kashmir Valley by domestic as well as international travellers.

The experience of army service during the thick of militancy in Jammu and Kashmir by Major P. Rajan in varying times coupled with the effervescent interest of Professor Dr. R Soundararajan on Jammu and Kashmir Tourism, who is the Academic Coordinator of Tourism Department, Directorate of Distance Education, Madurai Kamaraj University, Madurai, made this work an interesting literature. Since most people are dependent on tourism industry in Jammu and Kashmir, the adverse impact due to militancy in the State made them breadless during those times of militant threats. The present work is only a fair beginning by the authors to get into the empirical details, which are complex and complicated, as available to them, to probe into the ticklish question of Tourism and Terrorism and unravel the truth behind the decades long issues. Fortunately, the tourism industry has picked up its pace and tourists again started flocking the State which made this work more interesting with a smile of positive signs all around. Within the limitations of time and resources, all out effort has been made to analyses the problem in detail, with statistical data drawn from authentic sources, organizations and also thro questionnaires to various people associated with tourism and terrorism in the State of Jammu and Kashmir.

In as much Terrorism and Its Impact on Tourism in Jammu and Kashmir has been concerned, this work is a humble beginning and as a pioneering effort, it might suffer certain shortcomings, due to obvious reasons. However, an earnest effort has been made to present the theme with intellectual honesty and objectivity. We would like to put on record our gratitude and thankfulness to all those for their over-whelming response by providing us all details we sought after, in making this work possible. Finally, we express our heartfelt gratitude to KALPAZ PUBLICATIONS, DELHI, for their yeomen service in promoting the cause of Tourism in India by publishing well-written Tourism Literatures. For, KALPAZ PUBLICATIONS always stand as a synonym to international quality and standard.

Jai Hind

Dr. R. Soundararajan **Major P. Rajan**

Acknowledgements

We express our deep sense of gratitude, obligation and sincere thanks to **Dr Gurudev Singh, Scientist (Information), Dhanvantri Library, University of Jammu, Jammu (J&K)** for his immediate and timely help of providing material and continuous inspiration on all matters relating to this work.

We also express our deep and sincere thanks to **Mr Mohd Shoaib, Deputy Librarian and Mr Joginder Singh, Assistant Librarian (Documentation Section), Dhanvantri Library, University of Jammu, Jammu (J&K) and their worthy staff** who were very positive with us throughout the collection of data/study materials from the Library for successful completion of this work.

We also wish to acknowledge with deep appreciation the support extended to us by all the educational staff of **Basantar Library, C/O 168 Infantry Brigade** who responded to our requirements even at late hours. We are also thankful to all those who responded to the questionnaires and spared their valuable time for giving their opinion.

Mere verbal expression of thankfulness to the sincere service and '**legacy of Indian Army**' is not sufficient. For, their selfless effort in curbing Terrorism in Jammu and Kashmir has been history by itself. We thank whole-heartedly everyone in the Indian Army Service and we wish every citizen to render their support to their legitimate cause of eradicating Terrorism not only in Kashmir, but our entire Motherland too.

Jai Hind

Dr. R. Soundararajan **Major P. Rajan**

1
Introduction

As fewer overseas travellers packed their bags following 9/11 US attacks, millions of tourism industry workers worldwide were losing their jobs. Before September 11th, travel and tourism was the world's largest industry, accounting for one in every twelve jobs. When the massive $3.6 trillion industry almost ground to a halt after the terrorist attacks, the ripple aftermath effects extended well beyond the United States, exposing the vulnerability of countries too dependent on international tourism. The aftermath of September 11 has shown us how important travel and tourism are to the global economy and also how over-dependence on tourism can devastate lives and derail economies. Now, more than ever, it is time to put issues of sustainability at the top of the global tourism agenda.

Countries can redirect their tourism activities to make them more socially beneficial and environmentally sound. Wide ranges of positive efforts are underway to minimize tourism's negative impacts and to boost its benefits for local communities and the environment. Revenues from tourism have been especially important in the developing world, more so in India, which stands to suffer severe economic losses from the slowdown. Tourism is the only economic sector where developing countries consistently run a trade surplus. It is especially significant in poorer countries that have few other options; for the world's 49 so-called least developed countries, tourism is the second largest source of foreign exchange after oil.

Business communities in the developing world were particularly worried about the sharp drop and decline in bookings after 9/11. India and Nepal, which are close to Afghanistan, too felt the effects of a drop in demand. International tourism was expected to grow by only 1.5 to 2 percent in 2001, compared to the robust 7.4 percent rise in 2000. The adverse impact of 9/11 factor on the international tourism didn't continue too long as the organizations, such as Hotels, Tour Promoters etc, involved in promoting tourism adopted such conservation and booster measures and green practices that they were able recoup the revenue loss and falling occupancies in the succeeding years.

In India, terrorism continues to pose a serious threat in Jammu and Kashmir and the North East. Left extremism continues to claim its own victims in Bihar and Andhra Pradesh. In 1989, a popular movement demanding independence from India and backed by various militant groups badly disrupted life in the Kashmir Valley. Frequent curfews and strict security measures helped to ensure that hardly any tourists came to Srinagar and the famous houseboats on its lakes found deserted since 1990.

The economy of the Kashmir Valley flourished from the 1950s onwards, with very large number of tourists, both Indians and foreigners, visiting Kashmir almost throughout the year. However, the number of tourists started dwindling from mid 1980s and the tourism almost came to naught from 1989-90 onwards due to the insurgency in the State. Sadly, since about 70 percent of the population of the Kashmir Valley was dependent on the tourism industry, they suddenly found themselves without an occupation and no means of livelihood.

Jammu and Kashmir is again on the tourism map as has been revealed from the influx of the tourists in the State in the recent past. The recent trend confirms that travel, no more is limited to a few people, and rather has turned into a mass movement. It has become a typical expression of the present day society. Every successive year, more and more globe-trotters are setting out to discover the unknown, to pursue recreation, pleasure and fun or to just seek a change in environment.

Importance of the Study

(a) The study would be a model for similar researches in the field of tourism.

(b) It will help tourism planners and policy makers in framing plans and policies in view of the current situation.

Objectives: The present study aims at:

(a) To carryout a historical survey of the State of J&K.

(b) To analyse the worst of global terrorism.

(c) To find the background facts and present status about the terrorism in J&K.

(d) To make an updated and comprehensive survey about tourism in J&K.

(e) To review the pattern of tourist traffic in India and J&K State in detail.

(f) To study the terrorist attacks on J&K.

(g) To examine the impact of terrorism on J&K tourism.

(h) To understand the latest developments in the State of Jammu and Kashmir with regard to tourism.

Hypothesis

Terrorism has to some extent a negative impact on the tourist influx in Jammu and Kashmir State.

Limitations of the Study

Survey was conducted in the year 2004 & 2005.

Study is based on the information supplied by the respondents/supplemented by literatures.

Limitations of the statistical tools.

The purification of data is very much there.

Internet data consulted wherever necessary.

Sources of Information

The whole study has been devised as under:

1. **Primary Data**. A questionnaire targeting fifty people from each of the following segments of population who are associated with J&K tourism was developed and used for the present study:

   (a) Queries to the Tourist.

b) Queries to the Layman residing in/around the Tourist Spots.

c) Queries to the Security Forces/Government Officials.

2. **Secondary Data.** The rest of the data was collected from various Published Books, Magazines, Brochures, Internet and Newspapers etc.

Methodology Adopted

The present investigation is a study of "**Impact of terrorism on J&K tourism – a case study analysis**". The parameters required had led the investigator to use both Primary and Secondary data. Both historical and analytical approach has been considered to and the theme presented accordingly.

Statistical Techniques Used for Data Analysis

The statistical techniques employed for the analysis of the data in the present study are:

(a) Percentage Method.

(b) Graphical Representation of Data.

(c) Pie-charts

(d) Analysis Tables

Review of Literature

Terrorism in Jammu and Kashmir; Tourism in India in general and in Jammu and Kashmir in particular, are different subjects of much concern to the Professionals, Scientists, Organisations and to the Common people in the recent years. Though the subjects in general are not a new concept, the point of contention is that terrorism and tourism in J&K has taken a new twist and turn in the recent past. Astonishingly, there has been no recent study combining and comparing the ups and downs of both the issues of Terrorism and Tourism in Jammu and Kashmir. Terrorism in Jammu and Kashmir let loose in 1988 and ever since then the tourism in the state has been adversely affected due to the volatile situation in the Kashmir Valley and later in the following years the disturbance spread throughout the whole region of the State. An effort has been made in this study to anlayse the **Impact of Terrorism on Jammu and Kashmir Tourism** with the help of data collected from J&K Tourism Department, CID Headquarters, Jammu and also from various published literatures besides specially designed questionnaire.

To have a thorough understanding about the present status of terrorism and tourism in Jammu and Kashmir, it is necessary to study various aspects of the subject under consideration. Hence, an attempt has been made to review the existing literature pertaining to this study in the work on various aspects such as **Historical Survey of Jammu and Kashmir, Scenario of Global Terrorism, Terrorism in Jammu and Kashmir, Tourism in J&K** and **the Impact of Terrorism on J&K Tourism**.

For successful completion of this book, some of the published books/literatures have been exclusively consulted and they have been incorporated in the footnotes/endnotes wherever applicable. It would be seen that these evidences are the base and foundation of this work, which furnish authenticated details of information and data for reference for future studies.

The book entitled Kashmir Valley and its Culture, written by SR Bakshi[1] presents the brief historical survey of Jammu and Kashmir with details of political development in the State from pre-independence days, around Indian independence, Kashmir's accession to India and the successive Indo-Pak war of 1947-48, the cease-fire and the present status of Jammu and Kashmir; arts and crafts and society and religion of the State. Kashmir: Tourism, Monuments and Folklore[2] by the same author and publisher elaborate the cultural heritage of the state and the folklore.

Kashmir Through the Ages: Society, Economy, Culture, History, Architecture and Tourism of Kashmir, two different books, edited by Suresh K Sharma and Usha Sharma[3] are instrumental in depicting the architectural monuments, folk and lore of Kashmir.

The book entitled Cultural Heritage of Jammu, Kashmir and Ladakh, Three Volumes by Nagendra Kumar Singh[4] is an

Singh[4] is an encyclopedic attempt to portray the cultural heritage of the State of Jammu and Kashmir.

Regarding aspects relating to Global Terrorism, the book entitled The Worst of Global Terrorism, by LR Reddy[5] brings out the details of religious extremism and fanaticism, an analysis of global terrorism and the effect of 9/11. This book has been a very valuable contribution to this study. Besides, International Terrorism, a book by Perera Amrith Rohan[6] and another book entitled 9/11, by Noam Chomsky[7] served as useful sources of description of the topic.

In the fact finding chapter about the Terrorism in Jammu and Kashmir, the cause of terrorism in the state and its impact on socio- economic aspects of the people and the measures to curb terrorism in the state are the aspects that have been considered to have the review of literature.

Certain books written by the retired and serving Generals who are supposed to be the exponents on the subject Terrorism by virtue of handling it by themselves during their service career. The books entitled Operation Parakram: The War Unfinished; by Lt Gen (Retd) VK Sood and Pravin Sawhney[8], Threat from Within, India's Internal Security Environment; by Lt Gen (Retd) VK Nayar[9], Conquering Kashmir – A Pakistani Obsession; by Lt Gen KK Nanda[10], and Kashmir Diary : Psychology of Militancy; by Maj Gen Arjun Ray[11], are certain rare class of works known for their graphic presentation of an untold account of the most sensitive issues involving India's security concerns and her brilliant plans of retaliation. These works as told by her proudest sons' of the soil, in the service of the army, are contemporary documentation of facts about alien intrusion, obsession and violation of international regulations. A wide variety of the changing profile of the militants, Pakistan's apprehension about the changing situation, details of prominent militant groups, the concept of Jehad in J&K and the status of current militancy are some of the aspects dealt with in the present study.

Contemporary Data

In addition to them, the information from the National and State Dailies and various periodical publications have also been consulted and reviewed for updated information on the subject.

In continuation to the facts about the terrorism in the State, it is pertinent to study and review the literature on the tourism potential and avenues of the State to understand the relevance of the study of Impact of Terrorism on J&K Tourism. The literatures depicting the region-wise places of tourism attraction in J&K with geographical maps etc, and with special emphasis on religious shrines in the State, adventure tourism etc has been specifically considered for reference and review. These details have been compiled from various government publications such as J&K Tourism Department Brochures. It is like a comprehensive tourist guidebook of J&K State duly updated as a ready reference tool for the public concerned as well as the researchers, writers and expertise etc.

Here the book entitled India, a Survival Kit, by Geoff Crowther[12], has been a pace setter and guide to prepare the comprehensive paper with detailed information about Jammu and Kashmir. Among the J&K Tourism Department Publications, Yatra - a Guide to the Holy Pilgrimage of Shri Mata Vaishno Devi Ji[13], has been eye opener and elaborative information source. It is a must read and referral book for all.

The analysis of Impact of Terrorism on J&K Tourism incorporates the issues of the present status of J&K militancy, study of terrorist incidents, current case study of militancy in tourist spots and present status of tourism in the State. The entire analysis is based on the contribution of the government reports, Mass Media, various regular publications such as dailies, magazines, journals and other published works.

The News papers namely, The Hindu, The Times of India, The Hindustan Times, The Indian Express (The Himalayan Express), The Kashmir Times, The State Times, Daily Excelsior and The Tribune and the Magazines namely, India Today, Frontline, The Week and J&K Reporter have been exclusively consulted to Review the Current Situation in Jammu and Kashmir relevant to the topic. The role of the Mass Media in bringing out various facts and figures about the day to day incidents of the terrorist activities and reporting of the inner pulse of the public especially tourists immediately after such incidents on various incident related occasions have carefully been analysed and incorporated in the study. The dare devil Mass Media is the real and prominent contributor to the present study and the information provided in their respective field of coverage is salute-worthy.

The review of literature for the current study finds an accurate source of information from the Computerised Information Output System being maintained by the Documentation Section, Dhanvantri Library of University of Jammu. The information and incidents reported in various dailies on various subjects are systematically fed in the computer system maintained by the **Dhanvantri Library of University of Jammu.**

Chapter Headings

Present study **'Impact of Terrorism on J&K Tourism – a Case Study Analysis'** has been divided into six chapters:

Chapter I – Historical Survey of Jammu and Kashmir.

Chapter II – Scenario of Global Terrorism.

Chapter III – Terrorism in Jammu and Kashmir.

Chapter IV – Tourism in Jammu and Kashmir.

Chatper V – Impact of Terrorism on J&K Tourism.

Chapter VI – Review of Current Situation in J&K.

Summary of Chapters

Chapter One provides an **Introduction about the Jammu and Kashmir State** covering the Historical Survey, Geo- Politics of the State with three distinct regions viz. Kashmir Region, Ladakh Region and Jammu Region and Socio-Cultural Aspects of the State with special emphasis on the Cultural Heritage of J&K, the Architectural Monuments of Kashmir and the Folklore.

Chapter Two entitled the **Scenario of Global Terrorism** discusses the Worst of Global Terrorism; the 9/11 factors in detail with a review of Impact of Global Terrorism on the World Economy and the Measures taken by the international community to Eliminate International Terrorism with the contribution of India has also been presented.

Chapter Three, with the caption the **Terrorism in Jammu and Kashmir**, attempts to unravel the Cause of Terrorism in the State and its Impact on Socio- Economic aspects of the people. Also the measures to Curb Terrorism in the State have been discussed in detail.

Chapter Four is about **Tourism in Jammu and Kashmir**. It presents Region-wise Places of Tourism Attraction in J&K with Geographical Maps etc. Also Special Emphasis has been given about Religious Shrines in the State and Adventure Tourism etc. It serves like a Comprehensive Tourist Guide Book of J&K State duly Updated for any new visitor to the State.

Chapter Five entitled **Impact of Terrorism on J&K Tourism**, attempts to analyse the issues of the present Status of J&K Militancy, study the Terrorist Incidents, Case Study of Militancy in Tourist Spots and current position of Tourism in the State. Besides, the Case history of Issues pertaining to Tourism with data of Increase/ Decrease of Tourists, Role of State Government in Promoting Tourism, and its Overall Impact on J&K Tourism, plus finally Suggestions Towards a Better Future in J&K.

Chapter Six is an attempt to **Review of the Current Situation in the State of Jammu and Kashmir** relating to the Latest Development in Militancy, New Tactics to Fight Militancy, Impact of Indo-Pakistan Relationship on Kashmir, Contribution of Indian Army for J&K Development, Recent Social Developments in J&K and Current Developments in Tourism Sector.

To conclude, despite unforeseen hindrances and a lot of limitations of time and resources while working on this project, best of endeavour has been made to maintain a high degree of quality and standard. It will be appreciated, if this hard work and humble attempt is of any use to any one undertaking further research in the area.

Notes and References

1. Sarup & Sons, New Delhi, 1997.
2. *Ibid.*
3. Deep & Deep Publications, Jammu, 1996.
4. Jay Kay Book House, Jammu, 1997.
5. APH Publishing Corporation, New Delhi, 2002.
6. Vikas Publishing House Pvt Ltd, New Delhi, 1997.
7. Natraj Publishers, Dehradun, 2002.
8. SAGE Publications, New Delhi/London, 2003.
9. Lancer Publishers, New Delhi, 1992.
10. Lancers Books, New Delhi, 1996.
11. Manas Publications, New Delhi, 1997.
12. Lonely Planet Publications, Australia, 1987.
13. Shri Mata Vaishno Devi Shrine Board, Govt. of J&K, October 2003.

2

Historical Survey of Jammu and Kashmir

Introduction

Jammu and Kashmir State has an area of 84,000 square miles. Western Pakistan adjoins it on the west, south and south-east except for a small part of the boundary which Kashmir shares with the Gurdaspur district of the Punjab State of the Indian Dominion. The approach from the Indian Dominion to Kashmir is across this part of the border.

For administrative purposes, the State is divided into three Provinces- the Frontiers Province (districts of Ladakh and Gilgit), Kashmir Province (districts of Anantnag, Baramulla and Muzaffarabad) and Jammu Province (districts of Mirpur, Reasi, Jammu, Udhampur and Kathua). Besides these, there is the Poonch Unit which is a jagir of the Maharaja.

The State was transferred in 1846[1] by the British to an ancestor of the then Maharaja(Maharaja Gulab Singh) in return for a sum of 7 ½ million rupees (Nanakshahi) on condition that he acknowledges the supremacy of the British Government and *"in token of such supremacy, present annually to the British Government one horse, twelve goats (six male and six female) and three pairs of Kashmir shawls"*[2]. The treaty by which the transfer was effected has been referred to by political leaders as "the sale deed of 1846"[3] and the memory of this deal has inspired much bitter comment. In 1830 Gulab Singh brought Ladakh under his power and by 1842 had extended his control over

Baltistan and Gilgit[4]. The geneological tree of Dogra Rulers in Jammu and Kashmir is given in **Appendix I.**

The population of the State according to the 1941 census is four millions of which 3.2 millions are Muslims. The Muslims are in a majority in every province of the State. Even in the Jammu Province where they have the smallest proportion, they constitute 60 per cent of the population. The Maharaja's family belongs to the Dogra clan of Hindu Rajputs who have on that account always enjoyed special privileges in the State.

Political Development in the State

Throughout the history of Dogra rule, the State has been notorious for its autocratically wayward methods of administration and its religious intolerance. Killing a cow was a cognizable offence punishable with seven years rigorous imprisonment. There was a special tax on the slaughter of goats and sheep, which were sacrificed by Muslims once a year as part of religious ritual. A Hindu on conversion to Islam forfeited all inherited property. Under such a medieval and intolerant mode of Government, Muslim places of worship and pilgrimage within the State were not likely to have been respected by the rulers[5]. Many of them were usurped by the State and had to be restored to Muslims as a result of the enquiry into the affairs of Kashmir held by the Glancy Commission in 1931[6]. The Arms Act in force in the State exempted Hindu Rajputs from obtaining license for guns and swords. Schools and colleges were located so as to be easily accessible to the Hindu population. The Hindus man about 80 per cent of the services. Almost unlimited jagirs were granted to the Maharaja's kinsmen whose sway as unbridled landlords extended to over a hundred thousand acres of land on which the Muslims peasantry subsist as serfs. Taxation was arbitrary and was collected by extortionist methods; and forced labour was common. The police had vast powers. Administration by and large was in the hands of Hindus who also dominated the court. The masses of Kashmir, largely Muslim, had for the best part of a century, lived in squalor, penury and terror. As a natural reaction, therefore, the rise of political consciousness in the country as a whole in the second quarter of the last century was reflected much more strongly and led to more serious and more frequent clashes between the people[7].

Organized political activity within the State had its beginnings in the 1920s and was Muslim in origin. In the early 1930s it crystallized itself into the Muslim Conference, an organization whose leaders and workers form the backbone of the Resistance movement to-day. In 1938, during the regime of Gopalaswami Ayyengar the Maharaja's Prime Minister, seven out of the twenty members of the working committee of the Muslim Conference with Sheikh Abdullah as their head, founded a separate organization known as the **National Conference**. The National Conference as its name implies, claimed to be an organization of non Muslims as well as Muslims. As this coincided with the avowed creed of the Indian National Congress, Sheikh Abdullah and his followers developed Congress leanings and his organization became the favorite of the Congress leaders, who as a corollary to such an alignment, frowned upon the Muslim Conference. Sheikh Abdullah was the Maharaja's nominee in the Kashmir Government and the hope of the Indian Government. With the forceful development of Muslim politics in India and the demand for Pakistan, the Muslim Conference, on the other hand, developed powerful sympathies for the Muslim League and its ideology. Most of its leaders were either in prison or exile.

A study of the political upheavals in Kashmir since 1930 reveals the following facts[8] :-

(a) Both the Muslim Conference and the National Conference, despite their mutual rivalries, were anti-Government throughout and increasingly pressed for the transfer of power from the Maharaja to the people.

(b) In the repeated conflicts between the Maharaja and the people, the people's agitation took the usual forms like-political meetings, conferences, memorials, public demonstrations and the defiance of authority-and the Maharaja's Government adopted ruthless measures to suppress or disperse the popular movements by individual and wholesale arrest of political workers, ban on political meetings and processions, fines, floggings and shooting, confiscation of property and deportations.

(c) Although the National Conference claimed to be a non communal body, very few Hindus ever joined it or having joined, stayed in it for long. Since the Hindus are the ruling class in Kashmir and all popular movements tend to undermine their power, this was but natural. It is inherent in the situation, therefore, and inevitable that any major conflict within the State should, basically, take the form of Hindu versus Muslim. The only notable occasion when the law came down upon the Hindus was when about a hundred Kashmiri Pandits were arrested for opposing the recommendations of the Glancy Commission which sought to introduce a limited franchise in the State.

(d) Though not enamoured of either organization, the Maharaja's Government (and its advisers, who needless to say were practically always Hindus) when pressed to a choice leaned, for obvious reasons, to the National Conference. Thus when it was considered expedient in 1944 to appoint a Muslim from amongst the members of the State Assembly as a Minister, the choice fell on a National Conference nominee, although the next election confirmed the strength and popularity of the Muslim Conference.

Around Indian Independence

The approach of momentous constitutional changes in India quickened political activity in the State. In May 1946, Sheikh Abdullah launched the 'Quit Kashmir'[9] movement directed at the removal of the Maharaja. He was tried for treason and (in September 1946) sentenced to three years imprisonment[10]. In June 1946, the Muslims met at Srinagar and passed the "*Azad Kashmir*"[11] resolution demanding the establishment of a responsible Government and the summoning of a constituent assembly on the basis of adult franchise. In July 1946 a convention was called at Srinagar which passed the "*Direct Action*"[12] resolution calling upon the Muslims of the State to organize and prepare for a struggle. The annual session of the Muslim Conference to be held in October 1946 was banned. The working committee decided to defy the ban whereupon its prominent members were imprisoned. Elections to the State Assembly were held in January 1947[13]. The Muslims Conference captured fifteen out of the twenty one Muslim seats although its leaders were in jail. Widespread agitation against their continued imprisonment led to many clashes with the authorities who adopted drastic measures to suppress what was threatening to become a general rising. In July 1947, the General Council of the Muslim Conference declared in favour of accession to Pakistan.. The 'War Council' of the National Conference also met about the middle of August. Thirteen members attended, of whom eight voted for accession to Pakistan. A definite decision was however postponed pending consultation with Sheikh Abdullah who was then in jail. On the 15th August, *'Pakistan Day*[14]*'* was celebrated throughout the State. Pakistan flags were hoisted and resolutions were passed supporting the Muslim Conference stand on the accession issue.

There was also much political intrigue afoot. During 1946 and part of 1947, top ranking Congress leaders including Khan Abdul Ghaffar Khan, Dr Sinha, Chaman Lal, Asaf Ali, Acharya Kirpalani and Gandhi visited Kashmir and held consultations with Maharaja or his Government[15]. The RSS with its office at Jammu had been recruiting volunteers since 1942 and it was not long before the branches of this purposeful anti-Muslim organization were opened at Mirpur, Kotli, Samba, Udhampur and Kathua, i.e. at Hindu centers which were comparatively close to the Indian Union and could, therefore, maintain easy contact with it.

Kashmir's economy was inextricably linked with Pakistan: timber, which provided a third of the State's revenue, was marketed via Pakistan, as were most other produce and goods; all the food, fuel and power had to be imported, and all rail and all-weather road traffic was through Pakistan. The Pakistani leadership had geo-strategic considerations for integrating Kashmir into their country: their rivers originated in Kashmir; most west Pakistan cities were exposed to a potential military threat from a hostile Kashmir.

The Indian Independence Act of 17 July 1947 legally put forth the British decision to divide the British Indian Empire into two sovereign States – a Muslim majority Pakistan and a multi-religious India. It was a hastily made decision, reached by the British who were in a hurry to wind up their affairs in the Indian subcontinent. The Maharaja started toying with the idea of independence, despite wiser counsel by his Chief of Staff of the State Forces, Maj Gen Sir Henry Scott. His indecisiveness about what to do even frustrated Mahatma Gandhi; the Maharaja, rattled by Abdullah's growing support again, started negotiations with the Congress, while his Prime Minister did so with the Muslim League. Trouble brewed in July 1947, when a large inflow of Hindu and Muslim refugees, fleeing from communal violence in the plains, took place. Tension began to brew in Poonch principality, and Hari Singh took direct control, levying punitive taxes, and ordering Muslims to deposit their arms with the police. About, 60,000 Poonchis had served in the Indian Army during the Second World War, so Hari Singh had good reason[16]. But, the Muslims in his State force (above 80 percent) rebelled and the Poonch revolt began.

Kashmir's Accession to India and Indo Pak War 1947-48

Meanwhile, Independence came, and only three Princely States namely, Hyderabad, Junagadh and Kashmir, had not made arrangements with the new Dominions. The first two had Muslim rulers and predominantly Hindu populations, and neither was contiguous with Pakistan; while the matter was the opposite in Kashmir. Some people felt that India would take over the first two, while Pakistan would get Kashmir. Hari Singh would not make up his mind. He offered to sign a '*Stand still Agreement*[17]' with both Dominions, which Pakistan quickly accepted but India didn't respond. Jinnah, now the Governor General of Pakistan felt that Kashmir was slipping way. With the Poonch revolt gaining momentum, Pakistan ordered incursions by armed bands of tribals to fight against their brethren in Poonch.

Seeing that winter was approaching which would cut Kashmir off from India, Nehru suggested to his Deputy Prime

Minister Sardar Vallabhbhai Patel to take efforts to bring the Maharaja and the National Conference together so that there might be popular support against Pakistan. Sardar Patel got Hari Singh to release Sheikh Abdullah on 29 Sep 1947. Soon after Sheikh Abdullah went to Delhi for negotiations on Kashmir's future, news came that 5,000 of Pakistan's frontier tribesmen had invaded Kashmir[18]. The invasion roused the anger of Kashmiris. The tribals reached outskirts of Srinagar, committing atrocities along the way, most notably in Baramulla district[19]. The Maharaja had no option but to turn to India. He sent his Prime Minister, Mehar Chand Mahajan, to Delhi requesting Nehru for help, conveying his willingness to accede. Finally the Maharaja signed the **Instrument of Accession** on 26 October 1947 which was accepted by Governor General Mountbatten on 27 October 1947[20].

The Indian Army was rushed to Srinagar and pushed the invaders back till the declaration of UN ceasefire on 01 January 1949, though one third of Kashmir still remained to be liberated from the enemy[21]. The accession was legally, constitutionally and politically valid (also having the backing of the largest political party headed by Sheikh Abdullah). However, the Government of India expressed the following over the accession:-

(a) Firstly, a wish to make a reference to the people of the State to ascertain their wishes over the accession.

(b) Secondly, the issue of the invasion of the State was referred to the UN Security Council for a peaceful settlement.

(c) Thirdly, a war had to be waged to clear the State of invaders.

Cease-fire and Present Status of Kashmir

The Government wanted a plebiscite for not only was it sure of winning, but also it would help Hyderabad and Junagadh joining India. Pakistan, on the other hand, was afraid of losing the plebiscite, and when the Governors-General of the two countries met in November 1947, Jinnah even objected to a plebiscite held under UN auspices, calling such a thing "redundant and undesirable"[22]. The talks broke down, and India went to the UN Security Council. The UN Commission for India and Pakistan (UNCIP) resolved on 13 August 1948[23] that it would determine the status of J&K "in accordance with the will of the people" following an evacuation of Pakistani troops and nationals from the State. A phased withdrawal of Indian troops would follow Pakistan's total withdrawal. India accepted the resolution within a week; Pakistan evaded till 20 December 1948. A cease-fire was declared on 01 January 1949. The cease–fire line became the Line of Control (LOC) after the Indo-Pak war in 1971. The two countries never got around to the plebiscite and passage of time made it redundant.

India went ahead and drafted a Constitution which came into effect from 26 January 1950. Though the Constitutions of all States were embodied in the nation's Constitution, J&K was given time for its plebiscite; till its Constituent Assembly drew up the State's Constitution, Article 370 was incorporated in the Indian Constitution as "transnational and provisional". This provision limited the Power of Parliament to make laws for J&K; India controlled defence, foreign affairs and communications. In 1956, New Delhi amended the Constitution so that Kashmir became like any other State although Article 370 was retained[24]. In May 1957, J&K was put at par with other States in financial matters; the next year the All India Services were extended to Kashmir, as was the Election Commission of India[25].

Indo-Pak War 1965 and 1971

Following Indo-China war in 1962, a friendship pact came into existence between China and Pakistan. A convenient encounter at the Rann of Kutch, on the Gujrat border, a Sikh agitation in Punjab and language riots all over India encouraged the Pakistani decision to invade India at the beginning of August 1965. However, Pakistan was mistaken about several things. Firstly, the Kashmiris did not welcome them. It was they, in fact, who alerted the Indian Army units while the invasion was being mounted[26]. India then took Pakistan by surprise with a diversionary attack on the Punjab. The Indian Army was able to reach the outskirts of Lahore. On 23 September 1965, a cease-fire was accepted by both sides. At negotiations held in **Tashkent** under the auspices of the Soviet Union, the two countries agreed to withdraw to the pre-August positions, implying that the ceasefire line could be treated as a de facto international border as well[27].

Another Indo-Pak war broke out in 1971. By this time, the myth of a pan-Islamic nation in the subcontinent was exploded when a civil war erupted in Pakistan, leading to the formation of Bangladesh. A victorious Indian Prime Minister Indira Gandhi signed an accord with new Pakistani President Zulfiqar Ali Bhutto, at Shimla in 1972, stipulating that the two countries resolve their differences by peaceful means and through bilateral negotiations[28]. Sheikh Abdullah, jailed in 1953 was released in 1971 and rehabilitated in 1975. A six point accord/agreement was signed between him and Mrs Indira Gandhi which reaffirmed Kashmir's status as part of India, but conceded the continuation of Article 370. Sheikh Abdullah became the Chief Minister of the State. His popularity passed all tests in the 1977 elections; he remained Chief Minister for rest of his days. During this time, he proclaimed his son Dr Farooq Abdullah to be his successor. The sketch of Jammu and Kashmir with actual positions is given in **Annexure 1**.

Beginning of Militancy in Kashmir

Dr Farooq Abdullah's party won the Assembly elections of 1983, and he organized a conclave in Srinagar of leaders belonging to the opposition parties from the States around India. He fell out with the Centre, and, consequently, defections from his party led to his fall from power[29]. Instead of channelising this resentment, Dr Abdullah joined hands with Mrs Gandhi's son and successor, Rajiv Gandhi, and they together contested and won the 1987 elections in Kashmir, which the Muslim United Front(MUF), a conclave of major opposition parties in the State, somewhat exaggeratedly claimed were rigged. A consequence of this was that all the frustrated workers of the opposition parties, particularly the Muslim United Front, which had posted no real threat to the National Conference anyway, went underground. Political repression against them followed, and Pakistan found fertile ground for yet another attempt to fish in troubled waters.

Arms started pouring into the State in 1989[30]. Prominent political personalities were assassinated. In December 1989 the daughter of the Union Home Minister, Mufti Mohammed Sayeed, a Kashmiri, was kidnapped by the J&K Liberation Front(JKLF). Despite signals that the militants would have eventually released her, the then government caved in and acceded to their demands for the release of five of their associates. This led to an increase in kidnappings, not just in Kashmir, but all over India. Things went from bad to worse as Pakistan poured money, arms and mercenaries into the Valley. Every time it looked like that if somebody wanted to have a peaceful negotiation with the Government of India, the terrorists ordered that person dead. Terrorism have taken its toll on the people of Kashmir. The Government of India is anxious for means to restore peace. India is willing to admit its past mistakes and oversights. But Pakistan refuses to allow the people to come forward and negotiate their own destiny. The pro-Pakistan terrorists have openly announced that anyone who tries to settle things peacefully "will be dealt with". But drop by drop a trickle of a stream is beginning to flow.

The Kargil War[31]

Pakistan's military move into the Kargil sector exploited the element of surprise in warfare and proved to be a repetition of its earlier strategy against India. In the spring of 1999, as snow melted in the Kargil sector to the northeast of Srinagar, some 1000 or more infiltrators crossed the Line of Control from Pakistani-occupied Kashmir into the Indian Side. They established positions at heights above 14000 feet, overlooking the strategically vital road that connects Srinagar with Leh in Ladakh. Having acclimatized adequately, these intruders traversed the snow covered and glaciated ridges along the LoC and occupied certain dominating heights in Batalik, Kargil, Dras and Mushkoh Valley sectors, 5 to 6 kms inside the Indian territory. Although India and Pakistan had placed troops along their 1,875 mile border on high alert, India exercised restraint in not crossing the Line of Control, thus containing the fighting to the Kargil region within Indian Kashmir. **Operation Vijay** was the Indian Armed Forces retaliation to the Pakistani intruders. On 14 July 1999, India announced that Pakistani aggression and the intrusion into Kargil have been decisively turned back. More than 400 Indian soldiers had been killed; upwards of 700 infiltrators were dead. As India mourned its fallen heroes, tensions remained and militancy continued in the Kashmir valley.

Geo-Politics of Jammu and Kashmir

Introduction

The State of Jammu and Kashmir with an area of 222,236 square km[32] is a region of widely varying people and geography. In the south, Jammu is a transition zone from the Indian plains to the Himalayas. Precisely the rest of the state is Kashmir but in practice this title is reserved for the beautiful Vale of Kashmir, a large Himalayan valley in the north of the state. Here the people are predominantly Muslim and many ways look towards Pakistan and Central Asia. To the north- east is the remote Tibetan plateau region known as Ladakh. Only recently opened to foreign tourists, Ladakh is primarily Buddhist and Tibetan in its culture and a very clear contrast to the rest of the Kashmir, indeed to the rest of India. *Sandwiched* between the Kashmir and Ladakh regions is a long narrow valley known as Zanskar. This valley is even more isolated than Ladakh and has still been visited by comparatively few westerners, although this will change as the new jeep road into the valley is extended and improved. Jammu and Kashmir has always been a centre of conflict and bone of contention for independent India. The region is now divided approximately two- thirds to India, one-third to Pakistan, but both countries claim all of it. Furthermore, Kashmir's role as a sensitive border zone applies not only to Pakistan. In 1962 the Chinese invaded Ladakh, prompting India to rapidly reassess their position in this remote and isolated region.

Kashmir Region

Enshrined in towering mountain masses, the valley of Kashmir is one of the loveliest of lands. At 5,000 feet up the climate is delightful for the greater part of the year. Almost everything that grows in the temperate zone is found in profusion- peaches, nectarines, grapes, pears, apples, plums, strawberries and every kind of vegetables. In the spring the countryside is carpeted with irises: there is a welter of flowers through the summer and autumn. The lotus on the Dal lake in June are incredibly beautiful. The lake itself is a thing of beauty; the Mogul garden on its shores add to its charm; the glamour of an autumn sunset on its waters must be felt to be believed. Gulmarg, twenty-six miles away from Srinagar, is a succession of green meadows studded with flowers in the midst of pines and cedars. At 9,000 feet it is a delightful summer resort. The view from the ridge over the valley below to the great peak of Nanga Parbat eighty miles away is magnificent. No wonder that the valleys of Kashmir are beloved of the British in India. The valley of Kashmir is, however, but a small part of great State with its area of 80,000 square miles[33]. There are several provinces- Jammu, kistwar, Ladakh on the Tibetan border where the people are mostly Buddhist; outlying frontier regions like Gilgit, Baltistan, and semi-independent fiefs like Hunzanagar, Dardistan and Chilas on the Afghan borderland. Most of the country is a labyrinth of huge mountain ranges. The population of these remote regions is small. The bulk of the inhabitants are found in the provinces of Kashmir and Jammu at 60: 40 respectively. Eighty per cent of the population is Muslim.

Jammu Region

The Jammu provinces is almost entirely mountainous. It rises in a series of ranges from the foothills to the great Pir Panjal range, which separate it from Kashmir proper. There are over half a million Hindus, including Rajputs, and about fifty thousand Sikhs in Jammu[34]. The rest are Muslims. The Jammu people are known generally as Dogras whatever their origin. A considerable proportion of them have fighting qualities- Rajputs, Sikhs and Muslims. Beyond the northern mountain range in the Kashmir valley the people are utterly unwarlike, listless and cowardly to a degree. A thousand years of tyranny and oppression have sapped their virility. The "honour of Islam" has not given them self-respect: perhaps it is true, as sometimes asserted, that they are still Hindus at heart.

Rajouri and Poonch districts are located in the northwest of Jammu city comprising an area of 4304 Square Kms, of mostly hilly and mountainous terrain rising steadily from the plains of Akhnoor in the south to the 3000 ft ASL Outer Hills to between 11000 to 15000 ft high mountains in the north and the Pir Panjal Range[35]. The two important passes in this snowy tract are Darhali (13080 ft) and Budhal (14120 ft) over the Pir Panjal Range which have been traditionally used for crossing the range over to Kashmir Valley and vice-a-versa. The average heights of villages in this region is between 5000 to 6000 ft with cultivation taking place even at much higher levels. The region is well connected with road communications. It consist of 559 villages out of which over 75 per cent are Muslim populated and the rest mostly Hindus, including few Sikhs. The Muslim population is further divided into two major groups of Rajputs and Gujjars. The main economic activity is agrarian based coupled with government employment.

Ladakh Region

Ladakh, situated in the highlands of Himalayas is a district of Jammu and Kashmir and situated in the northern extremity of the State. Ladakh–the land of the *gumpas* and *lamas*, occupies a leading position among the Buddhists culture of the country. District Ladakh is bounded on the north by Karakoram ranges and on the east by Tibet. The districts of Baramulla, Srinagar, Anantnag and Doda of Jammu and Kashmir State are on the west, whereas southern part is flanked by the district of Lahaul-Spiti of Himachal Pradesh. The total area of the district is 95,876sq km[36]. The district is full with vast deserts, high plateau and rocky valleys, criss-crossed by high mountain ranges. The river Indus, cuts the district diagonally. It is inhabited by various population groups; and many socio-cultural and historical changes have taken place in the area. There is growth among the Ladakhi population due to ecological factors, as high altitude has effects on fertility. The map of J&K showing International Boundary and its various provinces are shown as **Annexure 2** and the Communal Groupings in the State are shown as **Annexure 3**. The area and population of the State as given in Census 2001 are tabled as **Table 1.1.**

Cultural Heritage

The culture of Kashmir sprang from Aryans and was influenced during the course of history by Jews, Greeks, Turks, Chinese, Muslims and what not. Writes Arthur Neve[37] "*Ancient India had nothing more worthily of its early civilization than the grand remains of Kashmir*". Says Kalhana[38] " *Kashmiris were called Shestrashilpira, i.e, architects*". Kashmir is a fusion of cultures and languages. The principal cultural division of the State are- (a) Dugar (b) Ladakh (c) Baltistan (d) Gilgit or the land of Dards (e) Mirpur -Poonch -Muzaffarabad (f) Valley of Kashmir, about thirteen languages and dialects are spoken in this area, chief being Dogri, Kashmiri, Pahari, Ladakhi and Dardi. The ancient script of Dogri was Takri and of Kashmiri Sharad. Kashmir shared fame as an important seat of learning and culture with Nalanda and Taxila. Kashmiri literature combines in itself Persian and Sanskrit traditions and Islamic and Hindu philosophies. A Sanskrit inscription on a tomb in the cemetery of Bah-ud- Din put up during the reign of Sultan Mohammad Shah in 1484[39] indicates that both Sanskrit and Persian were in use. A birch bark document in Sharda and Persian characters pertaining to Sheikh Makhdom Hamza, a Muslim saint of Kashmir, about 500 years old, reflects the Kashmiri's Catholicism of outlook.

Under the auspices of the State Academy of Arts and Culture, a Kashmir dictionary in Persian script was attempted claiming larger collection of words than *Grierson's*[40] which was based on the material collected by *Ishwar Kaul*[41] , a well known scholar. The first grammar of the Kashmiri language was published in 1886 by Rev T.R Wade. History of Kashmiri literature by *Abdul Azad* was compiled in three volumes. Translation of '**Nilamatpurana**'[42] by Dr. Ked Ghai is a valuable contribution. Jagan Nath Sheopuri's and Abdul Aziz's note book on **soofiana** music will carry forward this type of music which is an off-shoot of Indo-Iranian culture.

Mystics of Kashmir[43]

1. Grata Baba.
2. Sumbali Baba.
3. Madrasi Baba.
4. Mathra Devi.
5. Paltu Shah.
6. Akram Saib.
7. Lakhman Ji.
8. Nand Ram.
9. Gupa Joo.
10. Hari Ram.
11. Mirak Shah.
12. Nand Lal.
13. Lasa Saib.
14. Zaina Machi.

They are guarding the spiritual frontiers of Kashmir.

Village Life

Kashmiri villages are conspicuous in the landscape. There is usually a group of chenar trees, with light gray trunks, mottled with pale yellow, and massive curved limbs, with dense foliage forming dark green masses in summer and brilliant splashes of light red in the late autumn. Close by are two or three lofty poplars and lines of young saplings, bordering orchards of pear, apple and apricot, of market gardens enclosed by wattle fences. Mounds covered with large purple and white irises, brilliant and fragrant in the sunshine, mark the sites of the old village graveyards, and the hamlet itself shows as a collection of large high-pitched, straw-thatched gables, peeping out from among the mulberry trees. These homesteads embowered in trees are surrounded by thousand of acres of arable land, terraced squares and crescents of rice-field, irrigated from small channels. Rice ripens up to an altitude of about 7000 feet. It is the staple crop of Kashmir. There are at least sixty different varieties with distinct names; but there are two broad divisions viz., white and red. The former is considered greatly superior. The prominent variety of rice cultivated in Jammu and Kashmir[44] is given in **Appendix II.**

The Kashmiri is an absolute expert in rice cultivation and unless early frost steps in, continuous rain at harvest-time, or one of the disastrous inundation to which Kashmir is so liable, there is usually a splendid harvest. Throughout the valley there is very extensive irrigation. The water can be taken off at great heights from the tributary valleys, and there are also a large number of springs. The distribution is very wide and is said to be conducted on a system introduced by the Mughals[45].

Seasons of Cultivation

According to the Kashmiris there are six seasons in the year, each of two months. "*Wandh*", with a somewhat similar sound, corresponds to the English winter, or at least with the time from 15th November till 15th January. During this period and on till the end of March, the first ploughing for wheat and barley is done. Then rice, maize and the other autumn crops are thrashed; and when the snow falls towards the end of December the people weave woolen blankets, and attend to their sheep and cattle. "*Sont*" is the period from 15th March to 1st May. This is an extremely busy time. The fields have to be ploughed and manured for rice and is sown in nurseries, and the seedlings are planted out when they are nearly a foot high. Broadcast sowing gives better crops but entails considerably more labour in weeding. The wheat and barley harvest begins in the valley at the end of May, and during the whole summer the harvest goes on at the various altitudes. Linseed is a little later than wheat. From July to September the peasants are busy in the fields weeding the rice, maize and cotton. The last is a very pretty crop, with its large yellow flowers followed by snowy tufts. The real harvest of Kashmir comes on the September and October, called by the Kashmiris the season of "*Hard*". It is then that the rice and maize, millet, sesame, amaranth and other autumn crops are gathered in. And now the fruit trees are laden, and before long from all parts of the valley strings of ponies may be met, and lines of coolies carrying baskets of apples and pears and sacks of walnuts, most of which will fine their way to Baramulla and be exported from there by cart to the plains of India[46].

Kashmir is particularly rich in fruit trees. Many of these are indigenous and found wild in the forest. The people are quite clever at grafting. The stock is cut off rather low, and into the end three or four scions are wedged and supported by clay surrounded by birch bark. Ring budding is also successfully practiced. In addition to the ordinary fruit trees, currants, raspberries and gooseberries are found wild. Apricots are also common. The fruit has been all immensely improved by cultivation and the introduction of choice varieties. At the mouth of the Sind, there are some good vineyards producing delicious white and red dessert grapes. On the east side of the Dal Lake there are about 400 acres of wine grapes, and at the distillery, under skilled supervision, wines of the Barsac and Medoc type are produced. The vintage varies much from year to year. It is said that the soil is deficient in iron and phosphates, and that the frequent difficulty in obtaining perfectly ripe grapes affects both the quality and keeping powers of the wine. A large number of sheep are kept by peasants who live in the valley. The cows, which are numerous in the villages, are small, and they usually appear to be half starved. They seldom give more than six pints of milk a day[47].

As the autumn draws on in Kashmir the days remain bright and hot, but the cold at nights becomes increasingly intense. Early in September excellent snipe-shooting is to be obtained, and large number of ducks begin to fly over the valley. In the winter snow usually falls in the third week of December. After that, sometimes for six weeks, the whole country is snow- bound, clouds settle down upon the mountains and there is no sunshine. The cold then comes very great. Occasionally the Dal lake is frozen sufficiently to bear. There are occasions people skated from the distillery at the south end to beyond the Nassim Bagh, 3 miles to the north-west. It is not, however, very safe, as there are warm springs.

Small game is not nearly so common in Kashmir as might be expected. There are no hares nor wild rabbits in the valley.

On the hills the chikor partridge is common. It belongs to the genus of rock or sand partridge, and is found usually above the line of cultivation among the rocks. Covoys are often seen in the fields at harvest- time, and they are met with up to an altitude of 9000 feet. The monai pheasant is the most handsome of all Kashmir birds. The cock is magnificent, with rich peacock-blue plumage with golden-red sheen. These pheasants are not very common. They live chiefly at the upper margins of the forests.

Ploughing is done with small bullocks and the ploughs are small, for deep furrows are unnecessary. Rice cultivation is the great interest of most of the inhabitants of the valley. It speaks well for the fertility of Kashmir. It is in the village that we see the real Kashmir life. The language, dress, complexion, manners and customs of the people are quite distinct from those of any other country. Probably few people have undergone less change in the march of the centuries than this nation, in its isolated valley, separated by gigantic mountain ranges from all the countries around and, until the last quarter of a century, connected with. India only by a rough bridle track more than a hundred miles long.

The Folklore

Kashmiri, the vernacular of Kashmir, has descended from Sanskrit[48]. Actually Kashmiri is a very old language. During Muslim rule, it was enriched by Persian diction, and later on, in the modern period, Urdu and Hindi have been influencing it considerably. Kashmiri has had a rich literature. It yet lives in its songs, the folk-songs, which form a veritable *"literature of the people"* of Kashmir. In the Golden Valley with its abundant beauties of nature and man, it was but natural for some unknown hoary folk-bard to have started the immortal vogue folk-songs.

Kashmiri folk-songs present considerable variety in theme, content and form. They can be broadly classified into opera and dancing songs, pastoral lore, romantic ballads, play-songs, semi-mystical songs etc. Then there are other songs sung during particular seasons or in accompaniment to certain occupations. Boatmen, laboures, seed sowers, harvesters, embroiders, papier-mâché makers, milk-men, saffron reapers, shepherds, village belles fetching water, grinding, stacking or weeding paddy, sing their different melodious folk- songs, or at the birth and the naming of a child or at its circumcision or sacred thread ceremonies. Then there are wedding songs sung in chorus by women at and before marriage ceremonies. Dirges, popularly known as Van, are sung in chorus by the women after the death of old persons in the family.

Kashmir has an inexhaustible fund of folk-tales. They are, as folklorists have it, as old as the rocks. Many of the folk-tales of Kashmir like " *Himal and Nagiray*"[49], "*Zohra Khotan and Haya Bund*", "*Gulala Shah*" etc, are distinctly Kashmiri in origin. (Among these, "*Himal and Nagiray*" has been rendered into Kashmiri and Persian verse). Others, which constitute the large majority, are variants of popular tales of the East and the West.

Common Denominator

It is interesting to underline points common to folk-tales of Kashmir and the rest of the world. The demon or the lion or tigress, giving a tuft of hair or some such token to the ingratiating hero, to whom it serves as a useful charm, is a device common to Eastern (including Kashmiri and other Indian) and Western tales. The charming ring of Aladdin has many interesting variants in folk-tales of Kashmir. Besides, there are legends of man eating monsters in every country, whom the hero kills by ingenious means, these cannibal demons or vampires, for that matter, might have been a species of some mythical animal, whose fear universally persisted in the common man. The less awesome creature like Makara-half bird, half crocodile-was given other forms like half antelope and half fish, as the myth spread from India, influencing people's lore and arts as far removed as Java, Mongolia and China. The popular heroes, semi- historical or otherwise, who destroyed these terrors, won applause from the folk the world over. Apollo killed python. Hercules was the dragon-slayer. So were Beowulf and the heroes of "Percy's Reliques", in England, and Thor in Scandinavia. Variants of these legendary figures, woven into interesting stories, are to be found in Dravidian, German, Turkish, Tibetan and Kashmiri tales. The common denominator is and exotic admixture of the miraculous and the familiar, the myth and the reality. The hearer is transported into a new world, suspended between the known and an Utopia.

The prose of Kashmiri folk-tales is picturesquely colloquial. Nature's bountiful charms of the "*Vale of Cashmere*" add not a little to the beauty of the figure and the aptness of the diction. The faithfulness of the folk to the narrative is striking. It is largely the rural folk, young and old, who have preserved these treasures of the literature of the people in a mostly undiluted form. An old peasant, narrative a folk-tale, often intersperses it with fragments of narrative poetry which render the telling more effective.

Variety

Kashmiri folk-songs are current in almost every Kashmiri home, particularly in the rural areas. The songs present considerable variety in theme, content and form. The broad classification of the songs are:-

1. Love songs (*Lol-gevun*).
2. Ruf dance songs.
3. Pastoral songs.
4. Boatmen's songs.
5. Spring songs (*sont gevun*).
6. Harvest songs (*Lon-nuk gevun*).
7. Children's sporting songs (*Gindan gevun*).
8. Wedding songs (*Vanvun*).
9. Sacred Thread ceremony songs (*Yagnopavit gevun*).
10. Semi-mystic songs (current among the village holy men).
11. Opera songs (*Band Jashan*).
12. Dancers songs (*Bach Nagma Jashan*).
13. Ballads (Called Bath or Kath, literally meaning stories).
14. Cradle songs, lullaby, nursery rhymes (called Lalavun, meaning, to lull).
15. Dirges (*Van*).

Besides the boatmen's songs, mentioned already, there are songs galore sung to the accompaniment of certain occupations.

Seed-sowers, harvesters, embroiderers, papier-mache makers, saffron reapers, shepherds, village belles fetching water, grinding, spinning yarn,, or stacking paddy, or labourers doing the chores, sing their different occupational folk-songs in chorus. Then there are wedding songs sung in chorus by women at and before a marriage ceremony. Dirges, known as Van are recited in chorus by women of the family after the death of old persons. Variegated beauties of nature that surround the countryside form the theme of many a folk-song. Practically nothing is beyond the scope of the vehicle rendering of the rustic Muse, from subtle, philosophical thoughts to the romance and tragedy of love. The peasant women sing praises of the majestic tree of Kashmir, the Chinar, whose beautiful leaf recurs in the lovely motifs of the Valley. Besides their general appeal and entertainment value to all individuals who listen to or sing them, the folk songs form the main occupation of a section of people. It perhaps because they have the natural potentiality for at once playing the man and woman.

The Architectural Monuments of Kashmir

"Ancient India has nothing more worthy of its early civilization than the grand remains in Kashmir; the massive, the grotesque, the elegant, in architecture, may be admired in many parts of India, but nowhere there is to be seen the counterpart of the classically graceful, yet symmetrically massive, edifices of Kashmir which, though inferior to Palmyra or Persepolis in stateliness, are in beauty of position so immensely superior to either"–wrote a qualified European critic[50]. There are in Kashmir splendid and wonderful ruins, of cut lime-stone, dating from the third to the eighth century, to demonstrate that the ancient Kashmiris were great architects, and produced a beautiful and impressive style distinct from the Buddhist and Hindu architecture of other parts of India. It betrays, to some extent, Greek influence in its pediments, and its fluted columns with base shaft, and capital. But the pillars were spaced further apart than in Greek architecture, and pediments pitched higher and the temples crowned with pyramidal roofs tapering to a single lotus blossom, with the interior walls enriched with deep reliefs. In recent years much excavation and restoration have been carried out, and the results had been carefully recorded and surveyed, in 1933, by Mr. Ram Chandra Kak[51], in his excellent work, Ancient Monuments of Kashmir. This comprehensive and useful book should be kept handy by all visitors to Kashmir, interested in its many archaeological monuments.

The best preserved of these stone temples are at Avantipura and Martand, both within easy distance of Srinagar. Harwan has perhaps the oldest monument in Kashmir, containing the only remains of its kind in India. A temple and some tablets-built in the first or second century- have been unearthed here, which date the monument as belonging to the Kushan period, when Kashmir was closely connected with Central Asia. The remains are situated only a few furlongs below the water reservoir at Harwan which is close to Srinagar, and well deserve a visit for their great historic interest. The temple crowning the Takht-i-Suleiman, or Shankarachaya-which rises to the height of 1,000 feet above the plain, and overlooks Srinagar, and spreads away to the foot of the opposite but somewhat lower eminence called the Hari Parbat-is one of the earliest in Kashmir.

The little shrine at Payech on the Srinagar-Khanabal motor road comes next in point of antiquity, and in intrinsic beauty and elegance of outline is far superior to all the existing remains of similar dimensions. The cells, which is only eight feet square, and has open doorway on each of the four sides, is composed of only ten stones, the four corners being each a single stone, the sculptured tympanums over the doorways of four others, while two more compose the pyramidal roof, the lower of these being an enormous mass eight feet square by four feet in height. It has been ascribed by General Cunningham to King Narendraditya.

Of somewhat later date are the temples at Wangat, in two groups, up the Liddar valley, at the distance of a few hundred yards from each other, and consisting respectively of six and eleven distinct buildings. In close proximity is a sacred spring called Nagbal, and by it the footpath leads up the heights of

Haramuck to the mountain lake of Gangabal, a celebrated place of pilgrimage. The luxuriant forest growth had over thrown and buried almost completely several of the smaller temples, while on summit of the largest a tall pine had taken root. The architecture is of a slightly more advanced type than at Payech, the most striking feature being the bold projection and lofty trefoiled arches of the lateral. Of very similar character, but in more perfect preservation, is the temple at Bhaniyar, which stands on the very edge of the high road leading from Rawalpindi to Srinagar. The actual shrine is a cella of larger dimensions than usual, being 13 ½ feet square in the interior, with walls 6 ½ feet thick, supported on a basement, a 4 feet square, of singularly noble proportions. It is the earliest example that still retains its original enclosure a cloistered quadrangle measuring 145 by 120 feet. Though the final touches of the chisel have been effaced by time, the colonnade is in other respects almost perfect. The wall is pierced by a series of pedimented and trefoiled arches forming shallow recesses for the accommodation of priests and pilgrims.

The temple of Pandrethan is, next to Martand, the best known of all, in consequence of its close proximity to the capital. The domed roof is well worth inspection, being covered with sculpture of such purely classic design that an uninitiated person, who saw a copy of it on paper, would at once take it for a sketch from a Greek or Roman original. The temple is 18 feet square, with a projecting portico on each side, and displays a confused exuberance of decoration, more especially the repetition of pediment and trefoil, clear indications of a later date. It was erected by a Minister of King Partha, who governed Kashmir from 913 to 921 A.D. The details of monuments in the Kashmir Valley are given in **Appendix III.**

Jammu Region

So far little attention has been paid to archaeological remains of the Jammu Province by scholars of the subject. The forts of Reasi, Ramnagar, Bhaderwah, Gajpat, Basholi and the temples of Babore, Purmandal, Billawar, etc are magnificent monuments.

Jammu is known as city of temples. Amongst the temples in the city, **Raghunath Mandir** takes pride of the place. Situated in the heart of the city and surrounded by a group of other temples, this temple dedicated to Lord Rama is outstanding and unique in northern India. Work on the temple was started by Maharaja Gulab Singh, founder of the Kingdom of Jammu and Kashmir in 1835 AD and was completed by his son, Maharaja Ranbir Singh, in 1860 AD. The inner walls of the main temple are covered with gold sheet on three sides. There are many galleries with lakhs of 'Saligrams'. The surrounding temples are dedicated to various Gods and Goddesses connected with the epic Ramayana[52].

Ranbireshwar Temple: Located on Shalimar Road near the New Secretariat, and built by Maharaja Ranbir Singh in 1883 AD, Ranbireshwar Temple is dedicated to Lord Shiva. It has one central 'Lingam' measuring seven and a half feet in height (7.5 ft) and twelve Shiva 'Lingams' of crystal measuring from 15 cms to 38 cms and galleries with thousands of Shiva 'Lingams' fixed on stone slabs.

Bahu Fort: 5 Kms situated on a rock face on the left bank of the river Tawi, this is perhaps the oldest fort and edifice in the city. Constructed originally by Raja Bahulochan over 3,000 years ago, the existing fort was more recently improved and built by the Dogra rulers. There is a temple dedicated to Goddess Kali inside the fort.

Mubarak Mandi Palace: The oldest buildings in this Palace complex date to 1824. The architecture is a blend of Rajasthani, Mughal and even Baroque European influences. The most stunning segment is the Sheesh Mahal. The Pink Hall now houses the Dogra Art Museum which has miniature paintings of the various Hill Schools.

Conclusion

On a world map the Jammu and Kashmir appears remote and landlocked, isolated by successive ranges of mountains high above the plains of the sub-continent. Its apparent impregnability is, however, illusory. Over twenty passes provide points of entry and the valley of Kashmir is both a cross roads and a place of refuge. On account of its numerous tombs of saints and shrines, of which the holiest, Swami Amarnathji, lies in the eastern mountains of the Kashmir valley, it also attracted outsiders as a place of pilgrimage[53]. Over time the valley of Kashmir's political borders have expanded and shrunk and the very territories came under dispute.

The demand for independence in the Valley is not going to vanish overnight, but that should not discourage the policy makers from working out a constitutional formula, which would meet the legitimate political aspirations of all the regions of the State–the Kashmir Valley, Jammu and Ladakh. The revival of the political process is essential for any solution to the problems of the state, but simultaneously, all out efforts should be made to hammer out a framework of a solution which would be acceptable to most people, if not all. The government has to show a will and determination to deal firmly with the secessionist forces. It has to be a multi-dimensional policy encompassing all aspects of Kashmir problem – military, political, diplomatic and psychological. Pakistan is unlikely to reverse its policy of aid and abetment to terrorism in J&K and even when the people are getting disillusioned with Pakistan and terrorism[54].

Notes and References

1. SR. Bakshi, *Kashmir Valley and its Culture*, Sarup and Sons, New Delhi, 1997, p.247.
2. *Ibid.*
3. *Ibid.*
4. EA. Vas, *Without Baggage-A Personal Account of the J&K Operations Oct 1947*-Jan 1949, Natraj Publishers, Dehradun, 1987, p.4.
5. SR. Bakshi, *Op.cit*, p.248.
6. *Ibid.*
7. *Ibid.*
8. *Ibid*, pp.249-250.
9. EA. Vas, *Op.cit*, p.6.
10. SR. Bakshi, *Op.cit*, p.250.
11. *Ibid.*

12. *Ibid.*
13. *Ibid.*
14. *Ibid.*
15. *Ibid*, p.251.
16. Khurshid Salman, *Beyond Terrorism: New Hope for Kashmir*, UBS Publications and Distributors, New Delhi, 1999, p.49.
17. *Ibid*, p.50.
18. *Ibid.*
19. *Ibid*, p.51.
20. *Ibid.*
21. Rajiv Rajendra Kumar, *World Famous Wars and Battles*, Family Books Pvt Ltd, 1982, New Delhi, pp.105-106.
22. Khurshid Salman, *Op.cit*, p.51.
23. *Ibid*, p.52.
24. *Ibid*, p.53.
25. *Ibid.*
26. *Ibid*, p.55.
27. *Ibid.*
28. *Ibid.*
29. *Ibid*, p.56.
30. *Ibid.*
31. www.mastindia.com.
32. Crowther, Geoff, *India, A Travel Survival Kit*, Lonely Planet Publications, Australia, 1987, p.207.
33. Kr Sharma Suresh and Usha, *History, Architecture and Tourism of Kashmir (Kashmir Through the Ages)*, Deep and Deep Publications, Jammu, 1996, p.276.
34. Source: *Census 1981*.
35. S Bloeria Sudhir, *Pakistan's Insurgency Vs India's Security*, Manas Publications, New Delhi, 2000, p.16.
36. Kr Singh Nagendra, *Cultural Heritage of Jammu, Kashmir and Ladakh, Vol III*, Jay Kay Book House, Jammu, 1997, p.20
37. SR. Bakshi, *Kashmir: Tourism Monuments and Folklore*, Sarup and Sons, New Delhi, 1997, p.118.
38. *Ibid.*
39. *Ibid.*
40. SR. Bakshi, *Kashmir: Tourism Monuments and Folklore(Cultural Heritage)*, Sarup and Sons, New Delhi, 1997, p.121.
41. *Ibid.*

42. *Ibid.*
43. *Ibid*, pp.121-122.
44. Government of India, *Hand Book of Agriculture*, Directorate of Information and Publications of Agriculture, September 2003, p.779.
45. SR. Bakshi, *Kashmir: Tourism Monuments and Folklore(Cultural Heritage)*, Sarup and Sons, New Delhi, 1997, pp.124-125.
46. *Ibid*, p.128.
47. *Ibid*, p.130.
48. SR. Bakshi, *Kashmir: Tourism Monuments and Folklore(The Folklore)*, Sarup and Sons, New Delhi, 1997, p.146
49. *Ibid*, p136.
50. Kr Sharma Suresh and Usha, *Op.cit,* p.83.
51. *Ibid.*
52. Crowther Geoff, *Op.cit*, pp.208-209.
53. Schofield Victoria, *Kashmir in the Crossfire, Viva* Books, New Delhi, 1997, p.2.
54. Marwah Ved, *Uncivil Wars Pathology of Terrorism in India*, Harper Collins Publishers India, New Delhi, 1997, pp.150-151.

3

Scenario of Global Terrorism

The Worst of Global Terrorism

Introduction

Tuesday, September 11, 2001 witnessed the world in a state of stunned disbelief at the most audacious act of terrorism ever committed. In a devilishly brilliant plan designed for maximum impact, terrorists hijacked four planes and had three of them crash into America's most prominent buildings within a span of 60 minutes. Fallout of a serial assault by some faceless sky-faring terrorists on the citadels of America's economic and military might is unimaginably devastating. Utterly despicable are the four separate but transparently coordinated acts of terror that rocked America. Hardly concealed is the dastardly political motive of the criminals, but it has not been easy to determine the physical and psychological magnitude of a truly phenomenal tragedy.

At least several thousands of innocent people, Americans and many other nationals, have been perished in the stupendous aerial forays. Two separately hijacked passenger planes were piloted with deadly precision straight into the upper floors of the imposing Twin Towers of the World Trade Centre along New York city's showpiece skyline. It was not long before the towers collapsed in mighty implosions that were caused by the sheer impact of the aircraft intrusions. While some other terrorists commandeering and ramming yet another passenger plane as a flying missile into a corner of the Pentagon, America's civilian-military nerve center of power, it became increasingly clear that the perpetrators of the sequential heinous crimes were acting in concert. The terrorist blitzkrieg may indeed mark the beginning of a new defining war on civilized humanity itself. One more civilian aircraft, which too was hijacked, crashed over the U.S. homeland itself, and this completed a viciously bizarre pattern of anti-America vengeance[1].

Borderless Terrorists

Even as India celebrated her 57th Independence Day in a fairly contented manner, there were many areas of the world where violence held sway and near anarchy prevailed. Afghanistan saw frequent reminders of Taliban resurgence in the form of attacks on police stations and the killing of many Afghans. Israel and her Palestinian Arab neighbours once more resumed mutual killing, a bloody, negative spiral down which the Israelis as well as the Palestinian groups had been sliding rapidly for some years. The 'Road Map to Peace' in West Asia on which the US had worked so hard, was in tatters. There was internal strife in Iran as also terrorist violence in Saudi Arabia while Iraq, despite deployment of troops from the USA, UK and a number of other countries, was far from pacified. In fact, the UN of office in Baghdad was destroyed in a suicide bomb attack leaving the head of the UN mission and many others dead[2].

The attacks on 11 September 2001 are radically different from the ones America has encountered before. The US is no stranger to terrorism. Its citizens abroad, embassies and globally dispersed assets have long been the principal targets of international terrorism. The number of lives lost in these two other episodes of terror is also far from clear still. It is a poignant aspect of an immense modern-day marvel that the television networks have captured the live montage of an eerie aerial attack on the World Trade Centre. Also beamed across the world are some real time pictures of the other acts of terror as well. Those who plotted these suicidal missions could not have planned for more on a clear day of sunshine that turned into darkness for the entire civilized world. To empathise with the United States and its people and Government in their worst hour of crisis since the Pearl Harbour bombing during the Second World War, is to pay the minimal civilized homage to mankind.

With the borderless terrorists having struck at the heart of American power and pride, the US President should respond in a manner that will not at all aggravate the escalating instability of the global strategic and political order. There was a need to endeavour to enhance worldwide security in conjunction with all major and responsible countries. Some of the more significant instances relate to the bombings of two US embassies in Africa in 1998 and the ground level explosion at the World Trade Centre itself in New York in 1993. Yet, the apparent helplessness of the US authorities at the height of the latest saga of grief was a manifest testimony to the limits of America's present day power in the face of terrorists driven by a suicidal 'zeal' that may or may not owe its origin to a political or religious crusade.

No one is better placed than terrorists to wage unconventional warfare against even the most powerful states. Those opposed to the US were not going to fight it against its strengths. They were expected to target its weaknesses[3]. Few approaches other than terrorism give its practitioners the choice of time and location to spring the surprise. Democracies are specially vulnerable to terrorism, given their justified reluctance to curb the freedoms of their citizens and the built in opposition to draconian methods in countering terrorism.

Foreign Terrorist Organisations

Current List of Designation Foreign Terrorist Organisations[4] released by the Office of the Coordinator for Counter Terrorism, Department of State, USA as on 05 October 2001 are as under:

1. Abu Nidal Organisation (ANO)
2. Abu Sayyaf Group
3. Armed Islamic Group (GIA)
4. Aum Shinrikyo
5. Basque Fatherland and Liberty (ETA)
6. Gama'a al Islamiyya (Islamic Group)

7. HAMAS (Islamic Resistance Movement)
8. Harakat ul- Mujahidin (HUM)
9. Hisballah (Party of God)
10. Islamic Movement of Uzbekistan (IMU)
11. Al-Jihad (Egyptian Islamic Jihad)
12. Kahane Chai (Kach)
13. Kurdistan Workers's Party (PKK)
14. Liberation Tigers of Tamil Eelam (LTTE)
15. Mujahedin-e Khalq Organisation (MEK)
16. National Liberation Army (ELN)
17. Palestinian Islamic Jihad (PIJ)
18. Palestine Liberation Front (PLF)
19. Popular Front for the Liberation of Palestine (PFLP)
20. PFLP-General Command (PFLP-GC)
21. Al-Qaida
22. Real IRA
23. Revolutionary Armed Forces of Colombia (FARC)
24. Revolutionary Nuclei (formerly ELA)
25. Revolutionary Organisation 17 November
26. Revolutionary People's Liberation Army/Front (DHKP/C)
27. Shining Path (Sendero Luminoso, SL)
28. United Self-Defense Forces of Colombia (AUC)

Religious Extremism and Fanaticism

As the world began to witness the rise of identity politics it is evident from the above list of Foreign Terrorist Organisations that the groups which sought to promote their interests at the expense of other groups they had long lived with, terrorism and ethnic cleansing had become common across the world. Rise of religious extremism in the last few years in many parts of the world brought in another dimension to new right wing terrorism. In West Asia, extremist groups acting in the name of Islam had risen, nursing ideological and such other complaints against the US and the West. It threatens not only just America but also many of the regimes in the region itself. Terrorism was of course no monopoly of those misusing the name of Islam. The Subcontinent itself has been witness to various extremist groups of many different religious orientations. With the growing number of American citizens following the Islamic faith, the White House has tried to reach out to the leaders of the international community and convince them that its counter terrorism policies are not directed against any particular religion.

As a new spectre of terrorism haunts the world, no one has captured attention more than Osama bin Laden, the exiled Saudi-born millionaire, who has proclaimed far reaching political objectives and has pursued them across the world with unusual vigour. His alliance with the Taliban in Afghanistan reflects another important shift in the nature of international terrorism. The headquarters of international terrorism has moved from West Asia to the Subcontinent.

Although violence and terrorism have been on the rise again in West Asia, the Subcontinent has become the principal haven of international terrorism. The Taliban controlled Afghanistan has become a sanctuary for international terrorists as well as a breeding ground of extremist ideas that are driving the new scourge. All these trends have been well known and exhaustively debated in the US. The US has also recognized the importance of international cooperation with many countries, *including India*, in countering terrorism. But this cooperation has been too little in comparison to the scale of the threat that confronts the world as a whole. Despite the accurate assessment of the new sources of threat to international and regional security from terrorism, most states, including India and the US, have often had to compromise their counter terrorism goals in the face of other political and economic interests. But the war against the evils of terrorism and fanaticism cannot be fought by accommodating them and their sponsors, however tempting that course may be.

Modern technology and innovative ways of financing and global connections have given terrorists extraordinary capabilities that were demonstrated on 11 September 2001[5]. The simultaneous attack on so many different targets imply substantive preparation and coordination. The rise of suicide bombers has given terrorism a new edge and has made nations much more vulnerable. There has been fundamental change in the nature of terrorism over the last decade. In the past, left wing ideologies were the principal sources of inspiration for international terrorism.

Global Terrorism: An Analysis

The element of indiscriminate use of violence on innocent civilians, distinguishes terrorism not only from other criminal acts involving violence, but also from legitimate military activity and ordinary warfare[6]. The term 'terrorism' has neither a precise definition, nor one which is widely acceptable. The imprecise nature of the term means that with some accuracy it can refer to a specific set of fear-producing actions which can serve a variety of purposes. More generally it can apply to similar acts of violences-kidnappings and hijackings-which are not intended by the perpetrators to be terror-producing. The term is carelessly used as a synonym for rebellion, street battles, civil strife, insurrection, rural guerrilla war and coup d'etat. The indiscriminate use of the term not only inflates the statistics but makes understanding the specific character of terrorism and how to cope with it more difficult.

Defining Terrorism

Terrorism is by nature coercive, dehumanizing, a theatre of the absurd, and designed to manipulate its victims, and through them, a larger audience. Definition[7] of terrorism are notoriously difficult and imprecise. A nosology includes:

(a) Non-political terrorism, defined as the deliberate creation of fear for coercive purposes with an end goal of collective or individual, gain or terrorism engendered by seriously mentally disturbed individuals;

(b) Quasi-terrorism, defined as the application of terroristic techniques in situations that do not involve terroristic crimes as such, examples of this type abound and include the take of hostages in derailed bank robberies or prison riots as bargaining leverage to secure freedom or concessions;

(c) Limited political-terrorism, which involves ideologically or politically motivated terroristic acts, such as assassinations or the bombing of public buildings, but which fall short of seeking to overthrow established governments;

(d) Official or State-terrorism, defined as governmental rule-based on fear, oppression and persecution, and finally;

(e) Political-terrorism, defined as violent, criminal behaviour designed to create fear in a society-or in a substantial segment of it-for political purposes. When fully developed, political terrorism is revolutionary in character and seeks to subvert or overthrow an existing government.

Defining Terrorist Activity

The Immigration and Nationality Act of USA defines terrorist activity to mean: any activity which is unlawful under the laws of the place where it is committed (or which, if committed in the United States, would be unlawful under the laws of the United States or any State) and which involves any of the following[8]:

(I) The high jacking or sabotage of any conveyance (including an aircraft, vessel, or vehicle).

(II) The seizing or detaining, and threatening to kill, injure, or continue to detain, another individual in order to compel a third person (including a government organization) to do or abstain from doing any act as an explicit or implicit condition for the release of the individual seized or detained.

(III) A violent attack upon an internationally protected person or upon the liberty of such a person.

(IV) An assassination.

(V) The use of any-

(a) biological agent, chemical agent, or nuclear weapon or device, or

(b) explosive or firearm (other than for mere personal monetary gain), with intent to endanger, directly or indirectly, the safety of one or more individuals or to cause substantial damage to property.

(VI) A threat, attempt, or conspiracy to do any of the foregoing.

(a) The term "*engage in terrorist activity*" means to commit, in an individual capacity or as a member of and organization, and act of terrorist activity or an act which the actor knows, or reasonably should know, affords material support to any individual, organization, or government in conduction a terrorist activity at any time, including any of the following acts:

(I) The preparation of planning of a terrorist activity.

(II) The gathering of information on potential targets for terrorist activity.

(III) The providing of any type of material support, including a safe house, transportation, communications, funds, false documentation or identification, weapons, explosives, or training, to any individual the actor knows or has reason to believe has committed or plans to commit a terrorist Organization.

(IV) The soliciting of funds or other things of value for terrorist activity or for any terrorist organization.

(V) The solicitation of any individual for membership in a terrorist organisation, terrorist government, or to engage in a terrorist activity.

Rise in Terrorist Activity

Even though the data on the incidence and severity of terrorism, in all its forms, are sketchy, fragmented and therefore suspect, it appears that terrorist activity is rising the world over, that there is a trend towards more lethal incidents and injuries compared to years past and that US citizens and US property are being increasingly targeted. The October 1983 suicide bomb attack that killed two hundred and forty one US marines is but an example of the growing risk of terrorism and its increasing costs.

Given these trends, an increasing number of officials and private citizens will find themselves involved in terroristic crime, as victims of abductions and hostage-holding incidents or as targets for destruction. Some victims are deliberately targeted on the basis of their personal or professional characteristics or because they symbolize whatever has become the object of terrorist hate and annihilation. Other victims are chosen randomly and become victims strictly by chance. There is a growing body of literature on the subject of terrorism and its victims, but it is scattered and reflects many points of view, as well as many disciplines. The structural duality of terror/violence has also been a complicating factor. State or governmental terror has become far more pervasive and barbaric than individual or group terrorism. Only for the past two decades have social scientists been interested in terroristic violence. Some believed that it was a relatively rare phenomenon and others neglected it for different reasons.

The diversity of research methodologies used, such as retrospective studies of hostage experiences or laboratory studies of stress and sensory deprivation, presents major problems for generalizing from the information we do have. In the absence of epidemiological studies and base line data, it is difficult to chart psychological, social or physiological changes, much less predict future effects of terrorization on the victims of these crimes. Bound by the rule of law and due process, a democratic regime cannot resort to the same bloody methods used against it in combating terrorist crime. It is surely no accident that we do not hear much of revolutionary violence in totalitarian countries, where autocracies with limitless powers terrorise ethnic, religious or racial groups, and sometimes brutally subject entire populations. While the indiscriminate murders, maimings and mayhem associated with terrorism often appear to result from irrational behaviour by the terrorist, it is important to assume that violence, however barbaric, has its own rationality. This point may perhaps be difficult to accept but unless the responding forces and concerned officials do so, they will not be able to differentiate between terroristic violence and other forms of strife and will fail to understand the patterns that take place when the hostage-taker initiates an incident.

Terrorism is anti-democratic for at least two reasons[9]:

(a) First, sustained incidents of terrorism will inevitably produce governmental counter measures for the purpose of self defence. These in turn, can also become oppressive, thereby alienating the population from their government.

(b) Second, terrorist movements are clearly elitist, in spite of their alleged glorification of and identification with the masses. By seeking to coerce duly elected governments into concessions or even abdication, terrorists exert great stress on a country's institutionalized legal mechanisms and wholly circumvent the democratic process established to bring about orderly social and/or political change.

While there are no systematic studies of the effect of terrorism on the quality of life in nations experiencing sustained and serious assaults, there is growing evidence of encroachments of the civil liberties in such nations. Great Britain, for example, one of the oldest and more stable democracies in the world, in its struggle with sectarianism and periodic armed insurrection in Northern Ireland, has instituted such basically undemocratic measures as interment, in-depth interrogation, as well as arrests, searches and seizures without the benefit of warrants. There is also censorship. There has even been a relaxation of the rules of criminal procedure, such as trials without juries, the admission of hearsay evidence, a shift in the burden of proof from government to defendant, as well as an increase in penalties for activities classified as terrorism. West Germany and Italy, under sustained assault, have made comparatively benign procedural changes but have also significantly increased the penalties for terrorist related crimes. Governmental countermeasures such as these are not only understandable as mechanisms for self defence, but are also demanded by the public.

No form of political authority can long expect to survive continued, serious assaults on its institutions, and people, under the long recognized concept of 'social contract' do have a right to protection. Public outrage and demand for harsh action against terrorists seems to be the norm in nations experiencing serious problems with terrorism.

International Terrorism

Every society lays down its ground rules for abnormal and deviant behaviour. Those who do not stick to accepted norms are labeled as mavericks. In some-ways, militants are mavericks because they are non-conformists, independent minded and follow different rules of engagement. Their goals are political, not criminal, although the means they choose are violent. They passionately believe that violence and violence alone can awaken and arouse the passive population. Persons with such logic and insight cannot be described as abnormal. The militant is not a psychopath. He kills for a political purpose, the psychopath kills for pleasure[10].

During early periods of the 20th century, terrorism was perceived as a contest between two sides–a group of people or an organization vs a sovereign state. But, during the course of the second half of the twentieth century, various countries began to use terrorist organizations to promote state interests in the international domain. In some cases, states have established puppet terrorist organizations, whose purpose are to act on half of the sponsoring state, to further the interests of the state, and to represent its positions in domestic or regional fronts. In other cases, states sponsor existing organizations on the basis of mutual interests. The patron state provides its beneficiary terrorist organization with political support, financial assistance, and the sponsorship necessary to maintain and expand its struggle. The patron uses the beneficiary to perpetrate acts of terrorism as a means of spreading the former's ideology throughout the world, or in some cases, the patron ultimately expects the beneficiary to gain control of the state in which it resides or impart its ideology to broad sections of the general public.

Post-World War Scenario

After the First World War, international terrorist attacks were endemic in the new Balkan states and the internecine feuds of the Internal Macedonian Revolutionary Organisation(IMRO) split over into Vienna and Milan. Hence, it is a nonsense to suppose that international terrorism was invented by Latin American guerrillas in the mid 1960s. However, there has been a remarkable increase in the incidence of international terrorism during the past decade. A recent study of acts of international terrorism- i.e., attacks against foreign targets in the state of the terrorists' origin or attacks across international frontiers – recorded a total of 6,714 incidents between 1968 and 1980. The annual incidents climbed from below 200 in 1968 to 400 in 1970, over 600 in 1972 and over 800 in 1978. Explosive bombing remains far and away the most popular international terrorist tactic, but since 1975 there has also been a very steep rise in assassinations and attempted assassinations. Only a quarter of all attacks in this period caused death or personal injury, through a worrying trend since 1980 has been the increase in indiscriminate and lethal attacks such as massive bombings in public places and truck bombings: 1435 incidents between 1968 and 1980 caused at least one casualty[11].

Terrorism as a Tool

The high costs of modern warfare, and concern about non-conventional escalation, as well as the danger of defeat and the unwillingness to appear as the aggressor, have turned terrorism into an efficient, convenient, and generally discrete weapon for attaining state interests in the international realm. Terrorist violences were not the first choice of the freedom fighters; it was usually the last resort, during the period of imperialism. Today, it has come to be the instrument of governments to score over other nations. Terrorism is a very potent weapon in the armoury of guerrillas if it remains confined to limited or selective killings. It is a double edged weapon which if not used properly can cut the hands of the user. It has great potential of misfires or backfires. One has to be very discreet and careful in the application of terrorism. Unconventional terrorism is regarded the most threatening of all terrorist tactics. With the string of chemical-weapon terrorist attacks on various targets in Japan in early 1995, a formerly theoretical scenario has entered the realm of day to day reality.

Terrorism has become a very profitable business in which the investment is minimal and the dividends enormous. Kidnapping and hijacking are either to get their comrades released from jail or as a bogey to raise funds for their activities or just to create chaos in an established order. Some disgruntled and disillusioned hotheads have turned terrorism into a lucrative business proposition. Random shooting at Lod Airport, Tel Aviv, by the Japanese terrorists and at Rome and Vienna Airports by Aby Nidal's men calling themselves "*Martyrs of Palestine*" or the killing of innocent bus passengers by Sikh terrorists in Punjab and Haryana cannot be termed as calculated moves of highly motivated terrorists.

Current Trends

Present day terrorists are not interested in the affairs of their own country. According to a CIA report published in 1977, the terrorists of Turkey were using a Palestinian camp for training in Syria. The same report also revealed the growing involvement of Cuban terrorists in operations in Africa and Middle East. Cuban instructors were training the Palestinians in Syria, Lebanon and Cuba. *Shelter given to terrorists by various countries helps in spreading international terrorism.* The free world with its libertarian regimes of limited power, serves as a convenient breeding ground for the sprouting of international-terror. Terrorist organizations not only exploit the democratic countries but also the countries ruled by regimes of tyranny and terror, all under the cloak of revolutionaries. International affiliations have revealed that various terrorist groups do not have particular attachment to the happenings in their own countries.

Terrorists get a lot of publicity. With the improvement in mass communication system, the activities of terrorists get wide coverage. News-hungry newspapers, television, radio, etc always look for sensational news items and terrorists provide them with these. Terrorist activities are given a front page coverage. Coloured photographs are taken and published. The undue publicity given by the press encourages the terrorists to do many more acts of terrorism. It also gives an incentive to other fanatics to join the terrorist gangs[12].

By 1999, at least 64 out of a total of 96 active terrorist groups are clearly identifiable as being religiously motivated. This list is heavily tilted towards Islamic groups, but there are clearly many fractured Christian Catholic or Orthodox Church groups in the former Yugoslavia. Clearly if the terror let loose in Afghanistan is any guide, the "*jihad*" has killed more than a 1,00,000 in Kabul alone, - a figure far higher than anything that this data highlights. In Kashmir, more than 10,000 have died as a result of the jihad launched by Pakistan. In Kashmir, this is apparent enough with the movement for "*liberation*" centered since the early 1990's towards merging with Pakistan an objective that clashes completely with the original objectives that had sparked off violence. The Harkut-ul-Ansar and Lashkar-e-Taiba(to quote only the most well known groupings) are known to have an enviable communication systems, a publicity cell, a well thought out recruitment strategy, and huge recruitment reservoir that springs from the madrasas[13].

America-Prime Target of International Terrorism

In 1992, the State Department of USA recorded a total of 364 terrorist incidents worldwide, down from the 666 recorded in 1987. In 1993, total incidents increased to 427, but were it not for a series of coordinated incidents, the level of terrorism would have fallen in 1993 as well: the increase in 1993 over 1992 was caused by a campaign of 150 attacks carried out by the Kurdistan Workers Party against Turkish interests in Western Europe on two separate days, in June and November, with about 75 attacks each day. In 1994, the number of terrorist incidents world wide fell again, to 321, according to preliminary statistics available from the State Department.

According to the State Department, anti-US attacks fell to 88 in 1993, down from 142 in 1992. Anti US attacks fell again in 1994, to 66. By comparison, in 1986, there were 204 attacks against Americans. And about 21 per cent of world terror is targeted at the US[14]. In 1993, 109 people were killed and 1,393 were wounded in terrorist incidents worldwide, the highest casualty total in five years. Six of those killed and nearly a thousand of those wounded were Americans, all as a result of The World Trade Centre bombing. Prior to that, the most deadly attack against Americans was the downing of Pan Am 103 in 1988, in which 189 Americans were killed. In 1992, two Americans were killed and one was wounded in terrorist incidents. In 1991, there were 7 American fatalities and 14 other casualties. In 1990, 12 Americans were killed and 11 injured in incidents worldwide. In December 1994, the State Department's coordinator for counter-terrorism said that international terrorism was declining because of the Middle East peace process, the firm policies of the US and other governments, and the fall of the Soviet Union, which had provided support for terrorist organizations. But, the worst of the attacks was on 11 September 2001 on the World Trade Centre totally destroying the two landmark towers.

Weapon of Struggle

History tells us that in every recent struggle by national liberation movements, terrorism has invariably been adopted by some, if not all, of the movement's factions, as one of their weapons of struggle. Yet the Soviets, of course, angrily disavow the terrorism label for any of the campaigns or actions they support. They claim that, as the leading revolutionary power in the world, they have the duty to aid national liberation movements to the fullest possible extent, and they can even quote UN resolutions on struggles for self determination to support their claim that these activities are perfectly within the rules of international law. Hence, many Americans and other Western observers questioned the credentials of some of the national liberation movements the Soviets were sponsoring.

Keeping in mind always that terrorism has to be fought much more through the mind than by mere physical threat or persuasion, a strong media policy is as important than equipping the armed forces with weapons and technology that is suitable for anti-terrorist operations. In a war where the objective is in part to wear down the armed forces of a country, the standard customs of bring in huge numbers of armed forces into a conflict area must be resisted with the clear idea that this is playing into the hands of the enemy.

Financing

The 9/11 attacks cost somewhere between $400,000 and $500,000 to execute. The operatives spent more than $270,000 in the United States. Additional expenses included travel to obtain passports and visas, travel to the United States, expenses incurred by the plot leader and facilitators outside the United States, and expenses incurred by the people selected to be hijackers who ultimately did not participate. The conspiracy made extensive use of banks in the United States. The hijackers opened accounts in their own names, using passports and other identification documents. Their transactions were unremarkable and essentially invisible amid the billions of dollars flowing around the world every day. To date, we have not been able to determine the origin of the money used for the 9/11 attacks. Al Qaeda had many sources of funding and a pre 9/11annual budget estimated at $30 million. If a particular source of funds had dried up, Al Qaeda could easily have found enough money elsewhere to fund the attack[15].

Nuclear Terrorism

The widespread use of nuclear fission of uranium and plutonium for the release of large quantities of energy either in a relatively slow, controlled fashion, via nuclear reactors or in a short bomb-like burst referred to as a 'nuclear explosive device' has given rise to a very broad spectrum of possibilities for nuclear violence including the possibility of some terrorist groups resorting to such violence. Terrorists may secure radio active or fissionable material capable of being fabricated into a nuclear explosive device. Possession of a nuclear explosive device by a terrorist group and its threat to explode it in a populated area, would provide the group with a fantastic lever for extortion of concessions including weapons, money, release of imprisoned comrades, transport to a safe haven, alteration of government policies and so on.

Though there has been no incidents of nuclear terrorism so far, the possibility of such a violence is increasing. Factors contributing to the increasing probability of nuclear terrorism could be as under[16]:

(a) Terrorism is becoming more and more sophisticated and lethal with a view to increasing the shock value.

(b) Terrorism is being supported and in some cases even sponsored by some governments or government backed agencies.

(c) More and more nuclear reactors are available and terrorists could devise convenient plans for procuring material from any of the several places.

Impact on World Economy: The 9/11 Factor

US Markets were shut on 12 September 2001, with financial market participants reeling from an expected staggering human death toll a day after a wave of terror shook the nation, while European stocks and the dollar clambered higher. In Europe, safe-heaven bonds and gold lost ground. The NYSE was closed for a second straight trading day, the first-time since the end of World War II in August 1945[17]. The Federal Reserve Bank of New York pumped more than $38 billion reserves into the US banking system-about 10-times the size of a regular daily reserves action-to ease fears of a possible banking cash crunch. The Fed's injection of funds came in addition to the $80 billion in liquidity pumped into the financial system by the European Central Bank, the Swiss National Bank and the Bank of Japan. Those moves helped the dollar halve its losses from 11 September 2001.

Market Crashing

When investor confidence crumbled and panic set overseas, market dislocation prevented many fund management firms from pricing or redeeming funds, whipsawing European stock markets on thin volumes, with unusually high volume in insurance and airline stocks. The blue-chip FTSE 100 index seesawed in a 230-point range and climbed in late trading to close up 136.1 points or 2.87 percent at a high of 4,882.1, battling back from three year lows. The FTSE had fallen nearly 10 percent from its peaks before the 9/11 attack.

Declining Currency Value

Currency volumes in London-the world's biggest forex market fell by at least 50 percent amid severe logistical problems and as central banks and the main forex traders association urged restraint. The dollar was up more than a full percentage point against the Swiss franc, trading around 1.66 francs-well above the seven month lows the green back hit below 1.64 francs in the wake of devastating plane attacks. Against the yen, the dollar was trading around 119.35 yen in midday US trading, up 0.15 percent on the day. It eked out marginal gains from the losses of as much as three yen. ECB President Wim Duisenberg said in Brussels the central bank stood ready to provide liquidity to markets grappling with uncertainty over the impact of the US events on the global financial system. Meanwhile, fears of a full blown global recession rippled through Asia's markets on 12 September 2001 with nearly every stock index in the region falling.

Setback to Asian Manufacturing

Asia is a manufacturing base for a range of goods exported to the US market, and a main concern was whether the attack would trip a fragile American economy into a spiral and cause instability at a time when regional confidence was already weak. Tokyo's benchmark Nikkei average posted its eighth-largest percentage decline ever, ending down 682.85 points or 6.63 percent at 9,610.10, its lowest close since December 1983 and its first slide below 10,000 points since August. There are serious concerns that the tragic events in the US may have medium term and even long term fallout on the world economy and indeed, the Indian economy. Initially, India's exports were down by 2 percent in first five months and expected to affect further. Besides the financial markets, the real sectors of the Indian economy are in danger of being hit hard. India is dependent on imports for over 7- percent of its oil needs and spent $15.5 billion on imports last year. The flare up in global oil prices could cause inflation in the economy, send government's deficit soaring, strain the forex reserves and put pressure on the exchange rate of the rupee. The flare up in global oil prices since 2002 is the single most important cause of higher inflation in the Indian economy. There is a strong possibility that India's attempt at boosting growth would be jeoparadised.

Although the European Central Bank Kept its key interest rates unchanged, it pumped in fresh money to avoid cash crunch in banking systems unsettled by the terror attacks on the US. In a statement, the ECB signaled its readiness to act in concert with other major central banks to defuse any economic impact from the attacks by hijacked aircraft on landmarks in New York and Washington. Underlining their concern that European banks could face difficulties, the ECB and the Federal Reserve agreed to swap arrangement, under which the ECB would be able to draw up to $50 billion, while the Federal Reserve Bank of New York will get an equivalent amount of deposits in euros. European stocks were slightly higher in an uncertain mood without a lead from Wall Street.

Limited Impact

The Bank of Japan said there were no notable problems and international payments experts played down the impact, saying authorities had anticipated all sorts of problems stemming from disruption of trading systems at the World Trade Centre. Leading central banks and governments are coordinating their response to the financial effects of the terror attacks. The ECB said that while normal market conditions were expected to prevail in the period ahead, it would continue to monitor developments in financial markets and take action if necessary. Despite the scale of the human tragedy, these terrible events had only a limited impact on the international economy and global financial system[18].

Measures to Eliminate Terrorism

Combating Terrorism

One notices that every time a terrorist incident occurs like hijacking of an aeroplane, the tendency is to concentrate on solving the immediate problem of releasing the hostages. The situation eases as soon as the crisis is over. But if terrorism is to be eliminated anti-terrorist forces must work out better and stronger methods for protection against this menace. No anti-terrorist methods known at present can guarantee success. Several countries and international organizations are conducting intensive studies to find a solution to this problem.

There are no easy solutions to this problem since the attitude of nations towards terrorism is not uniform. In fact, their attitude ranges from outright condemnation of all terrorist acts whatever be the cause to active support to terrorist groups and their actions. The various international conventions held over the last 15 years to deal with one or more aspects of the problem failed to make any headway on account of differing views of the countries on the subject. If the menace of terrorism is to countered effectively all nations will have to cooperate with one another. Terrorism cannot survive without foreign support. Some nations not only provide safe sanctuaries, training, funds, etc, but also weapons to the terrorists. The problem becomes very serious if a neighboring country aids and abets terrorists.

1988 Document of India

A document prepared by the Government of India and submitted to Pakistan Government in 1988 and subsequent years outlined Pakistan's direct involvement in abetting terrorism in Punjab and later Jammu and Kashmir. The documents provided irrefutable evidence of Pakistan's attempt to create trouble in Punjab and Jammu and Kashmir by giving military training and weapons to the secessionists. Ironically

Pakistan's open help to militant groups in Punjab and J& K flies in the face of the SAARC convention on the suppression of terrorism which came into effect on August 22, 1988.

International Conventions

The various international conventions held over the last 15 years at Tokyo, the Hague, Montreal and other places including the European Convention of August 4, 1978 to deal with one or the other aspects of the differing views of the member states. Some countries are supporting terrorism. Libya has been a pioneer in abetting and aiding terrorism. Although Libya had denied supplying the IRA with weapons and ammunition, including surface-to-air Soviet missiles, British authorities claimed that Libyan plastic explosive was used in a bomb by the IRA on June 15, 1988 to kill British soldiers in Ulster. It was also learnt that the Japanese Red Army shifted its base from Lebanon to Libya. Israeli officials claimed Saudi Arabia by Sunni Muslim members of Islamic Jihad during 1988. While Saudis were paying for attacks, Israel said operational direction came from Jordan[19].

No-Surrender Policy

It is important in combating terrorism that there is no question of surrender on the part of the Government to the demands of terrorists. Such capitulation only reinforces that terrorists perception of the strategy as effective and encourages them in their actions. Another evil following from such capitulation is the emulation of successful terrorist techniques by others and new groups. Government must understand this and in no case should they bow before the terrorists. Yielding to the demands of the terrorist will encourage them to commit more heinous crimes and give them the feeling that they can get away from any situation and that too with rewarding results.

Intelligence

The most important job to counter terrorism is collecting timely intelligence. A support apparatus or a ground base is needed by terrorists in the target country. Likely targets are reconnoitered first by teams either based locally or sent from outside and then resources are mobilised and hit teams selected. Quite possibly, the local support organization may not have all the knowledge of the various stages of preparations, but high level intelligence obtained from the penetration of the support organizations may give useful leads to enable the security agencies to develop the information and take timely suitable preventive measures. Such sources may also help in investigating a terrorist crime after it has been committed. Penetration of indigenous terrorist organizations must also be attempted. Arrested terrorists provide significant clues and useful information. They therefore requires special treatment. They should be given all possible inducement and encouragement to change allegiances. Maximum advantage be taken of their ability to help the Government either by way of giving information or helping in identifying the culprits.

Pressure on Countries Supporting Terrorism

Countries suffering from terrorism must jointly explore the means of chastising the countries that harbour or support terrorists. As soon as any terrorist act takes place in one country, the other friendly countries in the region must denounce the act. The country which has given shelter and facility to the hijackers should be boycotted and economic sanctions imposed on it.

Check on Foreigners

Vast powers have been given to the law enforcing agencies to deal with foreigners in different countries and they should be exercised without any inhibition in regulating foreigners movement and activities. Cases of overstaying or seeking extensions for no ostensible reasons deserve special attention. Foreigners not reporting to the registration authorities, when required to do so, need immediate attention. Terrorists generally use forged travel documents. Fool-proof arrangements are, therefore, required to detect forgeries in the travel documents at the immigration check-posts on arrival and departure.

Political Process and Military Options

Political process of persuasion goes side by side the military options. Military action alone can not eliminate terrorism. It may retard terrorist activities for the time being only[20].

Multilateral Initiatives by UN

In dealing with the ongoing initiatives to prevent and combat terrorism, the study on the international initiatives on terrorism was undertaken several times in the United Nations. The question of terrorism was first introduced in the UN in the early 1970s at a time when Europe had become the theatre of terrorist activity of expatriate groups, such as the diverse Palestinian groups, as well as indigenous groups like the Baader-Meinhof, the Red Brigade, and the Basque terrorist group[21]. An Adhoc Committee On International Terrorism was established in 1973 consisting of thirty five members and was organized into three Sub-committees to study three distinct issues relating to the question of international terrorism. They were[22]:

(a) The definition of international terrorism.

(b) Underlying causes of international terrorism.

(c) Measures for the prevention of international terrorism.

Practical measures to Combat Terrorism were worked out by Several working groups of UK, USA, Sweden and Uruguay[23]. The efforts to curtain international terrorism still continues by the UN.

Regional and Other Organisations

In recent times, the movement towards regionalism has witnessed the growth of regional organizations and associations in different regions of the world, and consequently a trend towards adopting a regional approach in dealing with different political and economic issues concerning the international community. The **European Economic Community** (EEC), the **Organisation of American States** (OAS) and the **Association of South East Asian Nations** (ASEAN) are some of the early manifestations of this development, while the **South Asian Association for Regional Co-operation** (SAARC) is the most recent. The initiatives taken within some of these regional organizations on the question of international terrorism provide a good illustration of the particular advantages of a regional approach, in dealing with vital international issues[24]. Some of the initiatives are as under:

(a) European Convention on the Suppression of Terrorism (1977)[25].

(b) SAARC Initiative to Combat Terrorism in the Region-SAARC Regional Convention on the Suppression of Terrorism(1985)[26].

(c) OAS Initiative to Combat Terrorism in the Region (1970).

(d) Convention to Prevent and Punish Acts of Terrorism taking the form of crimes against Persons and related Extortion that are of International Significance, signed at Washington, February 02, 1971[27].

Constructive approach to the adoption of practical measures to combat terrorism in the background of the new international climate is also evident in parallel developments in UN fora and other regional conventions.

India's Contribution to Eliminate Terrorism

India's struggle against terrorism is a part of a world-wide struggle to promote the rule of law as against the rule of the gun, a struggle for democracy as against authoritarianism; a struggle for the triumph of reason, compassion and rationality as against forces which fan religious fanaticism and promote communal hatred; a struggle for a world order which celebrates human diversity and cultural pluralism, as against the imposition of a rigid, dull and monotonous uniformity. Responsible international opinion, whether in the media or in governments, cannot for long avoid taking a clear position on whether human rights are better protected by sympathizing with terrorists and their external sponsors or by supporting firmly democratic governments. Constant sniping at elected governments, thereby encouraging cross-border terrorism, even casually or unintentionally, is a sure recipe for destroying both democracy, the cradle of human rights, and the cherished offspring.

India seeks the world community's sympathy, understanding and support in its struggle against terrorism which aims at creating an environment in which, man's life will be poor, nasty, brutish and short. For whom would the bells toll if the terrorist groups which now challenge our territorial integrity succeed in their objective? They toll for all of us who believe in a world order where reason and rationality prevail, and in which men and women with diverse cultural, religious and linguistic identities can live and work together in a spirit of brotherhood and human solidarity[28].

Notes and References

1. LR Reddy, *The Worst of Global Terrorism*, APH Publishing Corporation, New Delhi, 2002, pp.1-2.
2. General S. Padmanabhan, *The Writing on the Wall-India Checkmates America 2017*, Manas Publications, New Delhi, 2004, p.59.
3. LR Reddy, *Op.cit,* p.17.
4. Chomsky Noam, *9/11*, Natraj Publishers, Dehradun, 2002, pp.120-121.
5. LR Reddy, *Op.cit*, p.17.
6. Perera Amrith Rohan, *International Terrorism*, Vikas Publishing House, New Delhi, 1997, p.5.
7. LR Reddy, *Op.cit*, pp.74-75.
8. Chomsky Noam, *Op.cit*, pp.123-124.
9. *Ibid*, p.76.
10. Maj Gen Arjun Ray, VSM, *Kashmir Diary –Psychology of Militancy*, Manas Publications, New Delhi, 1997, p.25.
11. Chomsky Noam, *Op.cit,* p.198.
12. DP. Sharma, *Countering Terrorism*, Lancers Books, New Delhi, 1992, p.55.
13. LR Reddy, *Op.cit*, p.142.
14. *Ibid*, p.210.
15. The 9/11 Commission Report: Executive Summary, *Strategic Digest, Institute of Defence Studies and Analyses*, New Delhi, Vol 34, August 2004, p.1145.

16. DP. Sharma, *Op.cit*, pp. 59 and 61.
17. LR Reddy, *Op.cit*, p.450.
18. *Ibid*, pp.452-454.
19. DP. Sharma, *Op.cit*, pp.229-230.
20. *Ibid,* p.231.
21. Perera Amrith Rohan, *Op.cit*, p.47.
22. *Ibid,* p.49.
23. *Ibid*, p.87.
24. *Ibid*, p.94.
25. *Ibid*, p.97.
26. *Ibid*, p.113. A Group of Experts reached an agreement on the following formulation which was a synthesis of the formulations in the Indian and the Sri Lankan Working Papers:

    "Murder, manslaughter, assault causing bodily harm, kidnapping, hostage-taking and offences relating to firearms, weapons, explosives and dangerous substances- when used as a means to perpetrate indiscriminate violence involving death or, serious bodily injury to person or damage to property".
27. *Ibid*, p.133.
28. Khurshid Salman, *Beyond Terrorism: New Hope for Kashmir*, UBS Publishers and Distributors, New Delhi, 1999, pp.33-34.

4

Terrorism in Jammu and Kashmir

Militancy in J & K:

Moves and Counter-Moves

"Kashmir is a garden of eternal spring or an iron fort to a palace of Kings". **(Mughal Emperor Jehangir)**[1]

In the summer of 1989, the air blowing from the Mughal Gardens of Srinagar carried more than the fragrance of flowers with it. It was heavy with the whiff of anticipation and the promise of independence. The murmurs were becoming louder by the day as more people joined the clamors of *azadi*. Terrorist activities in the Valley had almost doubled in one year. Yet, despite the nascent stage of violence, the movement spearheaded by outfits such as Jammu and Kashmir Liberation Front (JKLF), Ansar-ul-Islam and Hizbullah Islam Jamhooria, among others, was getting more popular support – both overt and covert. The political forces closeted in their insular edifices, however, could smell neither the rising dissension nor the seriousness of the changing mood of the greater population of Kashmir.

For chronological purpose, the year 1989 has been earmarked as the beginning of militancy in Kashmir. *That single year saw at least 2,154 incidences of terrorist violence in the State*, some as high profile as the kidnapping of Rubaiya Sayeed, the daughter of the then Union home minister, Mufti Mohammed Sayeed. The year also saw a systematic emasculation of the state machinery in Jammu and Kashmir (J&K). Apart from targeting innocent civilians, the militants were increasingly taking on the

J&K Police, the Central Reserve Police Force(CRPF) and the Department of Intelligence Bureau (DIB) personnel[2].

The local populace of Kashmir was also coming out in the streets chanting the *azadi* slogan in support of the militants. The State Government under Farooq Abdullah was either helpless or did not understand the gravity of the situation. It was no longer a law and order problem as government officials were dismissing it. In the absence of strong leadership at the top, the lower-rung civil and police official were reluctant and often scared to take action.

Background

The 1989 benchmark not withstanding, dissension or clamor for independence in Kashmir is as old as the Instrument of Accession, which Maharaja Hari Singh signed on October 14, 1947. Despite the period of calm that followed, and also the war which India fought with Pakistan over Kashmir, there have always been deep pockets of dissent in the State. India's original promise of holding a plebiscite to give the people a right to decide their future also keep the hopes of independence alive. So much so, that even a leader of the stature of sheikh Abdullah-who was proud of his friendship with Nehru and rubbished Pakistan's claim on J&K on the basis of religion – toyed and even went public with the idea.

Fuelled by various extraneous and local factors, and compounded by Delhi's ad hoc and inconsistent policies, the 40-year-old dissension simply took a violent turn in the late eighties. However, this outburst was essentially political in nature. Despite Pakistan's efforts at lending it a religious shade, the militant movement in Kashmir remained indigenous and above religious differences. Kashmiris (read, Muslims of the Valley) were seeking independence from India because of their perceived grievances and not because they felt unsafe in a country with a Hindu majority.

The main reasons for this was the very temperament of the Kashmiri people. Islam came to Kashmir through wandering Minstrels and Sufis, and not by the power of sword. The Muslims in this region hardly had any history of strife in the name of religion. They have always been tolerant people, simplistic in their faith and believing in the cult of Sufism. Even in 1947, when Pakistan raiders invaded Kashmir smug in the belief that the local population would support them on the basis of common religion, they were surprised to find the locals inimical to their designs. When Pakistan tried the same poly 18 years later in 1965, it was yet again surprised by the lack of local support for its cause. The Pakistan Air Marshal Asghar Khan later explained the reason for Pakistan's daredevilry. He said, "*It was assumed that widespread support existed within occupied Kashmir to make such a guerilla campaign a success.*"[3] To this day, for an average Kashmiri, the idea of a merger with Pakistan is more abhorrent than staying with India.

Though there have always been pockets of religious extremism in Kashmir and a few madrasas have been teaching the intolerant faith, the majority and terrorist outfits like the JKLF, largely remained indifferent to them. Even Jamaat-e-Islami had very few takers in Kashmir. The situation, however, started changing with the beginning of the eighties.

Sheikh Abdullah, who was considered the vital link between New Delhi and Kashmir, passed away in 1982. His son, the flamboyant Farooq Abdullah, inherited his father's mantle and proved his popularity by winning the 1983 elections. However, a term later he squandered his legacy by entering into an alliance with the Congress for the 1987 elections. The polls were massively rigged, pushing many fence-sitters who contested and lost the elections, including the now notorious Syed Salahuddin, the Chief of Hizbul Mujahideen, into militancy. Farooq Abdullah later regretted the unholy alliances as it put a permanent question mark on his credibility.

The 1987 debacle added to the rising discontentment among the local people. Though terrorist outfits (all indigenous) had started attacking and killing Kashmiri Pandits towards the end of 1989 in an effort to encourage their exodus from the Valley, the motive was political and economic, not religious. The Pandits of Kashmir were better educated than their Muslim counterparts and held better jobs, disproportionate to their population. Besides, they did not share the Muslim enthusiasm for independence from India. To the militants, they were stooges of the Indian Government. Besides, it made sense to change the demography of the Valley. Another pointer to the non–religious profile of the insurgency was the fact that militants did not target other religious minorities. Sikhs were not touched at all in the early years. Unlike the Pandits, Sikhs were largely peasants or small–time businessmen. They wielded little political power, and therefore did not pose any threat to the separatist movement. Terrorised by target killings, Pandits started moving out of the Valley by the beginning of the year 1990. However, of all the civilians killed by the terrorists till 1994, the majority were Muslims. Had it been a religious movement, the figures would have been different.

The Changing Profile

The nature of insurgency started changing once Pakistan hijacked the JKLF agenda under Prime Minister Benazir Bhutto. The rising levels of violence in Kashmir and the inability of the Indian Government to control the problem gave Pakistan the opportunity it had been looking for since 1947. It began by supporting the JKLF by way of funds, arms and training. Camps were opened in Pakistan occupied Kashmir (PoK) and the JKLF chairman, Amanullah Khan, ran the movement from there. But even as Pakistan was supporting the JKLF, it floated a number of other indigenous out-fits as early as 1989. Chief among these was the Hizbul Mujahiideen. *While the JKLF was fighting for the independence, the Hizbul agenda was a merger with Pakistan.* It made sense for Pakistan to weaken the JKLF and let the Hizbul run the campaign. The JKLF finally gave up the armed struggle in 1994, leaving the center stage for Pakistan dominated outfits led by the ISI-sponsored **Hizbul Mujahideen**[4]. Map showing an independent State of Jammu and Kashmir as sourced by JKLF is given in **Annexure 4.**

Pro-Pakistan Militancy

As pro-Pakistan militants gained ascendancy in Kashmir, the nature of movement started changing dramatically. Pakistan understood that the biggest sustainable force was religion, and hence it was necessary to wed freedom with religion. The internal situation in India also helped their cause. The demolition of the Babri Masjid and the communal carnage that followed in some parts of the country were used as fodder to foster communal intolerance. To further exploit the religious divide, terrorist activities were extended to the Doda district of Jammu by August 1992. Within a year, polarization along religious lines was complete.

Though Kashmir topped the Pakistan agenda, it was abetting another war around this time. Ever since the withdrawal of Soviet troops from Afghanistan in 1989, Pakistan, with the tacit encouragement of the Unites States, was providing support (financial and military) and training to Afghan mujahideen. Before 1989, these mujahideen were supposed to fight the Soviets. However, after their retreat and the fall of Soviet-backed President Najibullah, the guns were trained on the Kajik – dominated Burhanuddin Rabbani government. Gulbuddin Hikmetyar, with the support of the ISI, led the mujahideen (who were schooled in radical Islam in Pakistani madrasas) against the government of Rabbani. The ensuing civil was left bearly 10,000 dead. Even as the Pakistan-trained mujahideen were fighting the government in Afghanistan, Pakistan diverted over a thousand mujahideen into Kashmir in 1993. These were militants hardened by fighting against the Soviet army. This was the first time foreign mercenaries had entered into the movement in Kashmir.

As the battle line changed in Afghanistan, they changed in Kashmir too. The movement was no longer indigenous as it was the local population in Kashmir started coming out in favour of the mercenaries who were hailed as Islamic warriors and were controlled by the ISI in Pakistan. For the first time since the beginning of the militancy, certain sections in the media were actually talking about *"liberated zones"* (completely in control of the militants) in the pockets of Anantnag, Baramulla and Srinagar.

Pakistan Apprehension

To avoid being declared as a state sponsoring terrorism, Pakistan moved its terrorist base from Pakistan-occupied-

Kashmir (PoK) to Afghanistan in 1994. The ISI paid the Jalalabad Shura (warlords) to take these bases under its wings. To further wipe its hands from the charges of sponsoring terrorism, the government made various Islamic parties and organizations within Pakistan responsible for training and arming mujahideen who were to fight in both Kashmir and Afghanistan.

While in 1989 Kashmiri youth crossed the border to train in PoK, now they were doing so in Afghanistan alongwith Mujahids from other countries, including Pakistan, Afghanistan, Algeria, Yemen and even Saudi Arabia. As a consequence of this privatization of militancy, the Kashmir mujahids were exposed to militants from other nationalities. By the end of 1994, an even more conservative version of mujahideen emerged from the madrasas of Pakistan. This new group called itself the ***Taliban*** or the "students". They were stepped in the conservative school of Saudi Wahhabism and Deobandism. They were better trained and, more importantly, better motivated than the mujahideens of Hikmetyar who had not been able to make much headway against the Rabbani Government in Kabul, which was backed by the Tajik commander Ahmed Shah Masud. *The emergence of the Taliban changed the equations in Kashmir as well*[5], though not immediately.

Prominent Militant Groups

Presently, there are a number of extremist groups working in Jammu and Kashmir, and prominent amongst these are as under[6]:

(a) ***Hizbul Mujahideen (HM)*** of the Jammat-e-Islami: HM is essentially an organisation of indigenous Kashmiris. The recruits of HM got training in camps in Afghan territory by Instructors of Hizb-e-Islami and the Afghan mercenaries who came into Kashmir were followers of Heckmatyar. The HM describes its aim as liberation of Kashmir from India and its merger with Pakistan.

(b) ***Markaz Dawa Al Irshad***. Its militant wing is called Lashkar-e-Toiba and the Harkat-ul-Ansar(HUA).

(c) ***Al Badr.***

Lashkar-e-Toiba, Harkat-ul-Ansar and Al Badr are supporters of the Taliban. Their aim is the liberation of the Muslims in rest of India[7]. These organizations view Kashmir as the gateway of India and call for the creation of two more Muslim homelands – one in North India and other in South India.

In the forefront of the militant activities in Kashmir were groups like **Lashkar-e-Toiba** and **Harkat-ul-Ansar** that had a substantial number of foreign **mujahids** in their ranks. Though the majority still comprised the Kashmiris, they were now the hardened lot who had seen the battlefields of Afghanistan. Their respect for local traditions had waned after years of training abroad. And most importently, they were not contents to view the Kashmir issue in isolation anymore. The issue now encompassed the so-called Muslim brotherhood. However, the Indian Government dismissed these as mercenary voices. Some of them were foreigners, no doubt, but they were not fighting for money–they were fighting for their religion. The word jehad was now being used quite frequently to describe the freedom movement.

Taliban and Pakistan

The Taliban was the product of Pakistan's ill-conceived foreign policy for Afghanistan. The ISI funded militant madrasas propounding Saudi Wahhabism in order to create a force to fight the Soviets in Afghanistan. Once that war was won, these illiterate Pashtuns who knew nothing except a contrived interpretation of the Quran and how to wield weapons were expected to return to the madrasas. Unfortunately, that did not happen. As the civil war in Afghanistan spiralled out of control, the Taliban emerged yet again to restore order.

Free-Run

Pakistan decided to wait and watch in the beginning. However, as the Taliban gained control of one region after the other in Afghanistan with lightning speed, it started supporting them in the hope that through them it would get strategic space in Afghanistan. Pakistan also believed that with a malleable Taliban, it would be able to quash the demand of merger of the Pashtun- dominated areas in North Pakistan with Afganisthan. However, all these hopes were belied. Taliban refused to recognize the Durand Line, and terrorists all over the world had a free run of the Pakisan-Afghanistan border. The biggest irony of all was that they started fomenting sectarian violence within Pakistan. A large number of junior ISI officials and Pakistan's Pashtun population started sympathizing with them.

Pakistan could not upset the Taliban applecart for the simple reason that it was giving space to Pakistani groups operating in Kashmir. However, what it did not realize was that these groups were being distanced from Pakistan and the ISI because of their exposure to mujahids from other countries. Moreover, many junior level ISI operatives were also being swayed by the Taliban world view. Pakistan probably realized what was happening, but could not strengthen its weakening link.

Impact of Kargil War

The Kargil war in 1999 saw the end of Pakistan's already marginal influence over the Taliban. What was called Operation Badr by Pakistan had a two-fold strategy. The first part involved the regular Pakistan soldiers in civilian clothes intruding into Indian territory in the Kargil sector to try to alter the Line of Control. These were assisted by the mujhahids, who were now under the sway of the Taliban. At the same time, the Pakistan Army was to keep the border alive so that a large number of these mujahids could infiltrate in to Kashmir. The US intelligence later disclosed that the Harkat-ul-Mujahideen and Laskar-e-Toiba were involved in the Kargil war.

However, once the first part of the strategy failed, Prime Minister Nawas Sharif was compelled to call off the infiltration. But it was too late by then. The mujahids were no longer listening to Pakistan. When Nawas Sharifif's government fell and the Pakistan Army Chief Pervez Musharaf assumed power, he understood that his control over the mujahids was fast eroding. They were not only calling the shots in Kashmir, but also fomenting trouble in Pakistan. After all, if the Taliban model was the ideal then why shouldn't Pakistan embrace it as well?.

Final Blow

The final blow to the Pakistan government's influence over the Talibanised mujahideen was when Harkat-ul-Mujahideen hijacked the Indian aircraft IC 814 in December 1999. The hostages were released following a week-long drama after Indian external affairs minister Jaswant Singh personally escorted Maulana Masood Azhar, Mushtaq Zargar and Ahmed Omar Shaikh to Kandahar. The Taliban minister for civil aviation was present on the tarmac to receive Masood Azhar. Upon his release, Masood Azhar founded a suicide bomber outfit Jaish-e-Mohammad while Mushtaq Zargar started Al-Umar. Like Harkat-ul-Mujahideen, both had close ties with the Taliban. Pakistan or General Musharraf had no control over them. General Musharraf, in fact, was now voicing the jehadi agenda.

Jehad in Kashmir

Kashmir has increasingly become embroiled in this worldwide jehad. After the Kargil war, Mullah Omar declared his support for jehad in Kashmir. This was enough for militant elements every where in the world to embrace Kashmir as their cause. The post 1999 war of independence which the ethnic Kashmiris believed they were fighting against India turned into a jehad as the movement was now being led by the Taliban. Pakistan started losing ground rapidly as jehadi outfits like Lashkar-e-Toiba, Jaish-e-Mohammed and Harkat-ul-Mujahideen–inspired, trained and provided for by the Taliban and the Al-Qaeda–took over the armed struggle in Kashmir. Killings targetted at minorities-including the Sikhs increased, suicide bombers for ***fidayeen*** started hitting their targets with greater success and, most importantly, the terrorists started taking on the Indian Army with greater impunity.

Once upon a time, the Hizbul had made the JKLF redundant in post–1999 Kashmir, it was getting the same treatment from the Jehadi or the Talibanised outfits. Since it was being pushed to the corner, and since General Musharaf found it increasingly difficult to control the Jehadees, the Hizbul declared a cease fire in Kashmir in 2000. However, this was soon retracted as friction appeared within the Hizbul Cadre. Syed Salahuddin, the Hizbul chief based in Pakistan, derided the cease fire moves made by its commander Majid Dar in Kashmir.

Clearly, Syed Salahuddin could not ignore the Jehadis, especially since he was based in Pakistan. Between 1990 and 1994, Kashmiri youth were queuing upto join the Hizbul in 2000, they were going the Jehadi way. Compounding the situation was the changing attitude of the local populace. By the beginning of 2001, there were increasing demands for according the dead Jehadis a Martyr's burial. In 1994, the Hizbul was hailed as the liberating force; six years down the line, the same respect or awe being reserved for the jehadis.

Despite the overt similarities between the condition of the JKLF in 1994 and the Hizbul in 2001, the latter did not suffer a similar fate for the simple reasons that the Pakistan Government backed it. Besides, once it realized that it was getting marginalized by the jehadis, it started towing their lines, thereby ensuring its survival.

Leading to an Unfinished War

The immediate fall out of this was that the disarrayed jehadis became desperate. The first sign of this desperation was the suicide attack outside the Jammu and Kashmir Assembly on October 1, 2001, which killed 29 people. The Talibanasied Jaish-e-Mohammed took responsibility for the attack which was condemned by every one including Gen Musharraf, who was now back to his old tune of supporting freedom struggle in J & K. Hardly a year ago, he was talking of a jehad in Kashmir. The British foreign secretary, Jack Straw, linked the attack to Osama Bil Laden. Apart from that dastardly attack, there was a lull in the overall terrorist activities in the state. The jehadis were obviously groping in the dark. Their desperation was again evident in the ill – conceived attack on the India Parliament on December 13, 2001. Pakistan again rushed to condemn the attack, as did the rest of the world. However, by this time the

Indian leadership was obviously tried for waiting for the second phase of Operation Enduring Freedom to start, which the US promised would address Indian concerns (read, Kashmir).

The Indian Government decided to take matters in its own hands and announced a general mobilization of its troops, the biggest ever in Indian history. There was immense pressure on Pakistan to rein in the jehadis, but Musharraf was at pains to explain that he did not control them. In his address on January 12, 2002, directed towards both his compatriots and the West, he reiterated his commitment to fight terrorism. He declared that he would not allow any organization to run a terrorist movement from Pakistani soil. He also banned a number of jehadi and Islamic organizations, some of which were fomenting sectarian trouble within Pakistan. Among the banned outfits operating in Kashmir were Jaish–e–Mohammed and Lashkar–e–Toiba. There offices were sealed and the leadership rounded up.

Interestingly, the Hizbul was not banned. The general lull in terrorist activities continued in Kashmir, though sporadic killings did not cease. Despite the troop mobilization, the possibilities of war had receded. It appeared that India was looking for a face saving formula to demobilize its troops. It continued to harp on Pakistan handing over 20 criminals on India's list, including underworld don Dawood Ibrahim, an accused in the Mumbai bomb blast case. Also on the list were a few old Khalistan hands. Pakistan continued to ignore these demands.

On the Kashmir front, the mobilization seemed to have achieved practically nothing. With the onset of spring – the time when infiltration starts – there was a marginal increase in violence, but that was almost along expected lines. In May 2002, the suicide bombers started attacking various army camps in places like Rajouri, Jammu and Udhampur. The most audacious of these was the attack on the Kaluchak camp near Jammu. In a pre-dawn attack, the fidayeen killed 32 people–mostly the women and children of army personnel. Militancy has come full circle in Kashmir today. In 1994, the JKLF was sidelined, training camps were shifted from Pakistan to Afghanistan and the process of " jehadification" had begun. By 2001, the Hizbul was sidelined and the Talibanised jehadis were holding sway in Kashmir, looking up to Mullah Omar and Osama Bin Laden for inspiration, moral support and material sustenance. In July 2002, Mullah Omar was on the run and Pakistan once again appeared to be the only benefactor of the freedom fighters. They could no longer afford to be jehadis. The training camps that were earlier moved to Afghanistan now shifted back to Pakistan-occupied-Kashmir (PoK). A report in an Indian newspaper mentioned the existence of at least three active training camps in PoK.

Mind of the Kashmiri Militant

In the opinion of the Indian Government the real culprits have always been the militants, whom they hold responsible for terrorizing the people of Kashmir into open hostility against India and committing numerous extra-judicious executions[8]. The Indian Government also believes that militancy does not enjoy the popular support it had in the early 1990s. The militants lost some of their original élan due to a number of reasons: a continuous proliferation of groups, confusion and division in their ranks, regarding their ultimate objective, and Pakistan's changing policy towards different groups of militants. Indian authorities also allege that young men have been abducted against their will to become militants. In August 1993, The **Times of India** reported how Indian forces had intercepted a large group of 'Kashmiri Youth' who were being taken to Azad Kashmir at gun point by members of the Al Jehad militant group and that they had been promised sums ranging from Rs 2000 to Rs 10000.

Reports of rape by militants have also tarnished their image. While it is not clear that militant leaders have explicitly sanctioned such abuses, there is little indication that the militants have done anything to stop their forces from committing rape. *Some incidents of rape by militants appear to have been motivated by the fact that the victims or their families are accused of being informers*[9].

In the early days of insurgency, attacks were made on women for not adhering to the prescribed dress code, the wearing of the *burqah*. The Daughters of the Nation, an orthodox women's group, was particularly active in issuing threats and some women had to be hospitalized because acid was sprayed on their exposed faces. Due to adverse publicity, this has stopped and, especially in Srinagar, women do not feel obliged to wear the veil[10]. Allegation of corruption and drug dealing have also been leveled against some militants, in what the authorities call the 'criminalisation' of the movement, as well as military and government officials. Many of the orchards in Kashmir, owned by the Hindus, who fled, have now divided between the top militants. They are changing the deeds and so it will be impossible to trace their original owners.

The Kashmir situation is explosive, complex with serious internal and external ramifications. The normal law and order machinery and State Administration is incapable of handling it and of bringing about an environment whereby democratic processes can take place. It requires policy enunciation at the highest level and control and execution of the plan at the same level[11].

A New Phase

Pakistan informed the global community that it cannot hold the Kashmiri militants in leash indefinitely, and therefore India needs to initiate a dialogue with Pakistan at the earliest. However, what it did not say was more important. The freeze on militants would continue as long as it takes Pakistan to streamline its new policy on Kashmir. Hence, Gen Musharraf and the ISI were working overtime to isolate the pro-Taliban militant outfits.

The two primary Talibanised outfits, jaish-e-Mohammad and Lashkar-e-Toiba, were disbanded and their leaders, Masood Azhar and Hafiz Saeed, were detained and arrested respectively. The third group, Al Omar, run by Mushtaq Zargar, decided to relinquish its jehadi agenda and started towing Musharraf's line.

The militants who agreed to reinvent themselves were put at the disposal of either Hizbul Mujahideen or Al Omar. According to the newspaper reports coming from Pakistan, the idea was to make the Kashmir movement more organized and cohesive. In the early phase of the movement, Pakistan thought it wise to create a number of smaller outfits to deflect attention. However, now it appeared that it had started thinking that for a sustainable agitation with the respectability of a freedom struggle, it was important to create a single cohesive body, with an inbuilt political front. Further, it was imperative that such a body remain kashmiri in nature and not appear to be based in Pakistan.

Rumors were afloat in PoK about a new militant group, Kashmir Liberation Army (KLA), to be headed probably by Mushtaq Zargar. All the other groups were likely to come under its umbrella. Though KLA would enjoy Pakistan's tacit support, inclusive of weapons and funds, for appearances sake it would be a completely indigenous and independent body. The allegations that Pakistani nationals are operating in Kashmir would have been met by the reasoning that they were originally Kashmiris who fled Kashmir to escape Indian aggression. According to Mushtaq Zargar, " Whoever is fighting in Kashmir is a Kashmiri. The fact that those who fled from Kashmir in 1947 due to Indian repression and settled in Pakistan are now taking part in the freedom struggle along with their oppressed brethren does not impair the cause."[12]

The fact that the jehadi outfits are still refusing to fall in line with Pakistani policy implies that their source of sustenance, both physical and moral, has not dried up. If they feel that they can still fight the Indian security forces on their own, then obviously the American war against terrorism has not been entirely successful. If Mullah Omar, most of the top Taliban leadership and Osama Bin Laden are still at large, there is little possibility that this so-called jehad will end in the near future. There are reports already that in the absence of Osama Bin Laden, his son has risen in the ranks and is now directing the worldwide jehad.

Whatever the future of jehad in Kashmir may be, the insurgency was poised to enter a violent new phase in 2003 in spite of innumerable government initiatives. *Newspaper reports in India indicated that nearly 400 security personnel and 1,000 civilian died in terrorist violence during 2002. And this, when the Indian Army was mobilized and Pakistan has assured the world that nothing was happening on the Line of Control.*[13] Through the summer, there were a number of instances of infiltration –some of which were foiled and some successful. Interestingly, there were also reports about Musharraf training a new breed of young militants in PoK who would be the future freedom fighters. A report from the Indian home ministry indicated that a fresh movement of Kashmiri youth from Kashmir to PoK had begun. These young boys were being taken across the border by the militants in small batches of 10 to 15.

President Musharraf has already told the West that the freeze on militancy–India believes that there was never a complete freeze-will not continue indefinitely unless India initiates a dialogue. Pakistan was obviously waiting to complete the electoral process before increasing the tempo in Kashmir. As in on cue, Hafiz Saeed was released on November 19, 2002, and Masood Azhar on December 30, 2002. While Saeed started issuing threats to the Indian Government, Azhar has left for an unknown destination. There is no doubt that the tempo will increase. And this time, the initiative would rest with the Pakistan–trained and rechristened freedom fighters. In this fight, Nationality would be an important factor. So there may be Afghanistan-hardened militants, but they would be of Kashmir origin–at least officially.

To Sum Up:

From the foregoing discussion, the ground realities in Jammu and Kashmir can be analysed as under:

(a) The post-1989 insurgent movement turned against Pakistan because of her ulterior motives.

(b) The post-1992 Pak action of helping mercenaries supplant the indigenous Kashmiris again turned away Kashmiris from Pakistan.

(c) India need to give the people of the State of Jammu and Kashmir a good governance and a high degree of stake in it.

(d) There is an alienation in Pakistan Occupied Kashmir and Northern areas against Islamabad[14].

There are evidences to prove that Pakistan is a major international security problem. The reasons are as under:

(a) Pakistan is extensively involved in international terrorism.

(b) Pak orientation is towards religious extremism.

(c) Pak is a major narcotics trader and money launderer.

(d) Pak economy is not sound.

(e) It possesses nuclear weapons and the Army dominates its national decision making.

From 1993 onwards, the ISI's assistance to extremist groups was made conditional as under:

(a) The groups must support merger of Jammu and Kashmir with Pakistan.

(b) The group must agree to attack Hindus in Jammu division.

(c) The group should assist the alienated sections of the Muslim youth in the rest of India in developing a militant capability by training them in camps in Kashmir territory.

Current Insurgency

Kashmiri militancy has grown out of isolation, corruption, frustration and finally fundamentalism[15]. Corruption had its origin in the vast sums of money pumped into the Valley as subsidies, which were distributed by the people in power to further their aims. The sequence of specific causes for the current insurgency situation in Kashmir can be attributed to the following[16]:

(a) The questionable and disputed accession of Kashmir to India in 1947.

(b) The gradual dilution/emasculation of Article 370 of the Indian Constitution, which governed the accession of Kashmir to India, by successive governments at New Delhi.

(c) The dismissal of duly elected governments in Kashmir and their replacement with governments more pliable to the interests of the central government in power, at that point of time.

(d) The alleged rigging of the elections, in 1987.

(e) The appointment of governors in Kashmir without obtaining the concurrence of the State Government.

(f) Widespread corruption amongst the politicians, police and bureaucrats in the State.

(g) Low employment prospects for the people of the region.

(h) Shortages of electric power and food grains in the State, due to corruption, leading to a growing enchantment and alienation of the people against the prevailing economic situation.

(i) A singular ineptitude of governance and the use of external threats to justify governmental competence. The indifference and the blinkered perception of the civil administration and their inability to react to the developments in the State contributed to the escalation of the situation.

To sum up, a Muslim-majority State with a common border with Pakistan, having a disputed accession to India, was ripe for insurgency due to the sub-national fervor which arose on account of it being economically backward and being governed by a corrupt political and administrative set up.

The Indian Response

Indian's response to the changing profile of terrorism in Kashmir has been sporadic and reactive. Initially, when the insurgency broke out in the Valley in 1989, India treated it as a law and order problem. The State Police, and the paramilitary forces which were rushed to the valley, came down heavily on the people. The more people took to the streets, the more civilian heads were crushed with a vengeance. In a few months, the State administrative machinery had broken down completely. There were daily demonstrations in the Valley, and the police, instead of doing its job, switched sides and started eulogizing the power of the militant's gun. The years 1990 to 1992 witnessed the biggest deployment of army in the internal security operations in the Valley. While credit should go to the Army Chief, Gen S.F. Rodrigues, for overpowering militancy in the Valley towards the end of 1992, he unfortunately thought of the army's role as an "aid to civil power". This denied the army the opportunity to formulate an aggressive operational policy in the formative stages when the uprising was limited to the Valley.

Moreover, the army's morale took a beating when Gen. Rodrigues was criticized by the political leadership saying that "*good governance is the army's responsibility as well*". George Fernandez, who later became the defence minister – sought the General's resignation in Parliament. The honest General only said that, "the army had helped to overcome terrorism in the State of Punjab, and was now doing the same in the Valley". It was no secret that the political and administrative leadership had packed its bags and left Punjab in the eighties for the army to salvage the situation. The political leadership misinterpreted the General's remarks and concluded that the army's top brass were seeking a larger role in running the country perhaps reminds the maxim, "the devil quotes the scripture".

This incident, which was blown out of proportion by politicians, had its impact on India – Pakistan diplomacy as well. In February 1992, militants of the Jammu and Kashmir Liberation Front (JKLF) based in Pakistan – occupied – Kashmir (PoK) had threatened to cross the Line of Control (LoC) in Kashmir to show open solidarity with their cadres in the Valley. India warned Pakistan that if it did not stop them the situation could go out of control. Understanding India's seriousness, Pakistan stopped the JKLF cadres, but accused India of moving troops into forward locations to attack PoK. At this point, Gen. Rodrigues, after getting clearance from the Defence Minister, Sharad pawar, invited the Pakistan Army Chief, Gen.Asif Nawaz Janujua, to visit India. The visit did not materialize mainly because the Pakistani leadership estimated that it would weaken the militancy in the Valley. On India's part, the unsavory incident in the Parliament, which happened soon after the proposed JKLF march, had dampened Gen Rodrigues' spirits.

The General thereafter took little initiative for the rest of his term as chief[17].

Gen. Rodrigues' successor, Gen BC Joshi, sought to raise the morale of the army. Even before taking office, he publicly identified militancy in the Valley and asserted that it would be a long–drawn challenge to overcome it. One of the first things he did on assuming charge on July 1, 1993 was to inform the Prime Minister that the army's use for internal security duties would imperil national security. He suggested that the army be allowed to go back and train for its primary task at the border. He offered to raise more Rashtriya Rifle (RR) units in quick time for internal security operations. Even while Prime Minister P.V. Narasimha Rao concurred with his Army Chief, there was a clash of swords between Gen Joshi and the State Governor, Gen K.V.Krishna Rao–a former army chief–who had assumed office on Mar 12, 1993.

Governor Rao accepted his job only after the Prime Minister had agreed to his priorities, which were to curb militancy at the earliest, and then conduct assembly elections in the State. According to Governor Rao; "In essence, my view was that Kashmir was mismanaged over a period of time, and that militancy had to be put down before anything else could become functional in the State. Once militancy was controlled, efforts should be made to revive the assembly, which still had two years to go, and after a suitable period, try and hold elections–views that I set down in my letter to him (Prime Minister Rao) as a follow-up to our discussion."[18]

After discussion with the local army commander, Governor Rao sought two divisions worth of additional army troops and twelve BSF battalions urgently to establish an effective counter insurgency grid for the Valley. Gen Joshi expressed his inability to do so, but promised to raise more RR units. The Prime Minister, instead of resolving the issue, thought best not to take sides, and let matters drift. Problems were further compounded by the appointment of Rajesh Pilot, a junior minister in the Home Ministry, as minister–in–charge of Kashmir affairs in January 1993. On the one hand, the Army Chief and the State Governor publicly declared that they were answerable to the Prime Minister alone.

Afghan Mercenaries in Indian Soil

Around this time, Pakistan added to India's problems with a change in strategy. Foreign mercenaries who were well armed, trained and had fought in the Afghan war were inducted into the Valley. These hardened terrorists were skilled in the use of rocket propelled grenades and improvised explosive devices, which were responsible for the maximum number of casualties. The terrorists inside the country were now a mix of foreign mercenaries and Pro-Pakistan Hizbul Mujahideen, the former still in small numbers, who were bold enough to challenge the army in tactical battles. The terrorists also expanded their area of operation to the Doda district, where the situation was ripe for terrorists to inflame communal passions.

Against this backdrop, Gen. Joshi was busy with the raising of RR units and working on proactive means to combat terrorism; Governor Rao was determined to suppress terrorism at the earliest with the army, paramilitary forces and police that were available to him, and hold elections as soon as possible. The home ministry was busy sorting out differences between its two ministers; the external affairs ministry was occupied countering personnel; and the Prime Minister's office had little ideas of its own. *There was no cohesive thinking on how to fight terrorism; every one was working in isolation*. It was evident that whatever Governor Rao and Gen. Joshi were to do would have an impact on counter-terrorism operation in the following years. In an extraordinary issue like this, collective leadership would have gained us more but diametrically opposite views and clash of egos, had a counterproductive result.

State of Law and Order

There is complete breakdown of law and order and insecurity of life and property in Kashmir. The acknowledged figure of 24,000 Hindu families having migrated from Srinagar and the Valley is a clear indication of the gravity of the situation. The militants are calling the shots and have generated vocal public response to their deeds and cause, the so called liberation of Kashmir. Normal life has been disrupted; imposition of curfews to prevent further agitation has not succeeded. If at all it has given cause for further agitation. The militants have been able to gain moral ascendancy by imposing their will by public boycott of Government help to the public and are themselves looking after the deceased militants families. Militants have also succeeded in elimination of Government and other civilian functionaries, who can be termed as exploiters of Kashmiri Muslims or a symbolise dominance over their interests. To manifest their will, bundhs, change to Pakistan Standard Time and use of Pakistan currency had been brought about. By doing this they have systematically eroded the authority of the Government and established their own. They have also infiltrated, over a number of years, their sympathizers into Government Departments, the police and administration at all levels or converted amiable persons in the set up. This has further damphened the Government's ability to tackle the situation. It is almost a state of insurgency, with an identifiable popular cause of liberation. There are both internal and external factors, causes of both cannot be remedied overnight. A concerted long term view of the problem is necessary[19].

Rashtriya Rifles(RR)

First raised in 1990 under the Government Composition Table Part II, the RR is a non-field force at par with the Territorial Army, the National Cadet Corps and various paramilitary forces. At the time of inception, this was a good move as the government did not want to increase the strength of the Regular Army and it hoped that retired soldiers would gradually join the RR. The move was meant to provide both lateral employment to soldiers who are superannuated, and keep the army's annual allocation on pay and allowances in check. It was argued that the RR force so raised would be better trained and motivated than parliamentary forces for counter–insurgency (CI) operations.

Unfortunately, things have changed with the beginning of the insurgency in Kashmir in 1990. The retired soldiers did not join the RR and, in December 1993, Gen Joshi ordered the raising of 30 battalion and associated headquarters (about 40,000 troops) of RR in a record time of one year – and that too, from within the army resources. This was done to ward off international criticism instigated by Pakistan that India had increased its regular army strength in Kashmir, leading to an escalation in human rights violations. The other reasons for this move was Gen. Joshi's plans to hit the terrorist bases in PoK, which necessitated that the regular army revert to its operational role on the LoC.

Despite assurances to the army chief by Prime Minister Rao himself, the home ministry, responsible for all parliamentary forces refused to fund the RR until it weaned away from the defence ministry and came under its total control. This created a piquant situation: *the RR, which was a regular army by another name*[20], could not be under the home ministry. At the same time, it could not be what it actually was – a regular army due to the lack of funds.

Draw Backs of RR

Things continued to drift with a heavy cost for CI operations at two level. First, the Unified Headquarters (UH), which was formed in Kashmir in 1993 to ensure that all CI forces – various parliamentary forces, state police and the RR – work together, did just the opposite. The Border Security Force (BSF) as the oldest paramilitary force, argued that the RR should come under its command. The RR, on the other hand found the BSF and the Central Reserve Police Force incompetent. The two forces and their respective ministries could just not work together. This made the Unified Headquarters a non – starter, where CI forces worked against rather than with one another.

Besides, the RR manifested a host of internal problems, to the glee of militants and their Pakistani sponsors. A force which was culled out from various units and had a frequent turnover of troops *lacked cohesion, motivation, a regimental spirit*, and *plan*, good communications and weaponry. There were several reported and many more unreported instances of soldiers running amok. Cases of soldiers inflicting self-injuries to be eased out of the Valley were not uncommon. A few resorted suicide as the stress became unbearable. The commanding officers of most RR units had no communication at all with their troops. There was a discernible decrease in discipline and patience. Round-the clock vigilance, lack of sleep, and all-pervading psychological fear was taking its toll on the troops. Added to this was the shortage of young officers who could lead men by example from the front and infuse them with confidence. It was a Herculean effort for the army high command to bring about and acceptable normalcy and stability in the RR units a little before the 1999 Kargil War.

At the time of the Kargil War, the RR had a total of 36 battalions under two CI force headquarters (each equivalent to an army division headquarters) – "Victor" for the district of Anantnag, Pulwama and Badgam, and "Delta" for Doda district. The over all Force headquarters (OFH) under an officer of the rank of Lt Gen was the weakest link in the RR because it was an administrative rather than an operational headquarters. The operational control of the RR was with the local Corps Commanders in Kashmir. The CI grids were disturbed during the kargil War when regular troops supporting the RR were moved to the war theater and the two corps commanders – 15 and 16 based in Srinagar and Nagrota – relinquished their CI responsibilities. The commander, OFH, was moved from Delhi to Srinagar in Jun 1999 to assume command of the RR, and he replaced the corps commanders as the security advisor to the chief minister for CI duties. Unfortunately, even while the nation was fighting a war with Pakistan in Kargil, differences between the RR and other paramilitary forces in the UH did not diminish.

After the war, the CI situation detoriated for various reasons. As the commander of the OFH was unacceptable to the chief minister, he was sent back to Delhi. The local corps commanders reverted back to their additional CI task. Regular troops like the 8 Mountain Division, which had been involved in CI duties in Srinagar and were moved to Kargil for the war, were placed permanently under the newly raised 14 Corps headquarters in Leh. This created a grave imbalance in the CI grids at a time when Talibanised jehadis had started infiltrating into the State. The Government ordered the raising of two additional CI force headquarters – "Kilo" for Kupwara and "Romeo" for Rajouri were raised in September 1999 and January

2000 respectively. The earlier internal problems of the RR manifested themselves once again, and there was little co-operation between the RR, Paramilitary forces and the police. The stakes now were much higher as the Talibanised jehadis were different from the foreign mercenaries and indigenous militants. The army therefore raised another RR force headquarters called Uniform Force for the Udhampur area of Jammu division from within its own overstretched resources.

The present strength of the RR force is over 70,000 troops, divided into five force headquarters – Kilo for Kupwara, Victor for the Valley, Delta for Doda, Romeo of Rajouri and Uniform for Udhampur with the persistent overall shortage of young officers, and considering that the cream of the army holds the front line, the *RR unavoidably gets a step motherly treatment in terms of men, material and financial resources*. Even worse, the status of this CI force whether it is part of the regular army or a paramilitary force remains undecided. Moreover, its mandate to exist is being enhanced incrementally by the Government, with its latest term to expire on Marc h 31, 2004. To sum up, the RR, whose strength is over and above that of the regular army, remains an orphaned child being tossed between the defence and home ministries.

The Role of the Paramilitary Forces

The presence of the Army in strength had proved a major deterrent against armed infiltration across the LoC but their employment to deal with the civil population in congested towns should be studiously avoided. The paramilitary forces can certainly tackle such situations without the Army's assistance. The deployment of paramilitary force's posts within towns in educational institutions or other such places not only eats away essential strength but creates frequent problems with the locals. Such a deployment had resulted in constant friction between the public and paramilitary units and had led to avoidable clashes.

The CRPF and BSF units as they are organized presently are quite unsuitable for breaking up mass protests or hartals. All they can do is to open fire killing a large number of people.

The young children who witness these actions or young men who face such situations are hardly likely to make good citizens or remain loyal to India. Here, a common man believes that a reign of terror has been let loose. Moreover, an objective analysis of the role of the paramilitary forces will indicate that they are being put under undue pressure without any chance for rest or recreation. All actions of security forces have to be weighed against their political consequences if the State has to eventually win the war against terrorism sponsored or otherwise on the political battlefield. Nothing should be done to induce or push sensitive groups like students, unemployed youth and intellectuals into a corner with no exit routes, except terrorism and violence[21] .

Unified Headquarters(UH)

The brainchild of Governor KV Krishna Rao, the UH was formed on May 14, 1993. According to Governor Rao[22] ... "*What was set up was a Unified Headquarters and not a Unified Command, as erroneously referred to by some people. The unified concept comprised setting up a unified headquarters under the advisor (home) at the highest level in the State in order to coordinate between the security forces, intelligence agencies and civil departments concerned. At the field level, the two corps headquarters, in addition to their normal operational role of defence against external aggression, were to be responsible for anti-militancy operations in the State with the exception of Srinagar City. Under the corps, the divisions were to be responsible for anti militancy operations in their territorial jurisdiction, and all paramilitary forces meant for anti-militancy operations were to be under the operational control of the divisional commanders*".

It was never realized that the nemesis of UH lay within its own concepts. The paramilitary forces were most hesitant to work under the operational control of the army because the ethos, training, motivation, discipline, style of functioning and chain of command of the two forces were poles apart and impossible to bridge. The problem was further compounded when the paramilitary forces were required to work with the RR, which was practically the same as the regular army. Both indulged in one – upmanship and worked at cross purposes rather than with one another.

The Current Status of Terrorist Movement[23]

A brief survey of the achievements of terrorists and their failures attempted here is with a view to present the current status of secessionist-terrorist movement minus the rhetoric:

Achievement of Aims:

(a) The terrorists have achieved their aim of isolating the population in Kashmir valley morally and physically from the State.

(b) The aim of demoralizing State authority, paralyzing administration and subverting intelligence and police forces of the State has been largely achieved.

(c) The terrorists have proved that they have the capability to survive strong action by security forces and continue to mount attacks on selected targets.

(d) By creating an atmosphere of uncertainty and fear the terrorists have successfully brought all political processes to a standstill.

(e) They have successfully created an environment in which they can induce mass protests and prolonged confrontation between the people and the State at will.

(f) They have introduced religious fundamentalism in a secular society thus scoring a major victory for separatism.

(g) They have induced the State to use disproportionate force against its own population.

Failures:

(a) They have failed to make any substantial progress towards carving out a separate State.

(b) They have failed to convince all people that the methods they are using will lead to freedom from want or help in preserving a distinct Kashmiri identity.

(c) Terrorists have been unable to break the present stalemate and have not been able to graduate to full scale insurgency. They are in no position to tackle the Indian Army and have little hope of attaining such a capability.

(d) They have not been able to avoid Army patrols on the LoC thus suffering major setbacks.

(e) They have failed to induce Pakistan to escalate military confrontation all along the borders with a view to interfering with the Army's anti-terrorist operations.

The World Opinion on Kashmir Issue

USA: In the Unipolar World of the post Cold War, USA is the only super power left and has been arm twisting and forcing some countries to sort out their bilateral issues with or without their help. Earlier India and Pakistan were on a low priority for the US but since mid 1993 the focus has shifted on Kashmir on the basis of human rights violations. The statements of several US officials suggested the following:[24]

1 (a) The Simla Agreement has been a non-starter for so many years. No progress has been made and the position adopted by both sides is far too rigid to allow for any flexibility. By definition, therefore, the agreement is de facto.

(b) That whatever external support there may be for the militants in Kashmir, the US view is that "there are very strong indigenous elements to the insurgency and at this point it is really self-sustaining".

(c) That the underlying causes for the insurgency are not limited to external assistance but to the intensity of the anti-Indian mood in the Valley.

(d) That India needs to 'clean up its act' in terms of human rights violations in the Valley and try to restore some semblance of governance.

(e) That the US views the whole of Kashmir as disputed territory which makes itself evident that the Instrument of Accession(IOA) is also in dispute. That the dynamics of the Kashmir situation have changed dramatically since 1947 when the IOA was signed or the UN resolutions were passed.

(f) That Kashmir will increasingly lead to heightened tensions between India and Pakistan, possibly resulting in another regional conflict, this time involving nuclear weapons.

(g) That whatever solution is found to resolve the issue, it must have the support of the people of Kashmir.

UK: Britain's stand on Kashmir has been for quite sometime, that a, "bilateral dialogue under the Simla agreement" should be used to find a solution. They believe that UN resolutions on Kashmir have been overtaken by events and are not relevant now. They also maintain that, "the external support for the violence in Kashmir should cease and the human rights situation there should improve". Britain is totally against terrorism and believes that it cannot be a valid method to bring about political change.

Europe: The views of the European countries are similar to Britain. They are objective, are not willing to back terrorism and are against Pakistan's supporting the Secessionists, to bring about a political change in her favour. Generally, they are not for internationalizing the Kashmir issue but favour its solution through a peaceful bilateral dialogue between India and Pakistan on the basis of Simla agreement.

China: China was earlier committed to Pakistan and supported her in the diplomatic arena and the UN etc fully. Lately there has been a sea change. China now claims to be a friend of both India and Pakistan and has stated that she has a limited role to play in Indo-Pak dispute on Kashmir.

Organisation of Islamic Conference(OIC): The OIC is composted of all the Muslim countries, mainly from Sub-Saharan Africa and the Middle East. Pakistan has been managing to get the Kashmir issue on the agenda of the meeting of the OIC, sometimes directly, but mostly as part of the section devoted to "conditions of Muslims around the world" and has been successful in obtaining the support of the members. But for the OIC, there have been numerous other issues of greater importance than

Kashmir and the members have been offering moral support except Iran, Turkey and Saudi Arabia.

The United Nations Organisations(UNO): The UN has practically no role to play in helping India and Pakistan to solve the Kashmir issue. Pakistan keeps talking about the old UN resolutions on Kashmir, perhaps for domestic consumption, otherwise these are totally redundant. The UN Secretary General, keeping in mind the provisions of the charter of the world body, has categorically stated that, "there would be no UN mediation on Kashmir till both India and Pakistan wanted it". India, of course, would not agree to mediation, by the UN or for that matter any body else.

Responsibility of Media in Fighting Militancy

What is the role of media in a militancy situation? Media is the Fourth Estate and has a proactive role in dealing with militancy. The national media requires to do a lot of soul searching as perception of its role and obligations in Kashmir appear to be ill defined and hazy. Media needs to consider the following roles:[25]

(a) Mobilise public opinion and perceptions against violence. Towards this aim, the media ought to open debates for assessing achievements of militancy while playing down the glamour and cult of terrorism.

(b) Act as a citizens' watchdog on human rights violations by soldiers as well as militants, by articulating upon and informing about the aspirations of the masses.

(c) Prevent misuse of the media by militants.

(d) Discharge its obligation to keep the people informed of the factual ground situation.

(e) Maintain civilian morale and the nation's commitment to Kashmir.

(f) Pressurise the Government, Kashmiris and the militants to arrive at a conciliatory political meeting point.

Kashmiri Identity

Prime Minister Manmohan Singh told the press in Srinagar in November 2004 that India was willing to consider any proposals from Pakistan on Kashmir subject to two conditions. One, there would be no redrawing of international boundaries. Two, no division of the State on the basis of religion. According to Musharraf, there are two regions in Pakistan's part of the State and the rest of the five regions are on its Indian side. Three well defined regions-Kashmir, Jammu and Ladakh-on this side are well known. The other two as suggested by Musharraf can be formed only by dividing Jammu and Ladakh, on a religious basis. But why did he propose the division of Jammu and Ladakh on a religious basis? The essence of the most formulae on J&K is made up of religion as the basis of identity.[26]

Thrusts Towards a Solution[27]

(a) **Human Rights**. India must start paying full attention to it in right earnest straightway. The use of force, against the militants, must be kept to the minimum, commensurate with the requirements of security. The officials who are found to be responsible for human rights abuses must be appropriately dealt with.

(b) **Firm Stand**. In 1994, Ms Benazir Bhutto boldly declared that the "day was not far", when "Kashmir would be part of Pakistan". Even the official Pakistani spokesmen "address India in haughty and aggressive tones, virtually demanding that it should hand over Kashmir to them". Indian should have reacted angrily against such grave outbursts but she has been playing it cool and has kept her response at a low key. This kind of attitude has been sending wrong signals to Pakistan who started considering India to be weak and vulnerable. India must make firm stand and implement the same with determination.

(c) **Counter Insurgency**. Militancy in the Valley is too serious and cannot be just treated as a 'law and order' problem. The militancy has already spread in the areas of Doda, Udhampur and Jammu region too. Security Forces must ensure that the terrorists and the militants here are initially contained and subsequently eliminated in a short time frame.

(d) **The Economic Measures**. The following suggestions would be the beginning of winning over some sections of the people and will help in reducing militancy to some extent:

(i) **Educated Unemployed**. The educated young men who are willing to work but do not get jobs are the readily available resource for the Militants to exploit. They must be given jobs.

(ii) **School and College Education**. The rich and the well to do families of Kashmir have managed to send their children to schools and colleges outside the State and have secured their future. The Govt needs to step in and undertake to organize education of those poor children, outside J&K, in good institutions free of charge.

(iii) **Kashmir Arts and Crafts**. The world famous Kashmiri shawls, carpets, wood work and papier mache and other such articles which used to be sold to the tourists are hardly being manufactured now because there are no buyers. These industries should be encouraged to produce the articles and marketing facilities.

(iv) **Tourism**. The economy of the Valley flourished, from the fifties onwards, with very large number of tourists, both Indians and foreigners, visiting Kashmir almost throughout the year. Tourism almost finished during 1989-1990 and those who lived on this industry suddenly found themselves without an occupation and no means of livelihood. However, the tourism in J&K has flourished later and has recorded positive influx in the recent years[28].

(v) **Hiring of Civil Transport**. All the private trucks and buses which are not required in the Valley must be hired by the Government and the Security Forces for their use outside the Valley to help owners to earn their living.

(e) **Civil Administration**. The Kashmir administration has been generally believed to be corrupt and inefficient. To bring back normalcy the civil administration must be effective to implement the policy of the government.

(f) **Counter Offensive Against Militancy**. A proxy war is not an openly declared conflict in the traditional sense but is a *war all the same*. After containing the onslaught of the aggressor, in this case the Militants and the Secessionists, from the POK or from within the Valley and the foreign mercenaries, India needs to go on a counter offensive and take the War into Pakistan. A Proxy War is no different and the response needs to be similar. India, therefore, should also inflict a serious low intensity conflict in Sind and POK, and the Northern areas of Gilgit and Baltistan if possible and direct it by proxy through a similar agency like the ISI, and, of course, keep denying her involvement all the time!

(g) **Developmental Activities**. As soon as the insurgency in the Valley is reduced to manageable level, the developmental activities must start to create employment and provide means of livelihood to the local population[29].

(h) **Political Process**. Political process has already started in Jammu & Kashmir and elected government is functioning. Under no circumstances should the government bow down before the militancy.

(i) **Nodal Points**. A nodal point would mean a self contained village kind of a complex whore about 1000 Dogra families are settled. It would act as a firm base, in the hostile area of the Valley, to help the Security Forces to perform better. There are Village Defence Committees(VDC) in the Jammu Region who are armed by the government and defend their villages[30].

(j) **Psychological Warfare**. It is a highly technical discipline and should be left to the experts to organize. The army, in conjunction with the State administration, must counter the disturbing trend by launching a psychological war against all the terrorist organizations and the ISI with the sole aim of restoring confidence of the population in the administration and the security forces and in their commitment to protect them. The entire population of the Valley must be told through video cassettes, TV, radio and the print media about the atrocities being inflicted by the militants on the Kashmiri Muslims, etc.

(k) **Full Fledged Conventional War**. Pakistan has always, in the past, opted for an open conventional War when she failed to grab Kashmir by other means. India should also undertake a limited offensive in Kashmir. In a short war, the gains would be limited and, therefore, there is no requirement of planning large scale operations here.

(l) **The Nuclear War**. A nuclear exchange between the two adversaries though horrible, could happen and India needs to polish her strategy and plan to counter it.

Conclusion

Before considering the available options to India and Pakistan, for the resolution of the Kashmir problem, it would help to have a look again on their respective stands. Pakistan believes that the accession of Kashmir to India was manipulated and was a fraud and the Kashmiris must be given the option of exercising their right of self determination. India's stand on the other hand is that J&K acceded to India on its own. Despite the irreconcilable extreme positions of India and Pakistan, some options can be thought of and enunciated. These are:[31]

Option 1: Partition of J&K along the LC with minor adjustments. It is not acceptable to Pakistan. The Pakistan's version of a 'minor adjustment' was that India should hand over almost the entire Kashmir Valley to her but India offered to concede only some areas. As it did not satisfy Pakistan's aspirations, the talks failed.

Option 2: Partition of J&K and integration of Jammu and Ladakh Provinces with India and negotiating the status of the Valley, the POK and Northern Areas. Pakistan may accept it provided the disputed area is reduced to the Valley only. In its modified version it would not be acceptable to India.

Option 3: Integration of territories with India as mentioned in the preceding option, and have plebiscite in the Valley only, or convert into a UN trust territory for some years and then have a plebiscite after that. It is a non starter with India.

Option 4: Integration of territories with India as mentioned in Option 2, and grant of independence to Kashmir. If Kashmir means only the Valley, Pakistan may accept it but India will not. If it, in addition, includes POK and Northern Area, India may accept it but Pakistan will not.

It is obvious that in the present situation, as it obtains in the Valley, there is no viable option on the basis of which India and Pakistan can find a negotiated solution to solve the Kashmir issue. Recently, President Pervez Musharraf has talked about converting the LoC as International Border which has not been accepted by India. Musharraf also given a Kashmir formula in which he offered to *demilitarize entire Kashmir and invite foreign troops in Kashmir in the garb of United Nations Peace Keeping Forces*[32] which is rejected by India. Finally, despite India's rejection of third party intervention, Musharraf insisted during his two day official visit to the United Kingdom in December 2004 that he would like Britain to play a role in negotiations with India in resolving the Kashmir dispute[33].

Notes and References

1. Emperor Jehangir, *Tuzuk-I Jahanguri*, as quoted in Ajit Bhattacharjee, *Kashmir: The Wounded Valley*, New Delhi, 1994, p.21.
2. VK Sood and Sawhney Pravin, *Operation Parakram: The War Unfinished*, SAGE Publications, New Delhi, 2003, p.29.
3. Marvah, Ved, *Uncivil Wars*, Harper Collins, New Delhi, 1995.
4. VK Sood and Sawhney Pravin, *Op.cit,* p.32.

5. *Ibid.* p.34.
6. LR. Reddy, *The Worst of Global Terrorism*, APH Publishing Corporation, New Delhi, 2002, pp.341-342.
7. *Ibid.*
8. Schofield Victoria, *Kashmir in the Crossfire*, Viva Books Private Ltd, New Delhi, 1997, pp.266-267.
9. Asia Watch, *The Human Rights Crisis in Kashmir,* June 1993, p.98.
10. *Ibid.* p.268.
11. VK Nayar, *Threat from Within, India's Internal Security Environment*, Lancer Publishers, New Delhi, 1992, p.106.
12. In an interview to the Pakistani newspaper *Herald*, quoted in "Kashmir is an Indian Struggle", *The Indian Express*, 03 September 2002.
13. VK Sood and Sawhney Pravin, *Op.cit*, p.46.
14. LR. Reddy, *Op.cit*, pp.341-342
15. VK. Nayar, *Op. cit,* p.76.
16. Singh Harjeet, *Doda: An Insurgency in the Wilderness*, New Delhi, 1999, pp.14 and 15.
17. VK. Sood and Sawhney Pravin, *Op.cit*, p.47.
18. KV Krishna, Rao, *In the Service of the Nation*, Viking, New Delhi, 2001, p.428.
19. VK Nayar, *Op.cit*, p.74.
20. VK. Sood and Sawhney Pravin, *Op.cit*, p.50.
21. Karim Afsir, *Lancer Paper 2, Counter Terrorism, The Pakistan Factor*, Lancer International, New Delhi, 1991, p.126.
22. KV Krishna, Rao, *Op. cit,* p.448.
23. *Ibid*, pp.127-129.
24. KK Nanda, *Conquering Kashmir – A Pakistani Obsession*, Lancers Books, New Delhi, 1996, pp.332-341.
25. Ray Arjun, *Kashmir Diary: Psychology of Militancy*, Manas Publications, New Delhi, 1997, pp.87-88.
26 Puri Balraj, Respect the Kashmiri Identity, *The Indian Express*, Jammu, 25 November 2004, p.4.
27. KK Nanda, *Op.cit,* pp.341-358.
28. Excelsior Correspondent(New Delhi), *Daily Excelsior*, Jammu, 25 January 2004, p3. "Special National Tourism award for excellence was given to Jammu and Kashmir Tourism Department here yesterday for its outstanding performance in

tourism promotion during last year in a big way.... The award was given in recognition of the strategies adopted by J&K Govt to boost tourism, which is the mainstay of the state's economy and also provides livelihood to lakhs of people directly or indirectly".

29. Wani Izhar Ahmed, *India Today*, 29 November 2004, pp 30-32. "Prime Minister Manmohan Singh during his visit to Jammu and Kashmir on 17 November 2004 announced Central investment of Rs 24,000 crore for infrastructure development and creation of 24,000 government jobs and employment of 14,000 women in anganwadis".
30. ENS, *The Indian Express(The Himalayan Mail)*, 04 Nov 04, P 5. "The army, infact, is raising seven Home and Hearth battalions bulk of which would be locals".
31. *Ibid*, pp.363-365.
32. PTI, *The Indian Express(The Himulayan Mail)*, 31 October 2004, p.1.
33. Kashmir: Musharraf wants UK mediation, *The Times of India,* 07 December 2004, p.9.

5

Tourism in Jammu and Kashmir

Introduction

The State of Jammu and Kashmir is a province of widely varying ethnic mix and geography with three different regions. In the South, Jammu Region is a transition zone from the Indian plains to the Himalayas with majority of Hindu population. The Kashmir Region is the beautiful Vale of Kashmir, a large Himalayan valley in the north of the State. Here the people are predominantly Muslims. The natural beauties, the glorious climate and other attractions of the Kashmir valley have received such extravagant praise in the past that the new-comer is apt to picture to himself a **Paradise on Earth**[1] . *'Little Tibet'*, *'the Moonland'* and *'the Last Shangri La*[2] *'* are the names that have been applied to Ladakh Region, all with a bit of truth. Ladakh is a miniature version of Tibet - it is situated geographically in Tibet, which is a high-altitude plateau north of Himalayas. The people are Tibetan in their culture and religion and there are many Tibetan refugees.

The economy of the Valley flourished from the 1950s onwards, with very large number of tourists, both Indians and foreigners, visiting Kashmir almost throughout the year. Their number started dwindling from mid-eighties and the tourism almost came to grinding halt from 1989-90 onwards[3] . Those who depended on this industry suddenly found themselves without an occupation and no means of livelihood.

From a total of 503.62 thousands of tourists (both Indian and foreigners) arrival in Kashmir Valley in 1985, the number has diminished to 8.52 thousands in 1995, 9.98 thousands in 1996 and 16.13 thousands in 1997[4] due to the militancy in the Valley. However, the militancy in the Valley has been brought under control over a period of time, peoples' fear to visit the State due to sporadic acts of violence has reduced and *these acts by the militants have failed to stop the tourists from coming to visit the State*[5].

In the beginning of 2004, The Jammu and Kashmir has been selected for a Special National Tourism Award for its outstanding performance in tourism promotion in 2003. This is the first time that the State has received the coveted prize. It came in the wake of revival and promotion of tourism in the State, which has been badly affected by the one-and-a-half-decade old insurgency[6]. Due to the strategies adopted by the J&K Government to boost tourism and due to the tireless efforts of the Security Forces in the State, the tourism in the State has flourished again.

Jammu Region

General Information: Jammu is the second largest town in the State with a number of interesting attractions in the town. Jammu is still on the plains and in the summer is a sweltering, uncomfortable contrast to the cool heights of Kashmir. Romantic green meadows, majestic mountains, bewitching lakes and valleys is the ability of Jammu in surprising any visitor. Tucked snugly between glittering '*shikhars*' on ancient temples and holy shrines perched atop hillsides, lie the most picturesque scenes one can ever imagine. Jammu is actually two towns – the old town sits on a hilltop overlooking the river. Down beside the hill is the station for buses to other parts of north India and for the lower-class buses to Srinagar. Finally, several km away across the river is the new town of Jammu Tawi where the railway station is located. Map showing the places of tourist interest in Jammu Region are given as **Annexure 5.** Some of the valuable information of tourist interest are as under:

Vital Information– Jammu

(a) Area	: 20.36 sq kms.
(b) Altitude	: 305 Meters.
(c) Temperature	: <u>Maximum</u> <u>Minimum</u>
(i) Summer	43.0°C 23.4°C
(ii) Winter	26.2°C 4.3°C
(iii) Rain Fall	107 cms (July to September).
(d) Best Season	: September to April.
(e) Clothing	: Summer : Light cottons, Winter: Woollens.
(f) Languages	: Dogri, Hindi, Punjabi, Urdu and English.

Transportation

(a) **Air:** Indian Airlines operates scheduled services from Jammu to Delhi–and Srinagar/Leh. Jammu Airport is 08 kms from the city centre. Jet Airways also operates services between Jammu-Delhi and Jammu-Srinagar.

(b) **Rail**: Jammu Tawi is an important railhead of the Northern Railways serving the Jammu and Kashmir State.

The Trains Operating To/From Jammu are:

(a) Malwa Express, Superfast, Indore-Jammu Tawi.
(b) Jammu Mail, Delhi-Jammu Tawi.
(c) Jammu Express, Mumbai/Ahmedabad/Hapa/Jamnagar-Jammu Tawi.
(d) Shalimar Express, New Delhi-Jammu Tawi.
(e) Jhelum Express, Pune-Jammu Tawi.
(f) Himgiri Express, Howrah-Jammu Tawi.

(g) Himsagar Exp, Kanniyakumari/ Mangalore/Madurai-Jammu Tawi.
(h) Andaman Express, Chennai-Jammu Tawi.
(i) Chennai Express, Chennai-Jammu Tawi.
(j) Rajdhani Express, New Delhi-Jammu Tawi.
(k) Hemkunt Express, Haridwar-Jammu Tawi.
(l) Navyug Express, Mangalore/Madurai-Jammu Tawi.
(m) Hatia/Tata Express, Tatanagar-Jammu Tawi.
(n) Ahmedabad-JammuTawi Express.
(o) Lohit Express, Guwahati-Jammu Tawi.
(p) Gorakhpur Express, Gorakhpur-Jammu Tawi.
(q) Barauni Express, Barauni-Jammu Tawi.
(r) Ferozpur Express, Ferozpur-Jammu Tawi.

53 km long **Jammu-Udhampur** rail line has been built at a cost of over Rs 4,000 crore over a period of 20 years on a very difficult terrain. The line has been ready since March 2004 and trial runs of trains are going on. Besides being constructed in the difficult and hilly terrain, another significant feature of the line is that the railway bridge on River Gambhir is 70 metres higher[8]. The inauguration of railway services will commence on confirmation of the trial runs and security clearance at any time.

(c) **Road**. Jammu falls on the National Highway 1A and is connected by national highway network to all parts of the country. Some important road distances are: Amritsar-243 Kms, Chandigarh-436 Kms, Delhi-586 Kms, Katra-48 Kms, Srinagar-305 Kms, Manali-428 Kms, Patnitop-108 Kms, Mansar-62 Kms. Daily bus services operate to and from Jammu to Delhi, Amritsar, Ambala, Chandigarh, Ludhiana, Jalandhar, Pathankot, Shimla and Manali. Ordinary, Deluxe and Video Coaches are available on all routes. In addition to the J&K State Road Transport Corporation, bus service from Delhi, Haryana, Himachal, Punjab and Chandigarh State Road Transport Corporations also connect Jammu with various places in North India providing deluxe and ordinary services. All inter-state bus services operate to and from General Bus Stand in Jammu. Super deluxe, deluxe, video coaches and A-class buses to Srinagar operate from Railway Station. B-class buses to Srinagar leave from the General Bus Stand. J&K SRTC General Bus Stand is 0.5 Km from the Tourist Reception Centre. Besides, some travel agencies operate deluxe/video coaches on the main routes.

Local Transport

(a) **Coaches**: Luxury coaches are operated by the J&K Tourism Development Corporation and the J&K Road Transport Corporation. The reservation or bookings can be done at:

(i) Tourist Reception Centre, Vir Marg, (SRTC). Tele – 0191-2546851.

(ii) Tourist Reception Centre, Vir Marg, (JKTDC).Tele – 0191-579554, Fax – 0191 – 2546412.

(iii) Railway Station (SRTC) & (JKTDC) Tele- 0191-2530078.

(b) **Tourist Taxis**. Taxis for local sight seeing or any tourist destination can be hired by contacting special Tourist Taxi Association, Tourist Reception Centre, Vir Marg, Tele 0191-2246266.

(c) **Tariff.** Fixed tariffs are operational. Tariffs can be checked with the Tourism/ JKTDC/SRTC offices at TRC for rates. A sight –seeing tour of 2-2 ½ hours is also available covering certain important places like, Amar Mahal Museum, Dogra Art Gallery, Ranbireshwar Temple, Raghunath Mandir, Bahu Fort, Bagh-E-Bahu.

(d) **Scooter Rickshaws**. These are easily available from all points in the city. Rates are negotiable.

(e) **Mini Buses**. Most widely used as local transport, these cover the entire city on fixed routes.

Accommodation Network

Hotels: There are 'A' Category – Western Style Hotels with the rent ranging from Rs 900/- to 4500/- Room only. The 'B' Category Hotels are ranging from Rs 300/- to 1000/- Room only. And finally, the 'C' Category Hotels ranging from Rs 100/- to 400/- Room only.

Supplementary Accommodation: Accommodation to suit almost every pocket is provided by the J&K Tourism Development Corporation in the Tourist Reception Centre Hotel Blocks, Vir Marg; AC and Non-AC rooms are available. For railway passengers, AC and Non-AC rooms are available at the Railway Retiring Rooms, Jammu Tawi Railway Station.

Dharamshalas: In addition to the above, Gita Bhawan at Parade Ground, Aggarwal Dharamshala at Gurudwara Sunder Singh Marg, Hari Bhawan at Hari Market and Vinayak Dharamshala at Vinayak Bazaar are open to people of all faiths. The accommodation is available on first-come first-served basis and the charges are nominal.

Eating Joints: In Jammu, there are several popular restaurants where one can have a good meal. The restaurants provide food ranging from the simple to the exotic. Depending upon the mood, one can go in for regular north-Indian food or try some of the Kashmiri delicacies. For quick snack, there are many fast food outlets. Most restaurants and fast food outlets serve both vegetarian and non-vegetarian fare. A number of well-stocked bars in the city and wine shops provide a vast range of Indian and Foreign liquor. However, National holidays and certain other State holidays are dry days.

Places of Tourist Interest: Jammu Region

Peer Khoh. A cave shrine located on the Circular Road, 3.5 Kms from the heart of the town. There is a Shiva Lingam formed naturally in the cave; neither its antiquity nor its cause is known. And legend has it that the cave leads underground to many other cave shrines and even out of the country.

Ranbireshwar Temple: Located on Shalimar Road near the New Secretariat, and built by Maharaja Ranbir Singh in

1883 AD, Ranbireshwar Temple is dedicated to Lord Shiva. It has one central 'Lingam' measuring seven and a half feet in height (7.5 ft) and twelve Shiva 'Lingams' of crystal measuring from 15 cms to 38 cms and galleries with thousands of Shiva 'Lingams' fixed on stone slabs.

Raghunath Temple: Situated in the heart of the city and surrounded by a group of other temples, this temple dedicated to Lord Rama is outstanding and unique in northern India. Work on the temple was started by Maharaja Gulab Singh, founder of the Kingdom of Jammu and Kashmir in 1835 AD and was completed by his son, Maharaja Ranbir Singh, in 1860 AD. The inner walls of the main temple are covered with gold sheet on three sides. There are many galleries with lakhs of 'Saligrams'. The surrounding temples are dedicated to various Gods and Goddesses connected with the epic Ramayana[9].

Ranbir Canal: A small garden along the Ranbir Canal, 2 Kms from the heart of the town, provides a cool picnic spot during the summer. The Canal branches off from the river Chenab at Akhnoor, 32 kms away. Its water remains ice cold throughout the year. Its banks serve as good viewpoints and walkways.

Bahu Fort: 5 Kms from Jammu, situated on a rock face on the left bank of the river Tawi, this is perhaps the oldest fort and edifice in the city. Constructed originally by Raja Bahulochan over 3,000 years ago, the existing fort was more recently improved and built by the Dogra rulers. There is a temple dedicated to Goddess Kali inside the fort.

Bagh-e-Bahu: These extensive garden, laid around the Bahu Fort provide a pleasant view of the city. Open from 0800am to 0800pm.

Peer Baba: On the back side of the Civil Airport is famous Dargah of the Muslim saint, Peet Budhan Ali Shah. On Thursdays, Hindu and Sikh devotees vastly outnumber their Muslim brethren at the shrine.

Mahamaya Temple and City Forest: On the By-pass Road, behind Bahu Fort, the city forest surrounds the ancient Mahamaya Temple overlooking the river Tawi. A small garden surrounded by acres of woods provides best view of the city.

Mubarak Mandi Palace: The oldest buildings in this Palace complex date to 1824. The architecture is a blend of Rajasthani, Mughal and even Baroque European influences. The most stunning segment is the Sheesh Mahal. The Pink Hall now houses the Dogra Art Museum which has miniature paintings of the various Hill Schools.

Places for Excursions

Katra: 50 Kms from Jammu, this small town serves as the base camp for visiting the famous shrine of Vaishnodeviji in the Trikuta hills. The shrine is approachable on foot along a 12 kms[10], long well laid foot-path. Every year, nearly 4 million pilgrims pass through Katra on their way to Vaishnodeviji. Accommodation is available in Tourist Bungalows, Yatrika and a number of private hotels, besides pilgrims 'sarais'. A detailed study on this pilgrimage has been covered separately in this chapter.

Kud: 103 Kms from Jammu, this popular resort is situated on the Jammu-Srinagar highway, at an altitude of 1738 metres. Accommodation is available at the Tourist Bungalows of the J&K TDC as well as at several private hotels.

Patnitop: 110 Kms from Jammu, this famous hill resort is perched on a beautiful plateau, a an altitude of 2024 meters across which the Jammu-Srinagar highway passes. Enveloped by thickly wooded forests, Patnitop offers beautiful picnic spots, peaceful walks and breathtaking views of the mountain scape of the Chenab basin. In winter, the resort is generally covered with a thick mantle of snow thus providing opportunities for various snow games including skiing. For accommodation, there are a large number of huts and Tourist Bungalows, all managed by J&K TDC. Several private hotels also provide rooms to suit every pocket and preference.

Sanasar: 129 kms from Jammu and only 19 kms from Patnitop, Sanasar is a cup-shaped meadow surrounded by gigantic conifers. A place for a quiet holiday, the meadow has now been developed as a golf course. It also provides opportunities for Para gliding. Accommodation available in huts,

Tourist Bungalow and dormitory of the J&K Tourism Development Corporation.

Batote: 125 kms from Jammu, situated at an altitude of 1560 metres on the Jammu- Srinagar national highway, this resort straddles the forested slopes of the Patnitop mountain range, overlooking the spectacular lie of the Chenab gorge. Accommodation is available in huts, Tourist Bungalow and dormitory of the J&K TDC.

Sudh Mahadev: This holy spot near Patnitop is situated at an altitude of 1225 mtrs., about 120 kms from Jammu. The shrine is visited by pilgrims on the full moon night of 'Sawan' (July-August) to worship the "Trishul" (trident) and a mace which is said to belong to Lord Shiva. The Devak stream originates at Sudh Mahadev and disappears among the rocks a few kilometers down stream. Accommodation: Pilgrims Sarai of J&K TDC.

Gauri Kund: Short of Sudh Mahadev is the legendary spring where the Goddess Parvati used to bath before commencing Her daily prayers at Sudh Mahadev. This spring came to be named after her as 'Gauri Kund'.

Mantalai: Situated a few kilometers further away from Sudh Mahadev, Mantalai is surrounded by lush deodar forests, at an altitude of over 2000 metres. It is believed that Lord Shiva had got married to the Goddess Parvati here.

Mansar Lake: 62 kms from Jammu, it is a beautiful lake fringed by forest-covered hills. Boating facilities are available on the spot. Every year around Baisakhi, a food and crafts festival is organised here by J&K Tourism. Accommodation: Tourism Bungalow and huts of J&K TDC.

Surinsar Lake: 42 kms from Jammu, it is a picturesque spot with a lake surrounded by wooded hills. Accommodation is available in J&K TDC Bungalow.

Shiv Khori: 100 kms from Jammu, this holy cave, nearly a kilometer long with a 4-feet high naturally formed Shivling, is considered second only to the shrine of Vaishnodeviji. A major festival is held here on Shivratri day.

Dera Baba Banda: 75 kms from Jammu, it is a major Hindu-Sikh pilgrimage centre. Baba Banda Bairaagi was Guru Gobind Singh's favorite 'Saint–soldier', who had the Gurudwara constructed on the banks of river Chenab, where he spent his last days.

Purmandal: 40 kms from Jammu, just off the national highway leading towards Pathankot is the Purmandal Temple Complex built on the banks of the sacred, mostly underground river Devak. Often referred to as 'Chhota Kashi', its main temple is dedicated to `Umapati', while the other temples worship Lord Shiva. These ancient temples are associated with Shaivites of the Kashmir Valley. Regular bus service from Jammu is available. Accommodation is available in pilgrims `Sarai'.

Krimchi: On the way to Sudhmahadev–Mantalai, a short detour takes one to Krimchi, site of three of the oldest temples of Jammu. The architecture of the temple shows distinct Greek (Helenic) influences, Pancheri, a hill resort is a short distance away from here.

Jajjar Kotli: 35 kms from Jammu, on the national highway leading towards Srinagar is the Jajjar Kotli Tourist Complex, built on the banks of the Jajjar rivulet. The crystal clear, cool water of Jajjar attract picnickers in large numbers during summer, a Tourist Cafeteria, a Bar and a small Tourist Bungalow are the facilities provided here by J&K TDC.

Akhnoor: 32 kms to the West of Jammu situated on the banks of the mighty Chenab river is the historic town of Akhnoor. This town is associated with the legend of Soni-Mahiwal. Ruins of the Indus-Valley civilization are to be seen along the river bank commanding a panoramic view all around.

Salal Dam and Lake: 95 kms from Jammu to the west of the Holy Shrine of Vaishnodeviji is the Salal Dam and Lake. With an installed capacity of 400 mw of electricity, this is the largest Hydroelectric Project commissioned in the State so far. The lake formed behind the Dam is 33 kms long. The Dam site can be visited with the permission of the Project Authorities.

Baba Dhansar: 65 kms from Jammu, on way to Salal Dam, Baba Dhansar is a beautiful and cool picnic spot. Here, a huge spring gushes out the mountainside in a thick grove of trees and forms a number of small water-falls before flowing into the Holy Banganga. Next to the spring in a small grove in the rock face is a naturally formed Shivling on which droplets of water fall naturally all the year round. A big mela is held here during Shivratri.

Adventure Tourism

(i) **Trekking:** A range of trekking option is available in the Jammu area. Summer is the season when all the routes are open but some trekking routes are open in winter. There are excellent camping sites in the wilderness where one can camp when trekking for 2-3 days. The Sundarbani- Jungal Gali-Jasar Kote–Sanasar route in the Jungal Gali area lets one choose from any of the three exciting treks.

Facilities Available. The Tourism Department has 'Trekking Equipment Hire Shops' at Jammu, Kud and Rajouri. They stock local and imported trekking gear. Trekking parties and trekkers can hire the equipment at fixed rates. Equipment available are as under: Tents (Indian and Imported); 4-men tent (Indian); 2-men tent (Imported); Sleeping Bags (Imported); Carry mat (Indian and Imported); Jackets (Indian and Imported); Windcheaters (Indian); Rucksack (Indian and Imported); Trekking Boots (Indian and Imported). The equipment is issued against a cash security deposit equivalent to the cost or on a guarantee letter from any officer of the rank of Deputy Director, Tourism/Deputy Secretary of State Government or Central Govt. Some Travel Agencies in the city also organize trekking on different routes in Jammu.

(ii) **Skiing**: At Patnitop, ski courses are conducted in the months of January and February. During the winter months, there are introductory courses for tourists. The gently graded ski slopes of Patnitop are ideal for beginners. Madha Top(5-6 kms from Patnitop on the Sanasar Road) has excellent possibilities for all levels of skiing. After the newly planned ski-lift becomes operational, Madha Top will offer a range of skiing options for both professional skiers and beginners.

Facilities Available: For tourists taking the J&K TDC package tour, 40 sets of ski equipment are available at Patnitop and Sanasar. Also available are wooden sledges locally. For beginners and for people who want to brush up their skills, the J&K TDC Ski Instructors are available at Patnitop and Sanasar. Accommodation for skiers is available in huts of J&K TDC at Patnitop, Kud and Sanasar.

(iii) **Aero Sports**: J&K Tourism has introduced Paragliding at Sanasar and Jammu. Equipment can be hired from the Tourist Office in Jammu City. May-June and September-October are suitable months for paragliding at Sanasar. Other aero-sports like Parasailing and Hot-Air Ballooning will also become operational in the area.

Tourism Attraction in Rajouri-Poonch Districts

Rajouri-Poonch has been known for places of religious sanctity and historical interest. Budda Amarnath and Shahdara Sharief belong to the former, Chingus and Noori Chhamb come in the latter categories[11]. There are religion based tourism and attracting visitors to places of historical interest in these districts.

Religious Centres

Raghu Nath Temple: Located in the sylvan beauty of Channi Prat hills, about 10 kms from Sunderbani, is the lesser known 150 years old Raghu Nath Temple. It is a double storey structure with umbrella shaped Shikhara. It is said that one sadhu who used to mediatate in these forests requested Maharaja Gulab Singh to help him construct the temple. The temple consists of sanctum sanctorum surrounded by a Parikarma and verandah. A fair weather road leads up to the temple.

Mangle Mata The majestic and ancient shrine of Goddess Mangla is situated on a hillock near Naushera. It is believed to be as old as Mahabharata. Thousands of people congregate at the temple on every Dussehra.

Shahdara Sharief: This abode of Sufi Saint Baba Ghulam Shah is being venerated by Hindus, Muslims and Sikhs who visit in lacs every year to seek blessings. Funded by the offerings of the devotees, a massive effort has been underway to increase residential facilities and improve the surroundings.

Ziarat Chhotey Shah: Situated four kilometers away from Mendhar, on the road to Krishna Ghati is the Ziarat of Chhotey Shah, a highly revered Saint by the locals. Hundreds of pilgrims come to this place everyday.

Ram Kund: Few kilometers down the same road, a side road leads to the ancient temple of Ram Kund. Believed to be of Mahabharata vintage, the stones and architecture too indicate an ancient origin.

Nangali Sahib: This famous Sikh Gurudwara is situated on the Drungli Nallah, four kms short of Poonch town. The place has got great religious importance and attachment to devotees. Thousands of pilgrims of all religions throughout the year offer prayers here.

Budda Amarnath: Two kms ahead of Mandi is situated the ancient temple of Lord Shiva, carved out of a single rock. There are a number of mythological tales surrounding this famous shrine. It is believed that praying at this temple is equivalent to undertaking the pilgrimage to Amarnath. Thousands of devotees collect here on the day of Raksha Bandhan every year. In addition to the above, there are several tourist spots such as **Tatta Pani, Chingus, Dera Ki Gali, Noori Chhamb** and **Nandi Shool** which are regularly visited by local tourists.

Shri Mata Vaishno Devi Ji Pilgrimage Yatra

Vaishno Devi or Trikuta Bhagwati as the shrine is referred to in the ancient scriptures lies at a distance of 65 kilometers from Jammu out of which 53 km are covered by road and the last 12 kms by foot. The shrine is open through out the year and the pilgrims may visit it at their conveniences[12]. A pilgrimage to the Holy Shrine of Shri Mata Vaishno Devi Ji is considered to be one of the holiest pilgrimages of our times. Shri Mata Vaishno Devi Ji resides in a Holy Cave located in the folds of the three peaked mountain named Trikuta(Pronounced as Trikoot). The Holy Shrine attracts lakhs of devotees owing to the unflinching faith of the people who throng the Shrine from all parts of India and abroad.

Katra, a small but vibrant town, situated around 50 kilometres from Jammu (the winter capital of the State of Jammu and Kashmir), serves as the base camp for the journey to the Shrine. Vehicular approach is possible only till Katra, and in order to reach the Holy Shrine, a pilgrim is required to undertake a trek of around 12 kilometers either on foot or on ponies or palanquins. A helicopter service has recently been introduced for the benefit of the yatries, especially the aged and the infirm. The Holy Cave of the Mother is situated at an altitude of 5200 ft[13]. At the culmination of their pilgrimage, the yatries are blessed with the Darshans of the Mother Goddess inside the Sanctum Sanitorium–the Holy Cave. These Darshans are in the shape of three natural rock formations called the **Pindies**[14]. There are no statues or idols inside the Cave. Darshans are open for the yatries throughout the year.

Transportation

In order to visit the Holy Shrine of Mata Vaishno Devi Ji, one has to reach Katra; a small town situated around 50 kms from Jammu, the winter capital of the State of Jammu and Kashmir. **Katra** serves as the base camp for the yatra. Katra is well connected to Jammu and Jammu in turn, is well connected to the rest of the country by Air, Rail and Road. National Highway No 1A passes through Jammu towards Srinagar. At a point nearly 35 kms from Jammu, called Domel, the road branches off into two; while one road heads towards Srinagar the other leads to Katra.

Regular bus services from all major North Indian cities are available for Jammu as well as Katra. Ordinary and luxury buses are available from Jammu to Katra at a frequency of 10-15 minutes. While ordinary buses can be boarded from the State Road Transport Bus Stand around one km from Jammu Railway Station, luxury buses are available from just outside the Railway Station. It takes around two hours to cover the 50 km stretch from Jammu to Katra. The terrain is hilly and winding and passengers often experience nausea and vomiting.

Private taxies for Katra are available from the Jammu Tawi Railway Station and Jammu Airport. The official rates range between Rs 500-800 for one way travel depending upon the make of the vehicle. Many operators also offer taxies on a per seat basis. As with many other tourist destinations, it is not uncommon for passengers to be accosted at the Air port or the Railway station by taxi drivers. At the moment no train services between Jammu and Katra. However, work on the Jammu-Katra rail link is underway and Katra is likely to emerge on the rail map shortly[15]. Due to the disturbed situation in J&K, vehicles are usually stopped on the way by security personnel for security checks. Visitors have to cooperate with the authorities and comply with the security formalities.

Accommodation

At Jammu: For pilgrims to the Holy Shrine, Shri Mata Vaishno Devi Shrine Board provides excellent accommodation to pilgrims at its two guest houses called **Vaishnavi Dham** and **Saraswati Dham** respectively. These are strategically located just outside the railway station, Jammu and are thus ideal for passengers traveling by rail or luxury buses/taxies. The two *Dhams* cater exclusively to the needs of visitors to the Holy Shrine. In addition to Dormitory accommodation which is available at Rs 50/- per bed (Rs 25/- per bed for six hours), self contained air conditioned rooms and suites are also available. There is also a spacious restaurant on the ground floor where hygienically cooked pure vegetarian food is also available on no-profit basis and with a fair amount of variety. In addition, there is a Souvenir Shop where various souvenirs and mementos of the Yatra to Holy Shrine are available at a reasonable rate. Ample parking space, cloak room facilities and onward bookings for Katra are readily available.

At Katra: For the benefit of the Pilgrims, Shri Mata Vaishno Devi Shrine Board provides clean, well maintained and very economical accommodation at **Niharika Yatri Niwas** and **Shakti Bhawan** situated at bus stand, Katra. Rooms, both air conditioned and Non air conditioned are available. In addition, dormitory accommodation at Rs 50/- per bed is available in

Shakti Bhawan. Another 500 bedded accommodation in Sarai building is under construction near the Second Yatra counter (YRC II) and is expected to be available shortly. No loss no profit Bhojanalaya, a Souvenir Shop, a free Cloak Room and Free parking of private vehicles are certain facilities provided here. Accommodation for all Shrine Board Guest houses/dormitories can be booked at the reception of these guest houses or at the Enquiry and Reservation counter at Niharika complex. Advance reservation is possible by sending a demand draft of the required amount to the Chief Executive Officer/Dy Manager (E&R) payable at Katra. On line reservation facility is available at www.maavaishnodevi.org.

Free Accommodation at Katra: There is also basic accommodation for yatries on an absolutely FREE basis. This accommodation is available in the Niharika Complex and near the *Yatra Parchi Counter II (YRC II)*. Besides accommodation, blankets are also provided free of cost. During days of rush additional free accommodation is also made available to the yatries in the Niharika complex itself.

Other Accommodation Facilities at Katra: There are various Sarais/ Dharamshalas in Katra, which provide good accommodation to the pilgrims, either free of cost or at a nominal price. While some of them do provide facilities to the pilgrims, many of these places have passed in the hands of certain people with vested interests who insist on the pilgrims buying offerings from their own shops located in the premises of these Sarais. Pilgrims should be careful of such elements as they tend to sell items at a price many times higher than their original value. There are various lodges, Guest Houses, ordinary and luxury hotels, Cottages, Resorts and all types of accommodation facilities available too, which provide accommodation to the devotees. Pilgrims have a wide range to choose from depending upon their taste and budget.

Facilities on the Track: Refreshments like biscuits, cold drinks, tea, coffee, milk, mineral water, etc are available all along the way at Refreshment Units of the Shrine Board. Nearly all of these units are located at carefully selected locations, a total of 12 such locations or view points. The larger view points serve meals, bread, buns also, while the smaller ones only serve packed snacks and beverages. In addition, oxygen cylinders, cassettes, milk for infants is also available at these view points. There are several resting points with covered sheds with an approximate distance of 500 metres from each other. Toilets and drinking water facilities are also located nearby.

Accommodation at Bhawan: The Holy Bhawan houses the Sanctrum Sanitorium–they Holy cave which is the ultimate destination of the yatries. The Shrine Board has provided various facilities for the yatries at Bhawan, to facilitate comfortable Darshans. Self contained and furnished rooms are available on rent for the yatries at the Main Bhawan complex as well as Gauri and Vaishnavi Bhawan complexes. Dormitory accommodation is also available at Manokamna Bhawan complex. On line booking facility is available at www.maavaisho-devi.org. In addition, there are a number of large halls which are available for the yatries. This accommodation is free of cost and is made available on a first come first served basis. No booking or permission is required for using these premises since they are kept open round the clock and yatries can just go and occupy them subject to availability.

When to Visit the Holy Shrine

The yatra to the Holy Shrine is open though out the year. However, the summer months of May, June and July and the festival period of *Chaitra* (spring) and *Sharad, Ashwin* (Autumn), Navratras and New Year vacations witness peak rush. As a result of this rush, devotees have to often wait for 12-20 hours before having *Darshan*. For comfortable, quick and satisfying *Darshan*, the peak period of rush must be avoided.

Yatra Registration

The most important activity that a pilgrim has to undertake on reaching Katra is getting registered for the Yatra. All pilgrims **without exception** are required to register themselves before undertaking yatra. The registration is done by the Shrine Board which is the only **STATUTORY AND LEGAL** authority for the purpose. No other organisation, private or public is authorized to issue the *yatra slip*. The registration process is entirely FREE and is fully computerized. This process is carried out at the **Yatra Registration Counter**, popularly known **YRC**, situated at Bus stand, Katra. Registration at YRC is important because of the following reasons:

(a) All visitors, once they get registered at the YRC for their trek are automatically and compulsorily insured aginst any accidental casualty (a rare possibility) on their way to the Holy Shrine. This is a free insurance to all those who undertake this holy pilgrimage. The amount of insurance is Rs 1,00,000/- for majors and Rs 25,000/- for minors and is valid only in case of accidental deaths[16].

(b) Since the Shrine is located deep in the mountains, the Holy Mountain has its own limitations and saturation levels as regards its capacity to hold and sustain large crowds. Besides, the resources available to provide various basic services and facilities to the visitors are also limited. This is because, in absence of the road, even the most basic and essential items have to be carried either on ponies or by humans.

(c) Since the Holy Pindies are situated in a narrow Cave, group visits for Darshans are not possible. The system of Darshans is thus through a continuously moving queue, round the clock. Thus only a limited number of pilgrims can have Darshans everyday.

(d) Thus, because of all the above reasons, the number of pilgrims on the track and at the main Shrine Complex needs to be regulated. This regulation helps to avoid overcrowding and accidents and also ensures that all of them get basic facilities like food and water.

Porters, Ponies, Palanquins and Helicopter Services

Walking for 12-13 kms on the hilly terrain can be arduous and tiring for those not used to it. Many devotees have breathing problems or some other ailments and are physically challenged. All or some of them may need the services of ponies and palanquins. The Poly, Porter and Palanquin services are managed by the Notified Area Committee(NAC), a municipal committee organizing the local municipal affairs.

The rates of these services are fixed. The rates of the Palanquin Services(for 24 hours return journey) are as under[17]:

	Up to 100 Kgs (4 carriers)	**Above 100 Kgs** (6 carriers)
Katra to Bhawan and Back	Rs 1520/-	Rs 2140/-
Katra to Bhawan and back via Bharion	Rs 1750/-	Rs 2420/-
Sanjichhat Helipad to Bhawan and Back	Rs 450/-	Rs 600/-

There are helicopter services from Katra to Sanjichhat and Back.. Sanjichhat is located at an altitude of 6200 ft, about 3.25 kms from Adkuwari. The helipad is available here and yatries reaching by helicopter land at this place. From Sanjichhat, the remaining distance of 2.75 kms to the main Bhawan to be undertaken either by foot or by ponies/palanquins. The rates of helicopter services are as under:

Katra to Sanjichhat and Back (Return Journey) - Rs 4000/-
Katra to Sanjichhat (one way journey only) - Rs 2000/-

Landslides

The hills of Trikuta witness landslides at times. These are more common during the rainy season when the soil is loose. The Shrine Board has identified most of the potentially dangerous spots and covered them with sheds with a view to protect the unwary pilgrims. Notices about the same have also been put up near these potential landslide areas. Pilgrims are required to be cautious and refrain from resting near them.

Darshans and Aarti Pooja

The Divine Mother has revealed Herself in a natural rock form (*Pindies*) inside the Sanctrum Sanitorium. There are no statues, idols or photographs inside the Holy Cave. Pilgrims are required to focus their attention only on the Holy *Pindies*. There are three Holy Pindies, to the extreme left is the Pindi of **Mata Maha Saraswati** (the Supreme Energy of Creation), in the middle is the Pindi of **Mata Maha Lakshmi** (the Supreme Energy of Maintenance) and towards extreme right is the Pindi of **Mata Maha Kali** (the Supreme Energy of Dissolution). **Mata Vaishno Devi Ji** is believed to be an incarnation of all the three Supreme Energies.

The *Aarti* of the Goddess is performed twice a day, once during the morning at sunrise and again during the evening at sunset. The Holy Cave is closed for pilgrims during the period the Aarti is being performed and only the *Pujaries* are allowed inside. It usually takes around two hours for the Aarti to be completed.

The Shrine Board

The management of the *Yatra* and the governance and administration of the Shrine is done by the Shri Mata Vaishno Devi Shrine Board popularly known as the Shrine Board. The Board was set up in August 1986 under the provisions of **The Jammu and Kashmir Shri Mata Vaishno Devi Shrine Act, 1986.** The main objective of the Act was to provide for better management and governance of the Holy Shrine and its endowments including the appurtenant lands and buildings. The Governor of the State is the ex-officio Chairman of the Board. He nominates nine members to the Board. The Board discharges its duties through a Chief Executive Officer who is assisted by the Addl Chief Executive Officer, both these officers are senior officers of the Indian Administrative Service. The *yatra* figures (number of devotees visiting the Holy Shrine annually) which stood at 13.95 lakhs in 1986 jumped to 50.57 lakhs in the year 2001 and were recorded at 61.10 lakhs till 2004, the increased influx of pilgrims is due to the efforts of the Shrine Board which has created several facilities for the yatries.

Yatra Statistics since 1986, after the Shrine Board has been set up are as under[18]:

Year	*Number of Pilgrims*
1986	13.95 *Lakhs*
1987	18.57
1988	19.92
1989	23.12
1990	21.69
1991	31.15
1992	35.16
1993	33.68
1994	37.04
1995	40.12
1996	43.35
1997	44.34
1998	46.22
1999	46.70
2000	52.17
2001	50.57
2002	44.32
2003	54.00
2004	61.10

Note: No of Pilgrims in Lakhs. Annual Yatra figures are counted from January to December.

Tourism Attraction in Kashmir Region

Kashmir is the principal region in the State of Jammu and Kashmir, the other two supplementary units being Jammu and Ladakh. The Vale of Kashmir is an oval plain 140 kilometres (87 miles) long and upto 40 kilometres (25 miles) wide. It is surrounded on all sides by high mountains. Among the highest peaks are **Nanga Parbat** (8,114 metres or 26,621 feet), **Haramukh** (5,150 metres or 16,896 feet) and **Amarnath** (5,280 metres or 17,323 feet) as well as the magnificent **Pir Panjal**

Range with many peaks over 4,570 metres (14,993 feet). The fertile land of the valley, by the Jhelum River and its tributaries, produces crops of rice, maize, an enormous variety of fruit and saffron which has been cultivated in Kashmir for over a thousand years[19]. Over the years' Kashmir has come to love and look after its tourists' fulfilling their every whim. Tourists are everywhere, soaking up all that Kashmir has to offer-the walks, the pony treks, the cable car rides over Gulmarg resort, the Shikara rides at sunset on the Dal lake.

Season in Kashmir Region

For the natural beauties, the glorious climate and other attractions of the Kashmir Valley, a visit to this region can divide ones life into two halves-before and after Kashmir. Nestling in the lap of the dazzling, snow-capped Himalayas, the Kashmir valley is undoubtedly a jewel in India's crown. An inspiration for so much art, music and poetry, Kashmir is also a honeymooners' paradise, a nature lover's wonderland and a shopper's dream come true. The climate of Kashmir is as unlike that of the plains of India as possible, and is excellently suited to Europeans, either in health, when there is an enormous variety of out-door attractions, or during convalescence. Spring and autumn are entirely delightful, but during July and August the valley itself is too hot to be pleasant, while January and February are usually cold and damp[20].

Arriving at the **New Year**, the visitor will very probably find the whole valley covered with a few inches of snow. Days of sleet and storm will alternate with longer periods of fair weather. On most nights the thermometer will drop below freezing point and a good deal of skating on ponds, or the remains of summer floods, will be obtainable, while in really cold spells the Dal lake is sometimes safe. The weather in **February** is much the same as in the preceding month, but by the middle of March the spring sets in with a suddenness and determination that is quite unlike the hesitating approach which it makes in the British Isles, and in the space of a few days the willow trees begin to show a tinge of delicate green and some of the hardiest wild flowers burst into blossom. **April** which lives up to its showery reputation, and during which the days are still quite cool, sees the valley perhaps at its best. The spring is fully established; every tree and shrub has covered itself with new green leaves, and almond, apricot peach and early apple blossom cover large areas on the outskirts of Srinagar with clouds of white and pale-pink loveliness.

May is distinctly warmer, but, even in the middle of the day, the heat is by no means oppressive and the chenar trees, which are one of the chief glories of Kashmir, are a magnificent sight in all their fresh new foliage. Along the river banks drooping willows and graceful slender poplars make a cool and shady setting for the rows of moored house-boats, which by this time are rapidly filling with visitors, and the Golden Oriole, with its brilliant colouring, the friendly, cheeky Bulbuls, busy with domestic cares, and the slender, sinuous grace of the Paradise Fly-catcher all combine to tell us that summer has arrive. During this month roses and sweet peas, both of which grow to perfection, are among the chief glories of the garden, and on the outskirts of every village masses of mauve iris add to the beauty of the country-side.

With the advent of **June** the weather gets rather too hot to be pleasant during the middle of the day and the majority of the visitors move up to Gulmarg, or take a camp to the cooler uplands of Gurais, the Lolab, or the Sind valley. Apart from the increased temperature the valley loses some of its attraction, as the foliage has lost its first freshness and hangs in heavy masses of a darker green. Fruits come into season now; strawberries arrive first, followed soon after by mulberries, cherries, apricots, raspberries, and later by pears and apples.

In **July and August** the valley is definitely hot and oppressive and few Europeans remain voluntarily in Srinagar. But, visits should be made to the Dal and Manasbal lakes to see the famous Lotus Lily, which is then blossoming in all its glory. September marks the beginning of the autumn, and, as the month wears on, the evenings grow chill and the days cool. The weather from now until Xmas is almost invariably fine and clear, and autumn, with its russet tints and the rich colouring of the chenars, framed against the distant mountains of the Pir Panjal, which once again have been capped with while by the first falls of snow, closely rivals, if it does not exceed, the glories of the springtime.

The Delightful Kashmir

Any visitor will find Kashmir delightful, not only because of its pleasant climate, but also for the variety of amusements that it has to offer. If he is an artist, there is work for his brush at every turn. There is no day in the year on which the sportsman will not be able to amuse himself. The botanist has ranges of upland hill-sides, which are studded with scores of varieties of wild flowers for five months of every year. For the ordinary individual there are excellent golf courses and tennis courts in Srinagar and Gulmarg, there is the Dal lake in which to bathe and on the bosom of which to flirt, and there is the Club and Nedou's Hotel in which to dance and entertain. But all these things are summer joys, and, when the wind blows cold from the mountains and the leaves begin to fall, the visitors depart, the butterflies disappear, and only a handful of residents remain[21]. Map of tourist places in Kashmir is given as **Annexure-6.**

What to See!

Srinagar: The State's summer capital, is situated at an altitude of 1,730 meters above sea level. It is connected by Indian Airlines and Jet Airways flights directly to Jammu and New Delhi, and hence to every part of the national network. Srinagar is connected by an all–weather road to Jammu(National Highway 1A) which in turn is connected to many parts of North India. Srinagar's nearest railhead is Jammu which in turn connects all parts of the country, including Delhi, Kolkatta, Pune, Mumbai, Chennai and to the farthest Kanyakumari. The expanding city of Srinagar is home to half a million souls. It stretches along the bank of the Jhelum River, which is spanned by nine old and several other new bridges. Canals intersect the city and link the Jhelum with the spring-fed Dal Lake which is divided by causeways into four parts - Garibal, Lokut Dal, Bod Dal and Nagin. Part of the Dal Lake is covered by the famous *floating gardens*[22] made up of reed platforms moored to the lake bed and covered with heaps of weed and mud. These market gardens produce cucumbers, tomatoes and melons. At the Dal Lake end of town is the main Maulana Azad Road, on which are the Roman Catholic Church and the Golf Club(which has an 18 hole course and accepts temporary members). In the same area are the Tourist Reception Centre and the leading hotels, but it is the canal-crossed old part of the city with its wooden houses, colour and bustle which is most authentically Kashmiri.

Dal Lake: Much of Dal Lake is a maze of intricate waterways rather than a simple sheet of open water. Dal Gate at the city end of the lake, controls the flow of the lake water into the Jhelum River canal. Within the lake are two islands which are popular picnic spots. *Silver Island*(Sona Lank) is at the north end of the lake while *Gold Island* (Rupe Lank) is to the south. Both are also known as Char Chinar because they each have four chinar trees on them. There is a third island, Nehru Park, at the end of the main stretch of the lakeside Boulevard, but it is a miserable affair. North of here a long causeway juts out into the lake towards Kotar Khana, the 'house of pigeons', which was once a royal summer house[23]. The waters of Dal Lake are amazingly clear, considering what must be poured into them from the houseboats. On the lake there are houseboats that are definitely firmly attached to the bottom. And houses that look like they could float away. Most of the houseboats are at the southern end of the lake, although one find them on the Jhelum River and not on Nagin Lake. Each house boat has anything between two and four bedrooms in it with attached bathrooms and a common sitting and dining room. The charges of a houseboat always include all meals and a certain number of crossings by shikara to and from the houseboat. Houseboats offer far more personalized service than hotels because of the far higher host: guest ratio. On the other hand, fellow guests at the same house–boat tend to interact much more than if they were staying at the same hotel.

Jhelum River and Bridges: The Jhelum flows from Verinag, 80 kms south of Srinagar, to the Wular lake to the north. It's wide, swift flowing, muddy and picturesque as it sweeps through Srinagar. The river is famed for its nine old bridges. There are interesting mosques and other buildings near it; a stroll or bicycle ride through the narrow lanes near the river is rewarding.

Museum: The Shri Pratap Singh Museum is in Lal Mandi, just south of the river between Zero Bridge and Amira Kada, the first 'old bridge'. The museum has an interesting collection of exhibits relevant to Kashmir, including illustrated titles from Harwan. It is open from 1000 am to 0500 pm, closed on Mondays and admission is free.

Sankaracharya Hill: Rising up behind the Boulevard, beside Dal Lake, the hill was once known as Takht-I-Sulaiman, the Throne of Solomon. A temple is said to have first been built here by Ashoka's son around 200 BC, but the present Hindu temple dates from Jehangir's time. It is a pleasant stroll to the top, from where one have a fine view over Dal Lake-the Srinagar TV tower is also here. Alternatively there is a road right to the top.

Islamic Monuments

Shah Hamdan Mosque: Originally built in 1395, the all-wooden mosque was destroyed by fire in 1479 and 1731. The present mosque is shaped like a cube with a pyramidal roof rising to a spire. *Non-Muslims are not allowed inside.*

Pather Masjid: On the opposite bank of the Jhelum is the unused Pather Masjid. This fine stone mosque was built by Nur Jahan in 1623.

Tomb of Zain-ul-Abidin: Back on the east bank between the Zaina Kadal and Ali Kadal bridges is the slightly decrepit tomb of King Zain-ul-Abidin, the highly regarded son of Sultan Sikander. Built on the foundations of an earlier temple, the tomb shows a clear Persian influence in its domed construction and glazed tiles.

Jami Masjid: This impressive wooden mosque is notable for the 300 plus pillars supporting the roof, each made of a single deodar tree trunk. The present mosque, with its green and peaceful **inner courtyard**, was rebuilt to the original design after a fire in 1674.

Chasma Shahi: Smallest of the Moghul gardens at Srinagar, the Chasma Shahi are well up the hill side, above the Nehru Memorial Park. The gardens were laid out in 1632 but have recently been extended. These are one of the gardens with an admission charge.

Pari Mahal: Just above the Chasma Shahi is this fine old Sufi college. The ruined, arched terraces have recently been turned into a very pleasant and well kept garden with fine vieiws over Dal Lake. From the Pari Mahal one can descend straight down the hill to the road that runs back to the Oberoi Palace Hotel.

Nishat Bagh: Sandwiched between the lake and the mountains, the Nishat gardens have a superb view across the lake to the Pir Panjal mountains. Designed in 1633 by Nur Jahan's brother Asaf Khan, this is the largest of the Moghul gardens and follows the traditional pattern of a central channel running down a series of terraces.

Shalimar Bagh: Set some distance back from the lake but reached by a small canal, the Shalimar gardens were built for Nur Jahan, *'light of the world'*, by her husband Jehangir in 1616. During the Moghul period the topmost of the four terraces was reserved for the emperor and the ladies of the court. During the May to October tourist season a nightly *son et lumiere (*sound and light show) is put up on in these beautiful gardens. It is pertinent to note that a train namely *Shalimar Express* runs between New Delhi and Jammu Tawi daily.

Hazratbal Mosque: This shiny new mosque is on the north-west shore of Dal Lake. The mosque enshrines a hair of the prophet, but to non-believers it will be most interesting simply for its stunningly beautiful setting on the shores of the lake with the snow-capped peaks as a backdrop.

Nasim Bagh: Just beyond the mosque, these gardens were built by Akbar in 1586. Today this oldest Moghul garden is used by an engineering college and is not maintained as a garden.

Nagin Lake: The *'jewel in the ring'* is held to be the most beautiful of the Dal lakes and is ringed by trees. There are a number of houseboats on this quieter, cleaner lake.

Hari Parbat Fort: Clearly visible on top of the Sharika hill, to the west of Dal Lake, this fort was originally built between 1592 and 1598 during the rule of Akbar but most of the present construction dates from the 18th century. Visits are only possible with written permission from the Director of Tourism, J&K.

Pandrathan Temple: This small but beautifully proportioned Shiva temple dates from 900 AD and is in the military cantonment area on the Jammu road out of Srinagar.

Harwan: At the northern end of Dal Lake, archaeologists have discovered an unusual ornamented brick pavement near Harwan. Examples of these bricks can be seen in the Srinagar museum. The water supply for Srinagar is pumped from here and piped along the causeway across the lake.

Pahalgam: Also called the *Valley of Shepherds*[24], Pahalgam is about 96 kms from Srinagar and at 2130 metres above sea level. The beautiful Lidder River flows right through the town, which is at the junction of the Sheshnag and Lidder river and surrounded by soaring, fir covered mountains with snow capped peaks rising behind them. It is cool even during the height of summer. This is an ideal base for short day treks or for the longer treks to Kolahoi Glacier or Amarnath Cave. Pahalgam is the base for the Pilgrimage to the Amarnathji Holy Yatra. Pilgrimage to Amarnath Holy Cave is separately covered in this chapter. Pahalgam is also famous for its many shepherds. There are a common sight driving their flocks of sheep along the paths all around. A number of hotels and lodges cater to all preferences and budgets, from luxurious to unpretentious trekkers lodges, including JKTDC's delightfully romantic, fully furnished huts, partially concealed by giant pine trees. There is also a Government Tourist Bungalow. During the summer season the tourist office operates several tent sites with ready set up and furnished tents.

The route to Pahalgam from Srinagar passes through some interesting places. Only 16 km out of Srinagar is Pampore, center of Kashmir's saffron industry. Saffron is highly prized for its flavouring and colouring properties and is consequently rather expensive. Sangram, 35 km out, is a center for production of cricket bats. They are lined up by the road in their thousands.

At Avantipur are two ruined Hindu temples built between 855 and 883 AD. At Anantnag the road forks, the Pahalgam road turning north from here. There are regular bus service from Srinagar and taxies can be hired on need basis. Ponies can easily be hired in Pahalgam for trekking trips.

Gulmarg: The large meadow of Gulmarg is 56 kms from Srinagar at an altitude of 2730 metres above sea level. The name means *'meadow of flowers'* [25] and in spring it is just that. This is also an excellent trekking base and in winter it is *India's premier skiing resort*. The skiing equipment available is a bit primitive and limited but the costs are very low and the area would also be wonderful for ski touring. Gulmarg also has one of the world's highest green golf courses, as well as a club house which is a historical building in its own right. For a fun filled ride of a most unusual kind, Gulmarg's newly constructed Gondola lift from high above Gulmarg, through pine-clad slopes, is exhilarating.

There are several hotels catering for all classes of tourists. There are a variety of buses running from Srinagar to Gulmarg, many of them on day tours. On a day tour one have only a few hours at the hill resort, just long enough for one of the shorter day walks. At one time the road from Srinagar only ran as far as Tangmarg, seven km in distance or 500 metres in altitude below Gulmarg. The last stretch then had to be completed on foot or by pony. A road has now been completed over the last stretch, although some buses still terminate at Tangmarg. The winding road from Tangmarg is 13 kms in length, nearly twice as far as the more direct pony track. Riding or pack ponies can also be hired from Gulmarg to other sites around the valley. Rates are prominently posted at the car park.

Sindh Valley: There is a scenic area north of Srinagar through which the road to Ladakh passes. The Zoji La pass marks the boundary from the Sindh Valley into Ladakh. From Srinagar one pass the Dachigam wildlife reserve, once a royal game park. Anchar Lake is close to Srinagar but rarely visited and has a wide variety of water birds. There is a Moghul garden built by Nur Jahan at Manasabal Lake. Wular Lake is possibly *the largest freshwater lake in Asia*[26] and the Jhelum River flows into it.

Sonamarg, at an altitude of 3000 metres, 87 Kms from Srinagar, is the last major point in Kashmir and an excellent base for trekking. Its name means '*meadow of gold*', which could derive from the spring flowers or from the strategic trading position it once enjoyed. There are Tourist Huts, a Rest House and some small hotels here. The tiny village of Baltal is the last place in Kashmir, right at the foot of the Zoji La.

When conditions are favourable one can walk to the Amarnath Holy Cave from here. The *Zoji La is the watershed between Kashmir and Ladakh*[27] - on one side one have the green, lush scenery of Kashmir while on the other side everything is barren and dry.

Shopping

Everybody associates Kashmir's handicrafts with carpets, but there's a whole lot besides. Depending on the quality of one's purchase, one can either pay as little as Rs 10 or a few lakhs. Very many qualities exist side by side in Kashmir to suit a variety of budgets.

Shawls: There are pure wool shawls called raffal which have different counts of wool – 40, 60, 80 etc, and the shawl is progressively more expensive as the count increases. Shawls mixed with other fibres like cotton and cotton derivatives are far cheaper. On the other hand, woolen shawls mixed with *pashmina* will be far more expensive. Naturally, a pure *pashmina* shawl will run into thousands of rupees. Some shawls have gold zari embroidery worked on them in hook work and are highly priced.

Papier Mache: Here too, the quality of papier mache differs markedly, depending on two factors. The first is the papier mache in its raw state. Unless it is smoothened adequately to be silky to the touch, it is not considered high grade. On the other hand, inexpensive papier mache, brightly painted and varnished, makes a variety of gifts and souvenirs that do not cost a fortune. Eggs, Egg cups, candle and pen stands, kum kum boxes and cigarette boxes are just a few options at the low end.

Walnut Wood: Items made from walnut wood come from three parts of the tree; the branches, the trunk and the root.

The branches have the palest colour of wood, and the trunk the darkest. Branches have no veins. Objects made out of the root will be the costliest because of the wood used. As walnut is a soft wood, it takes carving very well.

Saris: Kashmir has extensive mulberry cultivation. Silkworms feeding on this produce resilient silk. Kashmiri silk may be thin, but it is strong nevertheless, as is chiffon. Kashmiri silk is used to make saris.

Cricket Bats: Kashmir's willow is so highly priced, that most of the national team uses cricket bats from Kashmir.

Other products of Kashmir include saffron, grown in Pampore on the way to Pahalgam. It is one of the only two places in India where saffron is grown, the other being Kishtwar, also in Jammu and Kashmir. Walnuts and almonds are available in the market throughout the year. Being substantially cheaper in Kashmir than elsewhere, they too make good gifts. Other food products from Kashmir are *shah zira* (also called kala zira), Kashmiri chillies and honey.

Amarnath Yatra

"The procession of several thousands of pilgrims in the far away cave of Amarnath, nestled in a glacier gorge of the Western Himalayas, through some of the most charming scenery in the World, is fascinating in the extreme. Of the psychological aspect and significance of such pilgrimage, done on foot for days and days, much could be written. Sufficient to say, that it is one of those ancient institutions which have above all, kept the fire of spirituality burning in the hearts of the people"-Swami Vivekananda[28].

Amarnath, lying at 3,883 metres in the Great Himalayan Range is the holy cave shrine dedicated to Lord Shiva, the most predominant deity of the Himalayas from Afghanistan in the West to Arunachal Pradesh and Tripura in the East and Kailas Mansarovar in the North to the Shivaliks in the South[29]. Situated in a narrow gorge at the farther end of Lidder valley, **Amarnath** stands 3,883 metres and is 46 kms from Pahalgam and 141 kms from Srinagar. Though the original pilgrimages subscribes that the yatra be undertaken from Srinagar, the more common practice is to begin journey at Chandanwari, and cover the distance to Amarnath and back in **five days**. Pahalgam is 96 kms from Srinagar. The route chart of Amarnath Ji Yatra given in **Appendix IV** be referred.

The trek to Amarnath, in the month of Sharavan(July to August) has the devout flock to this incredible shrine, where the image of Shiva, in the form of a lingam, is formed naturally of an **ice-stalagmite,** and which waxes and wanes with the moon. By its side are, fascinatingly, two more ice-lingamns, that of Parvati and of their son, Ganesha. The trek from Chandanwari to Amarnath cave is an old ancient peregrine route. The 30 km distance is covered in two days with night halts at Sheshnag(Wawjan) and Panchtarni. The distance from Pahalgam to Chandanwari (16 km) now be covered by vehicular transport, and the tail runs along the Lidder river. Pilgrims camp at Pahalgam or Chandanwari on the first night out.

The first day's trek of 12 km from Chandanwari is through spectacular, primeval countryside, and the main center of attraction is Sheshnag, a mountain which derives its name from its *seven peaks*, resembling the heads of a mythical snake. The journey to Sheshnag follows a steep in lines up to the right bank of a cascading stream and wild scenery untouched by civilization. The second night's camp at Wawjan overlooks the deep blue waters of Sheshnag lake, and glaciers beyond it., There are legends of love and revenge too associated with Sheshnag, and at the camp these are recounted by campfires, to the stillness of pine-scented, Himalayan night. The second day's 12 km trek steadily gains height, winding up across Mahagunas Pass at 4,600 metres and then descending to the meadow-lands of Panchantarni, the last camp enroute to the holy cave.

From Panchtarni to Amarnath is only six kms. But an early morning's start is recommended for there is a long queue awaiting entry to the cave. The same day, following darshan, devotees return to Panchtarni in time for lunch, and continue to Sheshnag to spend the third night out. They can also spend the night at Panchtarni itself returning to Chandanwari/ Pahalgam like the onward journey. Entrance to the cave is regulated, and darshan a hasty affair for there are many others waiting outside to pay homage before the awesome Shivalinga. The devotees sing bhajans, chant incantations and priests perform aarti and puja, invoking the blessings of Shiva, the divine, the pure, the absolute. For those who journey with faith, it is a rewarding experience, this simple visitation to a cave-shrine, the home of the Himalayan mendicant who is both destroyer and healer, the greatest of the Hindu Gods.

From 1996 onwards, the yatries coming to Amarnathji Holy Cave has increased to more than one lakh. According to the Director J&K Tourism, inspite of the prevailing situation in the Valley, there were 1.73 lakh yatries in the year 2000 and 1.19 lakh yatries in 2001 visited the Holy Cave[30].

Tourism Attraction in Ladakh Region

Ladakh's awesome bare granite mountains and the unique culture of its people – Sha Baltis, animist Dards and Buddhist Ladakhis – are the lodestones drawing an increasing number of visitors each year. Ladakh means '*land of several passes*' and its plateau, lying between 2,900 and 5,900 metres (9,500 and 19,350 feet) above sea level, is bounded on the north by the *Karakoram* chain and on the south by the *Himalayas*. The Indus River bisects this district, which accounts for 70 percent of the total area of Kashmir state, but its climate is so inhospitable that there are on averge only six inhabitants to every five square kilometers (two square miles). In summer, temperatures rise to 37 degree Celsius and in winter can drop to *minus* 40 degree Celsius. For seven months of the year Leh airport is the region's only link with the outside world. Leh, the capital is situated on a tributary of the Indus at 3,380 metres (11,090 feet) above sea level. Once a halt on the silk route to China, Leh is now a sparsely populated town whose transformation into a tourist resort has considerably changed the way of life[31].

Srinagar-Leh[32]

It's 434 km from the Vale of Kashmir to Ladakh and the road is surfaced most of the way. It follows the Indus River for much of the distance. Buses run along this road daily during the summer season and take two days with an overnight stop at Kargil. Sonamarg is the last major place in Kashmir, shortly before climbing up over the Zoji La Pass (3529 metres) and enter the Ladakh region. The road should be open from the beginning of June through to October, but in practice the opening date can be variable- sometimes mid-May, sometimes mid-June. There is a variety of bus classes run from Srinagar. Jeeps which take upto six passengers will permit additional stops and diversions along the interesting route. The return trip to Srinagar is at time complicated because buses may not turn up from Srinagar. The buses are very heavily booked in both directions at the height of the season ie in August. [A route chart of Srinagar-Leh is given in **Appendix V**].

Initially, Indian Airlines started flying to Leh in 1979 onwards, but now there are flights from both Srinagar and Chandigarh. The flight from Srinagar is very short (half an hour) and extremely spectacular as one cross right over the Himalayas, but also problematic. Flights can only be made into Leh in the morning and only when weather conditions are good. If it is possible that the conditions could deteriorate after arrival and the aircraft could not leave, the flight will be cancelled. End result is a lot of cancellations, a lot of flights that actually leave Srinagar but are not able to land at Leh since conditions can change very rapidly and a lot of frustrated passengers. At difficult times of the year, such as when the season is about to start but the road is still closed, the flights can be heavily overbooked. The answer is to book well ahead but be prepared for disappointment.

One of the major attractions of the Ladakh region is the tremendous scope it offers for trekking. The avenues available for this activity range from short, day-long treks up and down mountain slopes or across a ridge to enjoy the sheer beauty of the Himalayan scenery, to long trans-mountain traverses involving weeks of walking and camping in the wilderness. The western flanks of the region, particularly the Suru and Zanskar Valleys of Kargil district, due to their general lie along the Great Himalayan Range itself, offer a variety of routes across the world's greatest mountain range through various depressions or passes in its crest. For trekking in Ladakh to be a rewarding experience, it is not enough to be physically fit, intending trekkers must also be well prepared to face the rigorous of back country travel.

Kargil

The western parts of Ladakh comprising several river valleys, drained and formed by the Himalayan tributaries of the high Indus, constitute Kargil District. Prominent among these are **Suru** and **Zanskar,** which lie nestling along the northern flank of the Great Himalayan Wall, the lateral valleys of **Drass, Wakha-Mulbek** and **Chiktan** constitute important subsidiaries. About 15,000 sq kms in area, Kargil District has an agrarian population of approximately 120,000 people, who cultivate the land along the course of the drainage system wherever artificial irrigation from mountain streams is possible. About 85 per cent are Muslims mainly of the Shia persuasion, Islam having been introduced to the originally Buddhist population around the middle of the 16th century by missionaries from Kashmir and Central Asia.

Kargil town (2,704 metres), situated midway between Srinagar (204 kms) and Leh (234 kms) on the Srinagar-Leh highway, is the second largest urban center (approximately 8,000 inhabitants) of Ladakh and headquarters of Kargil District. Being located in the lap of the Himalayas, Kargil serves as an important base for undertaking adventure tourism and trips to the Zanskar Valley and other Himalayan regions. Visitors traveling between Srinagar and Leh have to make a night halt in Kargil before starting the second leg of their journey.

Kargil is a convenient base for undertaking adventure activities like trekking, mountaineering, camping, river-rafting etc in the high Himalayan valleys. It is also convenient base for taking excursions to the Wakha-Mulbek valley, where the chief attraction is a Nine metre high rock sculpture of Maitreya, besides other monuments. Another tour option is to visit the enchanting Suru Valley to behold the gradually unfolding panorama of the impressive Himalayan landscape. Yet another interesting excursion option is to visit Drass for sightseeing its famous features like **Tolo-ling, Tiger Hill** and the **Mushkoo** valley, well-known throughout India on account of the extensively televised conflict (Kargil war) on the LoC between India and Pakistan during May-August 1999[33].

Accommodation[34]

Hotel tariff in Kargil ranges from Rs 100 to over Rs 2000/- (with all meals) per day for a double room depending on the quality of accommodation and services offered, which range from barely basic to reasonably comfortable, with attached bath and running hot water in the top of the line establishments[35]. Down towards the river the *Crown Hotel* has basic and 'just about clean' doubles for a reasonable rate. The *International Hotel* is slightly better with doubles with bath at a higher price. Among the cheapies also include the *Hotel Greenlands*, behind the bus stand on the way to the Suru View, where clean doubles are available.

The *State Tourist Bungalow* near the river is simple, clean and adequate. It's about a half km from the main street. There are two *Tourist Bungalows with most rooms* at affordable price(between Rs 100 to Rs 150 per day); the one up the hill from the main street is good. In addition, Kargil has a *circuit house* and a pleasantly located *PWD Rest House*. There is also accommodation of some form or other at Drass, Mulbekh, Bodh Kharbu, Lamayuru, Khalsi, Nurla, Saspul and Nimmu. The *Tourist Bungalow* at Mulbek, which has attached catering arrangements, provides four furnished rooms at Rs 100/- each per day. Dormitory accommodation at much cheaper price is available with some Guest Houses attached with the teashops located near Mulbek Chamba. Alternatively, tourists can return to Kargil for the night. The *Tourist Bungalow* at Shergol also provides four fully furnished rooms at Rs 100/- each per day.

Transportation

The J&K SRTC operates regular buses (including deluxe coaches) between Srinagar and Leh/Kargil. Taxis of all kinds, including 4-wheel drive vehicles, can be hired at Srinagar and Leh for visiting Kargil. Local buses, including mini coaches for Mulbek and Drass, leave Kargil every morning and afternoon.

Sankoo, Panikhar and Parkachik are connected with Kargil by regular bus service. The bus ride from Kargil takes two hours to Sankoo, three hours to Panikhar and about four hours to Parkachik. Rangdum is serviced by the buses proceeding to Padum, which increases in frequency according to demand. Cars and jeep taxis can be hired from Kargil for visiting different places in the Suru Valley, including Rangdum, Penzila and the Zanskar Valley.

Mulbek

Situated 45 kms east of Kargil on the road to Leh, Mulbek (3,230 metres) is a predominantly Buddhist area. Many monuments of the early Buddhist era dot the landscape, among which the chief attraction is Mulbek Chamba, a nine-metre high rock sculpture in deep relief of the Maitreya, the Future Buddha, which reflects an interesting blend of esoteric Saivite symbolism with early Buddhist art. Situated right on the highway, it dates back to the period when Buddhist missionaries came traveling east of the Himalayas during the 7-8th century. **Mulbek Gompa,** the main monastery of the area is perched atop a rocky hill that dominates the valley below. It is easy to see why in the past this site served as an outpost to guard the caravan route between Kashmir and Ladakh. Further up, inside the picturesque upper part of the Wakha river valley, is **Wakha Rgyal**, an interesting hilltop village that appears like a medieval settlement of cave dwellings. Its mud houses, neatly white-washed and closely stacked, are built around caves dug into the face of a vertical cliff rising high above the valley floor. A small monastery, similarly constructed and occupying the top of the brown hillside, completes this interesting Buddhist village. Breathtaking views of the undulating hills crowned by rocky peaks can be had from the plateau, which is the terminal point of a 5 km long rough road linking the village with the main highway.

Shergol

Another picturesque village of the area, Shergol has a mixed population of Muslims and Buddhists, and can be approached through a link road from the main highway. The main attraction for visitors is a cave monastery visible from afar as a white speck against the vertically rising brown hillside from which it appears to hang out. Down below is a Buddhist nunnery with about a dozen incumbents. There is an interesting four day trek from here into the Suru Valley across two mountain passes, Safi-la and Rusi-la. **Urgyan-Dzong**, a meditation retreat tucked deep inside the surrounding mountains can also be approached via the nearby village of **Pho-Khar**. This natural mountain fortress conceals a circular tableland with a small Buddhist temple at its center, while the surrounding hillsides reveal several caves where high-ranking Buddhist saints are believed to have mediated in seclusion. At least one such cave is associated with the visit of Padmasambhava, the patron saint of Tibetan Buddhism.

Drass

Drass (3,230 metres), 60 kms west of Kargil on the road to Srinagar, is a small township in the center of a valley of the same name. Locally called Hembabs (or snow land), it is renowned as the ***second coldest inhabited place in the world***[36] because of the intensely cold winters and heavy snowfall. Winter temperature here is sometimes known to plummet to *40 degrees Celsius below zero.* During the four spring-summer months, however, the valley turns very picturesque as the surrounding hillsides transform into green pastures splashed with a variety of wild flowers. Lately, Drass has become famous all over the world due to the extensive coverage it received during the three month long conflict on the Line of Control(LoC) between India and Pakistan during ***Kargil war***. Its physical landmarks like **Mushkoo Valley, Tiger Hills, Tolo-ling** etc, have become part of India's modern national epic. A grand view of these features can be had from Drass town.

Suru Valley[37]

One of the most beautiful regions of Ladakh, the Suru Valley is the heartland of Kargil District. Nestling along the northern foothills of the Great Himalayan Wall, it extends from Kargil town, first southward for a length of about 75 kms up to the expanse around Panikhar, thence east ward for nearly 65kms up to the foot of the Penzila watershed where the Suru River rises. The natural beauty of this area is heightened by the magnificent perspective provided by the towering peaks of Nun(7135 metres) and Kun (7087 metres), which loom over the skyline in their crystalline majesty.

Sightseeing in Suru Valley

The drive into the Suru Valley takes one through the picturesque and sprawling village conglomerate of Trespone-Saliskut. **Trespone** (25 kms) is famous for its hilltop **Imambara**, which reflects a quaint mix of Islamic and Tibetan elements in its construction style and location. It is also the place where the tradition of making a derivative of the ancient **Scythian** bow is still carried out by some families.

Sankoo: The next major expanse of the Suru Valley, is a picturesque township surrounded by numerous villages and colourful rocky mountains all around. Dense plantation of poplars, willows and wild roses fill the bowl-shaped valley, giving it the ambience of a man-made forest. Two side valleys drained by large tributary streams of the Suru River, the **Kartse** flowing from the east and the **Nakponchu** descending from the west, open up on either side of the expanse.

Panikhar... and Beyond. 25 kms further ahead of Sankoo is Panikhar nestling under the shadows of the Nun-Kun massif. The first, full, photogenic view of Mt Nun(7135 metres), however, can be had from the roadside near the village of Thangbu, about 12 kms short of Panikhar. A beautiful expanse of the Suru Valley with about a dozen villages strung around, Panikhar comprises a series of intensively cultivated plateaux descending in level steps to the bed of the Suru River which receives the gushing waters of Chelung river, one of its major Himalayan tributaries. During summer, the area turns into a veritable valley of flowers when a large variety of alpine flora blossom.

Rangdum: The farthest and most isolated part of the Suru Valley, Rangdum (3657 metres) is surrounded by colourful hills on the one side and glacier-encrusted rocky mountains on the other. Situated 130 kms southeast of Kargil, it falls midway between Kargil and Padum (Zanskar). Visitors to Padum generally prefer to break the gruelling 240 kms long road journey for an overnight halt here. Set amidst spectacular surroundings, Rangum is a convenient place for camping in the Himalayan wilderness while being sufficiently near a road-head. Rangdum is also an important trekking base. The most popular trek from here leads to **Henaskut** on the Kargil-Leh highway, across the **Kanji** valley gorge.

Zanskar Valley[38]

About 20 kms southeast of Rangdum stands the Penzi-la axis across which lies Zanskar, the most isolated of all the trans-Himalayan valleys. Spread over an estimated geographical area of 5000 sq kms of mountainous territory, Zanskar is surrounded by high rise mountains and deep gorges. It remains inaccessible for nearly eight months every year due to heavy winter snowfall resulting in closure of all access passes, including the Penzi-la. This geographical isolation and the esoteric nature of Buddhism practiced here have enabled its inhabitants to preserve their identity, so that today Zanskar is the least interfered with microcosm of Ladakh. Closer observation of the lifestyle evokes admiration for a people who have learnt to live in perfect harmony with the unique environment.

Transportation

The 240 km long Kargil-Padum road remains open from early July to mid-October. The J&K SRTC operates a 'B' class bus service between Kargil and Padum. Tourist groups can charter Deluxe buses to visit Zanskar, including sightseeing within the valley. Jeeps and Gypsy taxis can also be hired at Kargil, but the charges are high due to the difficult road conditions. During June and early July, prior to opening of the road, it is recommended to trek to Zankskar from Panikhar or Parkachik onwards. The week-long trek provides an opportunity to enjoy the unending grandeur of the Himalayas and experience the rustic life of the inhabitants of the villages, which otherwise pass by fleetingly while traveling by a bus or taxi. By mid June, summer is at its peak in the region and the climate is ideal for trekking along a route free from vehicular traffic and the area is freshly rejuvenated into life after months of frigid dormancy.

Accommodation

The Tourist Complex at Padum has five furnished rooms at Rs 100/-, per room, per day. Catering arrangement is provided within the complex. There is also a camping place nearby for tourists traveling with personal tents. There are several private hotels also in Padum where rooms with basic facilities are available at reasonable price. At Karsha, basic accommodation is available in Guest Houses. In the distant villages like Stong-de, Zangla, Sani, etc, accommodation can be sought from the villagers on payment of suitable charges, which can be negotiated. Some monasteries may also take in guests, though more as a gesture of goodwill than on purely commercial consideration. Of course, the guest is expected to compensate the monastery suitably.

Sightseeing in Zanskar[39]

Padum: Once the capital of the ancient kingdom of Zanskar, Padum (3505 metres) is the present-day administrative center of Zanskar sub-division of Kargil District. Its old part comprising interconnected adobe houses and several high rise **Chortens** surround a boulder-strewn hillock, site of the erstwhile palace and fort. The new, upcoming township is fast encroaching upon the cultivated expanse downwards, and a small market is coming up along the newly built road. With a population of nearly 2000, Padum can be described as the most populous settlement of Zanskar, which is otherwise a very scarcely inhabited valley. Padum has also become famous as a major trekking base and a popular tourist destination.

Sani: The picturesque village is six kms west of Padum, on the road to Kargil. The main attraction here is the castle-like monastery, which unlike other monasteries of Ladakh, is built on level ground. By legend its origin is associated with Kanishka (Kushan ruler of 2nd century AD), on account of the Kanika Stupa, which stands in the backyard of the walled complex. Sani also associated with the famous Indian Yogi Naropa, which is said to have meditated here, housing a veiled bronze figure of the Yogi, which is unveiled once a year in late July on the eve of the **Naro-Nasjal** festival. People from all over Zanskar valley participate in this festival during which lamas from Bardan Monastery perform masked dances as ritual offering.

Karsha: The largest monastery of Zanskar, Karsha Gompa is an imposing complex of neatly white-washed building blocks comprising several chapels, besides residential cells for its nearly 150 lamas of the Geluks-pa sect. Karsha can be approached from Padum by the nine km long link road across an iron bridge over the Stod river. It can also be approached directly from the Tungri along a 17 km link road that branches off from the Kargil-Padum road at Tungri, about 12 kms before Padum.

Stong-de: Perched on a rocky outcrop overlooking the oasis-like village, the beautiful monastery of Stong-de lies 18 kms to the north of Padum on the Padum-Zangla road. An old foundation associated with the Tibetan Yogi Marpa, Stong-de is now the second largest monastic establishment of Zanskar, which is inhabited by a resident community of about 60 Gelukspa lamas. The while-washed monastic complex comprises a number of temples, among which the Gon-Khang housing several fierce-faced deities is of particular interest. The climb up to the monastery from the roadside is rather strenuous, but it is worth the trouble for the breathtaking scenery of the valley visible from here.

Zangla: About 35 kms further north of Padum, Zangle was ruled by a titular chief till his death about two decades back. The old castle, now in ruins except for a small chapel, occupies a hill overlooking the desertic valley below. Nearby is an old Buddhist nunnery worth a visit to observe the austere life style of the small monastic community of nuns. An old monastery situated in the nearby village of Tsa-zar, midway between Stong-de and Zangla, has exquisite frescoes which should not be missed.

Bardan: 12 kms south of Padum, Bardan is an isolated monastery with about 40 Drupka-Kargyud lamas in residence. Founded during 17th century as the first ever center of Kargyud order in Zanskar, Bardan controls several smaller establishments in the region, including the famous Sani monastery. The large assembly hall, around which all other structures are organised, has beautiful statues of Buddhist divinities and small stupas in clay, bronze, wood and copper. Perched atop a rocky crag rising vertically from the Lung-nak riverbed, Bardan falls right on the trekking trail to Manali. Nearby is the smaller monastery of **Muney**, also worth a visit for appreciating its art treasures.

Phugthal: By far the most spectacularly located monastic establishment anywhere in Ladakh, the Phugthal complex spills out of the mouth of a huge cave high up in the vertical mountainside of the lateral **Shadi** gorge through which a major tributary of the **Lung-nak** or **Lingti Tsarap** river flows. A visit to Phugthal including Bardan and Muney monasteries enroute, makes a good 5 day round trek from Padum.

Zongkhul: The other cave monastery of Zanskar, Zongkhul falls on the Padum-Kishtawar trekking trail, just before the ascent to the Omasi-la pass begins. Built like a swallow's nest on the rock-face in the Ating gorge, the monastery is associated by legend with the famous Indian Yogi, Naropa, who for meditation is believed to have used the two caves around which the monastery has developed.

Leh

Centuries ago this was an important stop on the old caravan silk route from China. Today, it is merely a military base of Indian Army and tourist centre, but wandering the winding back streets of the town is still fascinating. It is about 10 km north-east of the Indus in a fertile side valley. There is one main street with Leh Palace rising up at the end of it. The bus station and jeep halt is on the airport side of town. The airport, with its steeply sloping runway, is several kilometers out of town near the Spitok Gompa. There is a Tourist Office of J&K TDC and Indian Airline office and a noisy power generator in the middle of town; fortunately it shuts down at 11 pm. The Ecological Development Group has a solar demonstration house and a fantastic library on Ladakh.

As already brought out, there are flights from both Srinagar and Chandigarh to Leh and the road is open from the beginning of June to October. There are an amazing number of hotels and guest houses in Ladakh, many of which are open only during the tourist season. Prices are very variable-soaring in the peak season, plummeting at other times. The cheaper guest houses are generally just rooms rented out in private homes.

Places of Tourist Interest[40]

Leh Palace: Looking for all the world like a miniature version of the Potala in Lhasa, Tibet, the palace was also built in the 16th century. It is now deserted and badly damaged, a legacy of Ladakh's wars with Kashmir in the last century. The main reason for making the climb up to the palace is for the superb views from the roof. The Zanskar mountains, across the Indus River, look close enough to touch. The palace is still the property of the Ladakhi royal family, although they now reside at nearby Stok. It is open from 0600am to 0900am and after 0500pm.

Leh Gompa: High above the palace and also overlooking the ruins of the older palace, the Red Gompa was built in 1430. It contains a fine three-storey-high seated Buddha image. It's open from 0700am to 0900am and from 0500pm to 0700pm. The gompa above is in a very ruined condition but the views down on Leh are superb.

Sankar Gompa: It is an easy stroll to the Sankar Gompa, a couple of km up the valley from the town centre. This interesting little gompa is only open from 0700 am to 1000 am and from 0500 pm to 0800 pm with an entry fee. The gompa has electric lighting so an evening visit is worthwhile. Upstairs is an impressive representation of Avalokitesvara complete with 1000 arms and 1000 heads.

Around Leh[41]: There are some more places of tourist interest in around Leh, namely, **Spitok Gompa**. 10 kms from Leh, the temple is about 1000 years old. There are fine views over the Indus from the gompa. **Phyang**, about 16 km from Leh, on the road back towards Srinagar, the gompa has about 50 monks. **Beacon Highway**, probably the **highest road** in the world, crosses a pass at **5606 metres** ! The road is only open in September and October-it takes the whole summer for the snow and ice to melt for that brief time. **Choglamsar**, a Tibetan refugee camp has become an important centre for the study of Tibetan literature and history and Buddhist philosophy. **Shey,** an old summer palace of the kings of Ladakh built about 550 years ago. **Tiske Gompa**, visible from Shey is about 17 km from Leh. The monastery is very picturesque and superbly sited on a hilltop overlooking the village and the Indus.

Adventure Tourism

One of the major attractions of the Ladakh region is the tremendous scope it offers for trekking. The western flanks of the region, particularly the Suru and Zanskar Valley lie along the Great Himalayan Range and offer variety of routes for trekking. The Trekking Routes available in this region are given in the **Appendix VI**. There are several avenues for mountaineering in this region as given in **Appendix VII**. J&K Tourism maintains Trekking Equipment Hire Shops at Kargil and Leh. Equipment such as two-men tents, insulation pads, trekking shoes, sleeping bags and rucksacks are available to bonafide trekkers on reasonably daily and weekly rent, against security deposits commensurate with the cost of the equipment. Trekking equipment can also be hired from a number of trekking/ travel agencies operating from Leh and Srinagar.

J&K Tourism initiates and co-ordinates evacuation of casualties by Indian Air Force helicopters in the event of accidents or sickness while trekking, mountaineering or river-rafting in the remote parts of the State. Acute mountain sickness can occur to anyone traveling to altitudes above 10,000ft. The most common symptoms of Acute Mountain Sickness are headaches, disturbed sleep, and loss of appetite, nausea, coughing, irregular breathing, breathlessness, lassitude and lack of concentration. High Altitude Pulmonary Oedema (HAPO) and High Altitude Cerebral Oedema (HACO) are very serious forms of Acute Mountain Sickness which are life-threatening and require immediate medical attention.

Fauna and Flora[42]

Fauna: Kashmir offers great attraction to a sportsman as it possesses a large and varied animal kingdom. For a hunter there are snow leopards, barasingha, black bear, brown bear, markhor, ovis ammon (wild sheep), black bear, ibex, otter, weasel, musk deer, fox, marmot, etc. etc. Shooting season for big game lasts throughout the year except for (1) snow leopard, (2) musk deer, (3) brown bear, and (4) Kashmir stag, which have been declared as protected animals. Besides, there is a great variety of small game such as snow partriges, Ram chakor, (Snow-cock) monal pheasant (Sunal) and pheasants etc. etc.

Habitat and some particulars about some big game animals are given below:

Panther: Kashmiri name – *Seh*. These are not restricted to forests. They more often prey on dogs and domestic animals. They generally follow beaten tracks of animals through the forest.

Snow Leopard: Kashmiri name-*Shena Seh*. In summer generally found above the tree-line in rocks and cliffs and in winter follows the game to lower altitudes and prowls about villages in the lower foothills.

Brown Bear: Kashmiri name-*Gura Haput*. Inhabits bare, open peaks high above the snowline in summer.

Black Bear: Kashmiri name- *Haput*. In summer they may be found near the limits of treeline, 10,000 to 12,000 ft. In autumn maize fields in the foothills are a great attraction for them.

Ovis Orientalis: *Shapu or Urial*, found mostly in Ladakh-inhabits steep grassy hill slopes above forests.

Ovis Ammon: Ladakhi name-*Nayan*. Lives in wilderness and desolate plains and low undulating hills. They are migratory and wander wherever food and water is to be got. In summer they are found above 15,000ft.

Bharal or Blue Sheep: Ladakhi name-*Na or Sna*. Found in Ladakh and Zanskar. Seeks higher altitudes (16,000 ft) in summer and rarely below 13,000 ft in winter.

Markhor: Ladakhi name – *Raphoche*. Inhabits Pir Pantsal and Kazinag ranges. Lives in dense birch and pine forests whose grassy glens form their grazing grounds. Goes seldom higher than the snow-line. The ground they like best is precipitous crag and rock where they feel more secure from attack.

Serew: Kashmiri name-*Ramu, Halj, Salabhir.* Favours an elevation between 6,000 and 10,000 ft. Lives in recesses of thickly wooded gorges whose boulder strewn slopes and shallow caves give shelter from weather.

Kashmir Stag: *Hangul, Barasingh.* Limited to north side of the Kashmir Valley and adjacent valleys. Essentially a forest animal, roams from forest to forest to find good grazing. Spends winter in lower levels and summer on heights. Found in large herds in Dachhigam game preserve.

Ibex: Ladakhi name-*Skin or Sekin. Kashmiri Kale.* Favourite ground higher elevations above the treeline. Lives in the shelter and security of precipitous cliffs and ridges.

Musk Deer: Kashmiri name *roos, rous.* Generally met in birch forests above the zone of pines. At times they come to lower levels but always keep in thick cover.

Wolves: In barren uplands of Kashmir and Ladakh, they live as nomads, coming down to valleys in winter, migrating with game and grazing flocks to the snowline in summer. Holes, caves, cavities in rocks provide them with shelter in winter and thickets of reeds and scrub with a refuge in summer.

Red Fox: Kashmiri name *Loh*-found in Kkashmir and Ladakh, common in brushwood and cultivated land.

Lynx: Kashmiri name *Patsalav.* Found in Kashmir and Ladakh. Shelters in dense cover provided by scrub, patches of reed and tall grass and forests.

Common Otter: Kashmiri name-*Kula Oddur.* Generally makes its lair among rocks and boulders, in hollows, beneath the foots of trees growing by the water edge or lies up in reed beds, ferns, brakes and bushes. In summer many others go up the streams and torrents. Their upward movement coincides with the upward migration of carp and other fish for purposes of spawning. In winter they come down to the lower streams.

Stone Martin: Inhabits both forests and barren heights above the tree line, sheltering in hollows in trees, under logs, among rocks, or in holes in the ground.

Marmot: Kashmiri name-*Drin.* Found between 8,000 and 14,000 feet. Lives on grasses and seeds of various plants. When scenting danger utters a loud whistling scream.

Water Birds: A large variety of ducks visit Kashmir in winter and some of them also breed here, in Hokarsar and Haigam lakes. The shooting season begins from the First of September and lasts till the 31st of May. The game birds found in large clocks on its lakes are ducks and geese, mallard, pochard, gadwall, teal, snipe, grebe, coot, waterhen, white-eyed duck, dabchick, pintail, shoveller etc.etc. Haigam, Hokarsar and Mirgund are protected areas for small game shooting.

Fish: An angler finds the cold water streams such as Sindh, Lidder, Bringhi, Arapat and many of its mountain tarns such as Gangabal, Nundkol, Vishnsar etc, abounding in rainbow and brown trout. He can also find Mahaseer which comes up to breed at Ningal in June-July. The rivers are also full of various kinds of country fish. Mirror carp has recently been introduced and can now be found in abundance in the lakes and rivers.

Birds: Kashmir offers a vast field of study for a lover of birds. Numerous beautiful birds come here to breed in summer. Amongst them are golden oriole, thrushes, finches, bee eaters, tits, starts, dippers, flycatchers, swallows, wood peckers and the like.

Flora: For a collector of flowers Kashmir is a real paradise. In summer the meadows of Kashmir are literally a mass of a vast variety of flowers of varied colours, such as primulas, anemones, crocuses, gentians, aquilegia, saxifrage, marsh marigold, daisies, roses, purple and while irises, geraniums and numerous kinds of ferns etc besides some rare flowers such as blue poppy. Its forests and meadows abound in medicinal herbs, such as **Kuth**(Costus spacious) etc.

Wildlife Sanctuary

Out of a total geographical area of 137,876 sq kms, the forest area accounts for 21,000 sq km in Jammu and Kashmir State. The total area of the only existing sanctuary and 10 Wildlife Reserves, accounts for 500 sq kms which is 0.36 percent of the total geographical area and 2.03 percent of the total forest area[43].

The predominantly Himalayan (temperate and sub-trophical) fauna of the State contains certain critically endangered species like the musk deer, snow leopard, Kashmir stag and Himalayan black bear and brown bear. The details of the important Park/Sanctuary where these species can be found are as under[44]:

Important Parks/Sanctuaries

Name of the Park / Sanctuary	*Total Area*	*Species Found*
Dachigam Wildlife Sanctuary(Srinagar)	55 sq miles	Leopard, Blackbear, Brown bear, Serow, Musk deer, Hangul.
Raj Parian Wildlife Sanctuary(Anantnag)	20.50 sq miles	Brown bear, Black bear, Musk deer, Serow, Hangul & Chakor.
Shankarachari Wildlife Sanctuary(Srinagar)	310 acres Horizontal area	Chakor
Chumnai Basin Wildlife Sancturary (Anantnag)	N.A	Brown bear, Black bear, Leopard, Musk deer.

Conclusion

Among the states of the country Jammu and Kashmir enjoys wide variety of tourism products and places of attraction not only for the domestic tourists but also for the international visitors. The State Government has taken all the steps to improve the tourism industry by improving the facilities for the tourists and visitors in the recent past. Several infrastructures such as railway line connecting the Kashmir Valley from the rest of India, projects for more accommodation, and facilities to make the tourist enjoy the trip includes the mobile phone services in the State. Above all giving adequate protection to the visitors from disturbance and insurgency have been undertaken by the Government.

Notes and References

1. Nagendra Kr Singh, *Cultural Heritage of Jammu, Kashmir and Ladakh, Vol 2*, Jay Kay Book House, Jammu, 1997, p. 518.
2. Crowther, Geoff, *India, a Travel Survival Kit, Lonely Planet Publications*, Australia, 1987, p. 228.
3. KK Nanda, *Conquering Kashmir–A Pakistani Obsession*, Lancers Books, New Delhi, 1996, p. 347.
4. Govt of J&K, *Digest of Statistics 2001-2002*, Directorate of Economics and Statistics Planning and Development Department, Table No 20.00, p. 263.
5. SK. Sinha, Governor of J&K, *Kashmir Times, Jammu*, 05 January 2004, p. 3.
6. UNI, *The Hindu,* 23 January 2004, p. 3.
7. *J&K Tourism, Hindustan Thompson Associates Ltd*, Feb 2003.
8. PTI, *The Indian Express(The Himalayan Mail)*, 12 November 2004, p. 1.
9. Crowther Geoff, *Op.cit*, pp. 208-209.
10. Man Mohan Sharma, *Yatra. Pilgrimages in the Western Himalayas*, Trishul Publications, New Delhi, 1989, p. 15.
11. Sudhir S Bloeria, *Pakistans Insurgency Vs India's Security*, Manas Publications, New Delhi, 2000, pp. 218-233.
12. Man Mohan Sharma, *Op.cit,* p. 8.
13 Shri Mata Vaishno Devi Shrine Board, *Yatra- a Guide to the Holy Pilgrimage of Shri Mata Vaishno Devi Ji*, October 2003, p. 8.
14. *Ibid.*
15. *Ibid*, p. 20.
16. *Ibid*, p. 28.
17. *Ibid*, p. 88.
18. *Ibid*, p. 89.
19. Wright Gillian, *Hill Stations of India*, Penguin Books, New Delhi, 1998, p. 12.
20. Kr Singh Nagendra, *Op.cit,* p. 518.
21. *Ibid*, pp. 519-520.
22. Wright Gillian, *Op.cit*, p. 43.
23. Crowther Geoff, *Op.cit*, p. 213.

24. J&K Tourism, *Unforgettable Kashmir, Hindustan Thompson Associates*, Feb 2003, p. 11.
25. Crowther Geoff, *Op.cit*, p. 224.
26. *Ibid*, p. 226.
27. *Ibid.*
28. Man Mohan Sharma, *Op.cit*, p. 22.
29. *Ibid.*
30. Govt. of J&K, *Digest of Statistics 2001-2001*, Directorate of Economics and Statistics Planning and Development Department, p. 265.
31. Wright Gillian, *Op.cit,* p. 52.
32. Crowther Geoff, *Op.cit*, pp. 229 and 234.
33. GM. Kakpori, *J&K Tourism*, *Hindustan Thompson Associates*, Jan 2003, pp. 3-10.
34. Crowther Geoff, *Op.cit*, p. 230.
35. GM. Kakpori, *Op.cit*, p. 22.
36. *Ibid,* p. 14.
37. *Ibid*, pp. 17-21.
38. *Ibid*, pp. 24-33.
39. *Ibid*, pp. 26-29.
40. Crowther Geoff, *Op.cit*, p. 233.
41. *Ibid*, pp. 236-237.
42. NL. Bakaya, *Holidaying and Trekking in Kashmir*, Navin Press, New Delhi, 1998, pp. 24-29.
43. VB. Saharia, *Wildlife in India*, Natraj Publishers, Dehradun, 1982, p. 80.
44. *Ibid*, p. 244.

6

Impact of Terrorism on J&K Tourism

Introduction

Tourism has been identified as an industry with potential of development next to agriculture and horticulture in J&K. The industry was given special status with a view to generate year round activity. A special outlay of Rs 22.06 crores was made available during the 7th Plan period with which important schemes like Gulmarg cable car, development of Jammu and development of wayside facilities were taken up[1]. The result was that the tourist inflow has made considerable upward movement in mid eighties of the last century. However, the tourist trade has completed collapsed after the militancy in the State from 1989 onwards.

Recent events have once again generated some curiosity and interest in the issue of Jammu and Kashmir. Basic facts pertaining to the terrorism in Jammu and Kashmir issue are well established. However, there has been a concerted dis-information campaign that presents a distorted historical account of the developments that led to the irrevocable accession of the State of Jammu and Kashmir to India, the subsequent wars inflicted by Pakistan on India and the current situation in the valley. The involvement of Pakistan in fomenting insurgency and terrorism in the border states of India, especially Jammu and Kashmir, has been well documented and accepted by all impartial observers.

The demand for independence in the Valley is not going to vanish overnight, but that should not discourage the policy makers from working out a constitutional formula, which would meet the legitimate political aspirations of all the regions of the State–the Kashmir Valley, Jammu and Ladakh[2]. In a diverse country like India, disaffection and discontent are not uncommon. Indian democracy has the necessary resilience to accommodate genuine grievances within the framework of the sovereignty, unity and integrity. Government of India has expressed its willingness to accommodate the legitimate political demands of the people of the State of J&K. However, Pakistan sponsored terrorists have terrorized the intimidating or silencing voices of moderation that wishes to engage in dialogue. The human rights of the people of J&K have been systematically violated by such terror tactics and kidnappings and killings of innocent people by terrorists which has a great impact on over all economic development in general and tourism in particular.

Since the beginning of this century, several Central and State Government projects are underway to improve the overall development of the State and mark it as a tourist destination. Moreover, the recent developments in the Indo-Pak relations brought hope of peace in the State and as a result, there is a marked improvement in the domestic tourist inflow. The economy of the Valley flourished from the 1950s onwards, with very large number of tourists, both Indians and foreigners, visiting Kashmir almost throughout the year. During 1986, over 95 per cent of the funds allotted for Tourism developments in the State were expended for development of tourism in Kashmir region and 05 per cent was expended for Jammu region[3]. This clearly indicates the importance of tourism potential of Kashmir region. However, the number of tourists started dwindling from mid 1980s and the tourism almost finished from 1989-90 onwards due to the insurgency in the State. Those who lived on this industry suddenly found themselves without an occupation and no means of livelihood[4].

In late 1989, a popular movement demanding independence from India and backed by various militant groups badly disrupted life. Frequent curfews and strict security measures helped to ensure that hardly any tourists came to Srinagar and the famous houseboats on its lakes found deserted since 1990. About 70 percent of the population of Srinagar was dependent on the tourism industry and they looked forward to seeing the visitors come back again[5].

Due to the tireless efforts of the Government, Security Forces and the Public Support in some cases, the insurgency in the state has been put under check and controlled to a great extent from 1995 onwards. The year 1995 has been replete with stupendous and complex challenges for J&K State which has been beleaguered by Pakistan sponsored militancy from 1989 onwards. These challenges unfolded undaunting spirit, firm commitment and congealed determination on the part of the administration to come out stronger to restore normalcy and to initiate the political process for restoration of democratic set-up in the State. The developmental profile received impetus primarily due to liberal assistance from Central Government which helped the State Government to tide over its crucial financial problems[6].

Several projects were undertaken by the State/Central Government to revive the beauty of the Valley and to rejuvenate the tourism industry in the state. There is certainly an impact of the terrorism on the tourism industry in the state, yet, the Twenty First century saw a sea change in the tourists' influx to the state, both domestic and international. In the year 2003, The Jammu and Kashmir State has been selected for a **Special National Tourism Award** for its outstanding performance in tourism promotion[7]. The award was given in recognition of the strategies adopted by Jammu and Kashmir Government to boost tourism. It has also been stated by the State Governor Lt Gen(Retd) SK Sinha that the fear to visit the J&K state due to sporadic acts of violence have gone and these acts by the militants have failed to stop the tourists from coming to visit the state[8].

Key Militant Groups in the Valley

Pakistan's new game plan in the Valley has led to an alarming spurt in the levels of infiltration by militants in the mid of 2004. The major infiltration routes of the militants are given in the sketch. Civilians are the new targets apart from political leaders as terror returns with a vengeance. The key militant groups operating in the Valley and the number of militants as reported in **India Today** dated 13 September 2004 are as under[10]:

Number of Militants Operating in the Valley

(a) Hizb-ul-Mujahideen	- 880
(b) Lashkar-e-Toiba	- 520
(c) Jaish-e-Mohammed	- 279
(d) Harkut-ul-Mujahideen	- 129
(e) Harkat-ul-Jihadi Islami	- 148
(f) Al-Badr	- 107

Modus Operandi of the Militants

The militant's *modus operandi* is clear. They have made every effort to paralyse normal life, cause economic hardship to the people, make the administrative apparatus ineffective and destroy the age-old, culture and traditions of communal amity in the area. Their modus operandi then became one where they indulged in high profile mass killings, mainly of Hindu families. Presently, their activities generally are[11]:

(a) Killing of prominent political leaders[12].

(b) Attacks against soft targets to terrorise the public[13].

(c) Arson of government buildings and temples to demoralize the administrative machinery and population.

(d) Burning of timber dumps of the State Forest Corporation and any such assets of the government.

(e) Intimidation of Hindus to force migration[14].

(f) Sniping and ambushes against the security forces[15].

(g) Attacks on soft targets to show up the lack of ability of the government to extend security, e.g., bomb blasts in buildings, buses and crowded areas;

(h) Conduct of improvised explosive device attacks as well as standoff attacks against the security forces and their vehicles; and

(i) Fidayeen(Suicide) Attacks[16].

Incidents and Killings in J&K: An Overview

Since 1988, India has suffered a total of 59,186 terrorist incidents in J&K alone. Though in many incidents security forces were targeted but majority attacks involved civilians as 2,466 kidnappings and 791 extortion cases were reported since 1989. Pakistan supported terrorism also resulted in extensive destruction of property in J&K. There were targeted attacks on educational institutions (780) in a bid to destroy the modern education system, which the fundamentalist ideology of the terrorist did not approve. Since 1988, security forces have recovered very large number of weapons from terrorists in J&K. This included 889 rocket launchers, 347 rockets, 1525 rocket boosters, 1124 machine guns, 20,193 AK series rifles, 34,141 grenades, 21,332 kilograms of explosives and 1970 bombs.

The **annual variation of the terrorist incidents in J&K from 1988 to 2004 was as under**[17]. It is pertinent to note that there is a discernible improvement in the security scenario in the State with militancy subsequently declining as is evident from the figures:

Number of Terrorist Incidents in J&K

Year	*No of Incidents*	*Year*	*No of Incidents*
1988	149	1996	4866
1989	962	1997	2964
1990	3393	1998	2940
1991	2931	1999	3073
1992	4664	2000	3091
1993	4012	2001	4536
1994	6043	2002	4038
1995	6039	2003	3401
		2004	2565

To understand the trend of the incidents, graphical representation of the above mentioned data is shown as **Graph 1.** It clearly indicates that there is a drop in the level of terrorist related incidents in the State of Jammu and Kashmir from 1997 onwards and a bit of tension in the year 2001 and 2002 when the Indian Army and Pakistan Army were mobilized for OPERATION PARAKRAM along the international border, a possible conflict which was averted. Finally, the trend is sloping down in the recent years, a clear indication that the militancy is coming down in the State.

Between 01 Jan 1988 and 31 Oct 1998, there was a total of 38,753 Pakistan's sponsored terrorist incidents in J&K. During the same period, according to the Annual Reports on the Pattern of Global Terrorism issued by the US State Department, there were 4,411 terrorist incidents in the rest of the world[18]. As per the South Asia Analysis Group Paper No 192, the incidents during this period could be categorized as follows:

Targetted attacks on the Security Forces	- 18,064.
Targetted attacks on Civilians	- 9,793.
Indiscriminate killings with explosives and arson attacks	- 10,896.

It would be seen from the above figures that the incidents of violence in J&K was at its peak in 1994 and 1995 and started dwindling down thereafter. The number of attacks on Security Forces has been more than the attacks on civilians coupled with indiscriminate killings. **The details of militants killed in J&K since 1990** are as under[19]:

Year	*Militants Killed*	*Year*	*Militants Killed*
1990	-550	1997	-1075
1991	-844	1998	-999
1992	-819	1999	-1082
1993	-310	2000	-1520
1994	-1596	2001	-2020
1995	-1332	2002	-1707
1996	-1209	2003	-1494
		2004	-976

From the **Graph 2**, it is clear that the number of militants emerged for destruction of peace in the State of Jammu and

Kashmir has been reduced in the recent years. The graph line dips down from the year 2001 onwards and reached a low of 976 in the year 2004.

Present Status of Militancy

In an effort to neutralize the militancy, the Government of India has approved and implemented the Armed Forces Special Powers Act in the State from 1989. As a result, OPERATION RAKSHAK has been undertaken by the Indian Army and neutralized several militants and their hideouts. Ever since, security forces have also recovered very large number of weapons, explosives and ammunition from terrorists. The efforts of the government have shown the results and the situation has improved in the State.

There is a remarkable improvement in the security scenario in the State with militancy subsequently declining as is evident from the public disillusionment, their outbursts against militants, and their greater participation and cooperation in furnishing information leading to continuous successes[20]. Militants and even the foreign mercenaries who are finding it difficult to stand up to the forces, are now choosing soft targets and indulging in criminal acts like killing of innocent civilians, rapes, abductions, extortions, burning private and public property etc.

The J&K police has been re-activated particularly in combating militancy in conjunction with security forces in the affected areas and the mechanism redressal of the grievances has been sharpened. Administration with human touch has been the core element of strategy followed in dealing with militancy so that the sense of anomie and alienation amongst the people could be taken care of[21].

To analyse the present status of the militancy, the graphic details of terrorist related incidents in Jammu and Kashmir from January 2004 to June 2004 in comparison with the incidents in the previous year as brought out in *Frontline* dated 30 July 2004 are given as **Graph 3 to Graph 7**[22].

The fact remains that the infiltration has gone down since December 2001 when India adopted twin strategy of garnering international option against Pakistan and tried to intimidate Pakistan by deploying its armed forces on the border. According to available data, there were 2260 infiltrators entered in J&K in 2000, 2706 in 2001 and till July 2002, 748 infiltrators have been recorded[23]. The infiltration routes are shown in the sketch given in **Annexure 7.** The infiltration surge in the year 2004 is shown in **Graph 8.**

Militancy in Tourist Spots: Current Case Study

It is an irony of modern times that it is not the magnitude of violence or the barbarity of the act that defines the degree of tragedy but it is the identity of the victims. Or else, why would the calamity of 9/11 resulting in a few thousand deaths evoke global condemnation, while the one-and-a-half decade old catastrophe perpetrated by militants in Kashmir leading to over 50,000 civilian deaths, fail to stir up humanity's conscience?[24].

Till the commencement of militancy in J&K, large number of tourists, both domestic and foreign, visited the valley every year. By the mid eighties the tourists' annual figure had reached a peak of seven lakhs[25]. However, due to militancy since 1990, it came down to a dismal 10,000 or so in a year. Despite the militancy, tourists from other countries continued to visit the valley, although in driblets. Targetting or kidnapping tourists especially foreign tourists invited the international attention and of course international condemnation. The kidnappings and killings of foreign tourists took place in the initial phase of the terrorism in the State. However, the trend seem to have changed in the later stage in J&K.

Case History of Militants Targetting Tourists

Though the militants have not specifically targetted the tourists in the recent past, there were some incidents here and there which put fear psychosis in the minds of the people who are planning to visit the State of J&K. Moreover, the militancy in the State has also created inconvenience to the general public especially tourists due to the security checks at every halt. Fear of death and the inconvenience is, of course, a bad impact on the minds of the visitors. Reports of some of the details of such incidents where the tourists were targetted or the incidents in areas where tourists probably came under cross fire or other wise, collected from various publications and sources, in the recent past are compiled as under:

Kidnapping of Foreign Tourists

(a) On 26 June 1991, ***seven Israeli tourists and One Dutch tourist were kidnapped*** by a group calling itself Pasdaran-i-Inquilaabi Islam from a houseboat in Dal Lake. The two women among the kidnapped tourists were set free, but the men were tied and led out of the boat by armed men. Sensing imminent death, a young Israeli tourist in a dare-devil act managed to free one of his hands and snatched an AK-47 rifle from one of the kidnappers. He shot dead two of the kidnappers, but the others managed to escape. The unarmed youngster was able to free all the kidnapped persons. However, *one of them got killed* in the shootout that followed. One of the freed Israelis ran towards the city where he was captured this time by the JKLF activists, but he was ultimately released unharmed on 03 July 1991. The JKLF, on its part, ***condemned the kidnapping of foreign tourists***[26].

(b) **Abduction of 4 Foreigners by Harkat-ul-Ansar in Delhi, October 1994**[27]. The abduction of four foreign nationals (3 British and 1 American) from Delhi by the Harkat-ul-Ansar, a militant group of J&K, was carried out by a core group of five Pakistani nationals. The kidnappers demanded release of a number of terrorists in the custody of Indian Government. The kidnapping sent fear world across for the visiting foreigners since it took place at the very national capital of India itself.

(c) A group of 15 armed militants calling themselves the Al Faran group ***kidnapped five foreign tourists, including two Americans and two British***, on 04 July 1995 from Ledervat, 28 kms from Pahalgam. The kidnappers demanded the release of 22 militants in prison in exchange for the hostages. From all available evidence it appeared that Al Faran was a front organisation of Harkat-ul-Ansar based in Peshawar, Pakistan, though the Pakistan government has denied this. On 08 July 1995 one of the kidnapped persons, John Childs Donald of the US managed to escape. The kidnappers retaliated by kidnapping another tourist trekking in Pahalgam – Oflore Christafeen, a Norwegian, on 10 Jul 1995. He was later *killed in a most brutal manner* and his beheaded body with the words Al Faran in Urdu etched on it with a sharp-edged weapon was found near Anantnag after over a month. The militants suspected him to be a Jew. The whereabouts of the remaining four hostages are still not known[28]. *For the first time security experts from the US, Britain and Germany camped in Srinagar to assist the authorities*[29]. Later, about 40 persons were killed by militants in a landmine explosions and a fierce shootout in Pahalgam[30].

This was the first kidnapping case when the people and the separatist groups in the valley ***criticized the kidnapping of foreign tourists and even observed a bandh in protest***. The leaders of the All Party Hurriyat Conference also demanded the release of the hostages, but the kidnappers rejected the appeal. In a statement they said "*we are fighting against anti-islamic forces...Western countries were anti-islamic and America was the biggest enemy of Islam*[31]. The Pakistani hand is strongly suspected as most of the kidnappers were reported to be Urdu speaking.

Disrupting Amarnath Pilgrimage

(a) In July 1994, Harkat-ul-Ansar gave a call to disrupt the annual Amarnath Pilgrimage. However, Hizbul Mujahideen, who had earlier supported the call later disassociated from Harkat-ul-Ansar, following the settlement of the "bunkers issue" around Hazaratbal. Due to the militants threats, the local government employees and the private hotels, travel agents and shopkeepers refused to participate in the yatra[32].

Though the Yatra passed off peacefully, the Government had to get government employees, traders, and porters from Jammu as the local people boycotted the Yatra due to fear of the militants. Even "poly-wallahs" boycotted the Yatra[33]. It was yet another turning-point signifying the victory of the State Government over the militants.

(b) Harkat-ul-Ansar again announced a ban on the annual Amarnath Yatra in August 1995. Massive security arrangements had to be made to foil their many attempts to disrupt it. ***A government official was killed and some pilgrims injured in the bomb blasts at Pahalgam and Chandanwari***. A record number of pilgrims visited the shrine as compared to the last few years. This time militants did not completely succeed in persuading the local traders, pony-wallahs, and other concerned with the pilgrimage, not to offer their services to the pilgrims. This was yet another proof of the militants losing support among the people[34].

(c) The episode of August 1996, when about **243 people lost their lives** on the high region of Pahalgam had nothing to do with the militancy. It was **a natural calamity** of a sudden cloudburst, followed by heavy unprecedented snowfall when the yatris were caught unawares while moving along the track[35].

(d) In the 2002 pilgrimage, militants attacked Amarnath Pilgrims Camp near Pahalgam ***killing Nine people and injuring 26*** on 06 August 2002[36]. However, *The Hindu* reported on 07 August 2002 that at least nine Amarnath pilgrims, including a young girl, were killed and 50 injured in a militant fidayeen(suicide) attack on their highly fortified base camp at *Nunwan*(Pahalgam). Eyewitnesses said a blast shook the camp around 5.15 a.m. "*We heard a blast and didn't know what it was ... but when it was followed by heavy firing, **all of us ran for our lives***", said Savita, a pilgrim from Gujarat[37], the news paper added. **In**

spite of the attack, the yatra was not suspended and the pilgrims continued their journey from Jammu, the news paper further claimed. Al Mansuriyan, a militant outfit sponsored by the Lashkar-e-Toiba, claimed responsibility for the attack. In Delhi, the Deputy PM, Mr LK Advani said "In fact, some of the yatris who returned today to the base camp had **expressed satisfaction with the security arrangements**, but we are going to further strengthen the measures", concluded the news paper.

(e) *Daily Excelsior* dated 13 June 2004 reported that **apparently disturbed over the thick influx of tourists into Kashmir valley, militants struck on the famous hill station of Pahalgam on 12 June 2004. At least four persons, including two domestic tourists, got killed and 24 others sustained injuries in the grenade explosion.** The grenade attack took place in front of Purnima Hotel at Pahalgam at 1615 hours. Two employees of the hotel also died on the spot. **Since a thick tourist concentration appeared to be the target, at least 26 persons sustained splinter injuries.**

(f) Minutes after the blast, a dreaded militant outfit, known as *Al-Nasireen,* claimed responsibility. An unidentified caller who introduced himself as the spokesman of the guerrilla outfit **argued that the tourists were importing obscenity into the Valley which was "not acceptable",** news paper added. The attack was condemned by the State Government and the Office bearers of Kashmir House Boat Owners Association, Shikara Owners Association, Hotel Owners Association, Kashmir Chapter of the Travel Agents Association of India and Travel Agents Society of Kashmir.

Suicide Attack on Raghunath Temple

(a) Terrorist mounted suicide attack on Raghunath Temple in Jammu **killing eight people and**

injuring Seventeen on 30 March 2002[38]. The *Sunday Statesman* reported on 31 Mar 2002 that in a *fidayeen*(suicide) attack first of its kind in Jammu, terrorists stormed the Raghunath Temple complex in the heart of the city and gunned down seven people, including three security men, and injured 20[39]. The fidayeen attack took place at 10.20 a.m. on 30 March 2002. The *Kashmir Times* dated 31 March 2002 further added that panic gripped the entire city and the people were seen running helter-skelter. The news of the shoot out spread throughout the city like wild fire. All the shops and other business establishments were closed in most parts of the city soon after the shoot out began. Commuter traffic also remained effected for some time.

(b) Various social, political and religious organizations and individuals, including Jammu and Kashmir Liberation Front, have strongly condemned the Raghunath Temple shoot out. The news paper further reported that the recent incidents of Railway shootout, Trikuta Hills encounter and blasts near Ban-Ganga(Katra) in Jammu Region has already claimed its toll due to which ***Vaishnodeviji Yatra had considerably declined and now this incident despite all tight security arrangements and intensive checking by police personnel has exposed many loop-holes in the intelligence and security network.***

(c) Again in an effort to kill Hindus, terrorist stormed on Raghunath Temple on 24 November 2002 **killing 11 people including one woman and injuring 53**[40]. The *Hindustan* Times on 25 November 2002 reported that the Raghunath Temple in Jammu city once again became a scene of siege as a group of terrorists stormed the temple complex on 24 November 2002 evening. There was no clue as to how many terrorists were involved in the *fidayeen* attack which began with a series of explosion around the temple complex. There was panic all around when bombs started exploding and terrorists stormed in firing indiscriminately from their automatic weapons-are-run of the March 30 assault on the same temple in which ten people and two attackers were killed[41]. The crowded Raghunath Bazar was bustling with Vaishno Devi Pilgrims as well as local visitors when deafening blasts triggered panic and confusion. For both the attacks, the militant out fit Lashkar-e-Toiba claimed responsibility.

First Major Strike Against Vaishno Devi Pilgrims

(a) The attack on Vaishno Devi Pilgrims on 21 July 2003 at 2105 hours was successfully planned by the militants to terrorise the pilgrims, especially when the Amarnath Yatra was at its peak. This was an attack made on Banganga which is about two kilometers away from the base camp–Katra, to the holy cave of Vaishno Mata. About two grenade attacks were made within the span of 10 minutes which led to five killed including a child and 38 injured, eight of them seriously. Militant(s) managed to escape in the melee. July is the peak season for Vaishno Devi pilgrimage and on an average about 15,000 pilgrims used to visit the shrine everyday[42].

(b) The *Daily Excelsior* dated 22 July 2003 reported that *undeterred by the twin blasts, the pilgrims, drawn from different parts of the country, continued their march towards Mata Vaishnodeviji, the widely revered shrine, chanting "Jai Mata Di" and slogans against Pakistan and the militants. Authorities too didn't stop the yatra and allowed the pilgrims to proceed to the shrine after intensifying security arrangements at the base camp and 13 km hilly track.* The news paper also claimed that *tension gripped Ban Ganga for few minutes after the blasts.* ***However, the militants' strike failed to have any impact on the pilgrims, who went ahead with their journey.*** Army and para-military personnel were later deployed along the 13 km hilly track to sanitise the area and carry out a search for the militants.

(c) This was for the first time that the militants managed to break the multi-tier security cordon, put in force for Vaishnodeviji pilgrims, during 13 years of militancy despite making several attempts to do so. Prior to this attack, the militants had exploded bombs in Katra-bound buses but failed to cause much casualties. In 2002 also, the auto operators had alleged that a blast had taken place at their stand, a claim denied by the police. In the year 2001, four militants were gunned down by police in a mountainous area surrounding Trikuta hills. Police had claimed that the slain militants were headed towards the shrine, reported the newspaper.

Militants in Jammu Railway Station

Jammu Tawi is an important railhead of the Northern Railways serving the Jammu and Kashmir State. A critical situation had developed on 02 January 2004, when terrorists entered the Jammu Railway Station and were ***on the verge of slaughtering scores of innocent civilians***. Lt Triveni Singh of the 5th Battalion The Jammu and Kashmir Light Infantry neutralized the evil, designs of the terrorists and ensured that there was *no casualty to innocent civilians, women and children* present at the railway station, and sacrificed his life in the gun battle[43]. However, there remained fear in the minds of the people coming to Jammu Tawi Railway Station, though short lived.

National Highway Blast on 23 May 2004

The Hindu reported on 28 May 2004 that with the entire country reeling under intense heat wave, people have started flocking picturesque Kashmir valley in large numbers in search of respite. According to official figures, nearly 75,000 tourists visited Kashmir up to 28 May 2004 from beginning of the year against 24,000 arrivals in the corresponding period last year. Though the **deadly blast** on 23 May 2004 along Jammu-Srinagar National Highway in which **29 BSF personnel lost**

their lives proved a dampener, the arrivals have started picking up once again. Only 1253 tourists made it to the valley on the day of the blast as traffic was suspended for nearly five hours but the arrival of 1,708 persons the next day proved that **confidence of the tourists was shaken but not destroyed** [44]. According to Rajesh Kumar, a resident of Uttar Pradesh, who was on a holiday to Kashmir, the news of the **blast did send jitters down his spine but it did not deter him from visiting the valley as per his plans**, the paper reported.

Fidayeen Attack on Dal Lake Hotel

One or two militants sneaked into the **Hotel Leward** behind Nehru Park on the Dal Lake at 2015 hours on 27 July 2004. They fired grenades and AK-56 shots and made attempts to occupy the hotel, housing a unit of CRPF. The 65th Battalion of CRPF guarding the Dal Lake and sensitive installations around the lake, have been living at the hotel. Militants were suspected to have reached the protected site in a boat and sneaked into the hotel[45] . As per the version of The Tribune News Service, two militants and five CRPF personnel were killed. The encounter between the militants and the security forces continued till early morning of the next day[46] .

There were different opinion from various people on this attack. The Tribune dated 29 July 2004 reported that the J&K Tourism Minister Ghulam Hassan Mir brushed aside the attack, saying ***it won't have any impact on the tourism***. "This is an attack on a security picket. *This has nothing to do with tourists*", the Minister said, adding that "***all tourists in the area (Dal Lake) are safe***[47]". However those staying nearby the site of the suicide attack have panicked after hearing the gun shorts. "There is huge rush of tourists and all the houseboats in the Dal are fully occupied. *The attack has definitely caused panic among them*[48]", said the owner of Anarkali House Boat that floats in Dal Lake.

Attack on CRPF Camp Along the Bank of Dal Lake[49]

Two militants were killed on 11 November 2004 and a security officer was injured in a heavy exchange of fire after an abortive bid to storm CRPF camp in Srinagar, barely a week ahead of Prime Minister Manmohan Singh's maiden visit to Jammu and Kashmir. A group of militants, believed to be three in number, carried out the suicide attack on the camp at Konikhan ***along the bank of the Dal Lake*** at around 6.30 pm exploding grenades and firing indiscriminately on the troops in an attempt to storm the camp housed in a hotel. This has also given shock and fear to the tourists present in the Dal Lake area.

The World Tourism Organisation has rightly declared that tourism is a powerful tool for peace and dialogue amongst civilizations, an instrument that can spread international understanding and unity. The recognition of this positive potential of tourism sounds true today, especially after 11/9.

Tourism is a foe of terrorism although both share some similarities in its operations. Like both uses the high technology weapons, both aims at gaining the attention of the people from all over the world, both these activities are adventurous these are intangible in nature and the performers in both these activities does not know in advance the happenings of the future.

In both the tourism and terrorism, the people have to get out of their usual place of residence. And the risk of life is there in both these activities. Although there is a difference of nature in both these activities i.e. *the impact of terrorism is temporary where as the impact of tourism is lifelong or permanent.* But, at the same time, tourism is very much different from terrorism. Whereas terrorism feeds on intolerance and arrogance, tourism breeds tolerance and empathy. Terrorism seeks to erect walls of hatred between faiths and communities. Tourism breaks such barriers. Terrorism detests pluralism, whereas tourism celebrates it. And above all terrorism has no respect for human life. Tourism pays tribute to all that is beautiful in nature and in human life.

Hence, in the present case of Jammu and Kashmir, terrorism may have temporarily hit tourism in this metaphorical battle between the two, but it is an evident fact that a day will come when tourism will make a major contribution to the eventful defeat of terrorism in the State and will supplement the efforts of world powers to demolish the apparatus of J&K terrorism and uproot it from its last vestiges. Terrorism, no doubt, has left no stone unturned in removing the peace of the State, but at the same time, tourism has spread its tentacles and thus reaped the benefits from the terrorism.

Status of Tourism in J&K: Current Case Study

"Mercifully this season, Kashmir is not flowing but overflowing with tourists and I reckon we are back on the tourist map"[50] to quote **'Mr. Mohammad Saleem Beig'**, Director General, J&K Tourism Dept.

By 1988, many incidents of kidnappings, murders, killings etc had happened in J&K. And the end of 1989 saw militancy at its full flow in Kashmir valley. Besides politicians, government officials, professionals and educationalists, the militants also targetted foreign tourists during the peak of the militancy. But, gradually the situation has improved in the State in the recent past. The tourism, which is the major activity of the people for earning their livelihood, got a major setback for about a decade.

However, successful elections were held in J&K with 56 per cent turnout in 1996 and with 44 per cent turnout in 2002[51], a coalition Government came to power in the State. With the improvement in the situation, tourists have once again begun to throng the Kashmir Valley in large numbers. Peace coupled with discount packages by the corporations concerned have done wonders by making tourists, both domestic and foreign, flocking to the Valley in unprecedented number. This has not only led to generate revenue but also restore smile on grim and sullen faces of the people associated with the tourism industry. The Central and State Government have stepped in with various projects leading to promotion of tourism in the State and the Security Forces at the cost of their supreme sacrifices has brought the State close to restoring normalcy.

For the purpose of analyzing various factors leading to the current status of tourism in the State in spite of being adversely affected by the prolonged militancy, various published sources on Tourism in Jammu and Kashmir have been scanned and a case study on the current status of the tourism in the State has been conducted region-wise as given in the succeeding paragraphs.

Region Wise Case History of Issues Pertaining to Tourism

Jammu Region

It was felt by the people of Jammu region that the development of their region was being neglected by the Central and State Governments. The memories of 1952 Delhi Agreement, the 1975 Indira-Sheikh Accord and the 1987 Rajiv-Farooq Accord are too fresh to be forgotten. Each one of these stories have been that of betrayal of the people of Jammu because **they all pre-occupied with Kashmir alone**. During 1986, over 95 per cent of the funds allotted for Tourism developments in the State were expended for development of tourism in Kashmir region and only 05 per cent was expended for Jammu region. The on-going turmoil in the Valley of Kashmir should not be viewed in isolation from the geo-political crisis that dominates the distinct heterogeneous entitles of Ladakh and Jammu. Each region has its own identity and even while the Kashmiri dimension seems to pre-occupy, political imagination today, the crisis afflicting the Jammu and Ladakh regions cannot and must not be overlooked[52].

However, the Government has recently announced that it is committed to boost tourism in **all the three regions** besides consolidating basic facilities and infrastructure to change the socio-economic profile of the people of the State.

Amarnath Yatra base from Jammu to Pahalgam

The Hindustan Times published the news on 24 March 2004 that due to the improvement in the situation in the Valley, the government is planning to shift the Amarnath Yatra base from Jammu to Pahalgam. However, The All Jammu Hotels and Lodges Association has objected to what it called the "*continued neglect of Jammu in the tourism sector*"[53]. The Association indicated that the planned shifting of the Amarnath Yatra base from Jammu to Pahalgam was another indication of this "*anti-Jammu policy*" of the government. They also suggested various measures including cable car, improvements at Bagh-e-Bahu Fort and temple, better roads in Mansar, Surinsar and other places of the region, to boost tourism in Jammu.

The Travel Industry leaders of Jammu region has also demanded that the shops in the City of Temples i.e. Jammu, should be allowed to remain open till late hours. This would not only boost business but also help meet the needs of the large number of pilgrims and other visitors the city gets throughout the year. They also demanded that ***frequent security checks should be avoided so that visitors are not harassed***[54], reported *The Hindustan Times*, dated 13 July 2004.

Cabinet Sub Committee to Identify Tourism Potential in Jammu

Kashmir Times dated 06 February 2004 reported that the State Cabinet Committee has decided to set up a cabinet sub committee to identify potential tourist resorts in all the three regions and also to allocate funds and pinpoint other measures for promotion of tourism equitably in all regions. However, it was felt by the All Jammu Hotels and Lodges Association that the appointment of the sub committee was only a delaying tactics and proved Government's insincerity and non-seriousness in promoting tourism in Jammu Region. Earlier the Government had assured the Association that some concrete steps will be announced to compensate the Jammu Region for Central tourism incentives which was not being extended to Jammu. But by not announcing any concrete measures and putting the matter to a back burner, the Association felt that the Government had hoodwinked the tourism related traders in Jammu[55].

On the other hand, *The Indian Express (The Himalayan Mail)* dated 02 February 2004 reported that the Government has announced that it is committed to boost tourism in all the three regions besides consolidating basic facilities and infrastructure to change the socio-economic profile of the people of the State. The Minister for Tourism, J&K said that the Government has constituted cabinet sub committee under his chairmanship to *identify new tourist destinations in Jammu* as well as Ladakh so that project for development of such spots is formulated. The committee would also explore possibilities to trace out new tourist destinations in Kashmir valley also[56].

Ropeway Plan for Vaishno Devi

The Hindu reported on 20 April 2004 that The Vaishno Devi Shrine which has emerged as the second most revered shrine in terms of devotees after **the *Tirupathi Balaji shrine*** in South India, has registered over 54 lakh devotees paid obeisance at the shrine in 2003. In an effort to further boost *pilgrim tourism*, the Vaishno Devi Cave Shrine will be connected by a Rs 18 crore cable rope way project between Bhawan and Bhairon Ghati[57].

Rush in Katra

As per *Hindustan Times* dated 05 May 2004 with occupancy of hotels in Katra increasing from 25 to 50 percent in the summer 2004, it can be safely said that a large volume of tourists are flocking the town and the hotels were totally booked for the month of May and June. All the major tour operators are also leaving no stone unturned to bring the tourists to Jammu and Kashmir and are offering several special packages. Tourists plan their tour well in advance. Earlier they used to move towards Himachal Pradesh after visiting Vaishno Devi Cave Shrine, but now 90 percent tourists are going to Kashmir[58].

Yatra Registration Online

J&K State Governor, Lt Gen (Retd) SK Sinha inaugurated online Yatra registration facilities in Katra on 13 October 2004, reported *The Indian Express(The Himalayan Mail)*. Scheme for delivery of Prasad through speed post was also launched by him on the occasion and a UTI ATM facility also launched. The Government also launched a Rs 5 post card on Shri Mata Vaishno Devi, issued by the Postal department[59]. The online Yatra registration facilities would draw more pilgrims to the State as it would provide them ease and comfort before arriving Katra.

Resorts to Promote Tourism

The Indian Express(The Himalayan Mail) reported on 16 January 2004 that at a high level meeting chaired by the Chief

Minister of J&K, it was decided that an integrated tourist circuit comprising Patnitop, Kud, Batote, Sanasar, Sudhamahadev and Mantalai would be developed. Over 930 kanals of land has been identified there to set up a land bank for creating modern facilities ranging paragliding to gym, multiplex, artisan village, beautification of the mall and improvement of road communication. Instructions were given for formulating a detailed project for setting up of multi-facility convention centers at the tourist places to promote ***conference tourism*** in the State. It was decided that resorts with public-private sector partnership would be set up in the State. These resorts would have integrated modern facilities required to attract tourists. The sites for these resorts would be advertised and architectural plans sought for approval of the Government[60]. It was also decided for preparing a futuristic project for underground cabling with a common conduit system for electricity, tele-communication and water supply for these resorts. This would be on the lines in the developed countries and give better look to the tourist spots. It was also emphasized that the forest department would be exclusively responsible for afforestation, soil conservation and preserving and promoting green cover at the tourist places. Instructions were passed for setting up emporia at all the tourist resorts to promote *marketing of handicrafts*, handloom products and other artifacts of the State. A cable car project on Gulmarg-Gondola pattern from Pahalgam to Bisaran and Tulian has been planned and technical feasibility was being assessed [61].

Jammu-Udhampur Rail Service in January 2005[62]

The *Daily Excelsior* on 23 December 2004 reported that the much delayed Jammu-Udhampur rail service would commence its maiden journey in the first week of January with Prime Minister Dr Manmohan Singh inaugurating the prestigious link besides being the first passenger to board the rail. With the initiation of this rail service, a long pending demand of the people of the region would be fulfilled. The service is bound to result in socio-economic transformation of the people with **tourism and other allied sectors benefiting immensely** from the start of the rail service.

Projects to Boost Tourism: Jammu Region

As per *State Times* dated 13 July 2004, Jammu and Kashmir Government has formulated several ambitious projects to boost tourism and for further facilitating the ever increasing number of tourists thronging the winter capital of the State (Jammu)[63]:

(a) While, Rs 12 crore Tourist Reception Centre would soon be established in 500 kanals of land near Warehouse on the left banks of river Tawi, an International Convention Centre at canal road is proposed to be set up at an estimated cost of Rs 3 crore. The necessary finances for constructing these projects are being sought from the Centre.

(b) The high profile cable car linking Bahu-Fort with the city forest, ropeway at famous tourists spot of Patnitop and amusement park at Jajjar Kotli too would be established for which the proposals have been formulated and sent to the Centre for necessary funding.

(c) To promote the rich culinary of Jammu and Kashmir, both vegetarian and non-vegetarian, a world-class Hotel Management Institute at Jammu would also be set up and modalities are being finalized to make it one of the premier centers of the country.

(d) On the improvement of holy Katra town, which is base camp for more than 55 lakh pilgrims visiting Shri Mata Vaishnodeviji annually, Rs 1.25 crore is being spent to improve drainage system and sanitation in Katra.

(e) Tourism is on high priority list of the Government that hefty package of Rs 4.09 crore has been sanctioned for development of tourism in Jammu region against Rs 2.11 crore expended during the last fiscal.

(f) Projects such as setting up of a garbage disposal treatment plant at Katra, light and sound system in park, widening of Domel-Katra and Ransoo-Shivkhori roads, Construction of convention center, construction of artificial lake at Jajjar Kotli, development of Shivkhori track and shifting of railway station to general bus stand are under consideration and will be completed in a phased manner.

The details of yatries coming to Vaishno Deviji and Amarnathji Holy Caves as ascertained from the Dept of Tourism, J&K are given in the **Table 1.2.**

There is a co-relation between the pilgrimage of Vaishno Deviji and Amarnathji. The pilgrims from various States of the country plan to undertake both the pilgrimage together, the peak season being July-August. There has been an upward trend in the pilgrimage even when the militancy was at its peak. However, in 1990-1994, the pilgrimage of Amarnathji Yatra got a set back due to militancy in the valley. Katra being located in Jammu region, was not affected by militancy in the initial phase and there was no effect of militancy on the inflow of pilgrims.

Tourism being mainstay of the State, the rope way at Patnitop, cable car and amusement parks at Bahu-Fort would help in transforming the socio-economic conditions of the people living there. Jammu has all the potential to beat most sought after destinations. The pilgrimage to Mata Vaishno Devi at Katra in Jammu region, in spite of a terrorist attack in July 2003, has recorded an all time record of 54 lakhs in 2003. However, on 27 December 2004, the pilgrimage has surpassed all previous records and reached a historic high of **six millions**[64]. Government of Jammu and Kashmir has also taken adequate steps to improve the tourism potential of Jammu region as several projects have been announced for its upliftment.

Kashmir Region

The valley of Kashmir is the most beautiful region of the State. The Moghul rulers of India were always happy to retreat from the heat of the plains to the cool green heights of Kashmir, and indeed Jehangir's last words, when he died en route to the 'happy valley' was a simple request for 'only Kashmir'. The Moghuls developed the art of their formal garden style to its greatest heights in Kashmir and some of their gardens are beautifully kept even to this day. The most dangerous and terrific terrorists acts took place in this region since 1989 claiming about a lakh civilian lives, about 20000 security forces and damaged several public and private properties. However, the present century saw a change in the trend of militancy and several political initiatives also took place to reduce the Indo-Pak tension.

The inflow of the tourists during the winters to the State has gained momentum over the years and going by their ever increasing number, one can easily say that winter tourism is on revival path in the State in general and Kashmir Valley in particular. The domestic tourism in the Valley started to move towards a revival path and the State and Central government have proposed and implemented a lot of projects to promote tourism in the State especially in Kashmir region. The case study of such initiatives and projects for Kashmir Region from the published sources are tabled in the succeeding paragraphs.

Gulf Based Kashmiris to Invest in Tourism

The Indian Express(The Himalayan Express) dated 16 October 2004 reported that a group of Gulf based Kashmiris came to Srinagar and met the Chief Minister to explore the possibilities of investment in the tourism sector. The group intends to set up a tourist village at Sonamarg over the proprietary land of 70 kanals near Thajwas[65]. Interacting with the group, the CM said that the growing number of middle-class people with good purchasing power provide excellent market potential for J&K tourism. He further added that the world famous tourist destination of Gulmarg has been converted into an **all season destination** with the addition and up gradation of facilities at the site.

The Week dated 24 October 2004 brought out that Mohammad Tariq Reshi, Chairman of Gousia Group of Companies has invested Rs 400 crore in Jammu and Kashmir Tourism development. Reshi's family was one of the hundreds of Kashmiri families manufacturing carpets, shawls and other handicrafts in Srinagar. In the early '90s, when the situation worsened in Kashmir, the family set up Saudi Exports, a manufacturing unit, in Noida to export Indian handicrafts, particularly Kashmiri. By the mid 90s, Reshi had set up shop in Dubai and soon expanded his business to other west Asian countries and America. Now the Gousia Group has planned a solid and plastic waste recycling plant – expected to be set up in Srinagar in 2005 – heritage and amusement parks, and high end housing and tourism projects. The Rs 400 crore project will be completed in five years and it is likely to generate at least 2,000 jobs in the State[66]. The Gousia Wonder Land project will have heritage and amusement parks modeled on Disneyland. It will be located in picturesque spots like Zeethyar on the foothills of the Zabarwan range overlooking Dal Lake, and utmost care is being taken not to tamper with the environment. The Gulbagh Resort, set up in June 2004 on the slopes of Gulmarg, has received much appreciation. The resort comprises deluxe tents, with all the trappings of a star-class hotel room, pitched amid pine trees.

Wayside Tourist Facilities on Uri Road

Kashmir Times dated 11 January 2004 exclaimed that amidst talk of commencement of bus service between Srinagar-Muzaffarabad, the J&K Government has decided to create tourist wayside facilities on Uri road, while directing the authorities to formulate a comprehensive policy for developing resorts and tourist villages with private sector involvement for upgrading and expanding infrastructure facilities at popular picturesque spots in Jammu and Kashmir. The sites for the tourist villages would be identified for creating paying guest facilities at Laripora in Pahalgam and other tourist resorts where people would be provided necessary support in the shape of loan, grant, attractive and charming architectural designs to upgrade their houses to promote the tourism concept in the State by dove-tailing various schemes[67].

Tourist Traffic Flows in Pahalgam

The Indian Express(The Himalayan Mail) dated 14 February 2004 stated that for the first time since the inception of turmoil in the Valley, famous tourist spot Pahalgam is witnessing an influx of tourists both domestic and locals since the beginning of 2004. *The tourist visits stopped in early 90's. It was not only domestic but foreign tourists also started staying away from the spot* ***due to the fear***. Up to last year i.e. 2003, apart from Amarnath pilgrims only few groups of tourists used to visit the place. During the winter months, the entire Pahalgam town and it's peripheries used to present a deserted look, as no one used to show any interest in visiting the place. However, from the beginning of 2004, the tourist influx increased manifolds. The JKTDC is optimistic about the increasing inflow of tourists in the Pahalgam and hopes the rush will increase in the coming days too. After the eruption of turmoil, the Pahalgam used to give a deserted look during winters, the trend got changed in 2004, as several hundreds visited the place in January and February and many are enlisting their names for the bookings for the coming months. JKTDC has organized 385 package tours for the tourist resort alone, majority of them spent two to three days and many had extended their stay.

The news paper further added that most of the JKTDC hutments in Pahalgam were in shambles, however, renovation work already completed on some three dozen huts and tourists can enjoy comforts. Seeing the tourist rush JKTDC is planning to renovate more huts for the upper class people. Pahalgam is more attractive in summers but with the coming of amusement park many tourists started giving preference to the place. It is now encouraging that the place has the frequent visitors even during the winters. Apart from JKTDC, many tourists visited the place on their own and described their visit a memorable moment of their lives. "*It really gives pleasure to move around the place in the snow. I will love to visit the place in the next winter. Prior to visiting the place,* ***I was scared of the militants now I feel very happy as the place is a paradise on the earth***[68]", said Joshi, a tourist from Gujarat.

The news paper also claims that first-ever skiing course took off at Pahalgam on 15 February 2004. The winter sports which was hitherto remained confined to world famous Ski slopes of Gulmarg alone found its way to another tourist destination in Pahalgam with participation of scores of young skiers amid fanfare. It aims to bring in Pahalgam in the Adventure Tourism map of India. This would help give fillip to tourist influx to this fascinating spot even during winter months, thus, transform socio-economic conditions of those directly or indirectly associated with tourist trade. Another added attraction for adventurists at Pahalgam would be camping for which the scenic spot possesses ample scope and captivating sites that none could beat.

The *Kashmir Times* dated 01 June 2004 further adds that the locals are also turning up in good numbers in general and more so on Saturdays and Sundays. The locals assume that this health resort would be out of bounds for them as soon as Amarnath yatra gets underway. The amusement park which has started functioning from 2004 has added a new dimension to the beauty of the health resort. This has also given a fillip to the facilities being provided. The huge rush of the tourists has gladdened the hearts of the people who are directly involved with the tourist trade here. The hotels which used to present a scene of wilderness have started to show a lease of life since the tourists are thronging in good numbers to book their places in the different hotels. "***From the last 15 years we had been left jobless as very few people turned up to visit Pahalgam. This year we hope that there would be brisk business so that we are able to make good the losses which we were incurred by us from the last 15 years***"[69], said Mohammad Subhan, one of the hotel owners of Pahalgam.

Middle-East Tourists for Kashmir Visit

Kashmir Times dated 22 Janurary 2004 acclaimed that the Former DG J&K Tourism Mohamad Ashraf who was on a visit to Dubai on 21 January 2004 said that hundreds of people in Middle East especially in Dubai are interested to visit Kashmir. For the Middle East travellers, the Indian Airlines has already reduced the airfare from Delhi to Srinagar (just Rs 1200). In the beginning of January 2004 itself, Indian Airlines has sold 96 packages to Srinagar from Dubai alone[70]

Cable Car—Kashmir's Symbol of Hope

State Times on 22 July 2004 reported that deep in the snow-capped, forested mountains of Kashmir, Indian and French workers are building a cable car hoping to lure skiers from around the world to sample pistes ***within range of Pakistani artillery***[71]. For many in the area, the ambitious project is a symbol of hope following a fragile ceasefire between India and Pakistan, which for decades have claimed what is one of the world's most beautiful regions.

As per the statistics provided by the news paper, the cable car system is expected to be one of the world's longest and highest. Its backers hope it will prove a major tourist draw for a Kashmir region once called the Switzerland of the East. The project is estimated to cost $8 million and will attract lots of foreign skiers. The cable car covers five km reaching a height of 13,500 ft (4000 metres). Conceived in the mid 1980s, work on the cable car system contracted to French firm Poma Glaski, began in 1987. The first leg was almost complete in 1989 when separatists launched their revolt against New Delhi forcing the contractors to suspend work and return to France. They were persuaded to come back in 1998 to complete the first section. Work on the second, tougher leg began in June 2003[72].

The Tribune reported on 03 August 2004 that at least eight lakh tourists including two lakh domestic tourists, have visited Gulmarg till July 2004. Every day there are at least 3,000 local tourists visiting this spot while it crosses over 20,000 on Sundays[73]. Gulmarg gives new looks as several measures have been undertaken by the Gulmarg Development Authority(GDA) for its beautification. Efforts were also on to preserve the scenic beauty and environment of the area, without erecting any concrete structures. One of the measures initiated by the Government is the introduction of a tent village, which provides all facilities to the tourists without harming environment. The news paper adds the other measures taken by the Government to beautify the area to include:

(a) Fencing of the highest 18 hole golf course at a height of 13,500 ft.

(b) Shifting of shops to one area.

(c) Parking lots have been created and entry beyond a certain point has been restricted to keep the area pollution free.

(d) A water body set up in the area of old Gulmarg to add to the beauty of the area for attracting tourists.

(e) Besides a children's park, a Botanical garden is being raised in the area under the aegis of the University of Kashmir over an area of 220 kanals.

Tent Village to Attract Tourists in Gulmarg

The Tribune dated 29 July 2004 praised that as part of its efforts to promote tourism in Kashmir, the J&K Government set up unique tent village in Gulmarg, commonly known as the valley of flowers. A cluster of 10 tents with deluxe facilities for tourists over looking the green slopes of the picnic spot was inaugurated in July 2004. It is a significant development in the history of tourism in the State. While a large number of tourists were visiting the valley over the past couple of years, ***militancy continued to be at the centrestage***[74] . However, the tourism activities were going on normally. It is for the first time that such a step has been taken by the J&K Government *to overcome the lack of proper accommodation* in the health resort.

The Indian Express(The Himalayan Mail) dated 16 October 2004 brought out that The Chief Minister's Golf Cup 2004 was held at picturesque and one of the highest green golf courses, Gulmarg on 14 October 2004. The local horse and ponny-wallas demonstrated horse and ponny race which was an added attraction of the event witnessed by the golf lovers, visiting tourists and locals. While addressing the concluding function, the Tourism Minister said that measures are underway to develop J&K as **a full-season tourist destination** and the achievements of this goal would go a long way to supplement the socio economic profile of the people who are subservient to tourist influx[75] .

Winter Tourism on Revival Path in Gulmarg

The inflow of tourists during the winters is very much dependent on the games and sports available at the various health resorts of the State and in this regard Gulmarg is taking leading over the tourist spots of the State. The successful organizing of the fourth national winter games is a significant milestone in this respect.

Describing about **The Fourth National Winter Games,** *Kashmir Times* dated 09 March 2004 reported that these games were held in two stages at Gulmarg. The ice events of the championship were held from 28 to 31 January 2004, while as the snow events were held from 03 to 07 March 2004. Both the stages were held successfully which raised the hopes that this world renowned health resort would be able to hold events of international stature in the near future.

Gulmarg has the distinction of holding two national winter games in spite of all the hiccups and the turbulent situation. It was in 1998 that this world famous health resort played host to the participants of the first national winter games and it played host once again six years later to the participants of the fourth national winter games. Both the snow as well as ice events attracted attention not only at the national level, but also at the international level. The successful organizing of these games has led to the hope that the day is not far off, when the State of Jammu & Kashmir would host international skiing and other allied sports events. But for organizing an event of international repute, it is imperative that some drastic steps are taken.

The news paper further added that it was a matter of sheer bad luck for this world famous health resort that it was allotted commonwealth games long time back, but the tourney could not be organized due to the tumultuous situation in the State which has been prevalent right since the onset of militancy. But the hopes have re-kindled once again and there are chances that the State will now be able to hold an international skiing tournament[76]

Valley Shrinks in Space as Tourists Seek Dal Comfort

As per a Case Study on Dal Lake conducted in 1985, Dal lake is one of the main elements that comprises the successful tourist formula that makes Valley of Kashmir an important and famous tourist resort. It contributed about 16 percent of the State's income and about 1,60,000 people were provided employment in the mid 1980s. Of the total number of tourists visiting Srinagar in 1982, 3.7 percent stayed in the house boats. A high percentage of foreign tourists stayed in house boats than domestic tourists (18.2 percent of the former and 2 percent of the latter)[77].

After two decades, starved of cold comfort in the sweltering heat, people were flocking to the idyllic Dal Lake in the mid of 2004. As evenings set in and the silhouette of the giant houseboats show in the moonlight, hundreds of awe-struck tourists swarm the lake banks for a walk or to catch the "elusive" scenic splendour of the place. Not only this tourist attraction bristling with activity, the famous health resorts of Pahalgam, Gulmarg and Sonamarg too are brimming with life. The authorities expected the number to touch six lakh – five times more than the last year. ***Officials hope if there is no major militancy incident in Kashmir, the number can go up further***. They must have based this count on the 3,200 arrivals on one day – a record in the last 15 years – rather than the daily 600-700 tourists or the jam-packed hotels, houseboats and guest houses on the fashionable Boulevard running parallel to the lake. There was drastic space crunch in the city. Instances of four to five persons sharing a room has belied the government's claim that is ready to make tourists feel at home. Tourism officials admitted privately that there is a dearth of accommodation in the city. "The 6000 rooms including from 1,300 houseboats in city and another 1,200 in Pahalgam are not enough when you have a rush like this"[78], claims *The Indian Express(The Himalayan Mail)* dated 02 June 2004.

Efforts Afoot to Revive Adventure Tourism in J&K

Kashmir Times dated 22 March 2004 floated the news that the adventure tourism is all set to revive in the Kashmir Valley and plans are underway in this regard. Highland Excursions a group involved in the adventure trade has decided to take many innovative sites in this regard. The group has proposed to organize the events of Heli Skiing, Para Gliding and Hot Air

Ballooning in near future after taking clearance from the Civil Aviation Ministry. The group also wants to host river rafting events in the rivers and lakes of the State. They are also interested in introducing the chopper service to many a remote areas of the State to link the areas like Tanghdar, Kishtwar, Uri and Kargil. The group also wants to introduce the resort system for the accommodation of the tourists visiting they valley and they are hopeful that such a system would lead to the preservation of the environment. Eco friendly tourism and waste water management also figure in the priority list of the group. *The Highland Excursions is the group that has the distinction of holding the first Para Gliding event in the country*. It was in 1987 that this group ventured in to this field and held the event across Zabarwan hills and safely landed at Cheshmashahi[79].

Amarnath Yatra Now for Two Months?

Amarnath yatra to the holy cave is an annual ritual when thousands of devotees from all over India visit the shrine to pay homage to Lord Shiva. The yatra concludes on Rakshabandan day. Till 1989, the yatra was conducted over a period of three months or so, which facilitated the gradual movement of the yatris and their management at various staging camps. However, due to the changed security scenario since 1990 and need for extensive security arrangements for the yatris the yatra period was reduced to two to fifteen days only[80].

The Indian Express (The Himalayan Mail) dated 21 May 2004 reported the news that for the first time in the year 2004, it was announced by the Government that the annual yatra to the holy cave shrine of Amarnath, would be opened for the pilgrims for two months from Baltal route, instead of one month, as in the past. Necessary infrastructure like insulated Prefab huts, bunk beds, helicopter service for emergency aerial evacuation and hot water facilities for bathing and filtered drinking water for drinking purposes were also being provided[81].

However, on 23 May 2004, the same news paper reported that the State Government later decided to stick to one month duration for the pilgrimage in south Kashmir with base camp at Jammu as the ***proposal for two months duration could not be accepted due to the prevailing situation***[82].

Review of Amarnathji Yatra Arrangements

The Daily Excelsior, Jammu dated 16 July 2004 brought out the clear picture of review of Amarnath Yatra arrangements by the Chief Minister of J&K. It says that at a high level meeting held in Pahalgam on 15 July 2004, Chief Minister of J&K Mr Mufti Mohd Sayeed reviewed arrangements for the current year's Amarnathji Yatra and visited base camps and the holy cave site to interact with yatris and have a feed back on the arrangements put in place by various Government departments and agencies. After his visit and interaction with civil and police officials, voluntary groups and yatries, the Chief Minister expressed satisfaction over the arrangements. He said that the objective being smooth and successful conduct of the yatra, complete coordination has been among various civil, army, para-military and police agencies. The arrangements made by various departments for the smooth conduct of the yatra are as under[83]:

(a) The health department has posted 6 doctors at the cave site in comparison to only two last years.

(b) Medical camps have been set up at various places enroute to the cave and 450 oxygen cylinders made available along the route.

(c) The consumer affairs and public distribution department has stocked sufficient rations at various camps. The stocks are 10 per cent more than the last year's off take.

(d) Sufficient number of tents has been pitched for the yatries at Nunwan, Sheshnag and Panjtarni and deep trench latrines erected in good number.

(e) As many as 4126 ponies and 200 dandies have been registered for carrying the pilgrims and their luggage to the holy cave.

(f) Several langars (community kitchens) were put up by voluntary groups enroute to the cave.

The news further added that at Baltal the CM met a group of about ***30 South Africans who were on pilgrimage*** to

Amarnathji. The group was happy with the handling of the yatra by the Government and conveyed their pleasure to the Chief Minister.

Development Authority to Promote Tourism

The Jammu and Kashmir Government has constituted a development authority for Achchabal, Kokernag, Daksum and Symthan in Anantnag district which have tremendous tourism potential in different areas including adventure tourism, leisure and recreation, reported *The Tribune* dated 26 July 2004.. A similar development authority would also be set up for Lakhanpur, the gateway of J&K in Kathua district. The development authority would be on the pattern of Gulmarg, Pahalgam, Sonamarg and Patni Top, which were constituted by the State Government in the past two years. The news paper also said that the development of the new tourist places has become necessary in view of the increasing tourist inflow in to the valley[84].

Swiss Architect Engaged for Tourism Infrastructure

As per the *State Times* dated 10 June 2004, the State Government has engaged **world famous architect of Switzerland Karn Damschen** to develop the infrastructure at Sonamarg, Yousmarg, Kokernag, Pahalgam and Gulmarg tourist resorts to make them world class destinations.Damschen, who has a distinction of developing Kerala and Switzerland, visited Srinagar recently and toured different tourist places for on the spot review. According to the preliminary blueprint, the Government wants to have state of art facilities for boarding lodging and other facilities that will attract the tourists. Yousmarg, Sonamarg and Kokernag lack proper infrastructure and tourists who visit these resorts have to be back within a day. It has been noted that this does not work in favour of the people associated with the tourist trade there. Hence, small hutments will be constructed where tourists can reside and spend some days to enjoy the natural beauty[85].

Model Floriculture Centre in Srinagar

The Indian Express (The Himalayan Mail) dated 21 March 2004 states that the Model Floriculture Centre at Cheshmashahi(Srinagar) grows a lot of cut flowers. Besides being enjoyed by the tourists, the Government is taking steps to explore the commercial aspects of the flowers available in this Centre from the floriculture department on a major scale, particularly in foreign countries. Tulips, of different varieties having run a riot of colours, are grown in controlled conditions with the use of high technology to ensure their availability in winter also. The floriculture department has registered 114 private cut-flower growers, whose annual turnover exceeds Rs one crore. Besides being enjoyed by the tourists, they are exported by providing germ plasma and technical guidance by the department and their produce is collected through refrigeration van for export in fresh form.

The details of tourist inflow in Kashmir valley from 1951 onwards with the breakdown of country-wise foreign tourists collected from the Director Tourism, J&K are given in **Table 1.3 and 1.4** respectively.

It would be seen from the table that there has been changing trend in the influx of tourists both domestic and foreign in the State at varying time. However, it can be further noticed that the peak of tourism was enjoyed by the State in the eighties. From 1988 to 1994, the tourism industry of the State was destroyed by the militancy as no data is available swith the government about the influx of the tourists. Number of foreign tourists have started declining after the militancy due to the bad impact and bad publicity by the advisories of the countries concerned. From 1995 onwards, the State has started with a revival path in the tourism sector and the present century opened with very positive signs of tourism in the State.

Ladakh Region

Historically, relations between Ladakh and the outside world had been steadily deteriorating ever since the partition of

India in 1947. When Chinese troops marched into Sinkiang in 1949 and sealed the common border with Ladakh, Central Asian trade via Kargil and Leh became a thing of the past. In the wake of Chinese aggression in Ladakh in 1962, relations with Tibet were severed, as well. Only the bond with India, the mother country, became stronger; this could be seen in the reinforced presence of Indian troops in the area as well as in the construction of the strategically important road between Srinagar and Leh. Our picture of this remote region became more and more complete starting with the first accounts of Herodot-us about gold digging ants up into our time through scholars and adventurers. **International tourism, however, was only possible after 1974**[86], at which time the Central Government in Delhi opened the restricted area of Ladakh to foreigners. The Ladakhis must certainly have been astonished at the rapidly rising rate of tourism that immediately set in.

Tourism Boom in Ladakh.

Tourism boomed in Ladakh in the summer of 2003 after a lean season before. The tourists' inflow in the mere three-month season was almost four times more than the previous season's figure of some 9000, reported *Kashmir Times* dated 06 February 2004. This sudden surge in the tourists coming to Ladakh seems to have inspired the Travel Agents Association of Ladakh(TAAL) members to sit and plan seriously on going 'professional' in dealing with tourism henceforth. In view of the growing tourism industry and peace, the travel agents in Ladakh see a massive tourists influx ahead as never before. Thus, they decided to revamp the tourism norms, which were lying in oblivion so far.

The news paper further added that in a four-page proposal "*Tourism Promotion in Ladakh*"[87], the TAAL have charted a detailed way out of the problems in development and management of tourism in Ladakh. The proposal chiefly consisted of the following:

(a) All weather road to Leh with wayside facilities and encouraging the other other States' buses to ply on these roads to attract the low-income tourists.

(b) Government incentive for expansion of hotels, guest houses and restaurants; fixed schedule of flight operations etc.

(c) Resuming the helicopter service to Zanskar region in winter. A large number of tourists come during winter specially to do the popular *Chadar* trek (frozen river trek) to Zanskar. The tourists would prefer flying back to Leh rather than taking the same route while returning from Zanskar. This could prove very beneficial to the patients in the remote Zanskar region also.

(d) Noting the increased domestic tourists in the recent years, it was felt to develop amusement parks, shopping malls, entertainment outlets such as theatres, indoor and outdoor sports facilities.

(e) Further expansion of the scope in tourism by promoting Ladakh as special Buddhist place in countries like Japan, Korea and China.

(f) Need to identify new peaks and trekking routes for adventure tourists in Ladakh - a major part of tourism business in Ladakh region.

(g) Sought the tourism department's help in organizing special training to guides, cooks, waiters, housekeepers and cleaners. From now on the touts will be strictly dealt with and the Municipality Committee will see to it that the restaurants and others follow the regulations on such as food charges and other profits incurred from the tourists.

(h) Demand for strict actions against the possible threat to ecology.

Kargil has become a new tourist destination after the Kargil war in 1999. Visitors from all over the country want to see the place where the Kargil war was fought, where thousands of Indian soldiers sacrificed their lives for the protection of their country and to see a place which has become a symbol of bravery. Tourism was moving at a fast pace until the time when the great threat from across the LoC had struck the State. The flow of tourist in 1999 declined in this region, where as it has shown a tremendous increase in the year 2003. The tourist inflow to Ladakh region from 1974 to 2004 is given in **Table 1.5.**

After a long period of about 14 years, the tourist inflow in Ladakh has created the history in the year 2004 by attracting 35,091 tourists, thus showing an upward trend. Besides foreign tourists, it would also be seen from the above table that the domestic tourists have also started flocking to Ladakh region in the recent past. There is an alternative(different) route to Ladakh region through Kulu-Manali of Himachal Pradesh by which most of the foreign tourists reach this region these days bypassing the Jammu-Srinagar route. Moreover, there is no militancy in Ladakh region at present.

J&K State Case History: Issues Pertaining to Tourism

After studying the recent case history of region-wise issues pertaining to tourism, certain recorded news about the J&K tourism in the publications and other sources are analysed and studied in detail. It would be seen that the J&K State as such has taken adequate steps to save the tourism industry and promote tourism related activities in the recent past, like visiting of the State CM to various countries to promote tourism, attending various conferences including one at WTTC to give wide publicity about the tourism in J&K and also to impress upon the return of normalcy etc.

Adequate steps have also been taken to ensure the security and safety of the visitors by deploying adequate security forces in around the tourist spots and a positive thinking and approach towards the security without hampering the comforts of the tourists has also been planned, as in the case of creating **Tourist Police.**

Incidents and Reactions

Some of the recent incidents and the immediate reactions of the tourists as scanned from some of the dailies which are of interest to understand the mindset of the tourists are brought out in the succeeding paragraphs.

Despite Violence Tourists Flock to J&K

The Times of India dated 22 June 2004 reported that ***A week after the Pahalgam bomb blast which killed tourists (including some from Mumbai), the Kashmir tourism industry remains unaffected as hotels and travel agencies have reported no cancellations***[88]. Nilesh Vichare (27), a CA from Mumbai, who was in Srinagar for his honeymoon was one of the few tourists who visited the blast site the very next day. "We took photos of broken windows of the hotel and the security personnel. Many tourists were milling around. ***Everything was normal***"[89], said Vichare. Speaking to delegates of the Indo European Round Table Conference, Lt Gen(Retd) SK Sinha, J&K Governor said the situation was fast returning to normal as people wanted peace. Besides, *the ongoing peace process and Indo-Pak dialogue had a positive impact.* He further added that tourism will improve the economy. Against 28,000 in 2002 over 1.70 lakh tourists visited the Valley in 2003.

Militants Appealed Not to Target Tourist Spots

The Tribune dated 30 July 2004 brought out that the recent suicide attack in July 2004 on a hotel housing security forces in the Dal Lake area, the main center of tourist activity in Srinagar, killing seven persons, including militants and CRPF men, ***has hardly affected the flow of tourists***[90]. However, those associated with tourism have in a "**save tourism**" appeal urged militants not to choose the area for such activities and protect tourism in the valley. This was the first such attack by militants in the Dal Lake area, where tourists have been pouring in to enjoy staying in houseboats and hotels.

The news paper also reported that the tourists staying in house boats and hotels near the trouble spot felt scared while "the encounter was going on". For many, it was a nightmarish experience, but by the next dawn, they felt relieved and decided "***not to change their programme***" of staying in the valley. However, the incident created a sense of insecurity in the minds of tourists for some time. Recurrence of such incidents can prove fatal for the residents of the area. The association which appealed to the militants included the Houseboat Owners, Hotel and Restaurant Association, the Travel and Tours Operators Association. "*All associations concerned appeal that tourist places should not be chosen for such activities, so that thousands of families associated with the trade are not deprived of their livelihood*"[91], the appeal said.

The State Tourism Minister said it was ***wrong to say that the attack was on tourism.*** It was "***in fact an attack on a camp of security forces inside the Dal Lake area***". He added such incidents had been taking place across the valley over the past several years. He also referred to the June 12, 2004 grenade attack inside a hotel in Pahalgam and said it was not "an attack on tourism, but on a hotel", where tourists happened to be present.

Attack on Vaishno Devi Pilgrims

In a first major strike on Mata Vaishnodeviji pilgrims, the militants on 21 July 2003 night, at about 2105 hours lobbed two grenades on the devotees taking dinner at a langar(community kitchen) near Ban Ganga, about one kilometer from Katra town, the base camp of the shrine, killing five persons including a child and wounding 38 others, eight of them seriously.

Though the casualties were there in the grenade attack, but they were not the kind that would have satisfied the militants, if seen from the terrorist perspective. With this, although the overall figures did not have any affect on the flow of the pilgrims either to the Amarnath Cave or to the Vaishno Devi Shrine, yet there was an immediate affect to the tourist flow to both these places. It was seen that from July 09 to July 15, about 26,289 pilgrims left for Amarnath Shrine while 24,461 pilgrims left for the holy Cave during the second week from 17 July to 24 July. And on 20 July 2003, a batch of 3,372 pilgrims had left for the holy Cave shrine, followed by 3,423 on 21 July(the day of attack on Vaishno Devi Pilgrims) and 3,294 on 22 July 2003(the day of attack on Tanda Army Camp where a Brigadier was also killed). From then, yatra figures decreased to 2,810 on 23 July, 2,802 on 24 July, 2,516 on 25 July, 2,343 on 26 July. And the lowest ever 1,173 on 29 July 2003[92]. That speaks of the immediate impact of reduction of the pilgrims to the shrine.

But despite such terrorist attacks a record number of over 31 lakh pilgrims visited the cave till the end of July and it has gone up to a all time record of 54 lakhs. And in 2004, the pilgrimage surpassed all previous records and reached a historic high of six million on 27 December 2004. Alone in the month of the attack, i.e. July 2003, nearly 5.87 lakh devotees paid their obeisance in the holy cave. And not only that, there was also a record breaking number of the pilgrims to the holy cave Amarnath with about 1.75 lakh pilgrims visiting the cave in 2003.

UK and Australia Refuse to Oblige J&K Tourism

The Tribune deated 16 December 2004 reported that ***Australia and the UK have refused to oblige Chief Minister Mufti Mohd Sayeed by not withdrawing the advice against travelling to the militancy-infested Jammu and Kashmir***. Australia has also asked its citizens to be aware while visiting Kulu and Manali in Himachal Pradesh, particularly on some remote trekking routes, where several foreign citizens have been attacked or have disappeared.

The news paper has also brought out that the CM has time and again been urging these countries to withdraw the advisory that has badly hit the tourism sector in the State. However, the travel advice updated by *Britain and Australia on 14 December 2004 has again warned its nationals against visiting Kashmir, which they have described as an area with "high threat of terrorism"*.

The CM along with a team of officials had some time ago toured various countries to request them to withdraw the travel advisories against J&K. More than 4,00,000 British tourists visit India every year, but they have not looked towards Kashmir following kidnapping of five foreign tourists, including two Britons, by terrorists in 1995 and their subsequent killing[93].

The news paper further added that Although tourism has started picking up in the Valley, but the repeated terrorist incidents have created a scare among the people. Foreigners in particular were afraid of taking the risk of visiting here and were generally not traveling beyond Himachal Pradesh. *The travel advice of the Foreign and Commonwealth Office of Britain has warned that serious incidents of militancy continue in the Kashmir valley and Jammu province. Violent incidents have occurred recently in Public places. While such incidents are not normally directed against tourists, a hotel in Pahalgam was the target of attack on 12 June 2004 in which several Indian tourists also died. There is a danger of landmines in some border areas.*

The advice was "strongly against travel to J&K, with the exception to Ladakh via Manali or by air to Leh". The Australian Department of Foreign Affairs and Trade has also asked its citizens to "avoid all travel to Jammu and Kashmir". The advisory says that there is an ongoing risk of politically motivated violence and terrorist activity by militant groups. While there has been improvement in India-Pakistan relations since April 2003, the situation could change with little notice. Australians should take particular care if traveling to areas on the India-Pakistan border and should avoid all travel to Jammu and Kashmir. Australia has pointed out that serious security problems remain in Srinagar, as well as elsewhere in the Kashmir valley, and in other parts of the State.

Public Funds for Terrorism?

Frontline dated 30 July 2004 claimed after thorough research that not a single instance of looting from banks, government institutions or individuals by the militants since the end of March have been reported in year 2004. The three month break in cash seeking crime is the longest such gap in the history of violence in Jammu and Kashmir. By contrast, Rs 1,35,408 was looted from April to end June in 2003 out of a total of Rs 26,57,440 for all of 2003. In 2002, Rs 3,55,965 was looted in the April – June period, out of a total of Rs 53,73,865. Experts believe that the declining trend in looting is the outcome of large-scale diversions from the welter of large –scale public works projects that have been coming online in rural Jammu and Kashmir in recent years, notably in the irrigation and power sectors. ***Tourism operators in several areas are also believed to be making protection money payments***[94], as apple-orchard owners have done for at least the last decade.

Role of the Government in Promoting Tourism

The organizational chart of the Tourism Industry in India as well as the State of Jammu and Kashmir is given in **Appendix VIII.**

The success story of the J&K tourism has not come over night. There has been constant efforts both from Central and State government in promoting tourism in the State. There were several projects have been undertaken to attract the tourists and other steps by the government have helped return of tourism again in the State. Some of the news items scanned from the published periodicals puts us to understand the constant efforts of the Government. These are:

Centre's Support Package for J&K Tourism

(a) On 28 July 2004, *The Indian Express(The Himalayan Mail) reported that* the J&K government has proposed to set up ambitious Amarnath Yatra Complexes at Jammu and Qazigund, to provide a range of amenities to the Amarnath pilgrims. The State G overnment has already identified the land for the project and the Central Govt has agreed to sanction two Destination Development Projects for comprehensive development of tourist/pilgrimage sites. Rs 5 crore is to be provided to the State Government for each project from the Centre[95].

(b) It was also decided, the news paper brought out that, many shrines which were used as hideouts by militants, now partially destroyed or in poor shape in Jammu and Kashmir, will be given a facelift. As a package to the State, the Centre has provided Rs 10 crore to create infrastructure at historic religious places of Amarnath and Hazratbal. Also the State Government ***plans to organize an international film festival to boost its tourism prospects***, which has been lying low ever since the terrorism hit the State over a decade back.

(c) *The Statesman* dated 09 August 2004 claimed that the Union government also considering the possibility of having a separate police force called **tourist police**[96] in states having potential for tourism. However, the states have not responded to the concept of having tourist police so far, they would have to manage from the existing police force in their states.

(d) The Centre also started training courses in the valley to educate unemployed youth in various areas of tourism such as tourist guide, language guide and hospitality. The State Government extends stipend to the students of these courses. Besides, soft loans to Shikara(boat house) owners would also be given to renovate their boats in view of the good tourist season in the year 2004, *The Statesman* reported.

Tourist Influx to State on Rise

As per *The Hindustan Times* dated 15 March 2004, the tourist influx in the State has sharply increased in the recent past. After ceasefire on the International Border and the Line of Control, there has been a surge in tourists' arrival, which is expected to increase further in the future too. During the winter of 2003-2004, total influx in Gulmarg was three times higher than the winter in 1989 (prior to militancy) and 10 times than last year's graph[97]. More than five lakh tourists were expected during the tourists' season (April – May) as the hotel bookings for these months were full in advance. The State Tourism Department has made all arrangements and is ready for red-carpet welcome of tourists. The arrangements include:

(a) For accommodation, the Estate Department has been given directions and the State would be vacating its various properties so that the tourists do not feel neglected.

(b) Private hoteliers in the Valley have been sanctioned loans for renovations undor a Centre-funded scheme so that tourists have all desirable comforts.

(c) State Tourism Department has participated in five different *Travel Trade Marts at various places including* ***Chennai and Bangalore*** and the response was very warm.

(d) Corporate sector like TATA has shown interest to organize seminar in Kashmir and the Department would try to explore more such opportunities.

(e) As per *The Indian Express(The Himalayan Mail)* dated 21 March 2004, the Facelift of Mughal Gardens and other tourist spots in anticipation of tourist influx will be immediately undertaken[98].

(f) Cleaning and maintenance of the artificial lake at Botanical Garden in Srinagar which is situated at the entry point of the garden, should have clean water and a beautiful look.

(g) Extra toilet facilities in all the gardens of Srinagar to be raised to avoid any inconvenience to the tourists.

Indo-Pak Thaw Boosts Kashmir Tourism

On 19 April 2004, *Kashmir Times* brought out that the Indo-Pak thaw has started showing positive results on the ground in Kashmir. With peace in air, the ailing tourism sector of Valley has started reaping the benefits of the thaw. If the present tourists rush is any indicator, then around five lakh tourists were expected to visit Kashmir which would generate additional revenue of Rs 300 crore. Not only this, several **corporate houses of the country and abroad have also shown willingness to hold the conference in famous resorts of Kashmir**, adding to the goodwill generated by the Indo-Pak thaw.

Official figures suggest that the tourist arrival in Kashmir since January to March 2004 ending has been recorded at 26605 while as the tourist arrival in the corresponding period last year was only 1178. In the first three months of 2003 the number of foreign tourists visited was 847, but this year the number is 1094[99]. The reasons for the surge in tourists' arrival, as per the newspaper, are as under:

(a) There is Indo-Pak thaw which has generated a lot of goodwill.

(b) Overall situation in Kashmir is changing.

(c) The ***tourist arrival in India as a whole is increasing*** and Kashmir also do benefit from it.

The *Kashmir Times* further claims that the official figures also suggest that in 2003 nearly 1,91,164 tourists visited Kashmir. Of which 1,82,205 tourists were from different States of the country and 8959 were foreigners. The total revenue generated last year was pegged at Rs 100 crore[100]. In 2003 the tourists stayed for short periods of two to three days. But, in 2004 the trend has changed and the tourists are staying for longer period.

J&K Feel Good Factor: Tourism

After a long time, the State Government has some one, who is not knocking at their doors with a begging bowl in hand. Those, who have brought in feel-good factor, are Jammu and Kashmir Tourism Development Corporation (JKTDC) and Jammu and Kashmir Cable Car Corporation Limited (JKCCCL) – the corporations dealing with the tourism sector of the State, said *The Indian Express(The Himalayan Mail)* dated 07 March 2004. While rest of the corporations are neck-deep in debt, the duo after 14 years have once again turned into money-spinning machines. Peace coupled with discount packages by the corporations concerned have done wonders by making tourists, both domestic and foreign, flocking to the Valley in unprecedented number. This has not only led to generate revenue but also restore smile on grim and sullen faces of the people associated with the tourism industry. As per the figures available with the ministry of finance, out of the 18 Public Sector Units, 14 are running in losses[101], the details are given in **Appendix IX.**

In addition to generating revenue, the present situation in the State has the following feel good factors in the year 2003 as brought out in *India Today* dated 15 September 2003:

(a) Eighth Inter-State Council meeting attended by the PM, several Cabinet Ministers and Chief Ministers was held in Srinagar in August 2003[102]. The conference stands for the new-found peace in the Valley and a gateway to Convention Tourism in the State.

(b) Jammu and Kashmir finds a place in the Country's **cellular map on 18 August 2003**[103]. About 15,000 mobile connections have been distributed in capital cities of Jammu and Srinagar in the very first day. Mobile services have been made available in 14 district headquarters in the State, Katra to Vaishnodeviji and whole stretch of National Highway from Pathankot to Srinagar[104].

(c) The Amarnath Yatra goes off peacefully in 2003. As many as 1,75,000 pilgrims[105] undertook the yatra in this year and it was comparatively incident-free.

(d) Even the outbreak of SARS in Southeast Asia spelt good news for the Valley with high end domestic tourists changing their itineries and heading for the State. The State recorded 1,22,732 tourists visited the State from January to August (the peak of SARS), up from a mere 14,686 during the same period in 2002.

(e) More than 50,000 Kashmiri Pandits from all over India converged at Srinagar for the **Khir Bhawani** festival, but they did not stay for long.

Kashmir Figures as Tourist Destination at WTTC

The Indian Express(The Himalayan Mail) dated 02 May 2004 claimed that Kashmir has figured prominently as a tourist destination at the fourth World Travel and Tourism Summit (WTTC) held at Doha on 01 May 2004, with some operators pointing out the difficulties in going there. The moderator Nik Growning of BBC pointed out that Kashmir has been a trouble spot, but things have seen a change in view of the recent Indo-Pak test cricket series. The joint secretary in the tourism ministry, India said there was lack of understanding the geography of the country. ***One or two incidents should not necessary lead to advisories being issued over the entire country as it would have greater impact on tourism***[106]. He further added that isolated incidents only affected employment and livelihood of the people.

The news paper further added that the CEO of Qatar Airways Akbar Al Baker pointed out that *negative news was always played up* and pointed out the ***instance of four foreign tourists kidnapped by terrorists who were killed*** about a decade ago in Kashmir. The Indian status that "there has been 150 percent growth in terms of domestic tourist arrivals into Kashmir this year and international travelers were also visiting the State sometimes ignoring these advisories and that the private infrastructure is now being put in place in view of increasing tourist traffic" has been explained in the Summit.

J&K Fast Coming on International Tourist Map

Acclaiming that the J&K State will emerge as a magnet for tourists at the international level, the Governor of J&K, Lt Gen(Retd) SK Sinha said on 04 January 2004 while interacting with the students who were on tour of different States of the country that due to people's cooperation and their traditional cultural heritage, the winds of change have started blowing in the State, which is crown of India. He further said that the students of Himachal Pradesh, Uttar Pradesh and Madhya Pradesh will visit J&K State and carry a message of peace and mutual peaceful co-existence which they have themselves witnessed while visiting different parts of the State. By 2007, the State will become a hub of economic and tourist activities when *Srinagar and Baramulla would be connected with rest of the country by railway line.* Regarding peoples' fear to visit the J&K State due to sporadic acts of violence, Gen Sinha said that *"these acts by the militants have failed to stop the tourists from coming to visit the State" reported the Kashmir Times on 05 January 2004.*[107] *".*

Corporate Houses to Invest in J&K Tourism

The need for the private initiative for setting up resorts, camping sites and upgrading and expanding tourist infrastructure in Jammu and Kashmir has been stressed while discussing strategies for promotion of tourism in the State at a meeting with the representatives of Infrastructure Development Finance Company (IDFC) and Kuoni Travel (India) Pvt Ltd in Jammu on 24 January 2004 as reported in *The Indian Express(The Himalayan Mail)* on 25 January 2004. Moreover, private investments can help the State in creating a holistic investor climate wherein latest facilities would be created by the private players in key areas for developing tourist resorts, raising accommodation and soft adventure activities, airport strips, transport etc[108].

The same news paper on 23 May 2004 reported that as many as 20 places had been identified for the purpose of raising infrastructure facilities by private sectors in Jammu and Kashmir and besides raising infrastructure at the existing resorts, new places like Bangus, Dodhpathri and Mujpathri would also be developed[109].

Towards South India

The *Daily Excelsior* dated 22 December 2004 reported that in a bid to give a fillip to tourism in the State, the Jammu and Kashmir Government is looking **down south as the number of tourists from southern states was far less**, J&K Tourism Minister Jugal Kishore said in Chennai. He claimed that the tourists once again are thriving the State as militancy was under control for the last two years and the situation has been improving considerably. Earlier the minister had a meeting with his **Tamil Nadu counterpart.**

Stating that the Tourism Department had entered into an agreement with Tourism Corporations of Maharastra, Punjab and Karnataka to promote "two way tourism packages", the Tourism Minister said **this would be implemented soon in Tamil Nadu also**, reported the newspaper.

Rivals Join Hands to Hard sell Kashmir as Tourist Destination

At a reception held in the honour of a group of girl students from Jaipur, the ruling party and the opposition used the common platform to paint Kashmir as a "*must visit tourism destination*", as reported in *The Hindustan Times* on 24 January 2004. The newspaper added that for the first time, the ruling coalition of PDP and the Congress and the Opposition National Conference seem to have found a common agenda: to sell Jammu and Kashmir as the ultimate tourist destination. The Opposition leader Omar Abdullah, who also came to meet the girls at the function interacted with each one of them in an effort to wipe out their fearful impressions about Kashmir. He stressed that *"Kashmir is a beautiful place and we want that when you return home, you should persuade your parents to come along with you next time"*[110].

J&K Gets Special Award for Tourism

On 25 January 2004, the *Daily Excelsior* applauded that the Special National Tourism award for excellence was given to Jammu and Kashmir Tourism Department in New Delhi on 23 January 2004 for its outstanding performance in tourism promotion during 2003 in a big way. The award was given at an impressive function by the Union Minister for Tourism and Culture. The award was given in recognition of the strategies adopted by J&K Government to boost tourism, which is the mainstay of the State's economy and also provides livelihood to lakhs of people directly or indirectly[111].

The Indian Express(The Himalayan Mail) acclaimed on 22 January 2004 that this has become possible due to the strenuous efforts of the coalition government, particularly Chief Minister Mufti Mohammad Sayeed who interacted personally with those associated with travel trade not only within the country but abroad also. He along with a high level delegation including the tourism minister participated in World Tourism Mart in London to woo foreign tourists. A similar delegation from the State under the leadership of the Minister of State for Tourism had also visited Malaysia and Singapore in early autumn 2003 and held detailed discussions with those associated with travel trade there so that the tourist potential from the Far-East was fully tapped. The tourism department has also introduced package tours to lure domestic and foreign tourists to the State. All these measures have paid rich dividends immediately though these steps would have long-term benefit[112].

The Hindu said on 23 January 2004 that this is the first time that the State received the coveted prize. It comes in the wake of revival and promotion of tourism in the State, which has been badly affected by the one-and-a-half decade old insurgency[113].

Pakistan Pilgrims on Peace Mission in J&K.

The Indian Express(The Himalayan Mail) reported on 27 October 2004 that a group of pilgrims from Pakistan who, after the recent successful visit of media persons from neighbouring country, had come to Jammu and Kashmir in October 2004, obviously with a message of love and peace. "*We have come here to break the ice. I hope this visit will open the permanent road of love and friendship between the two countries*[114]", said Sardar Mohammad Alam, leader of 12 member Pakistani delegation soon after arriving at Jammu railway station. The delegation visited religious places belonging to all faiths and prayed for friendship between the two countries.

Security Forces to Vacate Hotels and Schools

On 11 December 2004, *The Tribune* brought out that the J&K government has ordered the Home Department to get the tourist infrastructure and schools vacated that were being occupied by the security forces while fighting terrorism in Jammu and Kashmir. The Home Department has planned to get such places vacated before the next tourist season. As many as 48 hotels and Commercial establishments in the Kashmir Valley are presently occupied by the security forces[115].

Travel & Tour Agents call on Abdul Aziz Wani[116]

On 23 October 2004, *The Indian Express(The Himalayan Mail)* reported that as part of commitment made by the present coalition government to generate employment opportunities for the unemployed educated youth in tourism and other vital sectors, the government is contemplating to provide various facilities to the people connected with travel and tourism. This was revealed by the MD, Tourism Development Corporation Abdul Aziz Wani, at a meeting of various travel agents, who met him on Thursday, with their charter of demands. The demands include exclusive reservation of six deluxe coaches and three mini coaches for tourists for bringing them to Valley for visiting various tourist spots, involvement of Valley Travel Agents in various packages floated from time to time by the TDC and also providing commission earning facilities, which is currently earned by travel agents of other States.

Kashmir in Kathmandu

The Tribune dated 16 December 2004 applauded that the Four-day deliberations on the Kashmir crisis in Kathmandu organized by the International Pugwash Foundation, which won the 1995 Nobel Prize for Peace, assumed significance in many ways. It was not just a gathering of nearly 60 thinking individuals, including Kashmiri separatist leaders, from India and Pakistan who exchanged their views on the festering problem. The Kathmandu Conference had the tacit support of India and Pakistan as both had sent their official observers. This means the outcome of the initiative may influence their future moves.

The Tribune further added that the meeting provided an occasion to the Kashmiris on both sides of the Line of Control to interact among themselves for the first time on a question that concerned them more than anybody else. **Interestingly, they disapproved of the use of violence to achieve their objective.** They supported the India-Pakistan dialogue process, expressing the view that peace could come back to Kashmir only through negotiations. Kashmiris in general are not bothered about which side of the LoC they are. They will be happy if they are able to meet their relatives on either side easily.

Pandit Migrants will Return to Valley Soon

The Times of India dated 07 December 2004 reported that the first batch of Kashmiri Pandit migrants will return to the Valley in less than five months. Revenue, Relief and Rehabilitation Minister of J&K State said the construction of 200 flats for migrants at Shekpora in Budgam is being expedited so that they could return as soon as possible. The previous government in the Centre had approved the rehabilitation programme for Kashmiri Pandit migrants under which 200 flats each were to be constructed at Sheikpora in Budgam and at Harnag in Anantnag in two phases. The project was worth Rs 20 crore for each phase.

The newspaper further reported that 3.5 lakh Kashmiri Pandits migrated to Jammu and other parts of the country in 1989-90 after the outbreak of militancy.

Rebirth: Indian Army to Induct Surrendered Kashmiri Militant[117]

It could easily come as a rebirth to a former gunslinger who fought security forces and later took on the militants. A new leaf in the life of Sheikh Tahir who is going to be the first surrendered Kashmiri militant to be **commissioned into the army**..... Tahir is going to join the Territorial Army as a commissioned officer, reported *The Indian Express(The Himalayan Mail)* on 04 November 2004.

Army Organises Educational Tour for Students[118]

To build confidence among youngsters of far flung and remote areas of J&K, Gurj Division of Army, as part of good will gesture, organized Sanskritic Sangam – Kashmiriyat-Ka Doab Se – a seven day educational tour to North India. Twenty nine students of IX and X standards participated in the educational tour which was flagged off by Maj Gen AN Aul, UYSM, GOC, 29 Infantry Division on 09 November 2004, reported *The Indian Express(The Himalayan Mail)* dated 10 November 2004. There are several such educational and adventure tours being organized by the army very frequently in J&K.

Army Lights Barari Homes[119]

People of Barari village in border district of Poonch has something to cheer at Maj Gen Vinod Chopra, GOC, 39 Mtn Div, who inaugurated mini-hydel Gharats at a remote village of Barari. It is pertinent to mention that Barari village has been devoid of electricity till date. The inauguration of mini hydel project by has brought smiles on the faces of the youngsters.... As a part of *Operation Sadhbhavna,* Army has already undertaken installing of mini-hydel Gharats in various parts of Jammu and Kashmir, applauded *The Indian Express (The Himalayan Mail)* dated 10 November 2004. For these projects natural streams have been harnessed to produce electricity for the benefit of the community.

It is amply clear from the above that the tireless efforts of the government supported by security forces have brought in the revival of tourism in J&K.

Analytical Conclusion

A careful and well balanced analysis from various published sources reveals that there was an adverse impact of terrorism on the tourism of Jammu and Kashmir as seen in the initial phase of militancy. However, the terror since turned to be a routine affair in the State and it has not succeeded in gaining ground because of return of normalcy especially in the field of tourism.

From the tables of tourists inflow(Refer Tables 1.2 to 1.5) to various regions, the following can be surmised:

(a) **Jammu Region**. The tourism in Jammu region is by and large pilgrimage oriented. Surprisingly it is found out that the inflow of the tourists to the Holy Cave of Shri Mata Vaishno Deviji at Katra, has shown a upward trend all the times in spite of having been targetted by militants in July 2003. The pilgrims have surpassed all previous records as on 27 December 2004 and has become the **second busiest shrine of the country after Tirupathi Shrine in South India as it has crossed six million pilgrim arrival mark in 2004**[120]. A number of new records have been achieved by the holy shrine. It is the fourth time that the five million mark has been crossed. The five million mark was previously achieved during the years of 2000, 2001 and 2003[121]. The anticipated tourists turn out is in no small measure due to the improvement in the law and order situation in Jammu region, especially the fall in militant related activities[122]. The graphical representation of the Yatries coming to Vaishno Deviji Holy Cave given in **Graph 9** clearly indicates that the militancy did not affect the overall tourist flow to the Jammu region especially to the holy cave at Katra.

(b) **Kashmir Region**. The tourism in Kashmir valley met with a set back due to insurgency from 1988 to 1995. The administrative machinery had failed to that extent that even there is no record of tourists' arrival available in the Government books for this period. Since there were several incidents of kidnappings and killings of tourists/visitors during this period, a fear psychosis affected the minds of people visiting the Valley in the ensuing years. However, because of the stringent actions of the Security Forces and the initiatives taken by the government, the militancy has been put under check and the restoration of normalcy was felt all over the country side. Now that there are several projects undertaken by the State Government in tourist places like Gulmarg, Sonamarg, Dal Lake, Pahalgam etc, the response from the tourists also on the positive side coupled with the increase of tourists to the country as a whole.

(c) It may be surmised that the tourist influx to the valley had a set back in the beginning of the militancy from 1988 onwards, but the situation was brought under control besides developing tourism oriented projects in the State. Thus, the confidence of the tourists was built so as to visit the valley from 1996 onwards. The present status of tourists' influx to the State shows that there is hardly any impact of terrorism on the tourism of the State, because every man associated with the tourism industry started enjoying his everyday bread and he is no more interested in helping militants and the cause of militancy. Since the Valley is the question of the dispute of claim and discussion being Muslim dominated and having support of the local populace for militancy and the fate of the locals dependent on the tourism industry who are left to discourage militancy. This realistic approach of the locals also led to reduction in insurgency and an input to increase in the inflow of tourists to the valley.

(d) Statistics reveal the fact that the impact of terrorism on the tourism in the valley is not negligible in the present day context as can be seen from the graphical representation of tourist influx to the valley both Indian and Non Indian from 1951 onwards. Where as the Indian tourist still throng the Valley without fear as indicated in the **Graph 10**, there is decrease in the number from 1995 to 1997 and drop in number after 2000. The number of foreign tourists have been decreased as can be seen in the **Graph 11** due to fear as well as the advisories of certain countries which doesn't recommend their countrymen visiting the valley.

(e) To visit the Amarnath Ji Holy Cave, the yatra begins from the Kashmir valley either from Pahalgam or Baltal. There is a very high degree of negative correlation between the militant activity incidents in the State and the tourist flow to the Holy Cave. There have been incidents of militancy in Pahalgam in 1994, 1995, 1996, 2002 and in 2004. From the graphical representation of the yatries coming to the holy cave from **Graph 12**, it can be seen that leaving aside the year of incidents, the performance of the yatra has been excellent. Moreover, the year 2004 has seen much more than the earlier years in spite of the yatries' having been targeted in the same year.

(F) There are two routes to reach Ladakh region, one through Kashmir and another through Kulu-Manali of Himachal Pradesh. Since there is a danger to pass through Kashmir valley because of militancy, several foreign tourists prefer to go through Rohtang Pass of Himachal Pradesh. Ladakh region is pre-dominated with Buddhist culture and Tibetan clans and there is no incentive for the militants of Muslim origin. The tourism in this region realized set back during Kargil war and thereafter the peoples' curiosity to see the battle field also helped in increasing tourist influx to this region. Overall, there is hardly any impact of terrorism on the performance of tourism in this region from 2003 onwards. The graphical trend of the tourists inflow in this region makes the situation very clear. Refer **Graph 13.**

The overall impact of terrorism on tourism of the State has been on the negative trend in the recent past. The Government and the Security Forces have taken time to stabilize the situation and understand the ground reality. Therefore, the delay occurred to restore normalcy and to encourage the visitors to plan their visit to J&K.

Assessment of the Situation by Opinion Survey

The scholar has prepared a questionnaire with queries relating to the above study aimed to collect a complete, valid and reliable information from fifty samples each from the following segments of people who are associated with the topic:

a. Queries to the Tourist.

b. Queries to the Layman residing in/around the Tourist Spots.

c. Queries to the Security Forces/Government Officials.

A copy of the questionnaire is placed as **Appendix XII**. The questionnaires were circulated to 50 people from each segment who responded with their valuable opinion. The information thus collected have been analysed and interpreted in the succeeding paragraphs.

Queries to the Tourists

Travelling groups. A mixed group of Employed, Business, Retired and Students were the respondents in this segment. It has been noticed that people mainly come in a group of 2-5 and they constitute 58 per cent of the total respondents surveyed. 19 per cent of the respondents were in the group of having 2-3 members in it and 18 per cent were couples/two members. Only 5 per cent respondents were traveling individually / single and did not have any company at all.

For an introductory question whether they are regular visitor to tourist/Pilgrimage spots of J&K, 72 per cent said that they are **regular visitors,** 8 per cent visited the State occasionally and 20 per cent said that they experienced the State for the first time.

(a) **Purpose of Visit**. The purpose of visit of these respondents are represented graphically as Fig 1.

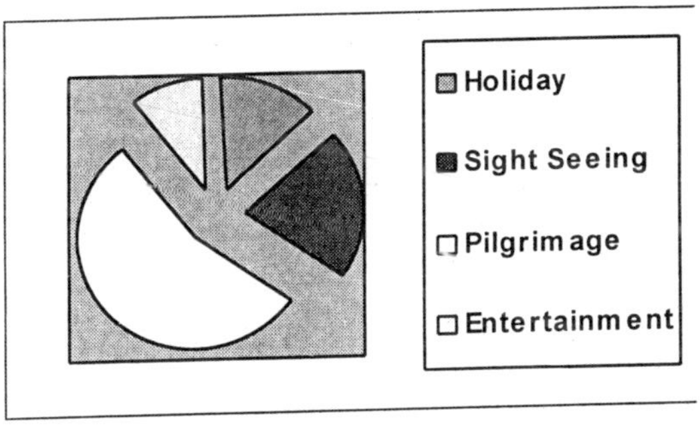

Fig. 1

(b) **Mind Set Before Coming to J&K**. On questioning the respondents regarding their mind set before coming to the State of J&K, 20 per cent of people say that it was fearful, 10 per cent say Worrisome, 42 per cent say Normal and 28 per cent say it was exciting. Refer Fig 2.

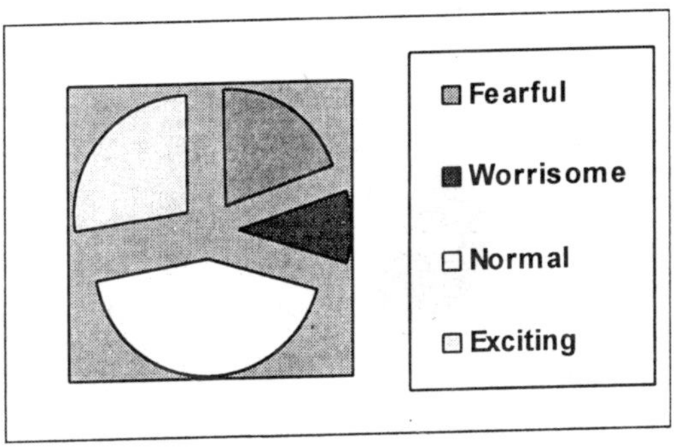

Fig. 2

(c) **Feelings After Arriving in J&K**. There is a positive feeling noted from the response of the people, as can be seen from the Fig 3 representing their answer on this question.

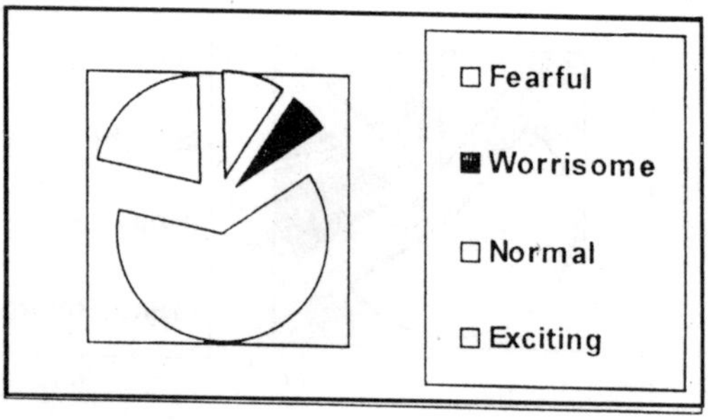

Fig. 3

(d) **Security Arrangements in J&K**. To understand the satisfaction level of the tourists, question regarding the security arrangements in the State especially in tourist spots was asked. 48 per cent say the security arrangements are Excellent, 42 per cent say Adequate and 10 per cent say Insufficient. Fig 4 shows the details graphically.

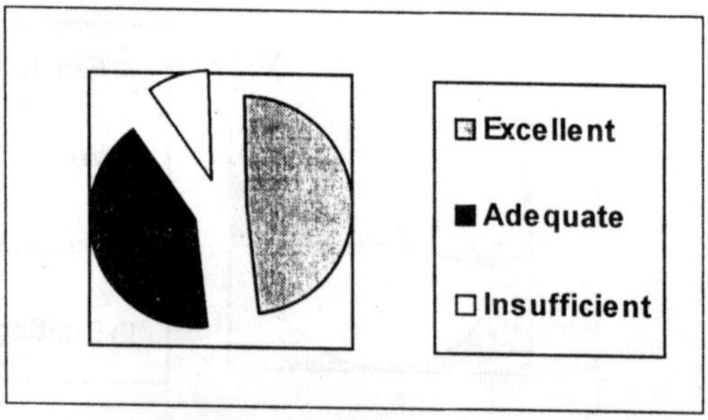

Fig. 4

(e) **Opinion About the Security Check**. Since security check is the most talked about issue concerning the tourists, opinion about the checks was asked from the respondents. 75 per cent say that Security Check is essential, 8 per cent say that it is troublesome and not required for tourists, and 17 per cent say it is boring as it puts ones mood off. We can understand about their opinion with the help of Fig 5.

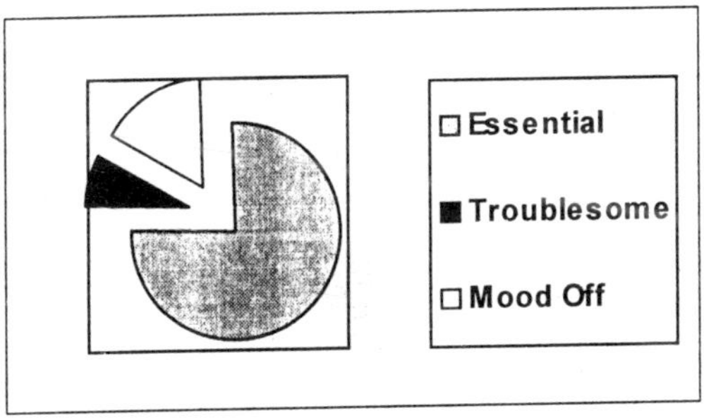

Fig. 5

(f) **Expectations About the Security Arrangements.** There are varying expectations from people for fulfilling their safety and security in the militancy-torn J&K. 32 per cent of people say the security arrangements are adequate and they have no more expectations, 34 per cent say they are good but the forces need more coordination among themselves, 22 per cent feel that the checking system is very conventional and need more equipment to effectiveness and 12 per cent feel the present security arrangements are not sufficient and should be thoroughly more vigilant.

(g) **Satisfaction Level of the Security Arrangements.** Fig 6 gives out the tourists' satisfaction level of the security arrangements in J&K.

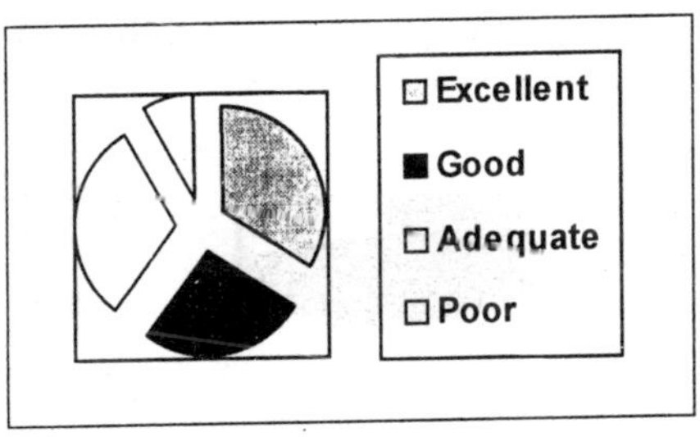

Fig. 6

(h) **Visiting the State Again**. The final question from the tourists - because of terrorism in J&K, whether they feel not visiting the State again, has brought out a scanty response as shown in Fig 7.

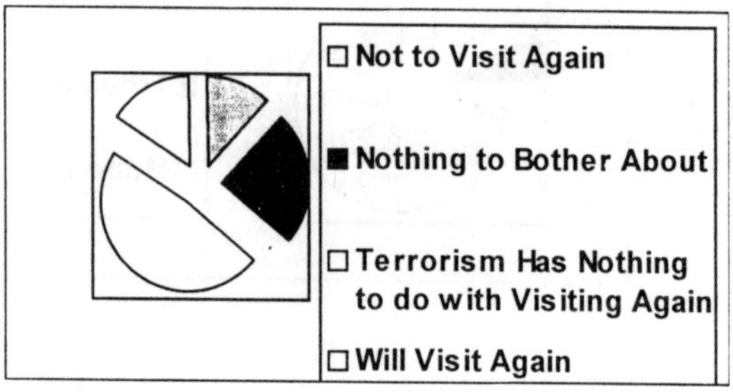

Fig. 7

Queries to the Layman residing in/around the Tourist Spots

The local residents of varying profession, diverse family size, varying age group and from different parts of the State of J&K were asked certain questions and their response has been very informative and interesting.

(a) **Impact of Terrorism on Tourism**. Since the locals are the real judge about the influx of tourists and the change in the situation in the State, the initial question regarding their feeling about the impact of terrorism on tourism in their respective areas were asked. 32 per cent of people say that there is an impact and 68 per cent of people say there is no change in the influx of visitors, hence there is no impact. Fig 8 refers.

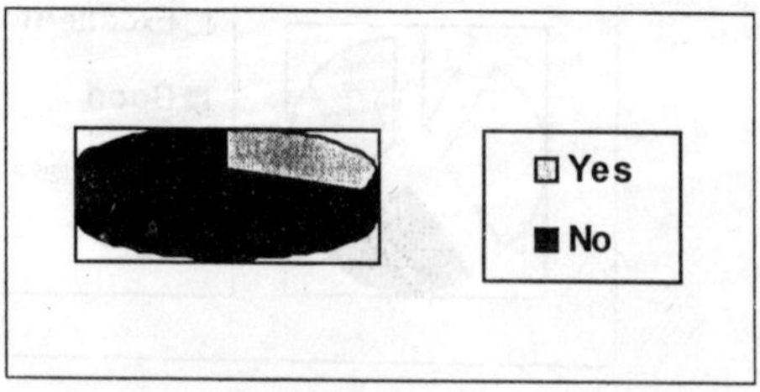

Fig. 8

(b) **Feeling Secured Living in a Tourist Spot?.** 54 per cent of people feel they are secured in their place, 12 per cent feel they are not secured and 34 per cent are not sure about any thing as there is no such problem in their locality as given in Fig 9.

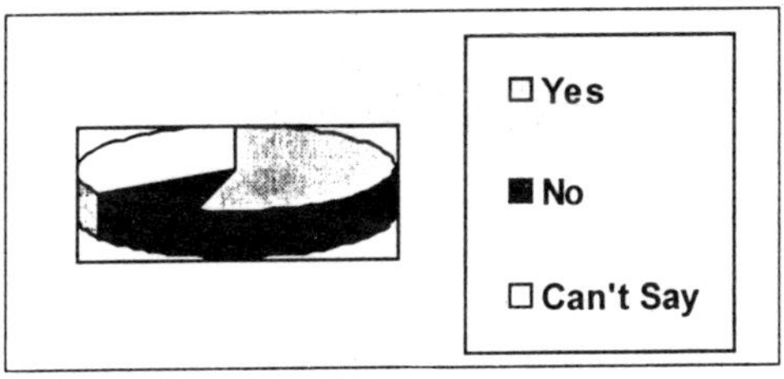

Fig. 9

(c) **Opinion About Security Forces**. There are varying response from the people with 52 per cent saying that they are good, professional and instill confidence in all of them, 32 per cent saying that they are strict and put everyone to lot of inconvenience, even do not consider the constraints of locals, 16 per cent saying that they are just duty bound and do not have humane approach to the locals, etc.

(d) **Inconvenience Caused to Locals.** For a question whether is there any inconvenience caused to the locals or to their family members or to their village members by security forces, the respondents have given their answers as given in Fig 10.

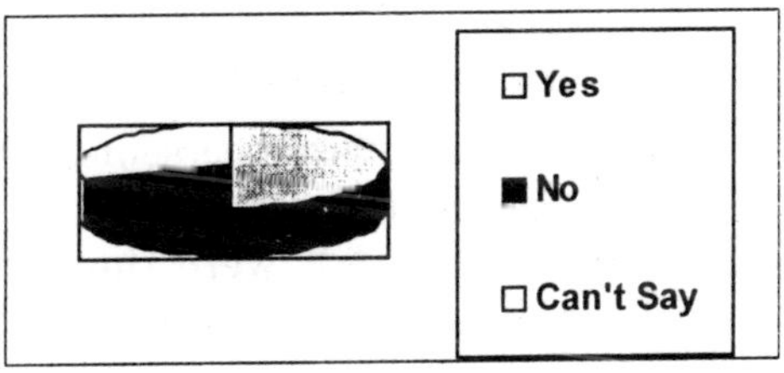

Fig. 10

(e) **Terrorists Taking Asylum in the Name of Tourists**. The locals response to this question is given in Fig 11.

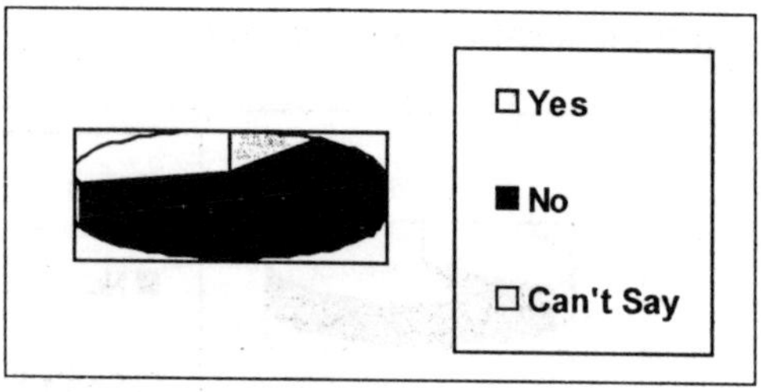

Fig. 11

(f) **Recommending New Security Arrangements to Safeguard Tourists and Locals**. The response has been very interesting with 66 per cent people saying Yes to new proposals and 34 per cent people happy with the present system, as graphically represented in Fig 12.

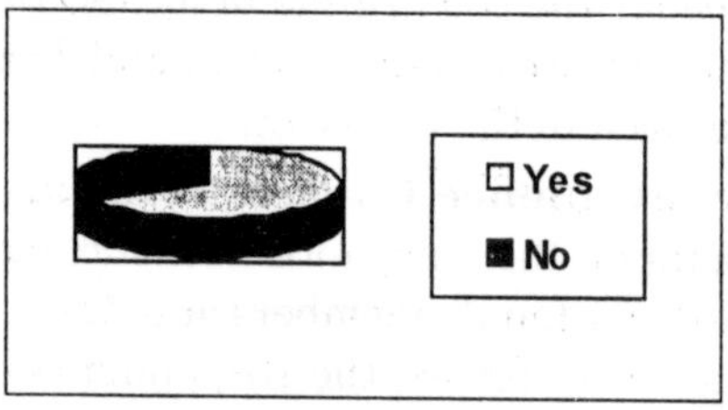

Fig. 12

Queries to the Security Forces/Government Officials

All ranks of Security forces personnel from Army, BSF, CRPF and Civil Police who are associated with tourism and Government Officials in J&K were the respondents. The questions put forth and the answers received are analysed as under:

(a) **Prime Role of Security Forces in Tourist Spots**. It has been found that majority of the Security Forces/ Government Officials i.e. 88 per cent feel that the

Security Forces role in Tourist spots relates to all the duties such as security of the tourists, monuments/ properties and the entire area, whereas only a few feel that it is given the responsibility of only one role as shown in Fig 13:

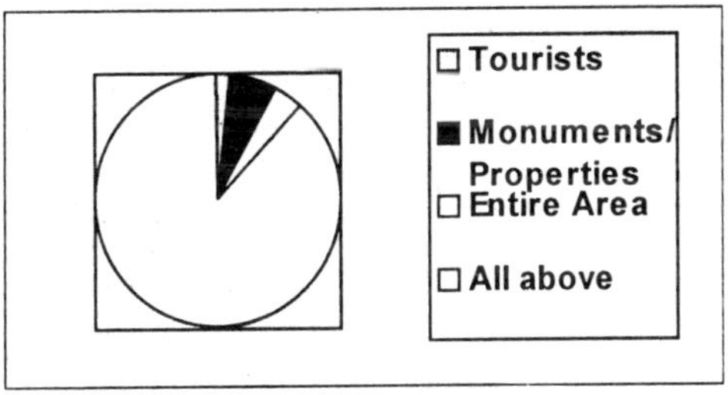

Fig. 13

(b) **Security Arrangements in Tourist Spots Fool-Proof**?. From the response, it has been found that 20 per cent of them feel that the Security arrangements are adequate, 24 per cent recommend more participation by Civil Police and Civilians and majority of them i.e. 56 per cent suggest various measures, such as combined effort of all Central and State Governmental agencies etc. The opinion is given in Fig 14.

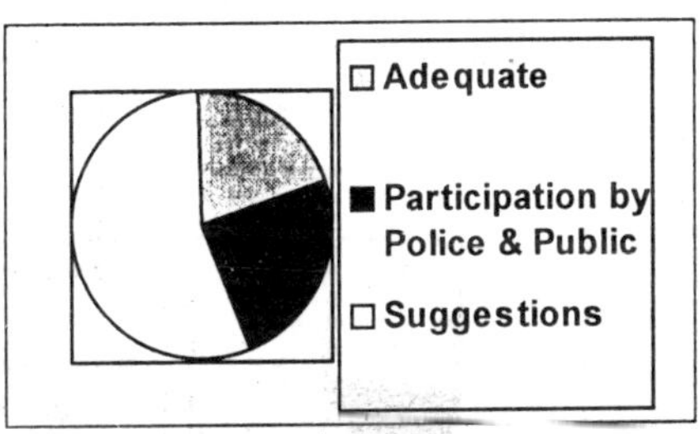

Fig. 14

(c) **Difficulty in Managing Security in Tourist Spots**. There is a wide opinion that when large number of tourists visit the place, it is difficult to enforce public control measures thereby enabling terrorists to take advantage of the situation easily. To this question, 66 per cent say tourists are generally outsiders, hence chances of terrorists visiting such places as tourists can't be ruled out; 14 per cent say that there is shortage of Security Forces, hence difficult to manage tourist spots much seriously; and 20 per cent people say that there is lack of cooperation from tourists as well as locals, these can be seen from the Fig 15.

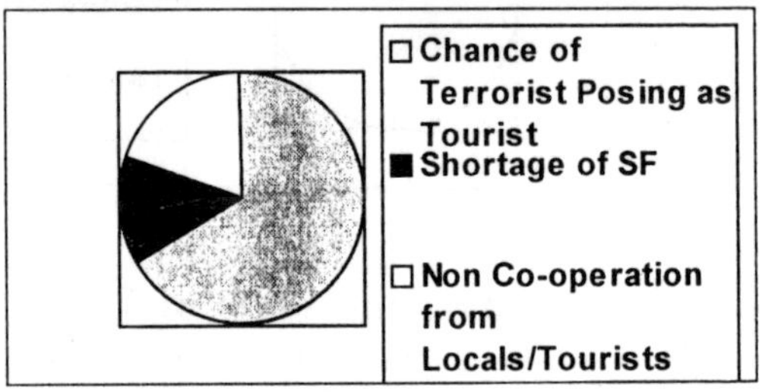

Fig. 15

(d) **Inconvenience Caused to the Tourists While Executing the Security Tasks**. Majority of the Security Forces and the Government Officials i.e. 58 per cent are of the opinion that tourists don't like to be checked; 16 per cent say that tourists don't cooperate with Security Forces; and 26 per cent say that tourists feel uneasiness to undergo security procedures as represented in the Fig 16.

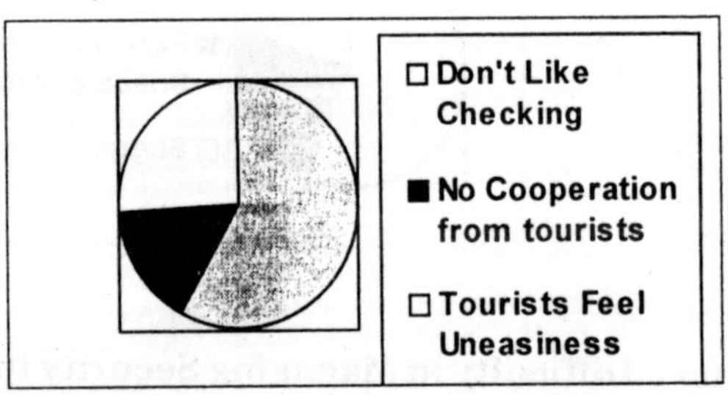

Fig. 16

(e) **Inconvenience Caused to Security Forces While Executing Tasks.** This question was aimed to obtain an introspection and to find out the self esteem of the Security Forces while guarding the installations of the State of Jammu and Kashmir and especially the tourist spots. 72 per cent say that it is a thankless job; 20 per cent say that security men are bored of the same routine without any fruitful result; and 8 per cent say that there is shortage of manpower in comparison to the influx of tourists in certain spots and it is very difficult to carryout hundred percent task leading to failure of duty. It can be seen from Fig 17.

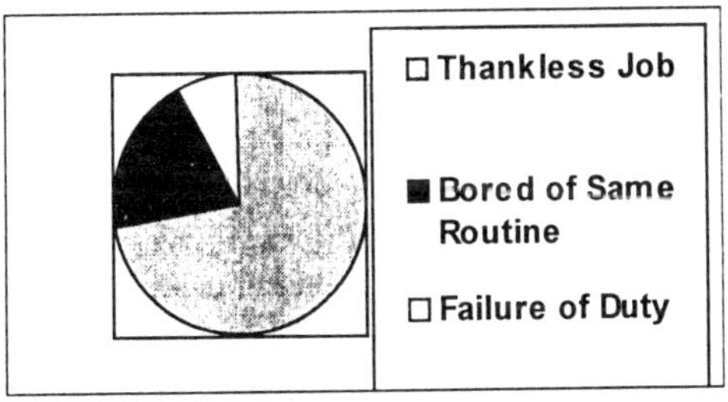

Fig. 17

(f) On a question as to any incentive given to the Security Forces Personnel deployed in such duties, all the respondents have confirmed that there is no such incentive being given to them.

(g) Regarding the general policy/strategy of protection to the people, the respondents have confirmed that there is nothing special as it is part of counter terrorism operations in the State. However, few of them emphasized that the security is generally enhanced to cater for pilgrimage tourists moving for Amarnath Yatra.

(h) **Level of the Intelligence Input from Locals.** To this question, 14 per cent of the respondents have confirmed that the intelligence input is Adequate; 62 per cent say it is Negligible; and 24 per cent say that there is no input at all. Let us refer Fig 18.

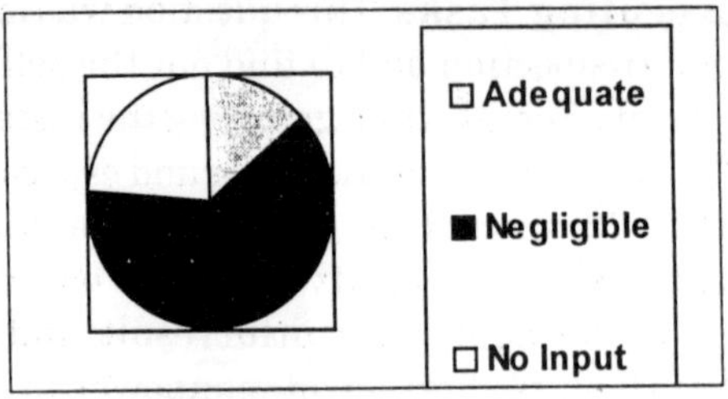

Fig. 18

(j) **Necessity of Security Forces in Tourist Spots in J&K**. When asked about the feelings of the Security Forces Personnel and Government Officials regarding the presence of the Security Forces in tourist spots, 88 per cent welcome their presence in tourist spots to ensure the safety of the tourists due to continuous terrorist related incidents in the State and 12 per cent feel that there is no need for Security Forces in such places. From the Fig 19 it is clear that till the time general security situation in the State improves, it is mandatory to have the presence of Security Forces in tourist spots, definitely because terrorism in J&K unlike any other State in India is a bitter truth.

Fig. 19

The survey was aimed at to find out the feelings of the people associated with tourism in J&K and found that there is a positive sign for the future of the tourism industry in the State.

Towards A Better Future in J&K

Tourism is the back bone of the Jammu and Kashmir's economy as the State is full of tourist attractions. Words cannot describe the beauty of Kashmir as it is aptly called the **Paradise on Earth**. Situated on the banks of the river Tawi, Jammu is the winter capital of the State, also called the city of temples. **Ladakh region** beckon for more than one reason as the land where snow never melts and only corn ripens' attracts tourists not only from India but also from the world. There are several issues to look towards the future of the State. Some of them are listed below:

Convention Tourism: A New Potential

Convention Tourism is professional travel with a specific purpose and different from vacation or recreational travel. International Conventions migrate from country to country. The participants are usually influential and have decision-making position, and therefore, actively promote tourism. The participants do not travel on their own savings but their costs of travel, accommodation, entertainment are covered by the sponsoring company or institution. Therefore, their spending power increases considerably. The present International Convention market is very large and has a very big future growth potential. Tourism is labour intensive and covers many professions. Convention Tourism requires professionalism and as such creates new professions.

Of late, the Government of Jammu and Kashmir have embarked upon an ambitious programme of getting benefited by the Convention Tourism. Expert advice has been sought to organize and market this type of Tourism. In this connection the State Government invited Mr D Hellstedt, MD, Stockholm Convention Bureau, Stockholm in 1976 who has given his recommendation in regard to management and marketing of the Convention Complex set up at a cost of Rs 10 Crores on the banks of Dal Lake. The entire complex will have three Department-Convention Centre, Common Service and Hotel Block built by Air India through Hotel Corporation of India which will have 275 rooms with five star amenities[123]. It would be interesting here to state that the State Government sent a team of senior officials and public men to some of the European countries, England and USA to study the marketing and sale of convention tourism and matters allied thereto so as to enable the State Government and Air India to formulate a plan of action for attracting international conventions to the Convention Complex at Srinagar.

In October 1980, a three member team headed by the Finance Minister Mr DD Thakur was sent to visit some of the West European countries, England and USA to study the marketing and sale of the Convention tourism. This team visited Frankfurt, Berlin, Amsterdam, Copenhagen, London, Hague, New York, Chicago, Washington, Paris and Geneva. The report of the team was under consideration of the Government and no concrete decision yet came out. It may not be out of place to mention here that to run the Convention Centre in Srinagar, joint efforts have to be made both at State as well as Central Government level apart from Air India and other airways.

Jammu and Kashmir is again on the tourism map as has been revealed from the influx of the tourists in the State in the recent past. Besides tourism, the Eighth Inter State Council meeting presided over by the PM was held in Srinagar in August 2003 which is a beginning of such a high level meeting in the State after a long time and some of the Corporate Conferences also started in the State. The need has arisen that the Government should make immediate arrangement to introduce the Convention Complex to the outside world. This will help in projecting Srinagar Centre amongst the world countries and particularly among the representatives of the international associations.

Concern for the Future of J&K

Though there are several world opinion for the settlement of the J&K dispute, by now one realizes that nobody amongst the International community is interested in the merits of the issue. They are not bothered whether Kashmiris want to be independent or join with Pakistan or remain with India. They simply see it as an irritant that bothers them specially now with possibility of a nuclear exchange between India and Pakistan[124]. The role of the State Govt and the Security Forces in curtailing the terrorism in the State and on the other hand promoting tourism to revive the livelihood of the Kashmiris cannot be left unnoticed.

The year 1995 has been replete with stupendous and complex challenges for Jammu and Kashmir State which has been beleaguered by Pakistan sponsored militancy for the last six years. These challenges unfolded undoubting spirit, firm commitment and congealed determination on the part of the administration to come out stronger to restore normalcy and to initiate the political process for restoration of democratic set up in the State. The developmental profile received impetus primarily due to liberal assistance from the Central Government which helped the State Government to tide over its crucial financial problems and wean the developmental process of the spectral of curtailment which was a recurrent phenomenon.

Even State Government machinery started operating smoothly. Ministers including the Chief Minister, attend office– a far cry from the days of Farooq Abdullah who preferred to rule from London[125]. The year 2002's assembly polls acted as a catalyst in restoring the faith of the Kashmiris in the Indian state. The CM and his daughter are always touring the Valley. Ms Mehbooba, the President of PDP and daughter of the CM visits the homes of the militants gunned down by the security forces. The CM, meanwhile, is aware of the importance of symbolism. By getting his MLAs to raise a crowd of almost 15,000 people to participate in the Independence Day celebrations, he sent out a powerful, visual appearance of normality. It was the same strategy of significance at work when he got the PM to address a public rally in Srinagar on 18 April 2003. Now that the shikharas are plying on the Dal Lake once again, the Hazratbal mosque is being visited by tourists instead of terrorists and Srinagar is suddenly the most sought after destination for politicians cutting across party lines[126].

With pressure of the forces increasing, the militants ranks are in disarray and they are on the run. Even the foreign militants, on whom Pakistan was more depending for sustaining militancy in Kashmir, were also finding it difficult to stand out forces[127]. With successful elections in the state in 2002, restoration of democracy along with peace ensured greater cohesive functioning and accountability of the Government machinery.

The Government has pulled out some of the regular troops from Kashmir in the end of 2004 keeping in view the improving situation in the State. It was also reported in the dailies that close on the heels of de-induction of troops, the Chief Minister of J&K is actively considering to reduce the strength of para-military forces in the Valley, especially in urban areas[128]. It is a clear indication that people are feeling more sense of security and are moving freely in their respective areas with out any fear even during mid nights.

PMs Address to the Nation(2004)

From the Ramparts of the Red Fort in New Delhi, Dr Manmohan Singh, PM of India, addressed the nation on 15 August 2004. Mentioning about the Terrorism in India, he addressed that "Both the North-East and Jammu and Kashmir are the most beautiful regions of our country. If we can work together to create an environment conducive to development and **tourism**, these regions will prosper more. Peace, social and political stability and communal harmony are essential for economic development. People want such peace and stability so that they can lead safe, secure and normal lives and go about their work, relax and enjoy life.

We might fight all anti-national and anti-social forces that try to disrupt normal life. Be they terrorists or communal and other such divisive forces. Terrorism is a threat to our normal lives and we must all unite in fighting it. Violence has never helped in the progress and prosperity of any society. We will fight this menace to civilized existence with determination. There should be no doubts on this scope. However, we are willing to talk to any group provided they abjure the path of violence"[129]. The above message of the PM is very clear to inform the environment about the policy and stand of the Indian Government.

The road to peace between India and Pakistan as brought out in The Times of India, 21 November 2004 is given in **Appendix X.** The Prime Minister's visit to Jammu and Kashmir on 17 November 2004 and the highlights of his announcement are given in **Appendix XI.**

Zero Infiltration During October 2004

Giving a thumbs up to normalcy, the General Officer Commanding of the 16 Corps, Lt Gen Ashok Kapur said that no infiltration geared towards inciting terrorism in the region has been detected in Jammu region during the month of October 2004[130]. It is clear that because of decrease in infiltration from Pakistan the militancy is likely to come down drastically.

Hizbul Mujahideen Ready to Help

The Hizbul Mujahideen, the single largest indigenous militant group operating in J&K, has said it is ready to provide any and every kind of help to resolve the Kashmir issue and asserted that it will never hesitate to participate in any meaningful talks which will lead to an honourable and acceptable solution of the contentious problem. The pro-Pakistan Hizb had announced unilateral ceasefire on 24 July 2000, but subsequently withdrew on 08 August 2000, after its negotiations with the Centre failed over the outfit's condition that Pakistan be involved in the dialogue, which was promptly rejected by the Government[131].

It is evident from the recent positive developments in the State that there is a better future for the State and the tourism industry is likely to uphold the economy of the State in the near future.

Notes and References

1. Om Hari, *Beyond the Kashmir Valley*, Har-Anand Publishers, New Delhi, 1998, p.179.
2. Marwah Ved, *Uncivil Wars Pathology of Terrorism in India*, Harper Collins Publishers India, New Delhi, 1997, pp.150-151.
3. Singh Nagendra Kumar, *Cultural Heritage of Jammu, Kashmir and Ladakh, Vol I*, Jay Kay Book House, Jammu, 1997, p.53.

4. KK Nanda, *Conquering Kashmir-A Pakistani Obsession*, Lancers Books, New Delhi, 1996, pp.346-347.
5. Wright Gillian, *Hill Stations of India*, Penguin Books, New Delhi, 1998, p.42.
6. Suresh Kr Sharma and Usha, *Kashmir Through the Ages, Vol 3, Society, Economy and Culture*, Deep and Deep Publications, Jammu, 1996, p.444.
7. UNI, Tourism Award for J&K, *The Hindu*, 23 January 2004, p.3.
8. KT News Service, *Kashmir Times*, 05 January 2004, p.3.
9. Singh Harjeet, *Doda: An Insurgency in the Wilderness*, Lancer Publications, New Delhi, 1999, pp.14-15.
10. Chengappa Raj, *A Deadly Revival, India Today*, 13 September 2004, p.42.
11. *Ibid*, pp.90-91.
12. As per *The Indian Express (The Himalayan Mail)*, 31 October 2004, p.1, "To regain the losing ground, ultras step up attacks on politicians. In the past five months alone, militants have killed 52 moderate politicians and made several unsuccessful attempts on the lives of various senior leaders of different organizations. The political leaders of all hues right from Chief Minister Mufti Mohammad Sayeed and Deputy CM Mangat Ram Sharma to opposition National Conference President Omar Abdullah and those belonging to All Party Hurriyat Conference, have come under attack from militants during 2004. Mr AR Veeri, Minister of State for Home, said "In view of the ongoing initiatives for restoration of peace and development in the state, militants have started looking at politicians as the main stumbling block in their nefarious designs. This is the reason that they have stepped up attacks on them". There are total of 28 ruling PDP activists have been killed by militants during these period, followed by National Conference (15) and APHC (3) and 6 of the Preachers and Social workers also killed. Officials of the Security Forces, however, say that these attacks were infact militants attempts to regain their lost ground in the State".
13. As per Swami Praveen, *Frontline*, 30 July 2004, p.118, "Indian Railways Construction Company(IRCON) engineer Sudhir Kumar Pundir and his brother Sanjay Pundir alongwith an IRCON subcontractor Farooq Ahmad Kucchai, and the driver of a leased vehicle, Shabbir Ahmad were kidnapped on 23 June 2004. Lucchai and Ahmad were let off some hours after kidnappers called IRCON's offices with Rs 50,00,000 ransom demand. The next night, the Pundir brothers were killed in the most gruesome

manner possible, by having their throats slit in ritual halal fashion.".

14. DD Saklani, *Kashmir Saga-A Bundle of Blunders*, Lancer Publishers, New Delhi, 1999, p.117. "Exodus from the valley....The killings, rape and other brutalities since the mid-eighties forced almost all the Hindu families to migrate. Since 1990 about 2,50,000 Hindus and 50,000 Muslims have migrated from the valley and sought refuge in Jammu, New Delhi and other parts of the country".
15. 'Militants Kill 4 Cops in Kathua Ambush", *The Tribune*, 11 December 2004, p.1, "Four police personnel were killed by a heavily armed group of terrorists near the Kindly post of the Special Operation Group(SOG) in Kathua district. The place where the terrorists ambushed the police party is in the Dudu-Basantgarh area near the Himachal Pradesh border. It is two hours trek to the spot from the road head".
16. Fidayeen Power, *Frontline*, 18 July 2003, p.22. "28 Fidayeen Attacks in 2001, 10 in 2002 and Seven attacks from Jan-Jun 2003 were reported in J&K".
17. *www.saag.org*, Raman, B, Pakistan Sponsored Terrorism in J&K, "*South Asia Analysis Group Papers*", Paper No 192 and Information collected from SSP, CID Headquarters, Jammu.
18. *Ibid.*
19. Sudhir S Bloeria, *Pakistan's Insurgency Vs India's Security: Tackling Militancy in Kashmir*, Manas Publications, New Delhi, 2000, p.349 and *Frontline* dated 17 January 2003, p.38 and Information collected from SSP, CID Headquarters, Jammu.
20. Suresh Kr Sharma and Usha, *Op.cit*, p.445.
21. *Ibid.*
22. Swami Praveen, Spring Far Behind, *Frontline*, 30 July 2004, p.118.
23. *www.ipcs.org*, Nayak Nihar, Institute of Conflict Management, Article No 990 dated 15 March 03.
24. Events that Changed India, *India Today*, 18 August 2003, p.73.
25. DD Saklani, *Op.cit*, p.123.
26. Marwah Ved, *Op.cit*, p.114.
27. www.waragainstterror.com.
28. DD Saklani, *Op.cit*, p.123.
29. Marwah Ved, *Op.cit*, p.144.
30. *Daily Excelsior*, 13 June 2004, p.1.
31. *Ibid.*

32. DD Saklani,, *Op.cit*, p.122.
33. Marwah Ved, *Op.cit*, p.138.
34. *Ibid*, p.148.
35. DD Saklani, *Op.cit*, p.122.
36. Diary of National Events, *India-2003-A Reference Annual*, Ministry of Information and Broadcasting, Govt of India, p.853.
37. *The Hindu*, 07 August 2002, p.1 and 11.
38. Diary of National Events, *Op.cit*, p.843.
39. *Sunday Statesman*, 31 March 2002, p.1and10.
40. Swami Praveen, "A Year after the Attack", *Frontline*, 17 January 2003, p.38.
41. *Hindustan Times*, 25 November 2002, p.1.
42. Katra Explosions, *J&K Reporter*, September 2003.
43. KT News Service, *The Kashmir Times*, 25 January 04, p.3.
44. *The Hindu*, 29 May 2004, p.3.
45. Excelsior Special Correspondent, *Daily Excelsior*, Jammu, 28 July 2004, p.1.
46. Tribune News Service, *The Tribune*, Chandigarh, 29 July 2004, p.1.
47. Express News Service, *The Indian Express, The Himalayan Mail*, 28 July 2004, p.1.
48. *Ibid*.
49. ENS/Agencies, *The Indian Express(The Himalayan Mail)*, 12 November 2004, p.1
50. Islah Mufti, *The Indian Express(The Himalayan Mail)*, 02 June 2004, p.1.
51. Barman Abheek, *Times of India*, New Delhi, 29 November 2004, p.12.
52. Singh Nagendra Kumar, *Op.cit*, p.52.
53. HT Correspondent, *The Hindustan Times*, 24 March 2004, p.3.
54. HT Correspondent, *Hindustan Times*, 13 July 2004, p.3.
55. KT News Service, *Kashmir Times*, 06 February 2004, p.3.
56. ENS, *The Indian Express(The Himalayan Mail)*, 02 February 2004, p.6.
57. *The Hindu*, 20 April 2004, p.3.
58. Khan Mohammad Shahid, *Hindustan Times*, 05 May 2004, p.3.
59. ENS, *The Indian Express(The Himalayan Mail)*, 14 October 2004, p.5.

60. ENS, *The Indian Express(The Himalayan Mail)*, 16 January 2004, p.1.
61. Excelsior Correspondent, *Daily Excelsior*, 16 January 2004, p.3.
62. *Daily Excelsior*, 23 December 2004, p.1.
63. ST News Service, *State Times,* Jammu, 13 July 2004, p.3.
64. *Daily Excelsior*, 28 December 2004, p.1.
65. ENS, *The Indian Express(The Himalayan Mail),* 16 October 2004, p.6.
66. Windfall in the Valley, *The Week*, 24 October 2004, p.30.
67. KT News Service, *Kashmir Times*, Jammu, 11 January 2004, p.1.
68. Mirehsan, *The Indian Express(The Himalayan Mail)*, 14 February 2004, p.5.
69. Rashid Jehangir, *Kashmir Times*, 01 June 2004, p.1.
70. KT News Service, *Kashmir Times*, Jammu, 22 January 2004, p.8.
71. *State Times*, Jammu, 22 July 2004, p.1.
72. *Ibid.*
73. Fazili Ehsan, *The Tribune*, 03 August 2004, p.6.
74. *The Tribune*, Chandigarh, 29 July 2004, p.6.
75. ENS, *The Indian Express(The Himalayan Mail)*, 16 October 2004, p.7.
76. Rashid Jehangir, *Kashmir Times*, 09 March 2004, p.1.
77. Mehdi Raza and Hanifa Bano, *Declining Impact of Tourism Economy: A Case Study of Dal Lake, Geography of Jammu and Kashmir: Some Aspects*, Compiled by Husain Majid, Ariana Publishing House, 1985, pp.285-286.
78. Islah Mufti, *The Indian Express(The Himalayan Mail)*, 02 June 2004, p.1.
79. Rashid Jehangir, *Kashmir Times*, 22 March 2004, p.1.
80. DD Saklani, *Op.cit*, pp.121-122.
81. ENS, *The Indian Express(The Himalayan Mail)*, 21 May 2004, p.5.
82. ENS, *The Indian Express(The Himalayan Mail)*, 23 May 2004, p.1.
83. Excelsior Special Correspondent, *Daily Excelsior*, Jammu, 16 July 2004, p.1.
84. *The Tribune*, Chandigarh, 26 July 2004, p.6.
85. KT News Service, *Kashmir Times*, 10 June 2004, p.1.
86. Singh Nagendra Kr, *Cultural Heritage of Jammu, Kashmir and Ladakh,* Jay Kay Book House, Jammu, 1997, *Vol III*, p.238.

87. Morup Tashi, *Kashmir Times*, 06 February 2004, p.3.
88. Manju andPandit Saleem M,Srinagar/Mumbai, *The Times of India*, 22 June 2004, p.7.
89. *Ibid.*
90. The Tribune, *Chandigarh*, 30 July 2004, p.6.
91. *Ibid.*
92. Over 50 percent Decrease in Flow of Amarnath Pilgrims, *Daily Excelsior*, 31 July 2003.
93. Sharma SP, *The Tribune*, 16 December 2004, p.6.
94. Swami Praveen, Public Funds for Terrorism, *Frontline*, 30 July 2004, p.119.
95. ENS, *The Indian Express (The Himalayan Mail)*, 28 July 2004, p.1.
96. Sanjay Singh, *The Statesman*, 09 August 2004, p.5.
97. Vijayanti, *The Hindustan Times*, 15 March 2004, p.3.
98. ENS, *The Indian Express(The Himalayan Mail)*, 21 March 2004, p.5.
99. KT News Service, *Kashmir Times*, 19 April 2004, p.1.
100. *Ibid.*
101. Dutta Pradeep, *The Indian Express(The Himalayan Mail)*, 07 March 2004, p.1.
102. Saghal Priya and Iyer Lakshmi, *India Today*, 15 September 2003, p.21.
103. Diary of National Events, *India 2004,- A Reference Annual*, Ministry of Information and Broadcasting, Govt of India.
104. *Daily Excelsior*, 18 August 2004, p.1.
105. Sagal Priya and Iyer Lakshmi, Op.cit, p.21.
106. PTI, *The Indian Expresss(The Himalayan Mail)*, 02 May 2004, p.8.
107. KT News Service, *Kashmir Times*, Jammu, 05 January 2004, p.3.
108. ENS, *The Indian Express(The Himalayan Mail)*, 25 January 2004, p.3.
109. ENS, *The Indian Express(The Himalayan Mail)*, 23 May 2004, p.1.
110. HT Correspondent, *Hindustan Times*, 24 January 2004, p.3.
111. KT News Service, *Kashmir Times*, 25 January 2004, p 3 and *Daily Excelsier*, 25 January 2004, p.3.
112. ENS, *The Indian Express(The Himalayan Mail)*, 22 January 2004, p.5.

113. *The Hindu*, 23 January 2004, p.3.
114. ENS, *The Indian Express(The Himalayan Mail)*, 27 October 2004, p.1.
115. *The Tribune*, Chandigarh,11 December 2004, p.1.
116. PTI, *The Indian Express(The Himalayan Mail)*, 23 October 2004, p.4.
117. ENS, *The Indian Express(The Himalayan Mail)*, 04 November 2004, p.5.
118. ENS/Agencies, *The Indian Express(The Himalayan Mail)*, 10 November 2004, p.6.
119. ENS/Agencies, *The Indian Express(The Himalayan Mail)*, 10 November 2004, p.7.
120. *State Times*, 28 December 2004, p.1.
121. *Daily Excelsior*, 28 December 2004, p.1.
122. Rocky Rakesh, *The Indian Express(The Himalayan Mail)*, 23 December 2004, p.1.
123. Husain Majid, *Geography of Jammu and Kashmir(Some Aspects)*, Ariana Publishing House, 1985, pp.317-320.
124. LR Reddy, *The Worst of Global Terrorism*, APH Publishing Corporation, New Delhi, 2002, p.343.
125. Saghal Priya and Iyer Lakshmi, *India Today,* 15 September 2003, p.21.
126. *Ibid.*
127. Suresh Kr Sharma and Usha, *Op.cit*, p.446.
128. *The Indian Express(The Himalayan Mail)*, 26 November 2004, p.1.
129. Dr Manmohan Singh's Address to the Nation, *Strategic Digest, Institute for Defence Studies and Analysis*, New Delhi, Vol 34, September 2004, pp.1274-1275.
130. ENS, *The Indian Express(The Himalayan Mail)* 27 October 2004, p.1.
131. Naqshbandi Aurangazeb, *The Tribune*, Chandigarh, 11 December 2004, p.9.

7
Review of Current Situation in Jammu and Kashmir

Latest Developments in Militancy

Militancy in Jammu and Kashmir has come to all time low level in the year 2004 and the year 2005 witnessed the multi-facet of militants with changed tactics. With the construction of 740 km long border fencing, the infiltration of militants from across the LoC has come to a standstill. The recent peace initiatives between India and Pakistan on various developmental issues linking both the countries, especially from across the LoC of the State of Jammu and Kashmir has given hope of improving the situation in the Valley. The foreign and domestic investment in the J&K industries, projects towards connectivity of the State by air and alternative roads, improvement of tourism infrastructure and the growth of the economy in the State-are the indicators of the situation getting stablised in the State. However, the militant groups are not in favour of giving up arms but continue fighting with changed tactics targeting the Politicians, public workers, civilians and not even spared the school children are spared in the recent times. The analysis of the recent developments in the State after a thorough study of the current situation on ground are given in the succeeding paragraphs.

Trouble Ahead in Kashmir?[1]

Tragic as it was, the May 24 (2004) bombing of a bus carrying Border Security Force troops and their families at

Lower Munda, on the Srinagar-Jammu highway, served no useful purpose. It provided the just sworn in new UPA Government in the Centre, especially Union Ministers for Defence and Home, the stark illustration of the challenges confronting them in J&K, **India's single largest security challenge**, as reported in the Frontline dated 18 June 2004.

More than four months after the initiation of the ceasefire along the Line of Control, Vajpayee's peace initiative has not yet led to any improvement in the ground situation. Pakistan believes India could concede some variant of the Chenab Plan, which contemplates a **communal division of Jammu and Kashmir**. In Pakistan's strategic wild-imagination, this communal carve-up could be delivered as part of a *quid pro quo* for an oil pipeline through its territory, key to securing and developing Reliance's oil interests in western India.

What needs to be done now? **First**, the government needs to draw some red lines; lines that cannot be crossed without jeopardizing the **détente** process itself. One red line, quite obviously, must be **terrorism**. The Hizbul Mujahideen, which carried out the Lower Munda bombing, is based in Pakistan, as is its supreme commander, Mohammad Yusuf Shah. As such, Pakistan cannot evade responsibility for acts of terrorism, which are executed by the organisation. **Second,** India's new government will need to start pushing for delivery on promises on the winding down of terror training camps and action against jehadi groups. Organisations like the **Jaish-e-Mohammad** and **Lashkar-e-Taiba** have resumed **fund raising and recruitment**, a violation of express commitments made by Pakistan's President, Gen Pervez Musharraf. One major obstacle Indian negotiators could confront is that Musharraf has already received part of the prize he sought through dialogue with New Delhi – notably, international legitimacy and aid.

Pak for Intifada to Keep J&K on Boil

Pakistan wants to bring a bit of Gaza to Srinagar so reported the **Times of India** (05 October 2004). While publicly waving an olive branch, Pakistani foreign minister Khursheed Kasuri and foreign secretary Riaz Khokhar privately met Kashmiri separatist leaders during their New Delhi visit and suggested that an ***Intifada*** was Islamabad's new strategy to keep Kashmir on the boil.

Recognising that cross border terrorism no longer delivers anything advantageous, Islamabad believes generating an *Intifada* is the new means to both bleed Indian security forces and keep alive the claim that India is suppressing people's aspirations. As Islamabad sees it, an *Intifada* has multiple plus points. The phrase will evoke global sympathy because of its association with Palestinian children throwing stones at Israeli tanks, an effective imagery of Davids pitted against a Goliath. Simultaneously, it keeps the door open for a low level form of terrorism that has the appearance of a homegrown origin, but will have the potential to harry India's security forces[2].

Less Violence in 2004

The year 2004 saw nearly a **one-fourth decrease in militant violence** compared to 2003, reported the **Times of India** (04 January 2005). There were 2,565 militancy related incidents in J&K from January to December 2004, as against 3,401 incidents during the corresponding period in 2003. Similarly, the number of civilian killings also came down from 836 in 2003 to 733 in 2004. There was a fall of about 14 per cent in the number of security and police personnel killed in action. As against 384 security personnel killed in 2003, 330 laid down their lives in 2004, the **lowest figure in the past five years**.

However, the year saw **62 political activists belonging to several mainstream parties being killed**. The ruling People's Democratic Party was the worst affected as it lost 35 workers, while its coalition partner Congress lost five and the opposition National Conference 16. Security forces eliminated 976 militants[3].

A Winter of Violence[4]

A ceasefire violation along the Line of Control and renewed armed offensives by militants broke the winter calm of Jammu and Kashmir. *Plus ca change, plus c'est la meme chose*(**The more things change, the more they remain the same**), the French saying holds true as for as Jammu and Kashmir goes. The year 2005 started on the usual violent note, reports the **Frontline** dated 11 February 2005.

By carrying out **series of suicide attacks on Central Government establishments**, the militants have issued a message, loud and clear, that urban militancy is still alive in the Kashmir Valley. At the same time, the signals received from the LoC have alarmed the security establishment. The **Id ceasefire** agreed upon between India and Pakistan armies on 26 November 2003. The 13 month long ceasefire with Pakistan, on which the peace process hinges, was violated for the first time in a major way on 18 January 2005 when Pakistan army pounded mortar shells across the LoC targeting Indian forward posts.

The Pakistan army's misadventure seems to be in line with the toughening of its government's political stand on Kashmir and its decision to take the issue of **construction of Baglihar dam by the Jammu and Kashmir government on the river Chenab to the World Bank.** Although the Pakistan army as usual, was quick to deny any violation of ceasefire, offices of the Northern Command of the Indian Army pointed out that, following the same analogy the Pakistan army had denied for a decade its involvement in facilitating the entry of militants to this side of the LoC.

PDP Councillor Resigns After Colleague's Killing

In the second such incident in as many days, militants shot dead a newly elected NC Municipal Councillor and a veteran freedom fighter Mohammad Maqabool Shah outside a mosque in Srinagar City on 09 February 2005. Shah, a staunch supporter of Sheikh Mohammad Abdullah, was elected to the Srinagar Municipal Corporation on 01 February civil polls on NC ticket, was shot at by militants when he was coming out from a local mosque after offering evening prayers, reports the State Times of 10 February 2005.

Also on 08th February, militants shot dead a newly elected Councillor and Chairman-designate of Beerwah Municipal

Committee, Ghulam Mohiuddin Mir in Budgam district of Central Kashmir. Mir, who was among 13 PDP councilors elected to the committee without contest was dragged out from his car and shot dead at Chakehama in the town.

In the aftermath of this killing, a Councillor of ruling People's Democratic Party has resigned from the party **asking the militants not to target him** after his colleague was killed by the ultras. Ghulam Rasool Khan, one of the 13 PDP candidates elected unopposed to the Beerwah Municipal Committee, announced his resignation from PDP through an advertisement in a local newspaper. In the advertisement, Khan **dissociated himself from the ruling party and appealed to all militant outfits not to target him**[5].

Income Tax and Passport Office Attacked in Srinagar[6]

The message of violence from the militant outfits for the urban areas too was no different. While local news papers in the Kashmir Valley linked the heavy rush outside the Passport Office in Srinagar to the possible opening of the Srinagar-Muzaffarabad road, Al Mansorian, a shadow out fit of LeT, issued statements warning government employees and the public not to go to government offices which house security camps. The warning was not taken seriously amid the claims of the security agencies that militancy in the State was waning as infiltration was at its lowest in 15 years.

The Let carried out its threat when it attacked the Income Tax and Passport Offices in Srinagar. On 07 January 2005, two *fidayeen* managed to sneak into the Income Tax Office mostly manned by Kashmir Muslims and guarded by the CRPF. A 24 hour joint operation by BSF, the CRPF and the State Police left four personnel and a watchman dead. The two militants were killed in a hide-and-seek drama that started at 0955 a.m and continued until 0400 p.m the next day. Almost a week later, heavily armed militants sneaked into the fortified Passport Office complex near the Bakshi Memorial Stadium. The complex was guarded by the CRPF from all sides. A 25 hour gun battle between the militants and the security forces ended with the death of two CRPF men and two militants.

Fidayeens Storm Divisional Commissioner Office

After a brief lull, two *fidayeens* from Pakistan stormed the Divisional Headquarters of the Jammu and Kashmir Government in Srinagar on 24 February 2005 with 250 people inside killing six persons, including three security personnel, and injuring two before being shot dead. The ultras had taken refuge in one of the revenue offices in the complex and were neutralized after a three and a half hour gun battle with security forces, reported the State Times of 25 February 2005. After a brief lapse, due to the inclement weather, which has reduced the number of casualties in militancy-related incidents, the ultras stepped up their attacks on government and security installations this time[7].

Terrorists in J&K Down to 2000 from 3400

Following stringent anti-terrorism operations in Jammu and Kashmir, the level of infiltration has almost come down to zero in recent months with number of terrorists dwindling to 2000 from 3400 reported **State Times** of Jammu on 13 February 2005. The forces have succeeded in causing severe blow to terrorist ranks by eliminating 74 top leaders of various outfits in the past few months while exercising maximum restraint during combating operations with a view that the civilian population is not harmed[8].

Terrorists to Strike Sufi Culture

Return of normalcy in the Valley has led to a revival of Sufi culture. "Ziarats", that were once neglected are now being restored and its religious activity is on the rise. The region is, after several decades getting back to its roots of Sufism and ideology of Kashmiriyat, reports **State Times**, Jammu dated 19 February 2005.

Foreign terrorists are aware of the fact that revival of Sufism and Kashmiriyat will sound their death knell. It will expose that the ideology of Jehad that justifies their presence in the Valley has been rejected by the people. They are perturbed as such by this enthusiasm of the people towards revival of Sufi culture. In order to subvert this inclination of the people towards reviving their distinct culture and identity, terrorists have been directed by their mentors from across the border to resort to coercive tactics to impose a restrictive, fundamentalist agenda upon the people.

The militants are sending messages to the people that **money should be spent on building and upgrading Madarsas that preach and breed *Jehad* and not on Ziarats for Sufi saints**. They spoke that *Jehad* and not Sufism is the path that a true Muslim is ordained to follow. Threats of physical elimination are being given in case of non-adherence to these dictates. However, people have clearly shown their disdain for the coercive tactics of the terrorists by coming out in large numbers to vote in the recently held civic elections[9].

Terror in J&K Down But Not Out

Is militancy dying? Well, not quite. From all accounts, militants are on the defensive, some lying dormant while some are taking foolish risks that is alienating them from the people. According to **Times of India** (17 April 2005), the backbone of militancy has not yet been broken but quite a few vertebrae have been smashed. **Insurgency, of course, can't be rooted out until the local people rise against it**.

In 2003, on average, ten people were killed in the State every day. The daily toll was down to seven in 2004, while it has been around five in 2005. Indian intelligence officers observe that the rise and ebb in militancy often depends on the nature of logistical and personnel support it gets from Pakistan. Right now, Pakistan has virtually turned off the terror tap. But it's estimated that 70-80 terrorist training camps - with about 2,600 militants - are still operational in PoK and elsewhere. Another 1,600-1800 militants are in J&K. They are under pressure but still capable of strikes.

Leaders of the various *tanzims* continue to enjoy the patronage of Pakistan and its Inter Services Intelligence (ISI). Hizbul Mujahideen Chief Syed Salahuddin, with ISI funding and protection, for instance, **lives in a fully air conditioned house in Islamabad**. Hafiz Syed Mohammad, leader of

Lashkar-e-Toiba, lives in Lahore. Maulana Masood Azhar of Jaish-e-Mohammad and Mushtaq Zargar of Al Umar have been **enjoying Pakistani hospitality** ever since they were freed by India following the IC-814 Indian Airlines hijack in December 1999. The list is longer. But the **number of Kashmiri youth going for training to terrorist camps has dropped**. In fact, a large number of youth who had crossed over now want to return home. But Pakistani authorities are not allowing them to do so[10].

Tourism Reception Centre Targetted by Terrorists

Barely 18 hours before the Srinagar-Muzaffarabad bus journey flagged off by the Prime Minister on 07 April 2005, the Tourism Reception Centre (TRC) was targeted by terrorists. For the Indian Government, the suicide attack is a serious setback, especially when viewed against the official hype given to the peace bus and the hope kindled among Kashmiris on both sides of the border. The massive security lapse that allowed the terrorists to enter the complex where the 24 passengers were kept, ostensibly in safety, was unpardonable.

The audacious suicide attack on the complex in the heart of Srinagar could have led to a major disaster if the terrorist, armed with rifles and hand grenades, had managed to reach the area where the passengers were housed. The militant was gunned down 200 yards short of his target, but not before injuring six people and putting the peace bus operation, described by the J&K CM as "**the mother of all confidence-building-measures**", in jeopardy and reviving the fear factor that had dissipated in the euphoria generated by the bus journey[11].

Both buildings of the Centre and Road Transport Corporation, where 21 prospective passengers has been lodged, were gutted in the exchange of fire between the militants and the security forces. The April 06 attack on the Tourism Reception Centre in Srinagar aiming at the passengers of the inaugural Srinagar-Muzaffarabad bus service has changed Pakistan's ambivalence towards the bus service into a firmer resolve to see that it continues. In PoK it has gathered a momentum of its own. The bus finally set off from Muzaffarabad at 11 a.m in a shower of rose petals.

HM Chief Rules Out Any Truce with Delhi

Two days after the pro-Pakistan Hizbul Mujahideen's top commander hinted at a possible truce on the conditions that "New Delhi announces a ceasefire that reflects on the ground," the outfit's supreme has ruled out any armistice in the near future, reports the **Indian Express** on 25 April 2005. In a statement to a news agency, supreme commander of Hizb, Syed Salah-ud-Din said that his outfit was not averse to talks but any dialogue process should have a definite goal, that is 'resolution of the Kashmir dispute'. Salal-ud-din, who is based in Pakistan said, **there is no immediate possibility of a ceasefire in Kashmir[12].**

Municipal President Killed

Stepping up attacks on political activists, militants on 03 May 2005 shod dead five persons including Chairman of Pattan Municipal Committee and three policemen, and wounded three persons even as police repulsed an attack on their camp in frontier Kupwara dist. Congress leader and chairman of Pattan Municipal Committee Mohd Ramzan Mian and three policemen, including his Personnel Security Officers, were killed and president of Beopar Mandal injured when militants opened indiscriminate fire at Pattan bazaar, 30 km from Srinagar, in Baramulla dist[13]. Militants also shot dead an Awami League block president in South Kashmir village on 03 May 2005. Al-Arifeen that opposed the Srinagar-Muzaffarabad bus service claimed the killing[14].

NC Corporator Shot Dead

Militants killed a National Conference Corporator, who was recently elected to the Srinagar Municipal Corporation, when he was passing through Bagwanpora locality of Baba Demb area of the city at around 1030 a.m, reported the **Times of India**. Militants have killed several corporators and councilors across the Kashmir Valley since the elections to local bodies were held earlier in 2005.

With militants having killed about half a dozen councilors since their election in February 2005 and around a dozen of them having resigned from their seats in fear, the valley-based civic body members seem to be giving up in the face of militancy, accusing the government of not providing them with enough security[15].

Hizb Favours Armed Struggle

Rejecting the call by moderate Hurriyat leaders to militant groups to take a backseat and support the political leadership to work out a solution to the Kashmir issue, Pakistan based militant group Hizbul Mujahideen has said the situation in the Valley warranted militancy to continue. "The situation(in Kashmir) had aggravated and in such circumstances the requirement for armed struggle had increased". Hizbul leader Sayed Salahuddin said from Muzaffarabad in Pakistan occupied Kashmir in response to the call by visiting moderate Hurriyat leader Mirwaiz Umer Farooq[16].

J&K Ultras Using Chemicals to Melt Fences

Militants are now using a new kind of chemical to melt the barbed wire fencing at some places along the LoC in J&K, say intelligence agencies. The chemical is easy to carry, does not set off any alarm bell and does not electrocute the person using it. Despite the confidence-building-measures between India and Pakistan, there has been no let-up in violence in the Valley by terrorist groups at the behest of their mentors across the border. The militants are trying their best to see that peace does not return fast in the Valley. The **Lashkar-e-Toiba**, which has a strength around 1,000 mostly comprising foreign mercenaries, is fast replacing local-based outfits like the Hizbul Mujahideen[17].

Level of Infiltration and Violence Down in 2005

The level of infiltration in J&K and terrorist related violence has been going up since snow began to melt in April. Figures with the intelligence agencies show that while in January, there were at least 19 cases of infiltration, in February and March the figure dipped to 5 and 7, respectively, as the mountain passes closed due to heavy snow making infiltration virtually impossible. However, in April, as soon as the snow started melting, infiltration suddenly peaked to 44 and was around 40 in May.

On the other hand, there was no such steep fluctuation in the level of militant-related violence during this period. There were 13- incidents of militant violence in January in which 123 civilians, 60 terrorists and 15 security personnel were killed. In the 87 incidents of violence in February, 74 civilians, 44 terrorists and nine security personnel were killed. In the 114 incidents of violence in March, 123 civilians, 71 terrorists and six security personnel were killed[18].

Car Bomb Back in the Valley

Separatist militants blew up a Maruti car packed with explosives on a busy Srinagar road during peak commute hours on 11 May 2005 killing at least one person and leaving 30 injured. The blast rippled through the city, damaging cars and buildings nearby and shattering glass panes up to three km away.

Al-Nasreen, the group which claimed responsibility for **burning down the Srinagar Tourist Reception Centre one day before the inaugural bus service to Muzaffarabad**, said in a statement it had executed the attack **to time it with the government's shift to the summer capital** of the State. The use of car bombs is rare in the State and marks a determination to use harder tactics and stepping up of attacks this spring[19].

Attack on Educational Institutions

Militants threw a grenade into Srinagar's oldest Christian Missionary School as children were pouring out after classes, leaving atleast 37 people, including 20 children injured, reported the **Times of India** (13 May 2005). The attack on main gate of Tyndale Biscoe Memorial High School, created in 1880, at Lal Chowk in the heart of Srinagar on 12 May 2005 afternoon was the second on a school since armed insurgency erupted in the state. Early in 2005, militants tossed a hand grenade towards a school compound at Handwara in Kupwara District, killing a student of class eight. In December 2004, militants had set school buses on fire to prevent children from attending army schools in Anantnag district[20].

Another school was attacked in the Valley on 17 May 05 while two persons were killed and 15 others injured as militants lobbed a grenade followed by firing on the mourners assembled at the fourth day ceremony of Abdul Gani Bhat, brother of former divisional commander of Hizbul Mujahideen, near Srinagar[21]. Yet another case of school attack was near **Pulwama School**. At least 16 people were killed and over 100 injured in the car blast outside a government school in Pulwama town of South Kashmir on 13 June 2005. Eleven civilians and three CRPF officers were killed due to splinter injuries[22]. No group has taken responsibility for the blast, which was suspected to have targetted school children reported the **Times of India** (15 June 2005). Strongly condemning the bomb blast in Kashmir, the United States lashed out at militant groups for resorting to violence whenever "peace overtures are underway"[23].

Attack on Temple in Kashmir Thwarted

Two days after the devastating attack on school children, militants in Kashmir on 15 June 2005 tried to attack the famous Kheer Bhawani temple where thousands of Kashmiri Pandits had gathered for a ceremony. (Times of India - 16 June 2005).

At least two militants were killed in a gun battle with the army. Acting on a tip off, security forces, already on a high alert following June 13th Pulwama car bomb blast which killed 16 people, moved in quickly around the temple in Tulla Mulla, about 27 Kms from Srinagar, blocking off a band of militants who were just one kilometer away from the temple. The militants were holed up in Sephora village and soldiers from 15 Corps quickly moved in, cordoned it off and laid a siege. A fierce gun battle erupted as the militants, who were planning to attack the crowd of Pandits who had congregated for the Zestha Ashtami ritual in the Kheer Bhawani temple, tried to break through the military cordon. Two militants were killed in the gun battle[24]

Million Dollar Notes in Valley

Militants in Jammu and Kashmir have struck it rich. Or so it would seem, with many of them nowadays brandishing one-million dollar currency notes for use in their nefarious activities. But now, the militants and their "over-ground workers" are not using them as hard cash. Instead, they are using the million-dollar notes as coded symbols to identify each other and collect consignments, especially huge amounts of cash through the infamous hawala channels. Though these currency notes look and feel like actual dollars, they are not genuine American greenbacks. They are actually collector bills printed on currency-grade paper from engraved steel plates, with the requisite watermarks and other intricate security features, just like real American dollars[25].

Mufti's Nephew Killed

In the first major casualty due to a militant strike in Jammu and Kashmir Chief Minister Mufti Mohammad Sayeed's family, his nephew, Ateequllah Shah, who was shot at and critically injured at his native village Bijbehara on May 01st, succumbed to his injuries in a hospital in Srinagar on 02 May 2005. According to **Times of India** of 03 May 2005, an unidentified youth shot at Ateequllah, eldest son of the chief minister's sister, when he was coming out of a local shrine adjacent to his house at Bijbehara in Anantnag district. The bullet hit Ateequllah in the abdomen[26]. This is another incident of killing of political workers and their kin which was condemned by various parties.

Funds to Fight Militancy Misused

"The Centre may be making available Rs 521 crore to the Jammu and Kashmir Government every year for security related expenditure(SRE) or combating militancy, but not all of it is used for tackling *fidayeens* or rooting out insurgency in the State" to quote the Times of India of 23 May 2005. For example, State bureaucrats enjoy the comforts of luxury huts at the tourist spot of Cheshmashahi on the foothills of Zabarwan mountain in Srinagar. The boarding and lodging of each of the babus costs the government Rs 1,500 a day, money for which is made available under the SRE head. The Estates Department of the State Government pays around Rs 29 lakh to Jammu and Kashmir Tourism Development Corporation every month as rent for the 65 luxury huts which the babus occupy.

A look at the past reveals more skeletons. Funds meant for security purposes were used by the former Farooq Abdullah Government to pamper its favorites. Crores were said to have been spent on the interior decoration of the official houses of these officials. For example, even a wardrobe in the house of a security officer of Farooq Abdullah was made from SRE money, exclaims the newspaper[27].

Terrorist Strikes from Across the World

Terrorism has not only terrorised the tourists of Jammu and Kashmir but also the people from across the world as it is evident from the recent matrix of terror revisiting Ayodhya, London, Bali, Beslan, Madrid and Egypt, the ascertained details given below[28]:

(a) **At Bali, on 12 October 2002**, Three bombs went off at the **Indonesian tourist resort**, killing visitors, many of them from Australia, one of the four countries that would invade Iraq. **Total 202 dead**.

(b) **At Madrid, on 11 March 2004,** Ten bombs triggered death in four Madrid trains at rush hour. Al-Qaida and an affiliated group Abu Hafs al-Masri Brigade claimed responsibility. **Total 200 dead.**

(c) **At Beslan, on 01 September 2004,** Chechen rebels loyal to Shamil Basayev took over a school for two days. A failed rescue operation ended in the death of 172 children, among others. **Total 350 dead.**

(d) **At Iraq, on 28 February 2005,** A suicide bomber steered a sedan full of explosives into a crowd queuing up for jobs at Hilla, 100 kms south of Baghdad. It was the single largest bomb attack since the insurgency in Iraq began. **Total 122 dead.**

(e) **At Ayodhya, on 05 July 2005**, Security forces averted a potentially devastating suicide attack by Laskhar-e-Toiba on the disputed Ram Mandir site. The toll included all five terrorists and a bystander. **Total 6 dead.**

(f) **On 07 July 2005, London** paid a heavy price for Britain's role in the "***war on terror***" as four bombs ripped through three underground trains and a bus leaving 52 dead and collateral damage to the assets. **Total 52 dead.**

(g) **At Sharm-el-Sheikh(Egypt), on 23 July 2005**, at least **88 people were killed** in a string of bomb attacks that rocked this **tourist-packed Red Sea resort.** Nine foreigners were among the victims and about 43 foreigners were wounded. Sharm-el-Sheikh has expanded at a furious pace in the recent years, making it a major player in Egypt's **vital tourism industry,** drawing Europeans, Israelis and Arabs from oil-producing Gulf nations. The last major attack was in 1997, when Islamic militants **killed 58 foreign tourists and four Egyptians** at the Pharaonic Temple of Hatshepsut outside Luxor in southern Egypt[29].

The first major attack after the 2001 war came in October 2002 in Bali where more than 200 people died in a suicide attack on a nightclub. Investigations showed this strike was the work of a group tangentially connected to bin Laden but acting semi-independently. The next major attacks – at Casablanca, Riyadh, Mombassa and Istanbul – revealed steadily diminishing amounts of central direction. Finally, in Madrid (in 2004), this process reached its logical conclusion. The attack, the most murderous so far, was the work of local militants who had been influenced by ideas of the global strand of Islamic militancy but had no contact with men like bin Laden at all[30].

Although London was predicted to be the next target after 9/11, the blasts would have robbed the city of its sense of quiet normalcy. The prime target of terrorists are underground lines, buses, trams, planes, cinema halls, railway stations, airports, tourists spots and any place where people congregate. In the past, hard-line groups had local grievances and directed their violence at the state, whether in Kashmir or in Israel. Today these groups form a larger global affiliation. Terrorists identify with the agenda of Al-Qaida but operate on their own.

There is no doubt that terrorism has become the **single greatest threat to everyday life of human being**. The US has deposed repressive regimes in Iraq and Afghanistan but in response terrorists have declared war on the world. Terrorism is now truly a global phenomenon. Terrorists strike wherever they choose, with no strategic advantage to be gained. The strike is an expression of anger, ***a message rather than a mission*** which the terrorists are willing to die for. In India, people have lived with terrorism for more than three decades. As Ayodhya has shown, there is no letting up. In Beslan, Russians paid for Chechen insurgency with the lives of their children. Post 9/11 and the declaration of the war on terror, attacks across the world have increased rather than decreased[31].

New Tactics to Fight Militancy

A Jehad Against Militancy: Village Defence Committee[32]

Having lived for long at the mercy of gun-toting terrorists, the people of remote hamlets in Surankote have launched a movement of armed resistance reports the **Frontline** of 14 January 2005. After having lived a subdued existence for years, people have now learnt to resist the violence as many of them volunteered to be Members of Village Defence Committee(VDC). While the Indian Government is engaging Pakistan to bring peace in Jammu and Kashmir-the efforts of these villagers, away from the media glare-have yielded results to an extent. Those in the vanguard of the resistance campaign are **local people who came back from Saudi Arabia in 2001-2002** to fight militancy in the State. The resistance which started in the Marrah area, is now spreading to other remote hamlets in Surankote in Poonch district, once considered the hub of militancy in the State.

The authorities help by providing the VDCs weapons. The Saudi-returnees provide training in the use of weapons. Training is given in the use of both weapons and communication equipment. The local people decipher with ease of code language of the militants. The money donated by the relatives of the villages based in various Arab countries gives financial backing to the campaign.

The reasons for the success of the **resistance campaign** are not hard to find. Militants had been using the homes of the local people for shelter, food and clothing. They even demanded the valuables of the families at gunpoint. The *Frontline* reported that Mohammad Qazim, one of the chief architect of the silent campaign to enlist local people into VDCs, saying "We know we are playing with fire. It is a date with death every day. To tell the truth, the villagers are scared as they have been oppressed by the militants for years now. But they are voluntarily rebelling against them. After all, it is a **choice between slavery and freedom from fear**".

Stung by the resistance, Laskhar militants have repeatedly threatened to kill anybody who takes up arms against them. On 24 July 2004, militants had killed 12 local residents who had dared to form VDCs. Though risk involved is high, the locals determined to resist the violence by forming VDCs.

Arms Training Camp for VDC

Three day Arms Training Camp for members of the Village Defence Committees of the borders areas concluded on 17 February 2005 at village Suchetgarh on the International Border. Ninety six members of twenty nine VDCs, which come under the jurisdiction of RS Pura Police Station, were given training in handling arms and ammunition, reported the State Times of 18 February 2005.

The camp was organized by SSP Border in collaboration with 157 Infantry Battalion of Territorial Army. The members of the VDCs were trained in firing, opening, cleaning and maintenance of weapons. The weapons have been provided by the State Government. The objective was to create security awareness among the people and involve them in creating a foolproof security environment.

The news paper further reports quoting the Army officers that the VDCs have played a very crucial role in checking the terrorist menace in different parts of the State, particularly in the border and hilly areas. These **people are local and know the area well and can play a vital role in fighting terrorism**[33].

CRPF to Replace BSF Soon in Areas Outside Srinagar

The Central Reserve Police Force (CRPF) will soon replace the Border Security Force (BSF) in maintaining internal security of the Valley. The information was given by the Director General, CRPF, at a function organised to honour the brave men of the security force on 20 May 2005. The decision to replace BSF with CRPF in a phased manner was taken by the Centre in 2004. **In its first phase, the CRPF replaced the BSF in Srinagar city**. However, the plan was put in abeyance as the *fidayeen* attacks on CRPF camps increased. The Union Government has now decided to withdraw the BSF personnel from other towns and rural areas of the Valley and replace them with CRPF men.

Gradually CRPF would be deployed throughout the Valley. It would be done in a phased manner. The force would need some time to acclimatize before deployment. Already, 38 CRPF battalions are present in Kashmir. By September 2005, another nine battalions are reaching the Valley. While five would be deployed in Srinagar, the rest would be posted in rural areas[34].

Four Tier Security Set-Up Put Along Border

A Four Tier security set-up has been put in place along 200 Kms of border in Jammu and Kashmir, following identification of 48 infiltration routes commonly used by militants. "We have identified **48 infiltration routes along 198 kms** of Indo-Pak border in jammu and Kathua districts, where a four- tier security set up is working round-the-clock to ensure that no cross-border infiltration takes place at all," Deputy Inspector General (DIG), Jammu- Kathua range, Niyaz Mehmood told in Jammu on 01 June 2005. Most of these routes lead to Udhampur and Doda districts and then to the valley. To quote the DIG, "we have been successful in breaking the (infiltration) notworks along these routes." BSF, Army, Police and Village Defence Committees (VDC) form the four-tiers of security set-up, he said. Besides Army and BSF, there are 45 border pickets and 430 VDCs guarding the border round- the-clock[35].

Governor Lauds Valour of Border People

Jammu and Kashmir Governor Lt Gen (retd) S.K Sinha has lauded the valour of border people in braving the situation and contributing immensely in heralding peace and bringing about normalcy in Jammu and Kashmir. Interacting with locals at border towns of Kupwara and Tanghdar in north Kashmir during his visit on 01 June 2005, Governor Sinha expressed happiness at the very **cordial relations between the Army and the local people**. The locals told him that the Army and civilians were living happily together as brothers[36].

Impact of Indo-Pak Relations on Kashmir

Srinagar - Muzaffarabad Bus from April 2005[37]

On 16 February 2005, a Press conference was held at the end of the talks between India and Pakistan Governments on the occasion of the first ever bilateral visit to Pakistan by an Indian External Affairs Minister since 1989. Both governments have agreed to allow travel across the LoC between Srinagar and Muzaffarabad by bus[38].

As India and Pakistan promised to open the Srinagar-Muzaffarabad road by April 07, Kashmiri youth exploded crackers at Lal Chowk in the heart of Srinagar. The only flyover in the city too was also illuminated. Indians will also be allowed to go to Gilgit and Baltistan, reported the **Indian Express** on 17 February 2005. The outline of the procedure agreed is:

(a) Application to be obtained from designated authorities.

(b) Once filled and submitted, forms will be sent across LoC for verification.

(c) Post-verification, a list of those cleared for travel will be handed over to respective designated authorities.

(d) These persons will travel up to the Immigration check post by bus, where entry permits will be issued for further travel by the country concerned.

(e) No passport, only entry permit.

(f) Open to all Indians and Pakistanis.

(g) Travel on Pakistan side to include Gilgit, Baltistan.

(h) Pre-verification mandatory.

Talks On for Jammu-Sialkot Road

Prime Minister Manmohan Singh on 27 February 2005 said talks were on between New Delhi and Islamabad about opening of a Jammu-Sialkot Highway connecting two sides of the LoC[39].

Thaw in the Air? India and Pak Discuss Siachen

India and Pakistan began talks to iron out differences over demilitarization of the Siachen Glacier, the world's highest battlefield reported Times of India dated 27 May 2005 from Islamabad. Defence Secretary Ajai Vikram Singh lead the eight-member Indian delegation for two day talks with his Pakistan counterpart Tariq Waseem Ghazi. The two sides were hoping to reach an understanding on demilitarizing Siachen during the ninth round of dialogue over the issue **to provide relief to the troops which are deployed in the most inhospitable conditions**. Pakistan is expected to maintain its old stand of willingness to agree for simultaneous pull back of troops to pre-1984 positions but would not authenticate the present positions held by India on Siachen on the maps as demanded by New Delhi.

India wants the 110 km long Actual Ground Position Line (AGPL) between NJ 9842 to Upper Saltoro Ridge on the **Siachen glacier to be authenticated by Pakistan** to safeguard the country's interest when disengagement takes place[40]. Defence Secretary Ajai Vikram Singh lead the eight-member Indian delegation for two day talks with his Pakistan counterpart Tariq Waseem Ghazi. The two sides were hoping to reach an understanding on demilitarizing Siachen during the ninth round of dialogue over the issue to provide relief to the troops which are deployed in the most inhospitable conditions. Pakistan is expected to maintain its old stand of willingness to agree for simultaneous pull back of troops to pre-1984 positions but would not authenticate the present positions held by India on Siachen on the maps as demanded by New Delhi.

On the Table for Siachen Talks

The differences between India and Pakistan stem from the varying perceptions both sides have on the extension of LoC beyond the coordinates NJ 9842. This was the point up to which the ceasefire line in 1949 and LoC in 1972 were drawn. The Karachi Agreement of 1949 mentions NJ 9842 as the terminal point and states "thence north to the glaciers". India suspected Pakistan of "cartographic aggression" in the 1980s when it backed a mountaineering expedition to the region. In 1984, India sought to pre-empt any such designs and gained military control of the area. It has since argued that the **line north of NJ 9842 would move along the Saltoro Ridge while Islamabad maintains that the line moves east of Karakoram**.

There have been eight rounds of talks between the Defence Secretary so far and both sides came close to reaching an agreement in 1989 when a press release issued at the end of the talks stated: "There was agreement by both sides to work towards a comprehensive settlement, based on redeployment of forces to reduce the chances of conflict, avoidance of use of force and the determination of future positions on the ground so as to conform with the Simla Agreement".

A broad understanding was also evolved in 1992 on a comprehensive solution to the Siachen issue, but no agreement could be reached. While either side blames each other for not sealing the issue then, the new found momentum in the on going peace process has once again given the impetus to evolve a road map for demilitarization of the glacier in an attempt to permanently settle the matter. In this connection, India looks to suggest certain specific measures with reference to the Actual Ground Position Line (AGPL)[41] . These would include:

(a) No increase in existing force levels in Siachen.

(b) No aggressive attempts at capturing additional points.

(c) Avoid lateral movement of troops on the glacier.

(d) Total commitment against using artillery fire.

(e) Strict compliance on avoiding exchange of small arms fire.

(f) No violation of airspace in the region.

PM Keen to Pull Out Troops from Frozen Frontier

Prime Minister Manmohan Singh has already consulted several retired generals and strategic experts about the possibility of pulling back troops from the Siachen-Saltoro Ridge region. (Times of India - 17 June 2005). While the defence ministry has frowned upon the pullout idea, Manmohan Singh is serious about converting the world's highest battlefield into a "**mountain of peace**" in keeping with his message to the troops deployed there during his visit on 12 June 2005. Pointing out that the deployment of soldiers in the glacial region has taken an enormous toll of jawans lives apart from entailing huge expenses, his aides said it was not necessary to set up a post at every important position along the frontier. The pull out has strongly been recommended by those asking India to walk the extra yard for the sake of peace process.

The defence establishment, too, favours disengagement but only after Pakistan agrees to "**jointly authenticate**" the Actual Ground Position Line on the Saltoro Ridge. The joint authentication will ensure tht any violation would be clearly evident to the international community at large[42]. The principal purpose of occupying the glacier in 1984 was to prevent Pakistan from gaining control of this undelineated area in the State of Jammu and Kashmir beyond NJ 9842, the last defined point on the LoC that was established in 1972 reports C Raja Mohan from Beijing in the Indian Express of 10 June 2005. While technology and best practices around the world could provide a credible verification mechanism, the Army's insistence on an "authentication" of present positions has become the principal deal-breaker in the Siachen negotiations with Pakistan.

Pakistan suspects that "**authentication**" of the current positions means legitimizing the current control of the Indian armed forces along the Saltoro ridge. If Pakistan is flexible, Indian diplomacy could surely find ways to get around the question of "authentication" by recording the current positions, for example by exchanging maps and withdrawal schedules that show geographic specifics about current disposition[43].

Kashmir Issue: An Early Solution - Musharraf

Pakistan President has suggested "**international guarantees**" for implementation of any pact with India on the Kashmir issue. He said a solution to the Kashmir issue could not be on any religious basis. Elaborating his new proposal, Musharraf said, "we are talking of guarantees which go beyond us"[44]. If we reach an agreement and we are reasonably sure that it will be followed, there is no harm why we should be so stuck up... I think we will have better permanence if the international community is involved in the guarantee", reports the **Times of India** (25 May 2005).

Pervez Promises 'Best Shot' for Peace

Speaking at the National Press Club in Canberra on 14 June 2005 President Musharraf expressed optimism over resolution of the Kashmir problem and said "there is no timetable but there ought to be some time table... and I have told Prime Minister Manmohan Singh that the best time table is that **it must take place within our tenures**[45]". "We have developed a kind of understanding between ourselves. There won't be a guarantee that future leaders will have the same focus," said Musharraf, (Times of India - 15 June 2005).

Business Revival in Valley

As India and Pakistan progressed on the peace talks, the business in Kashmir has picked up. In the recent times, many Indian business delegations visited the Valley and offered their support for the local economy. And of late, Kashmir is witnessing the boom in trade fairs. A mega trades fair, organised by the **Safeways Exhibitions** has been inaugurated at the lawns of the Hotel Centaur on the banks of the world famous Dal lake. And this trade fair has been a big attraction for the people of the Valley from its beginning. The trade fair, which is first of its kind in the Valley, has put on exhibition everything from Kashmiri handicrafts to computers and *Wazwan*, the special mutton delicacy of Kashmir, to glassware. The international brands from Italy and Germany were also on display[46].

J&K Traders to Cross LoC Soon

The Himalayan Mail (The Indian Express) of 05 June 2005 reported that with everyone wanting to cross the once-forbidden line to explore business opportunities, the Srinagar – Muzaffarabad road will soon witness heavy traffic. A business delegation of Jammu and Kashmir was ready for a trip across the LoC to explore the cross-border trade avenues. Chief Minister Mufti Mohd Sayeed said on 04 June 2005 that the delegation would soon travel to Muzaffarabad to look for possibility of trade with Pok[47].

Road to Happiness: Poonch-Rawalakot Link

At Jallas, the border village seven Km from Poonch, direct-to-home services brought the news that the 1947 route would see life again. Ahead of Jallas, at Salotri – the last Indian village– the panchayats are already making lists, with demands for a separate bus topping the list. It is just an announcement yet, but for the people in these area, the road is already a foreseeable reality. After all, Uri-Muzaffarabad happened, didn't it?[48] The reason for the euphoria isn't far to seek: In this part of Jammu, the Poonch-Rawalakot route has the same resonance as the Uri-Muzaffarabad road does in Kashmir, bringing people and opportunities within touching distance across LoC reported The **Indian Express** dated 25 April 2005.

Musharraf on Kashmir

A good augury was the rapport and the trust Musharraf and Manmohan seemed to have developed. Despite several meetings the personal chemistry between Vajpayee and the General was, according to an insider, "**near zero**". Manmohan and Musharraf share a refreshing bluntness and candour in their dealings. Manmohan's honesty, sincerity and scholarly approach appear to have convinced Musharraf that the new dispensation ruling India was capable of coming up with bold proposals. The Pakistan President presents a **new face to India- charming, affable and flexible** – and his recent Delhi visit on 18 April 2005 sees bold peace initiatives. **The big question: Is all this for real?** Has the General changed his stand on Kashmir? If the answer is an unequivocal yes, it is largely because Musharraf surprised everyone even before he landed by endorsing the Indian approach of having "**soft borders**" on the LoC. In his meeting with Manmohan, he talked of not just buses plying but also trucks, indicating that Pakistan was willing to look at permitting **trade between the two Kashmiris**. He even agreed to have meeting points on the LoC for divided families apart from allowing pilgrimages and cultural interaction. With Manmohan and UPA Chairperson Sonia Gandhi flagging off the bus from Srinagar, despite the attack on the Tourist Reception Centre the day before, India had for once read the mood of the Kashmiris right. The joyful scenes of reunion seemed to have changed the mindset of Pakistan's leaders.

The following statements of the General will reveal his attitudinal change on Kashmir issue[49] :

On Kashmir

10 January 2000: If we have to hold a dialogue with India, it will have to be on the Kashmir dispute first.

18 April 2005: There cannot be a rigid time frame to sortout Kashmir. But it cannot be indefinite too.

On Terror

22 October 2001: Kashmir cannot be identified with terror as it is a freedom struggle going on there.

06 January 2004: We would not allow any territory under our control to be used by terrorists.

On Dialogue

23 September 2003: Unfortunately, there has been zero, I repeat zero, returns from the Indian side.

18 April 2005: I am very optimistic. The achievements have been far more than I expected

On Soft Borders

21 June 2004: Any movement on cultural relation is putting the cart before the horse.

14 April 2005: The Srinagar bus service is the first step towards a soft border. I am in favour of it.

On Indo-Pak Relations

30 June 2003: We have fought three wars. So what is the guarantee there won't be any further action.

18 April 2005: The military option is not an option any more. Now is the time for conflict resolution.

The New Innings of Indo-Pak Relations[50]

For Musharraf and Manmohan, there is a range of critical issues on the negotiating table. These are:

(a) **LoC** progress on turning the 740 km dividing line into a soft border. Delhi and Islamabad agree on increasing the frequency of Srinagar-Muzaffarabad bus service and allowing trucks across the LoC to promote trade.

(b) **Wagah** India wants to open Wagah-Attari route for trade and raises transit rights with Pakistan, which is non-committal.

(c) **Khokrapar-Munabao Rail Link** First proposed by India in October 2003, the link to connect Rajasthan with Sindh has been lying in the back-burner. Musharraf has proposed that the link be operational by December 2005.

(d) **Siachen** The two leaders agree to expedite a solution on the world's highest battlefield. Pakistan wants India to disengage but the latter does not want to give the strategic heights.

(e) **Baglihar** Pakistan wants India to stop the construction of the 450 MW power project on the Chenab. After World Bank refused Pakistan's proposal to intervene in the issue, Manmohan and Musharraf have agreed to settle it through back-channel discussions.

(f) Additional bus routes to be introduced from **Poonch in J&K** and **Rawalkot in PoK.**

(g) **Movement of Trucks** across LoC to be allowed to enhance trade.

(h) **Divided Kashmiri families** to be allowed to meet at designated points.

(i) **Trade Consulates** to be opened in Mumbai and Karachi by the end of this year.

(j) **Gas Pipeline** from Iran to India via Pakistan[51].

Indo Pak Relations: Tracks to Cover[52]

Since India and Pakistan began the composite dialogue process in 2004, barely one-third of the 98 proposals have been implemented, most of them unilaterally by India. Some of the important pending issues are:

(a) **Consulate Concerns.** In June 2004 India and Pakistan agreed on reopening consulates in Mumbai and Karachi. Pakistan wants the Jinnah House in Mumbai but India has offered alternative properties.

Present Status: A new deadline has been set for reopening the consulates by December 2005.

(b) **Extradition Treaty.** India first made a proposal for an extradition treaty in July 2001 and then repeated the demand in September 2004. India has also proposed a mutual legal assistance treaty.

Present Status: No response from Pakistan as India is likely to seek the extradition of many wanted criminals.

(c) **Nuclear Hotline.** In June 2004, an agreement was reached to set up a secure and dedicated hotline on nuclear issues between foreign secretaries to prevent a nuclear flare-up in the subcontinent.

Present Status: While India has given the technical details to its neighbour, Pakistan has not reverted.

(d) **Railway Link.** The Munabao-Khokrapar rail connecting Rajasthan and Sindh was first proposed in 2003 during bilateral talks when Pakistan put emphasis on bus links.

Present Status: India had announced that it would start the link on 02 October 2005 but Pakistan has sought an extension till December.

(e) **Trade Links**. In 2004 proposals were made to open up trade and transit facilities on a reciprocal basis. India has also suggested an increase in the frequency of flights and to allow private airlines.

Present Status: Manmohan raised the issues with Musharraf but Pakistan is still non-committal.

India and Pak Talk Amritsar-Lahore Bus Service

India and Pakistan on 10 May 2005 held talks on the launch of Amritsar-Lahore bus service, restoration of communication links between the coast guards of the two countries and liberalizing procedures for repatriation of fishermen who stray into each others' waters reported the **Times of India** dated 11 May 2005. An Indian delegation of transport officials headed by secretary transport Alok Rawat discussed with the Pakistani officials modalities of Amritsar Lahore bus service linking the two Punjabs. The two countries had agreed in principle to run the bus during President Pervez Musharraf's visit to India in April 2005. India and Pakistan already run bus services between Lahore and New Delhi and Srinagar to Muzaffarabad and a train service between Lahore and Attari bear Wagah border point in Punjab[53].

Talks on for Kargil-Skardu Road

Prime Minister Manmohan Singh on 11 June 2005 said talks were going on with Pakistan for opening of roads between Kargil and Skardu in Pakistan-controlled northern areas. Laying the foundation stone for a 44-MW power project in Kargil, Prime Minister said converting the Srinagar-Leh road into national highway was under consideration and plans were afoot to make this road an all weather route. He also announced a grant of Rs 10 Crore for Kargil Autonomous Hill Development Council reported the Times of India dated 12 June 2005.

Recalling the 1999 Pakistani aggression of Kargil, PM Manmohan Singh said it had caused a lot of problems for the people of this region. “Our effort is to ensure that such dangers do not recur. That is why we have started talks with Pakistan government to ensure permanent end to mutual conflicts and so that people of two countries could live peacefully” he said. “In this regard, an important decision has been taken on opening of the Srinagar- Muzaffarabad bus service after 55 years,” he said. Singh noted that he has come to know that people of Kargil also want to revive trade relations with Baltistan and Gilgit[54].

Train To Sindh Gets Green Signal

There is jubilation in Rajasthan after the declaration in New Delhi on Sunday that the **Munabao-Kokhrapar rail link** would be restored and normal train service between India and Pakistan would start from January next year, i.e 2006. “Having worked in the Munabao-Khokharapar sector as a signaller in the erstwhile Jodhpur Railways, I know what benefits the rail link could provide to the people of the two countries. This will serve bigger purpose than the Attari rail link as most of the migrants from India are scattered in the Sindh province and traveling between the two countries would be far easier now. I am sure this would give **a boon to western Rajasthan's economy**,” said Ram Chandra Bora, a freedom fighter and a journalist who served in the Railways in Sindh, reported the **Times of India** (19 April 2005).

Pakistani Visthapit Sangharsh Samiti head Hindu Singh Sodha, who waged a battle to help Hindu migrants to cross over from Pakistan said, “A large number of Hindus spread all over Sindh would be able to meet their relations in Rajasthan. Muslims, who follow Peer Pagro, would be able to visit the holy place in Sindh province, while people from Pakistan could come using the rail route to visit the holy shrine at Ajmer”, added the newspaper.

With Pakistan having started repairs on the track on their side, most of which has to be dug out of sand, the Munabao-Khokharapr rail link could prove an ideal link between the two countries. Either a metre gauge existed between the two station, which is likely to be replaced by broad gauge. Munabao is connected with broad gauge rail link and a regular train between Samdari and Munabao is currently run on the Indian side.

During the meeting of the officials of the two countries four months ago it was proposed by Pakistan that it could finish the work on laying the track between Khokhrapar and Munabao by August- September this year (2005) and the traffic between the two countries could start in October. But it seems Pakistan would need more time to finish laying the track, hence they have sought extension of two months.

The **130 kms Munabao-Khokhrapar link was in operation till the 1965 war**. Both countries realise the importance of reopening the links between Munabao-Khokhrapar in the Thar desert as this was the nearest link, which connects the north western part of India with Sindh province in Pakistan. Presently, those traveling by rail from India have to take the longer route from Attari to Lahore and travel overnight to reach Karachi. The opening of the Munabao-Khokhrapar route will also lead to easy trade between the two countries as in the past[55].

Contribution of Army to J&K Development

Romeo Force Establishing Link Between Religious Tourism And Economy

Aiming at establishing link between religious tourism and local economy, the Romeo Force at now would help spread the perfume of sacred tree at Shahdra Sharief Shrine in Rajouri. And **taking part in this project would be the local woman**, who would find a way towards empowerment by making aromatic candles using the aroma of the scare fruit tree at the shrine of Baba Ghulam Shah Badshah in Jammu. The unique tree, which bears fruit throughout the year, has been revered by thousands as it had been planted by Saint Budshah himself, reports The **Indian Express** of 19 May 2005.

Also, as a part of the Army's bio-resource initiative, the **local women have been taught the art of making incense sticks** and also Tabruk (a local prasad). The women, who have been trained by the team of environmentalist Dr Anil Joshi, would directly send their product to the shrines trust, where it would be further sold out to the pilgrims visiting the shrine.

Major General GD Bakshi., GOC Romeo Force, said the idea is **to establish linkage between religious tourism and the local economy**, which will help enhance the incomes of house holds in the area. Recently a workshop was also held for the local women, where they were taught the art of making incense sticks, candles and even prasad. The workshop was attended by people from all over this district, including remote areas like Dera Ki Gali, Gamir, Azmatabad and Surankote[56].

Army Inaugurates Solar Steam Generation in Ladakh

In Ladakh sector, the Indian Army has taken a new leap towards effective, practical use of eco-friendly, non-conventional energy devices, with the inauguration of a new state of the art solar steam generation and cooking system by Lt Gen Hari Prasad, GOC-in-C Northern Command, at Leh, reported the **Indian Express** of 16 May 2005. The new facility makes use of the revolutionary technology using Shuffler dishes to heat water to create steam, which is further used for cooking food and heating purposes.

The system has been designed and supplied by M/s Gadhia Solar Energy Systems Pvt Ltd, who also provided that technical expertise. The complete system costed approximately Rs 20 lakh. With Ladakh being abundantly rich in solar energy, the new Solar Steam Generation and Cooking system would prove to be a very useful device for a variety of uses. Use of such devices will be a great boon for the fragile ecology of Ladakh which has been under strain due to increasing use of fossil fuels both by army and the civil population[57].

Operation Sadbhavna

On the occasion of the Army Day, the Northern Command of the Indian Army compiled the projects undertaken by the army in its Operation Sadbhavna, the people friendly activities, as published in the **Indian Express** dated **15 January 2005(Army Day)**:

(a)	Schools Constructed	-	56
(b)	Schools Renovated	-	355
(c)	Education Tours	-	39
(d)	Primary Health Centers	-	42
(e)	Artificial Limbs Provided	-	293
(f)	Community Development Centers	-	106
(g)	Vocational Training Centers	-	42
(h)	Roads Constructed (Km)	-	54 (Km)
(j)	Bridges Constructed	-	37
(k)	Electrification Schemes	-	145
(l)	Water Supply Schemes	-	502
(m)	Water Mills Renovated	-	294

Interview with Northern Army Commander

Lt Gen Hari Prasad, GOC-in-Chief, Northern Command spoke to Arun Sharma of Indian Express on 08 June 2005 on various issues. Following are the excerpts:

On a question about the **situation prevailing on the ground in Jammu and Kashmir**, the General said, the situation on the ground is **well under control**. Information is coming in and terrorists are being killed. A **large number of their commanders have been killed** during the last three months and this has led to an upheaval within terrorist organizations. Inter-*tanzeem* rivalry between the groups also reported. The **over-ground workers, who had been actively helping them, have started looking the other way, as terrorists have started accused them** too of passing on information. **Infiltration has come down** and I think the situation in Jammu and Kashmir is well under control, with security forces having an upper hand. However, the pattern of violence has changed. **The terrorists have started targeting civilians, including women and children.** They are deliberately doing it to create a fear psychosis among the people.

On a question regarding favouring **ceasefire in the Valley,** the General said, Ceasefire or no ceasefire, it is a political decision. But from our past experience when we did not launch combat operations, we witnessed the whole process, but the only thing that really helped in terrorism coming down were the operations carried out over a period. We certainly, are going to **be vigilant**. Whatever is the situation, **we are not going to lower our guard and make them consolidate**.

Regarding the percentage of **foreign terrorists** operating in Jammu and Kashmir, the General said, Earlier the percentage of foreign terrorists was much higher and they hailed from Pakistan, PoK and even Afghanistan. However, during the last 6-7 months, their number has decreased. This percentage has **reversed around 45 percent**. While the number of **foreign terrorists is dwindling, the local terrorists are increasing**. However, about the local terrorists, we have to get them back to the national mainstream as well[58].

Recent Social Developments in J&K

Municipal Polls After Two Decades[59]

The attacks on Income Tax and Passport Offices came in the wake of the ongoing municipal polls, which were being held after two decades. The polls have witnessed enthusiastic voting. The militants also struck at a National Conference rally, killing two persons, and killed a Congress candidate for the civil polls in Baramulla. Despite the fall in the overall level of violence in the State, the unilateral offensive by the militants in the urban areas has shown no apparent decline. In fact the number of attacks using grenades and improvised explosive devices has shown an increase in 2004. Comparative data revealed that 148 grenade and 139 IED attacks occurred in 2003, whereas in 2004 the figures were 182 and 244 respectively.

Hurriyat's Pak Visit: A Bus Ride for Peace between India and Pakistan[60]

For in more than 50 years of the bitter history of Jammu and Kashmir, a group of pro-secession political leaders took the first trans-LoC ride on 02 June 2005 from Srinagar to Muzaffarabad in Pakistan Occupied Kashmir. Seven separatist leaders of the All Party Hurriyat Conference(APHC) crossed the

LoC carrying Indian travel documents, which marks a shift. The journey was, however, marked with fissures. While the moderates, represented by Mirwaiz Umer Farooq who heads the dominant Hurriyat faction, were on board, hawks led by hardliner Syed Ali Shah Geelani, the staunchest supporter of Kashmir's accession to Pakistan, spurned the invite by Pakistani President Pervez Musharraf to visit Islamabad for talks in protest against the "shift" in Pakistan's policy on Jammu and Kashmir[61].

For India, letting the Hurriyat leaders cross the LoC marks a departure in the thinking of the Government. It had not allowed them to travel to Pakistan earlier and now it has facilitated their trip by issuing them emergency passports. The decision to let them go stems from the fact that while the Centre considers the Jammu and Kashmir Government as the true representative of Kashmiris, it is willing to let other groups in the state participate in the Indo-Pak peace process indirectly. The trip of the Hurriyat leaders follows a broad understanding between India and Pakistan that they should try to use their influence to prepare all sections for a solution to the vexed issue. The timing of the trip is significant. It comes close on the heels of Musharraf's proposal for "**maximum self-governance**" which entails demilitarizing a section of Kashmir and granting it autonomy. The proposal was welcomed by Prime Minister Manmohan Singh and Jammu and Kashmir Chief Minister Mufti Mohammad Sayeed.

Has the Government Handled Hurriyat's Pak Visit Properly?

Yes, it has not compromised on India's core interests claims Ms Navnita Behera, Reader, Delhi University in her article in **Times of India** of 26 June 2005. The Hurriyat visit is a useful input in to the peace process. India's fundamental stakes lie in safeguarding its secular principles and the plural character of J&K; winning over alienated segments and not making any territorial concessions. Manmohan Singh's stand that there will be **no redrawing of boundaries on religious grounds** and President Musharraf's public acceptance of these principles, which no Pakistani leader has conceded till date, secures our vital concerns.

The next challenge is to sustain the peace process; broaden its base and strengthen its political character. Hurriyat's foray across the LoC needs to be understood in this context. The visit fulfilled their long standing demand to consult the leadership in '**other Kashmir**' and helped Musharraf showcase it as evidence of India's flexibility to its domestic constituents. The visit confirmed that Hurriyat exercises no leverage over the ***jehadi*** groups and its political base remains confined at best to some pockets.

The gap between India's conception of '**autonomy for J&K**' and Musharraf's idea of "**autonomous Kashmir**", which Hurriyat is now supporting, is not unbridgeable. The challenge is to sell it to the people of J&K. New Delhi cannot accomplish this alone. Kashmir problem cannot be resolved without the broad based support of all the communities living on both sides of the LoC[62]

Ajai Sahni, Executive Director of Institute for Conflict Management debates that the visitors violated bilateral agreement by travelling beyond PoK. The bilateral agreement between India and Pakistan was violated both by the separatist leaders and by Pakistan when the visitors went beyond PoK. However, the PM has chosen, expediently, to focus on the violation by Pakistsn. Action should have been taken against the Hurriyat – or the government should explicitly have allowed travel beyond PoK. **The visit allowed General Musharraf to claim that this was a confirmation of the 'disputed status' of J&K by both countries, since they "have not come on Indian passports and visas issued by Pakistan"** [63]

Pakistan is keeping three channels of manipulation alive in J&K: **overground politics; terrorism; and government to government dialogue.** By thoughtlessly allowing Pakistan to enhance the status and apparent role of its own proxy, even as it continues to support terrorism in J&K, India has strengthened Pakistan's disruptive potential in the state. Hence, its bargaining position on the negotiation table.

Public Opinion

Is Opening of Srinagar-Muzaffarabad Road a Step in the Right Direction?

The Government of India has signed an accord with Pakistan to start the bus service between Srinagar and Muzaffarabad. There have been mixed reactions to this decision from the public. While majority of people has welcomed the decision, there are others who have apprehensions. *State Times, Jammu* interacted with many of its readers on the issue. Here are few view points published in the daily on 18 February 2005:

(a) I think it is a step in the right direction, said Balbir Singh. The talks were on for a long time and now we shall see a bus on this road after more than half a century. It will be **a dream come true for the separated families** on both sides of the border.

(b) This is a very good step for the people on both sides, as it will help in developing **better understanding amongst the masses**, opined Sameer Sharma. There have been many misunderstandings among the people, though they have a common heritage. Thus will help in bring the people closer.

(c) When we are **talking of fencing and sealing the routes of infiltration to check the terrorism** in the state, I do not understand how is it going to help our cause to start a bus service from Muzaffarabad, said Joginder Paul expressing concern.

(d) I welcome this step, as it is a **historic piece of diplomacy**, said Anoop Sharma. A large number of people who are residents of Muzaffarabad and had to leave their homes and relatives behind will have a chance to see their native land and meet their separated relatives.

(e) It is a good step, said Mansoor Hadi. But, **the aspect that there will be no visa restrictions on the Pakistani citizens crossing over to India needs to be looked into** carefully. In my view this should be opened on the same pattern, which is prevalent in

(f) Chander Mohan Sona held that the service has been started on experimental basis and **both sides will have to be extra vigilant to keep the distractions away**. This will however, provide an opportunity to the separated families to unite again[64]

A Landmark Visit[65]

For the first time since Partition a Left party delegation, comprising leaders of the Communist Party of India (Marxist) and Communist Party of India (CPI), visited Pakistan between 24 February to 04 March 2005. While the overall objective was to contribute to the thaw in India-Pakistan relations, the delegation, led by CPI(M) General Secretary Harkishan Singh Surjeet and CPI General Secretary AB Bardhan, went along with the broader understanding that any improvement in the ties would help the democratic and progressive forces in the long run. On Kashmir issue, the CPI (M) general secretary said that the Kashmir issue had been **over-sentimentalised** in Pakistan by both the Army and the mainstream parties and that the first requirement was that it had to be "**desentimentalised**", reported the ***Frontline*** dated 22 April 2005.

Kashmir Pandits Up in Arms Over Return Policy

Terming the move for return of Kashmiri Pandits to Valley as a "conspiracy" against the displaced community by the State Government, hundreds of Pandits held a protest demonstration in Jammu on 13 Jun 2005. The Kashmiri Pandits assembled in front of relief commissioner's office and protested the government's "forcible move" to take them back to Kashmir Valley in phased manner from July this year[66].

Hurriyat's Latest Proposal: United States of Kashmir

Chairman of the moderate faction of Hurriyat Conference, Mirwaiz Umer Farooq, has propounded a new concept for resolving the Kashmir issue - one of the **'United States of Kashmir'**, where people would be able to move about freely. "We desire to be citizens of the United States of Kashmir and

"We desire to be citizens of the United States of Kashmir and we desire India and Pakistan to give a free hand to the Kashmiri leadership to come up with new proposals," he said, adding that Hurriyat Conference has decided to take the initiative reported the **Times of India** dated 12 June 2005 from Islamabad.

Mr Mirwaiz addressing a "**Symposium on Kashmir; looking towards the future**". Organized by Pakistani daily *Dawn* in collaboration with Human Rights Commission of Pakistan, Pakistan Peace Coalition and Islamabad Council for World Affairs in Karachi on 10 June 2005. Farooq said, **Conversion of LOC into a permanent border or status quo is not acceptable**. We are ready to explore other options. Decisions should not be imposed from New Delhi or Islamabad. As India is not ready for tripartite negotiations, the moderate Hurriyat leader said, a way out could be triangular talks between Kashmiris and Pakistan, between Kashmiris and India and between Pakistan and India.

Farooq said United Nations, Organisation of Islamic Conference and the international community have failed to address the Kashmir issue and mitigate the agony of the people of Kashmir. We should forget about the international community and the people of Kashmir should choose their own course. People of Kashmir were never in favour of a violent course, the situation was imposed on us, he said adding that Hurriyat supported the peace process. He also sought to clarity that their visit to Pakistan did not mean that there was a complete unanimity of views on the issue. JKLF chairman Yaseen Malik said it was not for New Delhi or Islamabad to represent the people of Kashmir or to decide who was their leader. Kashmiris should be included in the dialogue process as equal partners. Former Hurriyat Chairman Abdul Ghani Bhat said sensitivities of India and Pakistan had to be taken into consideration in resolving the issue but the two countries cannot move ahead unless they took the Kashmiris into confidence and engaged them as equal partners in the dialogue process[67].

Separatists Lead Life at Odds with Their Cause

They may clamour for independence and think the Indian State draconian, one that has perpetuated control over Kashmir through its military might. But, when it comes to availing of resources of that State for their personal security and convenience, **separatist leaders in Kashmir are very much Indian subjects, that too chosen ones** who feel they even have a right to its misuse, reports the Times of India of 25 April 2005.

Living in palatial houses in up market colonies, protected by security personnel armed with lethal weapons, driving around in bullet-proof cars with a red beacon flashing atop which they are not allowed to use, theirs is a life which seems much at odds with the cause they espouse.

The offices they operate from are no camps that "freedom fighters" would identify with. Located in posh residential colonies of Srinagar city, these were purchased at throw-away prices–remember the mass exodus of Kashmiri Pandits from the valley–or have been taken on rent[68].

Srinagar Girls Refill Vehicles

Till the other day, Kashmiri women were shackled under Islamic orthodoxy. Fundamentalist and militant diktats asked them to remain under purdah, stay caged in the four walls of home and be faithful, obedient and committed towards their family and husbands. While women in the rest of the world moved ahead in all spheres, Kashmiri women went backward in time. So much so that the women abandoned wearing trousers and western outfits which they had started doing in the late 1980s. Whosoever defied militant diktats had to pay a heavy price, with extremists resorting to tactics like throwing acid on their faces.

So, after almost a decade and a half, when some girls have bravely stepped out of their homes to face the world, it is indeed a special occasion. Breaking shackles of orthodoxy, the girls reach Petrol Pump at 9 am in their uniforms, refill vehicles the whole day and leave at six in the evening. The work is not easy all the time. Sometimes conservative customers pour scorn at the girls and advise them to stay at home[69].

Work On Historical Mughal Road

The reconstruction work on historical Mughal road being developed as an alternate link connecting the valley with rest of the State via border districts of Poonch and Rajouri would be started by July next. During current financial year(2005-2006), Rs 50 crore would be spent on the road project involving a total cost of Rs 160 crore. This was stated by Minster for Works GA Mir while inspecting various sites along the road from Shopian side on 23 May 2005.

Minster of State for PHE, Sayed Bashir Ahmad, Minister of State for Social Welfare, Ghulam Hassan Khan, Chief Engineer R & B, Farooq Ahmad Bakshi and a team of engineers and officers were accompanying the R &B Minister. The minister said the 84 km road from Shopian to Bufliaz, Surankote having 157 meter long bridges and would be completed in three years. Two new R&B divisions are being established at Shopian and Rajouri for the early completion of the road. Interacting with people of Shopian and adjacent villages, the Minister said that the construction of the road would provide better road connectivity to backward areas of this part of Valley and cut the distance from Poonch to Kashmir by hundreds of kilometer, besides promoting trade and commerce **it would also promote tourism** in these areas.

The road connectivity is must for ameliorating the socio-economic lot of the people of an area and in this context **Government is endeavoring hard to provide better road connectivity to all unconnected areas by 2007**. Emerging peace in the State following the steps taken by UPA Government under the leadership of Prime Minister, Dr Manmohan Singh and Sonia Gandhi for improving relationship with Pakistan has been hailed world over as new beginning of cooperation and progress in the sub-continent. The Minister called upon the people to cooperate with the government agencies for implementation of various state and centrally sponsored projects so that the benefits of all development schemes percolate down to grass root[70].

Recent Developments in Tourism Sector

Tourist Flow Remains Despite TRC Attack

Despite militants' attack on the Tourist Reception Centre (TRC) in Srinagar on 06 April 2005, the **flow of tourists is expected to remain unaffected**. As of the end of April, there was 40 percent booking of tourists in hotels and houseboats along the Dal Lake with a total occupancy of over 3,000 rooms, reported The Tribune of 30 April 2005. The **booking was full for the month of May** in hotels mainly catering to the economy class tourists[71].

J&K to Move Summer Capital to Baramulla

To develop Srinagar as an exclusive tourist resort, J&K plans to shift the summer capital to Parihaspora in Baramulla district, 20 kms from Srinagar. The proposal for a new capital city outside Srinagar has received the Centre's nod, which would be ready within next three years at an estimated cost of Rs 3,500 crore.

The **objective of the project is to decongest the summer capital of the state by moving the government offices out and develop the city as an exclusive tourist resort with heritage villages and other amenities to make it among the most attractive tourist destinations on the globe**. Finance and planning minister Muzaffar Hussain Baig visited the site of the proposed capital at Parihaspora which served as the capital of King Lalithiadatiya[72].

Sufi Music and Poetry to Reverberate in Valley

After 15 years of violence, first-ever Sufi musical festival planned in Valley; shows in Uri, Karnah and Baramulla. **Sufism and mysticism had been the prized heritage of the Valley**. With the years of violence, the traditional culture might have seen a push to the backdrop, but now it is again breathing. The revival of sufi music and poetry has now been put as the main focus of cultural activities, with a drive being initiated to spread it across all corners of the violence-hit State.

To begin with, the J&K Cultural Academy will take Sufi artists to border areas in the Valley, with programmes orgainsed in Uri, Karnah and Baramulla. Talks are also on to hold the first-ever sufi festival in the Valley, with artistes from Egypt, Iran and rest of the country to be roped in[73].

Over 20 Lakh Pilgrims in First Five Months

More than 20 lakh pilgrims from all over the country visited the holy cave shrine of Shri Mata Vaishno Devi Ji during the first five months of 2005 reported the Indian Express dated 02 June 2005. The exact number of pilgrims who have visited till 31 May 2005 were around 20.39 lakh. During the month of May alone, over 6.51 lakh devotees paid their obeisance at the holy cave shrine[74].

Dal Lake Bracing Up for a Change

The show piece of Valley, Dal Lake, is bracing up for a change. That is not only coming from the Prime Minister Manmohan Singh's reconstruction plan, but the State's rehabilitation package as well. The state government is seeking to **relocate some 50000 lake dwellers from the 58 hamlets within the Lake to the colonies in Srinagar city to save the Dal from 'dying'**, reports the **Himalayan Mail** on 03 May 2005.

This is to go along with the Prime Minister's assistance for the conservation of the Lake. The newspaper further added that the State Government had prepared a detailed project report **to shift over 4800 families to the colonies outside the Lake**. For this whole exercise, the State Government has worked out an expenditure of Rs 497 crore. The Lakes and Waterways Development Authority has acquired around 700 kanals of land to set up the residential colonies for the people living within the Dal Lake. Likewise, around 600 kanals of land has been notified at places like Hadoora, Sadpora and Bakra to shift the families to these colonies. "The **rehabilitation programme will commensurate with the conservation plan of the Central Government. This is to restore the Lake to its pristine**

glory", said Vice Chairman of Lakes and Waterways Development Authority Tanveer Jahan.

The Government has programme to **provide septic tanks to the houseboat** owners to save the Dal Lake from getting polluted. The condition of Dal Lake, with the pollution rising up in it, has drawn up sharp criticism from the environmentalists who have been expressing concern over the shrinkage of this world famous Lake and the pollution that flows into it from the adjoining areas. However, the Government is seriously working on to conserve this Lake. Under the rehabilitation plan, the **families which will be shifted to the new upcoming colonies, will be provided payment of the land** where they will be rehabilitated, compensation for their structures that will be pulled down and also the six month rent while they rebuilt their houses. For this a rehabilitation committee headed by the Divisional Commissioner, Kashmir, would meet to decide on the relocation of the Dal dwellers. Officials of the Lakes and Waterways Department said that while trying to shift the families to new colonies, the State Government is seeking to discourage further encroachment of the Dal Lake which has been caused due to the making of floating gardens in the Lake[75].

Public Opinion: Is Govt Doing Enough to Boost Tourism in Jammu Region?

Majority of the Jammuites feel that the state government has still long way to go to **boost tourism industry in Jammu region**. The cross-section of the people *The Indian Express* talked to feel that the State Government has not been spending enough for the development of tourist infrastructure in Jammu region[76]. The views of the locals as reported in the *Witness Box*, The **Indian Express** dated 09 May 2005 are:

> .... State government has so far failed to bring Jammu in the map of tourism. This can be achieved only if government pays enough attention to develop many a tourist resorts in Jammu–**Hansraj, Mutton Merchant**.
>
> It will not be fair if I blame State Government for lack of tourist flow to Jammu region. All of us have to

make efforts to see that the influx of tourists throngs several resorts in the region–**Rakesh Choudhary, Industrialist**.

Unless and until the Government provides proper infrastructure to various health and tourist resorts the visitors - both domestic and foreign will remain elusive. Many a times people on their visit to Bagh-e-Bahu complain that there is no proper drinking water facility. In such pathetic situation how come we will be able to attract tourists–**Hemant, Businessman**.

Only Jammu mela and similar other programme will not fetch good results. The State Government will have to take due care of infrastructure. Something that is very important to attract tourists-**Subash Dogra, Teacher**.

The State Government has yet not done enough to enhance tourism flow in the region. The money they utilise in building infrastructure will in future help them add to their State exchequer by getting more and more tourists–**Jaipal, Mechanical Engineer**.

Tourism potential in Jammu region is plenty, but the problem is that the same is not properly tabbed. J&K Government is concentrating more on Valley. Jammu should get equal priority–**Ankush Gupta, Student**[77].

Heavy Snow Fall: Red Alert in Valley

Nearly 1,080 vehicles were stranded at different places on the 300 km Jammu-Srinagar National Highway was closed for vehicular traffic on 18 February 2005 following landslides and fresh snowfall[78]. Owing to the heavy snowfall and poor weather condition, the State Government sounded high alert in Jammu province whereas Red alert was declared in Kashmir Valley on 19 February 2005, where army was called in to standby, following the **heaviest snowfall in 15 years** reported the **State Times** dated 20 February 2005.

It was first snowfall in the history in Ramban and Chanderkote belts with a record of 11 feet recorded at Jawahar

Tunnel and 7 feet at Patnitop Hill Resort. In Kashmir Valley, Srinagar and most of adjoining and far-flung cities were covered with a thick blanket of snow that paralysed normal life and vehicular movement. Heavy snowfall also forced the closure of the Srinagar-Jammu National Highway and cancellation of flights. **Many tourists also stranded due to the heavy snowfall**. The snowfall has also damaged communication towers and phone lines. Three to four high tension electric towers too have been damaged snapping power supply to Kashmir[79].

The Mata Vaishno Devi Pilgrimage was also suspended after an avalanche hit the track and blocking the track to the holy cave shrine in Trikuta Hills. **Stranded pilgrims were being housed in a 700-bed hostel of the Shrine Board free of cost**. Around 4,000 to 5,000 pilgrims have been visiting the cave shrine daily despite the snow and rains.

Stranded Tourists Airlifted Out of J&K

The Jammu and Kashmir Government on 25 February 2005 came to the rescue of 396 foreign and domestic tourists, airlifting them from the Kashmir Valley after avalanches and landslides shut down the Srinagar-Jammu National Highway. Many of the airlifted tourists returned with empty pockets–a result of their forced overstay in hotels – and found themselves flying out of the valley to Jammu in Indian Air Force planes meant to carry essential items, reported the Times of India of 26 February 2005. The state tourism has shifted all tourists from the avalanche-prone resorts in Sonamarg, Gulmarg and Pahalgam because of the threat of blizzards in the upper reaches of the valley. Forty two foreigners have also been shifted from Zanskar and Nubra to Leh in Ladakh. More than 600 tourists (500-plus Indians and 100-plus foreigners) were trapped after heavy snowfall lashed the Valley. They were provided free transport, medical and lodging facilities. Vehicles were sent to different tourist spots, asking them to come forward if they required anything, including money[80].

Jammu-Udhampur Rail Line

Over hundred years after famous Dogra ruler Partap Singh conceived the idea of connecting Kashmir valley with the rest of the country through rail, it was a dream come true for the people of the state when Prime Minister Manmohan Singh **inaugurated the 55-km Jammu-Udhampur rail line** on 13 April 2005. (Times of India dated 14 April 2005). The Jammu-Udhampur rail line is the first phase of Rs 7,000 crore Jammu-Udhampur-Srinagar-Baramulla national rail line project to connect the State with the rest of the country. The newspaper further adds that the official files of the archives department revealed that the first plan to connect Kashmir valley with rest of the country through a rail line was first conceived by Maharaja Partap Singh in 1898. **In June 1898, the Maharaja had engaged a British engineering company M/s SR Scott Stratten and Co for survey and execution of Kashmir rail project**[81]**.**

Promotion of J&K Tourism: Kashmir Cultural Festival at Ahmadabad

As a result of concerted efforts of the coalition government in Jammu and Kashmir and general scenario becoming quite conducive for tourism revival, the people of Jammu and Kashmir expect better days to come for picking up State's economy as the tendency among the nature lovers, holiday makers, pilgrim tourists and winter sports lovers is gaining momentum across the country **to attract good number of domestic tourists for visiting Jammu and Kashmir tourist destinations in year 2005.**

At the inaugural function of 3-day Kashmir Cultural Festival(KCF) at Ahmadabad in Gujarat on 17 February 2005, Minister for Tourism and Urban Development, J&K Govt, Mr Gulam Hassan Mir lauded the role of tour and travel operators operating from Gujarat and Maharastra, adding that the maximum number of domestic tourists among 8 lakhs, who visited Jammu and Kashmir last year were from Gujarat and Maharastra. Amidst cheers Mr Mir offered **free training courses in Gulmarg for Gujarati winter sports lovers** during next two years and said that the State Government will be pleased to host good number of domestic tourists visiting Jammu and Kashmir tourist destinations during the current year[82].

Mufti Hard-sells Kashmir to Woo Gulf, Europe

Kashmir tourism is poised for a big leap with the Gulf travel trade expressing willingness to sell the Himalayan valley as a favourite destination. Meanwhile, the International Golf Society in Dubai announced weekend trips for golfing in Srinagar even as the Indian Airlines has offered a special package for intending Kashmir bound Gulf tourists reported the State Times of 14 February 2005. All this follows a hectic Kashmir Promotion Campaign led by the Chief Minister Mufti Mohd Sayeed here and supported by Minister for Tourism, Gulam Hassan Mir and his team of officers who have been camping here for some days now. The Chief Minister had also visited London, a hub of tourism and travel trade in the world.

Mufti Sayeed was successful in influencing some decisions of far reaching consequence for promotion of tourism in Kashmir taken by tour operators and travel trade in Dubai. He held a series of meetings with them in an effort to create awareness in the Gulf about Kashmir as a global destination.

In a significant development, the Dubai and Sharjah based travel trade has decided to form a consortium titled Kashmir Bureau for selling Kashmir to the Gulf. Lending its support to the effort, the India Tourism would hold a workshop in April next (2006) and provide training to front office staff and managers of tour operators and airlines. In yet another important decision, the Indian Airlines has offered special package from Dubai to Srinagar and Sharjah to Srinagar including travel to and three nights stay in the summer capital of Jammu and Kashmir[83].

Five Lakh Pilgrims Expected in Amarnath Yatra-2005

At its 8th Board Meeting in New Delhi on 15 February 2005, the Shri Amarnath Shrine Board (SASB) chaired by Governor, Lt Gen (Retd) SK Sinha chalked out broad contours for upgrading facilities and developing infrastructure on the base camps of Pahalgam and Baltal besides various points enroute the Cave Shrine. Last year's(2004) four lakh pilgrim arrival had been the highest ever number of yatris paying obeisance at the shrine during 2-month pilgrimage which reflected fast changing security scenario in the trouble-torn valley, Lt Gen SK Sinha said, hoping their number to touch five lakh this year. This calls for **massive arrangements like health and hygiene, maintaining environment, creating facilities at various camp sites besides ensuring supplies and electricity** etc.

The SASB decided to put up 2100 pollution free toilets and 650 bathrooms at all the points including base camps. Of these 550 toilets and 250 bathrooms have already been put up. The expertise of Sulabh International will also be made adequately available for environment friendly toilet and bathroom facilities[84].

Amarnath Yatra for Two Months in 2005

Putting all speculations to rest about the period of the year's Amarnath Yatra, J&K Governor Lt Gen SK Sinha (Retd), who is also chairman of the Shri Amarnath Shrine Board(SASB), has made it clear that the Yatra would be for a period of two months. The SASB is the final authority to decide about the arrangements and about the period of the Yatra[85]. The All Jammu Hotels and Lodges Association has demanded that Baba Amarnath Yatra **be extended to three months**, starting from the beginning of June alongwith the opening of Gumeri pass[86].

Registration Counter For Amarnath Yatries: DUDF

Rajinder Kumar, advocate and President of District Udhampur Development Forum (DUDF), Udhampur has demanded the opening of Registration counter for Amarnath yatries at Udhampur. In a memorandum submitted to the Government who is the head of Shri Amarnath Shrine Board, Rajinder Kumar alleged that under a well planned conspiracy the Registration Counter, which used to function at Udhampur a couple of year ago was closed without assigning any reason. It has been pointed out in the memorandum that Udhampur town is connected by two prominent roads of J&K National Highway and Dhar Road. Similarly, with the inauguration of Railway Station, a number of pilgrims would directly come to Udhampur from rest of the country and abroad. Under these circumstances

Udhampur is the natural choice for a number of pilgrims for getting themselves registered for yatra purpose, reports the **Indian Express** of 09 May 2005.

Rajinder Kumar has reminded the Governor that in a recent judgment on the management of Amarnath yatra, the High Court of J&K has Suo-Moto suggested that a yatra counter should be opened at Udhampur town. It was further requested in the memorandum that the Governor should understand the regional discrimination towards the hilly district of Udhampur by vested-interest who are doing so since decades[87].

Amarnath Bhawan

It has been promised three years ago - a commitment that came in 2002 for building a Amarnath Yatri Bhawan. Even after three years, the idea has not gone beyond the identification of site for the proposed project reports The **Indian Express** of 27 May 2005. With a few weeks left for the Amarnath Yatra to begin and five lakh pilgrims expected, the project Amarnath Yatra Bhawan to house the Yatris - comes under scanner again. Even though the State Government has announced last year (2004) too that the work on the project would start in months, nothing has been done so far, brought out the newspaper. **During the three years, the only activity on this front had been selection of 50 kanals of land** near the Bacchan Depot - the area in the vicinity of Balidan Stamb. Earlier the land was identified near the Silk Factory, but the idea was contested on the basis that it would add on to congestion in the area. **The land, which is currently selected, also has been mired by controversy**, with the Forest Department also raising objections to it[88].

Threat to House Boats

A report from Srinagar has brought into sharp focus the threat of extinction being faced by houseboats in Dal and Nagin lakes. The condition of the majority of them has deteriorated. There is shortage of water-resistance cedar wood needed for repairing and building them. In addition, skilled craftsmen no more find making of houseboats a gainful activity and are shifting their attention to other more profitable pursuits. Admittedly, the long period of militancy has played havoc with these floating beauties as with everything else in the State. There are more than 1200 houseboats in the two lakes and they are normally **sought after by affluent tourists or those who want to enjoy privacy in idyllic surroundings**[89]. It is time that adequate steps are taken to maintain them with genuine concern.

Will Indo-Pak Thaw Melt into a Tourism Bonanza?

The recent thaw in ties between India and Pakistan has raised hopes of the tourism and hospitality sector which sees the road to the neighbouring country as a passage of opportunities not to be lost sight of. Tourism experts say a liberalized visa regime and further **opening of the road, rail and air links could give a shot in the arms to tourism industries in both countries**. Several Pakistanis are desirous of visiting India to meet their families, others wish to visit religious destinations such as Ajmer Sharif, Nankana Sahib and the Golden Temple. **Chennai and Bangalore are major centers of medical tourism**. The day is not far when one can think of going to have lunch in Lahore on a Sunday afternoon or a young man bikes it down to the city. Once such a thing happens it would not be difficult to increase the present Pakisitan arrivals which are roughly 45,000 to become 4,50,000. The opportunities that will follow the softening of borders are simply mind-boggling[90].

J&K May Put Uri on Tour Map

A year ago, few in Kashmir were familiar with Kaman Bridge, Urs or Salamabad, all en route to Muzaffarabad. But, now these places, witness to the making of history, have become household names which many want to visit. Kaman, Salamabad and Red Bridge were the focus of every news channel on April 07 as the Srinagar-Muzaffrabad road opened after 57 years and Kashmiris saw villages beyond Uri for the first time. Now, **beauty, historical importance and curiosity has kindled hope among Valley people to visit these places at least**

once. J&K Director General of Tourism Mohammad Saleem Beig says the Department is planning to **develop Baramulla and Uri on the tourist map**. Land has been purchased at Salamabad to develop it as a tourist destination[91].

Fly From Delhi To Srinagar in Only Rs 1,230

The Indian Airlines has decided to fix the rates for Delhi-Srinagar flight at 100 Dirham (Rs 1,230) **for those passengers who will be coming from Dubai to Srinagar**. This was revealed at a meeting between Chief Minister Jammu and Kashmir Mufti Mohammad Sayeed and Union Minister of State Civil Aviation Praful Patel in New Delhi on 24 May 2005. Sayeed underlined the need for opening the Srinagar airport to international flights by March, 2006. He said the economy of the state and **tourist industry will get a huge push with the arrival of international air carriers**. Appreciating the state government's demand for increasing the number of daily domestic flights from Delhi to Srinagar and Jammu to Srinagar, the Union Minister said a decision to this effect will be taken soon. The increase in frequency of domestic flights will help cater to the huge rush of tourists to Srinagar. It was also agreed in the meeting that steps will be taken for transfer of Centaur Hotel Complex to Jammu and Kashmir Government after reasonable evaluation of the cost of the structure is made.

A decision was also taken to let the Jammu and Kashmir Government run its own domestic district air service on the pattern of North-East states. The Chief Minister asked the officers of the State to prepare a plan for submission to Government of India for earmarking funds for this purpose. It was felt that **inter-district state flights will further boost tourism industry** and help strengthen the economic scenario. The Union Minister for Civil Aviation assured the Chief Minister that Civil Aviation Ministry will give **full support to state government to cater to the huge rush of tourists**. He directed the officers concerned to **launch an information campaign to apprise the people outside the state about the improvement in the ground situation** in the state[92].

Valley Expecting 10 Lakh Tourists in 2005

The Valley expects **10 lakh tourists this season**, including for the first time, **two golfing groups from Pakistan, and two more from the Gulf**. At the scenic Royal Spring Golf Course overlooking the Dal lake, the Indian beauty queen, Ms Sushmita Sen, the new brand ambassadar, too, was stirred by the beauty of the Valley. Kashmir is really a paradise. **A heaven is a heaven, no matter what happens, the circumstances cannot change it,** exclaimed Ms Sen. Inaugurating the TAG Heuer Golf tournament, the Chief Minister said that this is a successful golf tournament and will **boost the tourism** in the state. He further added that "we are developing **more golf courses at Pahalgam, Sonamarg, Jammu** and other places to boost the game and tourism"[93].

Pollution Toll

It is slow poisoning of the water that is daily killing a part of the Dal Lake, which has been the major attraction in Kashmir Valley. The Pollution Control Board's report 2003-04 says that the Dal is dying slowly as **pollutants were six to eight times more than the permissible limit** (as prescribed by the Water Act (Prevention and Control of Pollution) and also by the Central Board for Control of Pollution (CBCP), reports The Indian Express (01 May 2005). The report also says that construction and design deficiencies of the treatment plant was leading to its poor functioning. Besides the known factors like human settlements (60,000 people), hotels (300), floating gardens, and even *dhobhi ghats* on the periphery, are generously contributing to the lake's slow death. The lake, which has **shrunk from 75 sq kms to mere 11.56 sq km** has ammonical nitrogen of over 1.57 mgl, with the maximum permissible limit being 0.5 mgl. Another indicator is the chemical oxygen demand (COD), which was 41.8 mgl at the Nehru Park basin. Though the permissible level of COD is 9 mgl, it varied from minimum 18.76 mgl to maximum of 41.8 mgl, says the report.

The phosphates concentration, which should be less than 0.1 mgl, was also found to be increasing, with1.18 mgl recorded at Hazratbal Basin, and a constant increase recorded all through the Lake. The report also states that the dissolved oxygen was found to be declining at various basins of the Dal. The pH value was also put on a higher alkaline side, with 7.39 at Nehru Park basin to 8.16 at Nageen basin. Dr Bilqees Ara, senior scientist with the PCB, says most of the pollutants are found two to six times higher than the permissible limit. Ara says that quantity of bio-mass is ever- increasing, reducing the penetration of light, and that is why the red algae is blooming in the lake. The **depth of the lake has also decreased from 17 feet in 1970s to less than nine feet**. The regular surveys of Lake and Waterways Development Authority (LAWDA) have also shown a rise in pollutants though the department authorities say that the government was seriously working towards saving the Dal. Vice Chairman, LAWDA, Tanveer Jahan says that over six sewerage treatment plants are being set up, and of these, two has already started working. There is a plan to shifting dwellers from the Dal to various pockets of the city, says Jahan[94].

J&K Wounds are Healing

Terrorist violence has dipped substantially. Cross border infiltration is virtually zero. Tourists are arriving in hordes. Economic development is picking up. And to top it all, people enthusiastically voted in the recent civil elections despite militant threats and boycott calls. At the peak of militancy "tourist arrivals" had slid to 6,000 a year. It rose to 28,000 in 2002, followed by 1.9 lakh in 2003. In 2004 there was a tremendous quantum jump to 3.76 lakh. Depsite the winter, 20,000 arrivals were recorded in January 2005[95].

Terrorist Incidents Down by 24 per cent in J&K

Describing **fencing on 750 km border in J&K as a major achievement**, Governor Lt Gen (Retd) SK Sinha has said that infiltration and effective combat operations have resulted into **24 percent slash in militancy-related incidents** in the State during the past year(2004), reported the **Indian Express** dated 15 January 2004. The Governor said that 2,500 incidents were recorded during 2004 against 3,400 in the year 2003. The terrorists have suffered heavy casualties with their 40 to 50 top leaders having been eliminated in several encounters during the year 2004. The border fencing will have a good impact on the situation in hinterland soon.

As a result of improving situat ion, the Governor said that tourism showed a big spurt with 3.76 lakh tourists, including over 18,500 foreign tourists making Kashmir their destination during the last season. "**We are expecting a big tourist arrival this year, as the hotel accommodation in Srinagar has already been fully booked till June 2005**" said the Governor, reports the newspaper. The religious tourism also registered a record high of over four lakh to Shri Amarnath Shrine in south Kashmir and 60 lakh to Mata Vaishno Devi Shrine in Jammu during the by gone year. The tourist arrivals to the Valley in the previous years – 28,000 in 2002 and 1.60 lakh in 2003[96].

Gulmarg to See Skiing Champs

International skiers will dot the thick snow covering the undulating meadows of Gulmarg, for the first time, making winter warmer for the people associated with the tourism industry. The Federation of International Skiing, Switzerland, approached the Winter Games Federation of India that an international skiing championship be held on the Gulmarg slopes. The J&K government agreed without wasting any time and put its best foot forward to provide facilities for international skiers, reported the Indian Express of 15 January 2005.

More than **100 sportspersons** from Iran, Japan, Hungary and some from the SAARC nations will be participating in the International Skiing Cross Country Championship to be organized from 19-21 February 2005. This **will not only be the first international skiing event to be organised in Gulmarg, but in India too.** This is the reason why Winter Games Federation of India in collaboration with the Gulmarg Development Authority and JKTDC do not want to leave any stone unturned, as they want to send across the message that they have facilities to organize such events in the future too[97].

Another High For Gulmarg: World's Highest Cable Car Ropeway

Known all over for one of the highest golf courses-Gulmarg, the country's famous health resort in north Kashmir is about to achieve another distinction-run the **world's highest cable car ropeway**. The completion of the **second phase of Gondola Cable Car ropeway from Kongdour to Apparwat (2.65 km)** has helped Gulmarg achieve this feat. From February 2005 onward the second phase of the cable car would start operating, thus giving winter sports a new boost, reports Indian Express (19 January 2005). It will lift tourists from Kongdour to Apparwat - situated at a height of 13,500 feet. The project costing Rs 11 crore was **completed by a French agency**, Poma Galski, in January 2005. After successful trials the Jammu and Kashmir Government has decided to start its commercial run. For projection of cable car ropeway, the JKTDC and Gulamarg Cable Car Ropeway Project have coined a catchline: "**The joy of traveling is not where you go, but how you get there**. There are some journeys of which this is truer than other. Gulmarg cable car is one of them."

To have a glimpse of the virgin slopes in Gulmarg heights, Cable Car Corporation has fixed Rs 300 per person for the to and fro ride. Already, queries from several ski lovers from the European nations have started pouring in. The coming of the cable car from Kongdour to Apparwat will serve as a boon for the skiers of the international repute as **one here has choice of slopes**, ranging from beginners run and slalom slope to sharper descents for more experienced skiers. Earlier, the skiers had to remain contended with Kongadour slopes only. For reaching Apparwat, one had to hire a helicopter which was not easy, "With the coming of this cable car, they can move up and down without any hassles. Travelling via ropeway will make one enjoy true nature-open, liberal, warm and sensuous-in the biting winter," says Farooq Shah, Chief Executive Officer, Gulmarg Cable Car Ropeway.

Till date, only Venezuela, a country in South America, can boast of the highest cable car ropeway. However, the same is said to be out of order for quite long. The first phase of the cable car is already doing brisk business. It operates from Gulmarg to Kongdour and has a capacity of 1,500 passengers. **To woo the international tourists, JKTDC has flashed the pictures of the cable car ropeway on its**

website. "With the cable car ropeway, you can enjoy world' best skiing slopes at rates 10 times cheaper than Europe," says Aziz Wani, General Manager, JKTDC[98].

Foreign Consulates In Kashmir

While expressing her satisfaction over the upgradation of the Srinagar airport to an international level, Mehbooba Mufti, MP and president of the ruling PDP, asked the Centre to allow foreign countries to **open their consulate offices in Srinagar to boost tourism**. Mehabooba said that there was a need to improve the infrastructure of the travel industry in the state, adding that the foreign office consulates of different countries had to be opened here, so that lack of visa facilities do not hamper tourists spending time here. She said that an **international airport would attract more tourists in the State**, thus breathing life into the tourism industry of the State, which had passed through its worst phase in the 15 years of turmoil. Mehbooba said it was time to upgrade the airport to fulfill the expectations of the tourists. She informed that the extension and up gradation of facilities at the airport had already begun at a cost of about Rs 60 crore and added that sophisticated communication and navigational aids had already been put in place[99].

The Kashmir Chamber of Commerce and Industry (KCCI) while hailing New Delhi's decision to upgrade the Srinagar airport, said, it was long pending demand of the KCCI which had been raised with New Delhi for long. They attributed boost in exports of the State's handicrafts to this decision, and also rise in of tourist inflow. The Kashmir Hotel and Restaurant Owners' Federation also hailed the Centre's-decision and expressed its gratitude.

Hoteliers Demand Better Tourism Promotion

Welcoming the allocation of Rs 4,200 crore for the J&K's annual plan for the year 2005-2006, all Jammu Hotels and Lodges Association has demanded that the State Government should make adequate allocation in its plan for tourism promotion. A meeting of the association held in Jammu on 16 February 2005 demanded that an **equitable share shall be**

earmarked for promotion and development of tourism in Jammu. (Indian Express - 17 February 2005). The association said that there is ample scope and potential for pilgrim tourism in Jammu region and alleged that out of Rs 24,000 crores announced by the Prime Minister, to be provide to the State in the next four years, for reconstructing its shattered economy, no funds have been earmarked for tourism development in Jammu. The Central and State Government in the past have neglected tourism in Jammu, further alleged the association.

The association proposed that the project of Tawi face-lift, in Jammu city should be taken in hand, on top priority and demanded that an artificial lake should be created in the Tawi river between the main old bridge and the new bridge, near Bagh-e-Bahu. Both the banks on Tawi between these points be provided steps and ghats for the devotees to offer Aarti there daily. This will help promote pilgrim tourism in Jammu and will be an attraction for the Vaishno Devi to stay in Jammu for a long or so. The association also demanded installation of cable car between the points from Mubark Mandi to Bagh-e-Bahu and from there to Maha Maya city forest. Similarly light and sound system should be set up at Mubark Mandi, Bagh-e-Bahu and Rajinder park[100].

Valley Preferred Tourist Destination: Mir

Militancy has come down considerably in Jammu and Kashmir and law and order has improved, making it a preferred destination among tourists, J&K Minister for Tourism, Ghulam Hasan Mir said in Ahmedabad on 16 February 2005. "Kashmir is once again slated to be **preferred destination for tourists which is affordable, secure and full of fun and adventure**," he told reporters at a **three-day festival of Jammu and Kashmir** in Ahmedabad. The minister said in an **effort to woo the Gujarat tourists**, who constitute a huge chunk, the Jammu and Kashmir government has started a promotional campaign in a big way. The State Government has specially organised free training facilities for Skiing for Gujaratis, Mir said, adding that facilities and infrastructure, including waterways, roadways, communication, civil aviation and accommodations have been upgraded. Last year 45.000 tourists had visited the State while a total of 60 lakh pilgrims visited Vaishno Deviji temple, to quote the **Indian Express** of 17 February 2005.

The domestic tourist inflow last year (2004) was over 3,58,000, while the inflow of foreign tourists was more than 18,000, which is much more that the previous years. The State Government contemplates to involve Ahmedabad based Centre for Environmental Education (CEE) to create awareness about conservation methods and technology for famous Dal lake and other water bodies in the State. The center has already prepared an educational manual on environmental education and the State Government is actively considering to utilise this facility and possibilities would be explored to apply the method on the conservation would famous Dal lake[101]. The year 2005 will witness a major influx of tourists from metropolitan cities to the Valley, especially from Delhi, reports the Indian Express of 04 January 2005. J&K Tourism Minister Ghulam Hassan Mir interacted with a team **of Delhi based tour operators**, who were on a familiarisation tour to Kashmir. The delegation comprised representatives of All India Domestic Tour Operators Association, Tour Operators Federation of India and other Travel Trade Bodies. The tour operators have decided to workout packages for Kashmir, which include the adventure, sight seeing, Golf and nature watching to get in newer clients[102].

Paradise Once Again

Don't head for Kashmir this summer-Every square inch of space in Srinagar, Gulmarg, Sonamarg and Pahalgam is booked, appealed the **Times of India of 06 January 2005**. A huge tourist rush has taken even the State Government by surprise. **With hotels fully booked, it has had to put up tents**. And the security forces are being turfed out of hotels to make rooms. In 2004, the J&K Government had budgeted for 2.4 lakh tourists, considerably higher than the 1.25 lakh it had the year before, only to get skeptical sniggers. But, by the time the year ended, the tally was a healthy 3.6 lakh–the highest since 1990, when terrorism hit the state. If 2004 was good, 2005 is shaping up better as within four days of the New Year, J&K has already been sold out for summer 2005. It is a story the State Government had not scripted. Unknown to it, **tourists seem to have pushed the threat of terrorism behind them and come in large numbers.** Tour operators were overjoyed. They were making **huge bookings** while State Government officials were on their toes to provide infrastructure for incoming tourists. The State was once dependent heavily on tourism until it became a playground for militancy[103].

Effective Monitoring of Dal Lake Project

Implementation of comprehensive plan formulated to restore pristine glory of famous Dal Lake and development of its catchment area including face lifting its peripheries besides retrieving Dole Demb water body was discussed in Jammu threadbare at 14th meeting of board of directors of J&K Lakes and Water Ways Development Authority (LWDA) on 04 January 2005, reports the **Daily Excelsior** of 05 January 2005.

Apart from reviewing the decisions of 12th and 13th board meetings, detailed discussion was held over the current years action plan and several decisions were taken in the four hour long meeting to remove the bottlenecks hampering smooth take off of the various schemes. These include speedy **completion of 3 sewage treatment plants, retrieving Dole Demb, Rehabilitation of Dal Dwellers, sanitation process with thrust on solid waste management of houseboats, besides implementation of alternative programme launched making Dal Lake Polythene free zone**[104].

Bollywood Response to Kashmir

Asking the Bollywood to practically display its penchant for the theme of patriotism, Chief Minister Mufti Mohammad Sayeed called upon movie makers **to review its Kashmir connection and contribute to the improvement in J&K situation**. He said the film world should take a lead from the industry and travel groups of the country in supplementing the forces of peace in the State. He said the industry and tour and travel operators have strengthened the confidence of the people of Jammu and Kashmir by reviving their activities in the State and he would like the movie makers to follow the suit[105].

New Highway to Connect Jammu–Kashmir

After opening of the Uri-Muzaffarabad road, Jammu and Kashmir residents have something to cheer at. To get rid of ageing Jammu-Srinagar National Highway, the work for an alternate road connecting two capitals of Jammu and Srinagar is in the offing. The blue print for the project to be taken under the **North South Corridor Express Highway** has already been prepared. This alternate four-lane National Highway is supposed to shorten the distance by 70 Kms and will be operational from 2008. As per the blue print, the road would have underground tunnels at Nowgam and Kud and would be capable of withstanding extreme weather conditions. Special attention was being paid to the road connectivity under the Prime Minister Reconstruction Plan. This new highway would save people from using the weather-beaten 93 year old Jammu Srinagar National Highway which has 29 major and 19 minor landslide prone areas[106].

Conclusion

Peace initiatives with Pakistan, the mentor and promoter of terrorism in Jammu and Kashmir has brought in prosperous hope for development of the State as a whole and tourism sector in particular. Taking the opportunity of the improved situation, the Tourism Ministry of Jammu and Kashmir Government is also leaving no stone unturned for development of the tourism infrastructure. The ministers are touring other parts of the country and giving wide publicity not only in our country but also in abroad.

Development of roads connecting the areas across the LoC, declining number of terrorist incidents, increased tourist influx in the state and willing participation of the civil population in civic activities are the definite indicators of the return of normalcy in the State. To cap it all, the role of the security forces especially the Indian Army in restoring normalcy by eliminating the militants and providing necessary support to the civil population living in far flung areas through **Operation Sadbhavna** is praise worthy. May peace prevail in Jammu and Kashmir and prosperity flourish in the State.

Notes and References

1. Swami Praveen, *"War and Peace", Frontline,* 18 June 2004, p.16.
2. Bagchi Indrani/TNN, *Times of India,* 05 October 2004.
3. Pandit M Saleem, *Times of India,* 04 January 2005, p.7.
4. Luv Puri, *"A Winter of Violence", Frontline*, 11 Februrary 2005, pp.40-41.
5. *State Times*, Jammu, 10 February 2005, p.1.
6. Luv Puri, *A Winter of Violence, Frontline,* 11 Februrary 2005, pp.40-41.
7. *State Times*, Jammu, 25 February 2005, p.1.
8. *State Times, 13 February 2005, P.1.*
9. STNS, *State Times,* 19 February 2005.
10. Mishra Bisheshwar and Pandit Rajat, *Times of India,* 17 April 2005, p.8.
11. Ramesh Vinayak, *"Trail by Fire", India Today*, 18 April 2005, p.21.
12. ENS, *The Indian Express(The Himalayan Mail),* 25 April 2005, p.1.
13. *Times of India, 04 May 2005, p.9.*
14. Ehsan Mir, *The Indian Express(The Himalayan Mail)*, 04 May 2005, p.1.
15. Pandit M Salim/TNN, *Times of India,* 08 May 2005, p.6.
16. *Times of India,* 13 June 2005, p.6.
17. Mishra Bisheshwar, *Times of India,* 13 June 2005, p.6.
18. Mishra Bisheshwar, *Times of India,* 13 June 2005, p.6.
19. *Times of India, 12 May 2005, p.7.*
20. Pandit M Saleem, *Times of India*, 13 May 2005, p.9.
21. *Times of India,* 18 May 2005, p.6.
22. TNN and PTI, *Times of India*, 14 June 2005, p.1.
23. *Times of India*, 15 June 2005, p.7.
24. Pandit M Saleem, *Times of India,* 16 June 2005, p.7.
25. Pandit Rajat/TNN, *Times of India,* 09 June 2005, p.7.
26. TNN, *Times of India*, 03 May 2005, p.10.
27. Pandit M Saleem/TNN, *Times of India*, 23 May 2005, p.4.
28. *India Today,* 25 July 2005, p.28-35.
29. *The Hindu*, 24 July 2005, p.1.
30. *India Today,* 25 July 2005, p.42-43.

31. Aroon Purie, *India Today,* 25 July 2005, p.3.
32. Luv Puri, "*A Jehad Against Militancy*", *Frontline*, 14 January, 2005, pp.33-35.
33. *State Times, Jammu*, 18 February 2005, p.4.
34. Masood Bashaarat, *The Indian Express(The Himalayan Mail)*, 21 May 2005, p.1.
35. PTI, *The Indian Express(The Himalayan Mail)*, 02 June 2005, p.1.
36. ENS, *The Indian Express(The Himalayan Mail)*, 02 June 2005, p.8.
37. Samanta Pranab Dhal/*Islamabad* and Jaleel Muzamil andBali Pawan/*Srinagar, The Indian Express(The Himalayan Mail),* 17 February 2005, p.1.
38. Reddy Muralidhar, "*A Bus Ride for Peace*", *Frontline*, 11 March 2005, pp.31-32.
39. *State Times*, 28 February 2005, p.1.
40. *Times of India,* 27 May 2005, p.6.
41. Samanta Pranab Dhal, *The Indian Express(The Himalayan Mail)*, 26 May 2005, p.1.
42. Roy Bhaskar and Pandit Rajat, *Times of India*, 17 June 2005, p.11.
43. Raja Mohan C, *The Indian Express*, 10 June 2005, p.1.
44. *Times of India,* 25 May 2005, p.1.
45. *Times of India,* 15 June 2005, p.7.
46. ENS, *The Indian Express(The Himalayan Mail)*, 24 May 2005, p.6.
47. ENS, *The Indian Express(The Himalayan Mail)*, 05 June 2005, p.1.
48. Bali Pawan, *The Indian Express(The Himalayan Mail),* 25 April 2005, p.5.
49. Raj Chengappa and Syed Talat Hussain, *Has the General Really Changed?*, *India Today*, 02 May 2005, pp.19-25.
50. *Ibid,* p.26.
51. *The Times of India*, 19 April 2005, p.1.
52. *Ibid*, p.28.
53. *Times of India, 11 May 2005, p.13.*
54. *Times of India*, 12 June 2005, p.7.
55. Bhandari Prakash/TNN, *Times of India,* 19 April 2005, p.5.

56. ENS, ENS, *The Indian Express(The Himalayan Mail)*, 19 May 2005, p.5.
57. ENS, *The Indian Express(The Himalayan Mail)*, 16 May 2005, p.2.
58. *The Indian Express(The Himalayan Mail),* 09 June 2005, p.1.
59. Luv Puri, *A Winter of Violence, Frontline*, 11 Februrary 2005, pp.40-41.
60. Reddy Muralidhar, *A Bus Ride for Peace, Frontline*, 11 March 2005, pp.31-32.
61. Shukla Saurabh and Vinayak Ramesh, *Cross Border Traffic, India Today*, 13 June 2005, pp.33-35.
62. Behera Navnita, *Sunday Debate, Times of India*, 26 June 2005, p.14.
63. Sahni Ajai, *Sunday Debate, Times of India*, 26 June 2005, p.14.
64. *State Times, Jammu,* 18 February 2005, p.3.
65. Rajalakshmi TK, *A Landmark Visit, Frontline*, 22 April 2005, pp.20-21.
66. *Times of India*, 14 June 2005, p.7.
67. *Times of India*, 12 June 2005, p.7.
68. Pandit M Saleem, *Times of India,* 25 April 2005, p.6.
69. Singh Aarti Tikoo/TNN, *Times of India*, 16 June 2005, p.7.
70. ENS, *The Indian Express(The Himalayan Mail)*, 24 May 2005, p.5.
71. Fazili Ehsan, *The Tribune*, 30 April 2005, p.4.
72. *Times of India,* 13 May 2005, p.8.
73. Bali Pawan, *The Indian Express(The Himalayan Mail)*, 02 June 2005, p.1.
74. ENS, *The Indian Express(The Himalayan Mail)*, 02 June 2005, p.4.
75. Naseem Ishfaq, *The Indian Express(The Himalayan Mail)*, 03 May 2005, p.8.
76. *Witness Box, The Indian Express(The Himalayan Mail),* 09 May 2005, p.3.
77. *Ibid.*
78. *State Times,* 19 February 2005, p.1.
79. *State Times,* 20 February 2005, p.1.
80. Pandit M Saleem, *Times of India,* 26 February 2005, p.10.
81. *Times of India,* 14 April 2005, p.9.
82. *State Times*, 18 February 2005, p.1.

83. *State Times*, 14 February 2005, p.1.
84. *State Times,* 16 February 2005, p.8.
85. ENS, *The Indian Express(The Himalayan Mail)*, 19 May 2005, p.1.
86. ENS, *The Indian Express(The Himalayan Mail),* 26 April 2005, p.3.
87. ENS, *The Indian Express(The Himalayan Mail)*, 09 May 2005, p.3.
88. ENS, *The Indian Express(The Himalayan Mail)*, 27 May 2005, p.3.
89. *Editorial, Daily Excelsior,* 26 April 2005, p.6.
90. *Daily Excelsior,* 26 April 2005, p.7.
91. Ehsan Mir, *The Indian Express(The Himalayan Mail),* 25 April 2005, p.8.
92. ENS, *The Indian Express(The Himalayan Mail)*, 25 May 2005, p.1.
93. ENS, *The Indian Express(The Himalayan Mail)*, 04 June 2005, p.6.
94. Bali Pawan, *The Indian Express(The Himalayan Mail)*, 01 May 2005, p.1.
95. Pandit Rajat/TNN, *Times of India,* 18 February 2005, p.7.
96. ENS, *The Indian Express(The Himalayan Mail),* 15 January 2005, p.8.
97. Dutta Pradeep, *The Indian Express(The Himalayan Mail),* 15 January 2005, p.1.
98. Dutta Pradeep, *The Indian Express(The Himalayan Mail),* 19 January 2005, p.1.
99. TNN, *Times of India*, 31 January 2005, p.4.
100. ENS, *The Indian Express(The Himalayan Mail),* 17 February 2005, p.6.
101. ENS, *The Indian Express(The Himalayan Mail),* 17 February 2005, p.6.
102. ENS, *The Indian Express(The Himalayan Mail),* 04 January 2005, p.6.
103. Pandey Vineeta, *Times of India,* 06 January 2005, p.1
104. *The Daily Excelsior,* 05 January 2005, p.3.
105. *State Times*, 01 May 2005, p.1.
106. Dutta Pradeep, *The Indian Express(The Himalayan Mail),* 15 April 2005, p.1.

8

Conclusion

The revival of a constructive political process is essential for any permanent solution to the problems of the State, but simultaneously, all out efforts should be made to hammer out a framework of a solution which would be acceptable to most people, if not all. The ***government has to show a will and determination to deal firmly with the secessionist forces***. It has to be a multi-dimensional policy encompassing all aspects of Kashmir problem–military, political, diplomatic and psychological. Pakistan is unlikely to reverse its policy of aid and abetment to terrorism in J&K and even when the people are getting disillusioned with Pakistan and terrorism.

The Tribune (dated 11 December 2004) reported that the underlying problem of Jammu and Kashmir is not economic. It is political and administrative. ***The State does quite well in terms of socio-economic development***. Its literacy level (64.8 percent) is almost on a par with the national level (65.4 percent). Its sex ratio (923/1000) too is almost on a par with the national average (933/1000). J&K's birth rate (19.9/1000) is lower than the national average (25.8/1000). Its death rate (5.4/1000) is also lower than the national average (8.5/1000). Its infant mortality rate (45/100) is also superior to the national average (68/100). For the 10th Five Year Plan J&K got a per capita allocation of Rs 14,399 where as the national average was only Rs 5,668. It can thus be nobody's case that J&K did not get enough. All the ***money sanctioned by the Centre has gone down the tubes in J&K***. There are hardly any public works contributing to the common good and higher productivity to show. Roads are in a terrible condition. The power situation is miserable. There is no public sanitation worth the name and all the sewage seems to flow into the Dal Lake, and then carried into Pakistan by the Jhelum River.

The J&K Government's books have not been audited for over a decade and no one really knows what was spent where and who got what. Talk to even the most ardent Pro-India Kashmiri, and there are some, and he will tell you that the politicians and bureaucrats have stolen most of the money. It is believed that *every second house belongs to a government employee* or one connected with it. Relate this to the low poverty line in the State and it would seem that trickle-down economics works!

The Government job is much sought after in J&K, irrespective of its rank and status because it enables the employee to make easy money without much effort by resorting to malpractices. A young graduate or above prefers to be even a peon in State Government service rather than looking for some better avenues outside. Some of the class III/IV officials have alternative jobs and businesses. They would normally be absent from duty for most part of the month. They would show their face in the office at the end of the month to collect the salary. The liberal and un-monitored funds allotted by the Centre to the State went into the pockets of those who mattered. The basic needs and the much required developmental works in the state were adversely affected. Consequently the have-nots became disillusioned and easy prey to the design of the militants. The corruption in the State has to be contained for bringing peace and tranquility, otherwise it will be perpetually exploited by the anti-national elements and the adversaries.

The only effective antidote to insurgency is the restoration of good government and order. In J&K we had neither. The forces meant to impose order are themselves often quite disorderly. The Indian Army and the various para-military forces work independently of each other and often at cross-purposes. Worse still they work independent of the popularly elected government. We must wonder if powerlessness makes the State Government purposeless as well.

On the economic front, the Government of India has been most liberal with grants and aids to Jammu Kashmir right from the beginning, underwriting most of the development needs of the State from the Central resources. While the infrastructural facilities have multiplied many times and income generation has also shown a constant upward trend, the distribution of wealth between the regions as also within a region between various sections of people has not been equitable. This has generated heart burning amongst regions, groups and individuals giving rise to discontentment, which has been, according to some observers, one of the factors contributing towards rise of militancy in the State. The often heard charges of wide spread corruption, almost institutionalized during some of the regimes, further compounded the sense of disenchantment amongst the local population.

Travel and tourism are as old as coming of man on the planet earth. In ancient times pilgrims, traders, scholars and adventurous people used to undertake journeys to distant places and countries in order to satisfy their respective urges. Daring wanderers of the by gone eras transformed the vast neighbourhood, of course, their ***journeys were full of adventure and risks*** due to the antiquated transport facilities, entrance paucity of information and lack of wayside safety and comforts. In spite of such difficulties and risks, the travel and tourism continued. However, for these reasons, the early travels were confined either to the well to do class of society or to highly spirited souls. As of now, the scenario has altogether changed.

Travel, no more, is limited to a few people, rather has turned into a mass movement. It has become a typical expression of the present day society. Every successive year, more and more globe trotters are setting out to discover the unknown, to pursue recreation, pleasure and fun or to just seek a change in environment. This unprecedented increase in tourist traffic has already made tourism, the most flourishing industry of the world that provides job opportunities to millions of people and influences almost every sector of economy the world over. For many countries tourism has become the economic mainstay while for many more it serves as the single largest source of foreign exchange earning. Realising the socio-cultural, political and environmental benefits of tourism besides its economic contributions, tourism now finds a prominent place in the central planning of India. Jammu and Kashmir, lacking in other natural resources is heavily dependent upon tourism for its development which has started giving profits to the Government. **Terrorism in the State, hence, as a matter of fact, cannot stop the inflow of the tourists to the state in future.**

Due to the tireless efforts of the Government, Security Forces and the Public Support in some cases, the insurgency in the State has been put under check and controlled to a great extent from 1995 onwards. Several projects were undertaken by the State/Central Government to revive the beauty of the Valley and to rejuvenate the tourism industry in the State. There is certainly a positive impact of the terrorism on the tourism industry in the State, but the Twenty First century saw a sea change in the tourists' influx to the State, both domestic and international. In the year 2003, The Jammu and Kashmir State has been selected for a Special National Tourism Award for its outstanding performance in tourism promotion. The award was given in recognition of the strategies adopted by Jammu and Kashmir Government to boost tourism. It has also been stated by the State Governor Lt Gen(Retd) SK Sinha that the fear to visit the J&K state due to sporadic acts of violence have gone and these acts by the militants have failed to stop the tourists from coming to visit the State.

Appendix I

Geneological Tree of Dogra Rulers in Jammu and Kashmir

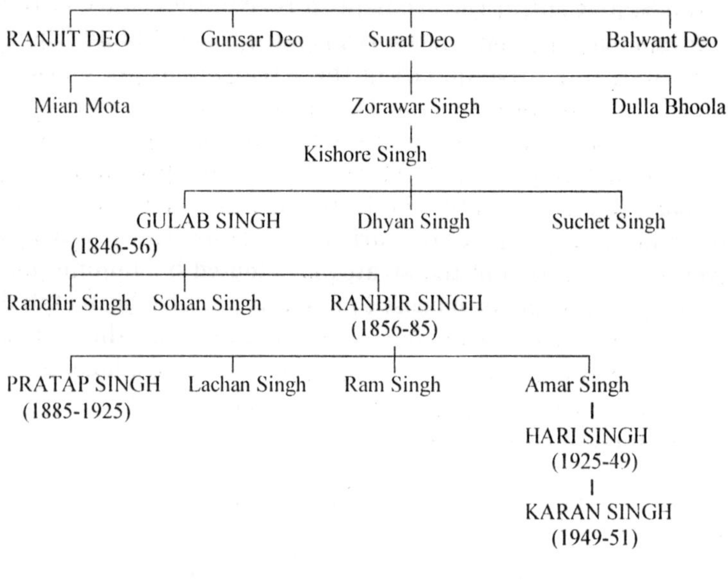

Source : Anand AS, ***The Constitution of Jammu and Kashmir-Its Development and Comments***, Universal Law Publishing Co Pvt Ltd, Delhi, 2004, p.6.

Appendix II

Rice Varieties Cultivated in J&K

Kashmir Region

Season of Cultivation	- Last Week of April to October.	
Varieties Commonly Grown:		
Kashmir Plains	'CH 988',	Niver,
(Very Early and Early)	'CH 972',	'K 84',
	'CH 1039'	'K 116',
	Budgi,	Larbaol.
Kashmir Hills	Niver,	'K 332',
(Early)	Quadir Garai,	'K 333',
	'K 78.13',	
	Madeo,	
	Siga.	

Jammu Division

Season of Cultivation	-	June to November.
Varieties Commonly Grown:		
Very Early	-	'CH 988',
		'CH 1039'
		Ratna,
Medium	-	Jaya,
		Basmati 370,
		Giza 14.

Source: Government of India, ***Hand Book of Agriculture***, Directorate of Information and Publication of Agriculture, September 2003, p.779.

Appendix III

Monuments in Srinagar and Its Vicinity

From	*To*	*Distance*	*Mode of Travelling*	*Remarks*
Srinagar	Sankaracharya temple	2½ miles	By carriages to Mission Hospital and thence on Foot.	
Srinagar	Patthar Masjid, Shah Hamadan's Mosque		By boat to Badhas and thence by carriage to Jama Masjid, or throughout by carriage	3 to 4 hours
	Zain-ul-Abdin's, Hari Parbat Mosque of Madin Sahib Vistar Nag Chasma-I-Shahi		5½ miles by motor road from Srinagar.	
	Pari-Mahal and back	1 ½ miles on foot Chasma-i-Shahi	Srinagar to Harwan by road	11 ½ miles

Contd.

Srinagar	Nishat		2½ miles by motor road
	Shalimar		2 miles by motor road
	Harwan		1½ miles by motor road.

Monuments above Srinagar

From	*To*	*Distance*	*Mode of Travelling*	*Remarks*
Srinagar	Pandretha	3½ miles	Motor road	
	Avantipur	18 miles	Motor road	
	Laduv	16 miles	Road Partly Unmettalled	Tents and necessaries to be taken
Avantipur	Payer and back	12 miles	Briddle-path.	
	Narasthan	20 miles	-do-	
Srinagar	Achhbal	39 miles	Motor road.	
	Martand	39 miles	Motor road.	Rest house at Matan; Dak Bungalows at Achhbal..
Achhbal	Kother and back	6 miles	Motor road and bridle path	
Martand stages	Mammal, two	30 miles	Motor road to Pahalgam, opposite to which, across the stream, is Mammal.	

Contd.

Martand	Bamzu and back	2 miles	Motor road.
Srinagar	Verinag	50 miles	Motor road. Dak Bungalow at Munda within 5 miles.

Monuments Below Srinagar

From	*To*	*Distance*	*Mode of Travelling*	*Remarks*
Srinagar	Parihasapura	14 miles	by the Baramulla cart road, and 3 miles on foot or pony beyond	
	Pattan	17 miles		Rest house
Pattan	Baramulla and Ushkar	17 miles		
Baramulla	Fathgarh	3 miles	over the hill	
Baramulla	Naranthal	3½ miles	on pony	
	Buniar	14 miles		Dak Bungalow at Rampore
Buniar	Bandi temple	9 miles		
Srinagar	Manasbal	18"	by motorable road, or by Boat.	
	Wangath	33 miles	18 miles by motorable Road as far as Wayil, thence Bridle-path.	

Source: ***Sharma, Suresh Kr and Usha,*** *History, Architecture and Tourism of Kashmir- The Architectural Monuments of Kashmir*, Deep and Deep Publications, Jammu, 1996.

Appendix IV

Route Chart: Amarnath Ji Yatra

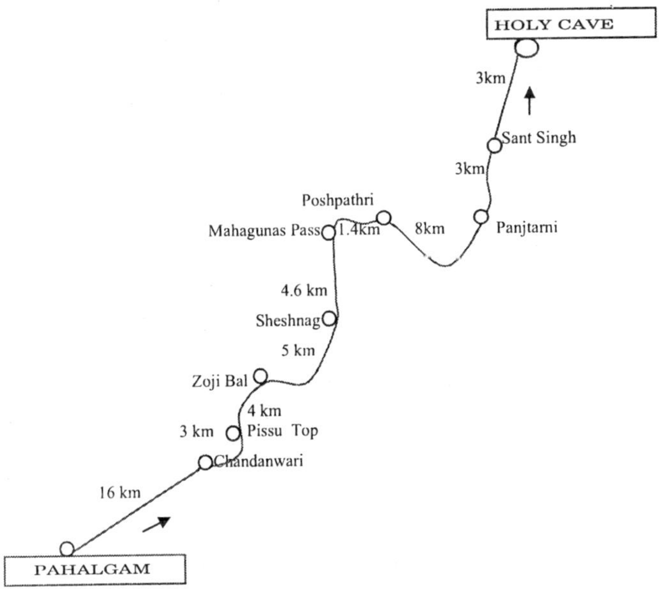

Altitudes

1. Chandanwari - 2895 Mtr.
2. Pissu Top - 3377 Mtr.
3. Sheshnag - 3352 Mtr.
4. Poshpathri - 4114 Mtr.
5. Mahagunas Top - 4276 Mtr.
6. Panjtarni - 3657 Mtr.
7. Holy Cave - 3952 Mtr.

Source: *Amarnath, Trek the Holy Pilgrimage* , Issued by Director Tourism, J&K.

Appendix V

Srinagar-Leh Route Chart

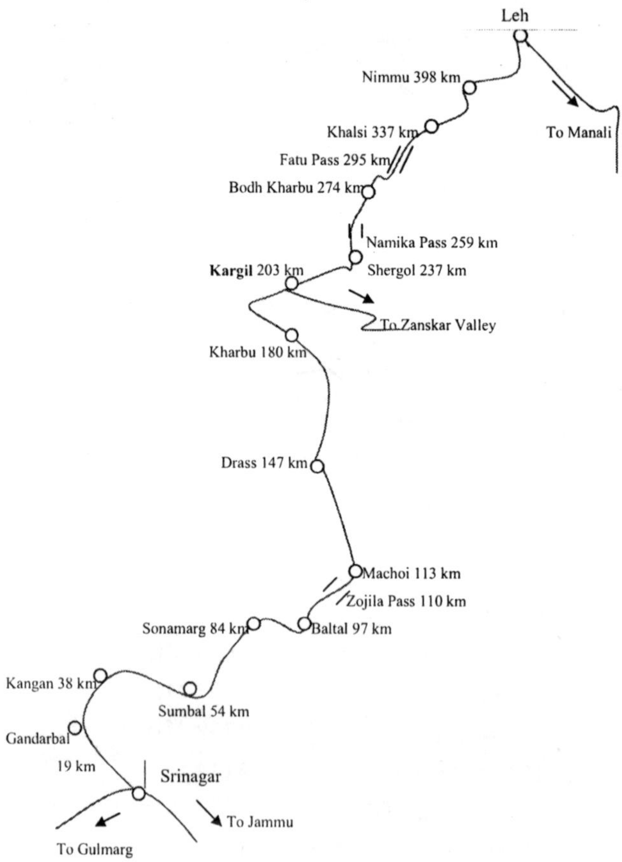

Source: Crowther Geoff, *India, a Survival Kit*, Lonely Planet, 1987, pp.232-233.

Appendix VI

Trekking Routes in Ladakh Region

1. **Base: Sankoo.**

(a)	Sankoo-Stakpa-Umba	-4 hours
(b)	Umba-Umbala (3350 metres) camp	-5 hours
(c)	Umbala Camp-Lamochan-Drass	-4 hours
(d)	Sankoo-Thasgam Valley-Rusila Base	-5 hours
(e)	Rusila Base-Rusila (4930 metres) Sapi	-5 hours
(f)	Shergol-Mulbek via motorable road along right bank of Wakha river.	- 1 hour

These treks can be combined together to make a weeklong trekking programme from Drass to Mulbek, by-passing Kargil. From Mulbek one can take a bus to Leh or back to Kargil.

2. **Base: Panikhar.**

The main treks originating from Panikhar lead to different points in the Kashmir and Kishtwar valleys, across the main ridge of the Great Himalayan Range. The first few stages are common to all, till access to the head of the Warvan valley is gained. It is from the Upper Warvan that different routes are to be followed for different destinations. The first five stages are as follows:

(a)	Panikhar-Chelong Valley-Dunara (Sumdo)	-4 hours
(b)	Dunara (Sumdo)-Bhotkol Pass (4600 m) -Kanital Camp	-8 hours
(c)	Kanital-Humpet Camp	-4 hours

(d) Humpet-Sukhnis Village -6 hours

(e) Sukhnis-Inshan Village -7 hours

From Inshan one can either trek up the Margan Pass and descend to Lehinvan in the Kashmir Valley or follow the Warvan Valley downstream to reach Kishtwar in the Chenab Valley.

To Kashmir:

(a) Inshan –Margan Pass (3380m) -Camp Lehinvan -6 hours

(b) Camp Lehinvan to Srinagar-By road transport

To Kishtwar:

(a) Inshan-Yordu -7 hours

(b) Yurdo-Hanzal/Sondar -4-5 hours

(c) Hanzal/Sondar-Ikhala to Kishtwar (by bus) -6 hours

To Pahalgam:

The Pahalgam trek branches off from Humpet instead of following the Warvan Valley to Inshan. The stages are as follows:

(a) Panikhar to Humpet in 3 stages as described above;

(b) Humpet-Permandal -5-6 hours

(c) Permandal-Gulol Gali (4500m) Sheshnag 5-6 hours

(d) Sheshnag-Chandanwari -5-6 hours

(e) Chandanwari-Pahalgam -By road transport

3.**Base: Rangdum**:

Two trails originate from Rangdum: one across the Kanji La and through the Kanji Gorge to Henaskut on the Kargil-Leh highway; and the second, more difficult Himalayan traverse involves crossing the glaciated Chillung La behind the Nun Kun massif to terminate in the Kishtwar Valley. The trekking itineraries are as follows:

(a) Rangdum-Henaskut Trek.

Rangdum-Rusgogdo	- 5 hours
Rusgogdo-Kanjila Base	- 5 hours
Kanjila Base-Kanjila (5270m)-Camp	- 7 hours
Camp-Kanji Village	- 4 hours
Henaskut to Kargil or Leh	-By road transport

(b) Rangdum-Kishtwar Trek.

Rangdum-Tashi Tongze-Chillungla Base	-5 hours
Base-Chillungla (5200m)-Sar Camp	-4 hours
Sar Camp-Mandiksar Camp	-6 hours
Mandiksar-Fariabad	-6 hours
Fariabad-Metwan	-4 hours
Metwan-Tatapani	-4 hours
Tatapani-Yurdo	-4 hours
Yurdo-Sondar	-5 hours
Sondar-Ikhala-Kishtwar	-6 hours (By bus)

(c) Rangdum-Penzi La Trek.

Rangdum-Tashi Tongze-Penzi La Base	-4 hours
Penzi La-Base Penzi La- Drang Drung Glacier	-6 hours
Drang Drung-Rangdum (return)	-6 hours or 2 hours by road transport.

4.**Base: Padum(3505m)**.

Four major treks involving crossing of the main mountain ranges originate from Padum. These are as follows:

(a) Padum-Manali Trek.

Padum-Muney/Raru	- 6 hours
Raru-Purney	- 6 hours
Purney-Phugthal Gompa-Purney	- 5 hours
Purney-Kargyak	- 6 hours

Karghyak-Lakung (Singkun La Base (5100m)-Ramjak	- 7 hours
Ramjak-Darcha	- 7 hours
Darcha-Manali	- By bus in 7 hours

(b) Padum-Lamayuru Trek.

Padum-Pishu (by road via Zangla)	
Pishu-Hanamur	- 5 hours
Hanamur-Snertse	- 5 hours
Snertse-Haluma La(4800m)-Lingshet	- 6 hours
Lingshet-Singey La Base	- 5-6 hours
Singey La Base-Singey La(5060m) -Photoksar	- 5-6 hours
Photoksar-Sirsir La(4805m)-Hanupata	- 6 hours
Hanupata-Wanla	- 5 hours
Wanla-Prinkiti La (3726m)-Lamayuru	- 4 hours

(c) Padum-Kishtwar Trek.

Padum-Ating (by road transport)	- 22 kms
Ating-Huttra	- 6 hours
Huttra-Omasi La(5434m)-Bujwas	- 10 hours
Bujwas-Machail	- 8 hours
Machail-Atholi	- 6 hours
Atholi-Kishthwar	-By road transport

(d) Padum-Hemis via Markha Valley.

This hard but exciting trek is recommended from late August onwards till late September because between Zangla and Markha many streams have to be crossed and re-crossed enroute, and in summer the water level is too high to negotiate.

Padum-Stongde-Zangla (By road transport)	-4 hours
Zangla-Chharchar La Base	-4 hours
Chharchar La Base (5170m)-Chhup Chak	-7 hours
Tomto-Tilat Sumdo-Kurma Sumdo	-6 hours

Kurma Sumdo-Rebrang	-5 hours
Rebrang-Rebrangla (3900m)-Thaltak Baho	-5 hours
Thaltak Baho-Umlung	-5 hours
Umlumg-Nimaling	-4 hours
Nimaling-Kongmaru La(5230m) -Camp below Kongmaru La	-4 hours
Camp-Chhogdo	-4 hours
Hemis-Leh	-By road transport

In addition to the above treks, several internal round treks are also available from Padum. Detailed briefings about these circuits may be requested from the Tourist Offices at Kargil, Leh and Padum. There are also several less beaten tracks across the Himalayan range on the one hand and the Zanskar Mountains on the other. Guides well-versed about these treks may be required to be engaged from Padum.

Source: *Kargil-Zanaskar (Ladakh)*, J&K Tourism Department, Jan 2003.

Appendix VII

Mountaineering in Ladakh Region

The Suru and Zanskar Valleys are adorned with a number of majestic mountain peaks, which attract climbers from all over the world. In particular, the Nun-Kun massif serves as the focus of increasing mountaineering activities in the region. Its easy accessibility by road and the shortest possible approach to reach the base camps makes the Nun-Kun massif one of the most attractive mountaineering destinations in the Western Himalayas. Nearby is the Zanskar massif with several challenging peaks surrounding the Drang-Drung Glacier, adjoining Penzi-La. This massif too is accessible by road up to the base of the glacier and the approach trek to the base camp is at a day's trek from the road head.

Nun-Kun Massif

The most frequented climbing area, the Nun-Kun massif comprises several peaks, chief among them being Nun(7135m) and Kun(7087m). Kun was the first to be conquered in 1913 by the Italian mountaineer Piacenza, while Nun, the highest summit of the massif, was first scaled by the Swiss climber, Madame Claude Kogan in 1953.

The Massif falls on the Kargil-Zanskar road. It is approached both from Tangol(70 kms from Kargil) and Gulmatongo (110 km from Kargil), depending upon the route of ascent allotted by the Indian Mountaineering Foundation. Some approaches are also made from Parkachik (90 kms south of Kargil) along the Parkachik glacier. The approach from Gulmatongo involves crossing the Suru river over a footbridge.

The base camp can be reached after a day's trek both from Gulmatongo and Tangol.

Other known peaks in the massif are Pinnacle (6930m), While-Needle (5600m), Z-1(6400m) and D-41 (5600m). In addition, there are many unnamed peaks in the altitude range of 5500m to 6509m in the same area. Adjacent to the Nun-Kun massif is the Bobank Peak(5971m), which is also frequented by foreign climbing expeditions. It is approached via the Chelong Valley, westward of Panikhar.

The Zanskar Group

This massif lies adjacent to the Nun-Kun massif. Most frequented area in this group is along the Drang-Drung Glacier below Penzi-la, on the Kargil-Zanskar road. Its base camp can be approached in a day's trek from the road head. The best known peaks in the group are Z-2(6175m), Z-3(6270m) and Z-8(6050m). In addition, there are many unnamed peaks in the area in the altitude range of 5000m to 6000m.

The climbing period in the region extends from early June to mid–October, the main climbing period being June-August when most of the Himalayas elsewhere remain inaccessible due to the monsoon, while the Ladakh Himalayas are unaffected.

Permission for Expedition

Every foreign mountaineering expedition has to obtain permission in writing from the Government of India through the Indian Mountaineering Foundation. A booking fee depending upon the height of the peak is charged and a Liaison Officer is deputed with each climbing team. A list of peaks and application forms, etc, can be obtained from Indian Mountaineering Foundation, Benito Juarez Road, New Delhi-110021. Tele: 011 2671211, 2622245.

Source: *Kargil-Zanaskar (Ladakh)*, J&K Tourism Department, Jan 2003.

Appendix VIII

Organisational Chart of Tourism

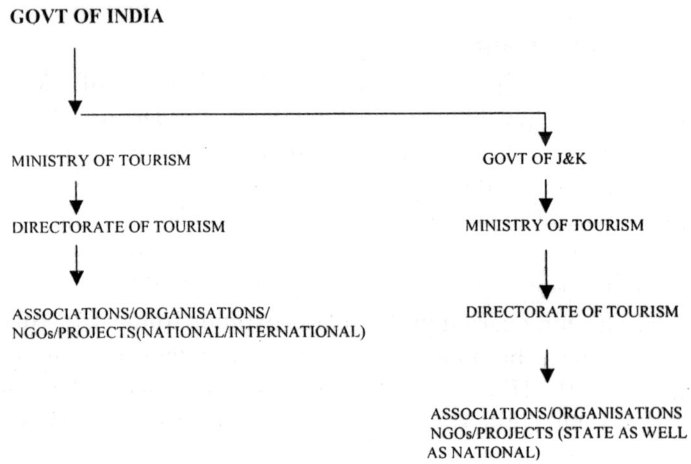

Appendix IX

J&K Feel Good Factor : Tourism

Name of Corporation	**Loss (in crores)**
J&K Industry	Rs. 2729.91
J&K Small Scale Industry Development Corporation	Rs. 98.75
J&K Handicrafts (SE) Corp	Rs. 483.93
J&K Minerals Ltd	Rs. 2700.73
J&K Handloom Development Corp	Rs. 701.00
J&K State Industrial Dev Corp	Rs. 573.00
J&K Women Development Corp	Rs. 31.20
J&K SC/ST/OBC Development Corp	Rs. 98.99
J&K Agro Dev Industries Corp	Rs. 184.59
J&K Horticulture Pro and Mktg Corp	Rs. 1424.62
J&K Financial Corporation	Rs. 1146.91
J&K Power Development Corp	Rs. 464.18
J&K State Road Transport Corp	Rs. 4722.00
Money-Spinning Projects	
Name of Corporation	**Profit**(in crores)
J&K Cements Ltd	Rs. 225.47
J&K Cable Car Corporation Ltd	**Rs. 9.39**
J&K Projects Const Corp Ltd	Rs. 100.00
J&K Tourism Development Corporation	**Rs. 16.30**

Appendix X

Road to Peace Between India and Pakistan

There is a marked improvement in the relations between India and Pakistan in the recent years after prolonged tension between both the counties following the attack on Indian Parliament in December 2001 which is evident from the following events:

April 2003: Former Indian Prime Minister Atal Behari Vajpayee offers the "Hand of friendship" to Pakistan in a landmark address in Kashmir. He was speaking after months of tension following an attack on the Indian Parliament in December 2001.

May 2003: India announces the resumption of a bus service between Delhi and Lahore. Both sides name high commissioners. Delhi says it will release Pakistani prisoners after a similar move by Islamabad.

August 2003: For the first time in history, Indians and Pakistanis hold joint independence day celebrations.

November 2003: The two countries order troops to halt firing along the LoC.

December 2003: India and Pakistan agree to resume direct air links from January 01 after a two-year ban.

January 2004: At a regional summit in Islamabad, President Musharraf spends an hour with Vajpayee, their first meeting in nearly three years.

February 2004: India and Pakistan begin their first formal talks in nearly three years.

March 2004: Around 30,000 cricket fans watch India beat Pakistan in their first tour of Pakistan since 1989.

May 2004: Pakistan welcomes a pledge made by Prime Minister Manmohan to seek friendly relations.

June 2004: India and Pakistan renew a ban on nuclear weapons tests and set up a hotline to alert each other of potential nuclear risks.

September 2004: The two countries' foreign ministers meet in Delhi and Musharraf and Manmohan Singh meet in New York. For the first time, leaders of both countries discuss "options" to solve the Kashmir dispute.

October 2004: Musharraf unveils some radical proposals to bring an end to the dispute.

November 2004: India begins to withdraw some troops as Manmohan Singh visits Kashmir and announces a Rs. 24,000 crore package for the state.

Source: **Roy Ranjan,** *Sunday Times of India*, **New Delhi/ Chandigarh, 21 November 2004, p.6.**

Appendix XI

PM's Kashmir Visit

Even before Prime Minister Manmohan Singh landed in Srinagar on 17 November 2004, he had taken one of the biggest steps by an Indian leader to reduce tensions in the Valley since terrorist violence spiraled out of control in 1989. By announcing the scaling down of troops in the Valley, the PM signaled that he was ready to smoke the peace pipe provided Pakistan kept puffing it too and stuck to its commitment made to India on cross-border terrorism. For separatist groups, including the Hurriyat, the PM sent a clear message that while he was willing to talk to everyone unconditionally, there would be no further cajoling to bring them to the negotiating table. Nor would they be allowed to place conditions like a visit to Islamabad. The following are the signals of PM during his visit to J&K:

(a) **Troops Withdrawal:** Army presence in the Valley will be scaled down. Presently, there are about five lakh troops in J&K. About 40,000 troops will be withdrawn.

(b) **Infrastructure Development:** Rs 24,000 crore to be invested in infrastructural development of the State over the next four years.

(c) **Peace Talks:** Government willing to talk to all factions, including the Hurriyat, without any preconditions.

(d) **Border Redefinition:** No redrawing of the international border. Any proposal that involves further division is not acceptable to India.

(e) **Unemployment:** Creation of 24,000 government jobs and employment for 14,000 women in anganwadis.

The PM urged the unemployed youth "who have deviated from their path and taken up guns" to come forward and join the mainstream. He also asserted that those who are using terrorism as a tool to get their political aspirations fulfilled, "will not succeed". "We are not going to bow down before terrorism", he said.

Source: Wani Izhar Ahmed, *India Today*, 29 November 2004, pp.30-32 and Tikoo Aarti, *The Times of India*, New Delhi/ Chandigarh, 19 November 2004, p.1.

Appendix XII

Questionnaire

Major P Rajan, a Post-Graduate in Defence Studies from University of Madras and Diploma in Creative Writing in English from Indira Gandhi National Open University is presently posted somewhere in Jammu Region of J & K. He is a registered scholar of **M.Phil (Tourism Management)** from Madurai Kamaraj University, Madurai (TN) under the guidance and supervision of **Dr. R. Soundararajan, M.A, M.Phil, M.Ed, Dip in Arch, Ph.D**, Professor and Academic Coordinator, Department of Tourism Management, Madurai Kamaraj University. The topic registered in the University for his dissertation is **"Impact of Terrorism on Jammu and Kashmir Tourism : A Case Study Analysis"**. The queries relating to the above study aims to collect a complete, valid and reliable information from the following segments of the people who are associated with the topic:

a. Queries to the Tourist.

b. Queries to the Layman residing in/around the Tourist Spots.

c. Queries to the Security Forces/Government Officials.

The Scholar and the Guide request the concerned to kindly fill in their valuable answers in the appropriate columns. There is no need to write your name. Data will be kept confidential.

Queries to the Tourist

1. Please record your personal details:

   a. Age ______ Years b. Gender: Male/Female

   c. Profession: Employed/Business/Retired/Student/Any Other__________

d. Address:District and State ______________________

e. Are You a Regular Visitor to tourist/pilgrimage spots of J&K? Yes/No. If Yes, how often____________

f. How big is the party (family or group) you are in this Visit: ______________

2. What is your Purpose of Visit?
   - a. On Holiday.
   - b. Sight Seeing
   - c. Pilgrimage
   - d. Entertainment

3. What was your mind set before coming to J&K?
   - a. Fearful
   - b. Worrisome
   - c. Normal
   - d: Exciting

4. How are you feeling after arriving in J&K?
   - a. Fearful
   - b. Worrisome
   - c. Normal
   - d. Exciting

5. How do you feel about the Security Arrangements in J&K especially in Tourist Spots:
   - a. Excellent
   - b. Adequate
   - c. Insufficient

6. What is your Opinion about the Security Check:
   - a. Good; Security Check is Essential.
   - b. Troublesome; It is not required for Tourists.
   - c. Boring; These checks put your mood off.

7. What is your expectations about the Security Arrangements?
   - a. Security Arrangements are Adequate, No more expectations.
   - b. They are good but the Forces need more coordination among themselves.
   - C. Security Check System is very conventional, need more equipment to effectiveness.
   - D. Security arrangements should be thoroughly more vigilant.

8. What is your satisfaction level of the Security Arrangements in J&K?

   a. Excellent b. Good

   c. Adequate d. Poor

9. If your reply to question No 8 is 'Poor', please state reason:

----

10. Because of terrorism in J&K, do you feel not visiting the State again:

    a. Yes, I will not take chance again.

    b. No. There is nothing to bother about as everything is normal here for a visitor.

    c. Terrorism has nothing to do with my visiting again to J&K.

    d. I have confidence in our Security System, I will have no problem visiting again.

Queries to the Layman Residing in/around the Tourist Spot

1. Please record your personal details:

   a. Age ______ Years b. Gender: Male/Female

   c. Profession: Employed/Business/Retired/Student/Any Other___________

   d. Address:District & State ____________________

2. How long are you living in this area?

   ____________Years.

3. What is the Size of your Family? ___________Elders and __________ Children.

4. Do you feel there is an impact of terrorism on tourism of this place, if so at what level?

   a. Yes. ______________________________

   b. No. There is no change in the influx of the visitors.

5. Do you and your family feel secured living in a Tourist Spot because of militancy in the State?

a. Yes. I am secured in this place, I have confidence in our Security System.

b. No. There is no security to the layman, we are at the disposal of the God.

c. Can't say .... Till now there is no such problem in our locality.

6. What is your opinion about our Security Forces?

a. They are good, professional and instill confidence in all of us.

b. They are strict and put us to lot of inconvenience, even do not consider the constraints of locals.

c. They are just duty bound and do not have humane approach to the locals.

d. They are troubling the locals for want of information about militants.

e. They are basically show pieces, a deterrent to militant attacks.

f. Any other____________________________

7. Is there any inconvenience caused to you or your family members or to your village members by Militants?

a. No, there is no disturbance to us from militants.

b. Yes, there are/were some disturbance to our villagers from militants.

c. There is no such militancy in this area.

8. Is there any inconvenience caused to you or your family members or to your village members by Security Forces?

a. No, there is no inconvenience to us from Security Forces.

b. Yes, there are/were inconvenience in the form of Security Checks, due to which we got delayed to our work.

c. Yes, there are/were cases of interrogation of villagers in search of terrorists.

d. Any other____________________________

9. Do you think Terrorists take asylum in the name of Tourists in this place:
   a. No, there is no such cases known to me.
   b. Yes, there are chances but not confirmed.
   c. Yes, there have been some such cases in the past.
10. Do you recommend any Security Arrangements to safeguard the interest of the Tourists as well the locals?
   a. Yes. ______________________
   b. No, I think the present system is sufficient.

Queries to the Members of the Security Forces/ Government Officials

1. Please record your personal details:
   a. Age ______ Years b. Gender: Male/Female
   c. Profession: Army/BSF/CRPF/Civil Police/Retired/Govt Officials
   d. Address:Unit ______________________
2. What is the prime role of Security Forces in Tourist Spots:
   a. Security of the Tourists.
   b. Security of the Monuments/Properties etc.
   c. Security of the entire Area.
   d. All of the above.
3. Do You feel the Security Arrangements in the State especially Tourist Spots are fool- proof?
   a. Yes. The Security Arrangements are adequate.
   b. No, We need more participation by Civil Police and Civilians.
   c. Any other______________________
4. What is the difficulty in managing Security in Tourist Spots?
   a. There is no such management problem.
   b. Tourists are generally outsiders, hence chances of terrorists visiting such places as tourists can't be ruled out.

c. There is shortage of Security Forces.

d. There is lack of co-operation from tourists as well as the locals.

e. Any other ____________________

5. What is the inconvenience caused to the tourists while executing the security tasks?

a. Tourists don't like to be checked.

b. Tourists don't cooperate with Security Forces.

c. Tourists feel uneasiness to undergo security procedures.

d. Any other____________________

6. What is the inconvenience caused to the Security Forces while executing tasks?

a. It is a thankless job, every tourist dislike to be checked.

b. Security Men bored of the same routine, without any fruitful result.

c. The influx of tourists at certain places are more and the number of Security personnel are very less to carryout 100 per cent task leading to failure in the duty.

d. Any other____________________

7. What is the incentive of the State Government for the forces deployed in such duties?

a. No incentive.

b. Yes... if any____________________

8. What is the general policy/strategy of protection to the people?

a. Nothing special, it is part of counter terrorism operations.

b. A special care is required when dealing with civilian people that too when they are on recreation/holidaying, hence a humane touch in our operational style.

c. Any other____________________

9. What is the level of the information input about terrorists in the area from the locals?
   a. Adequate.
   b. Negligible.
   c. No input.
10. Do you feel the presence of Security Forces in tourist spots are mandatory in J&K?
   a. Yes, because of certain incidents in the recent past.
   b. No,...give reason________________________

Annexure 1

Sketch of Jammu and Kashmir Showing Actual Positions

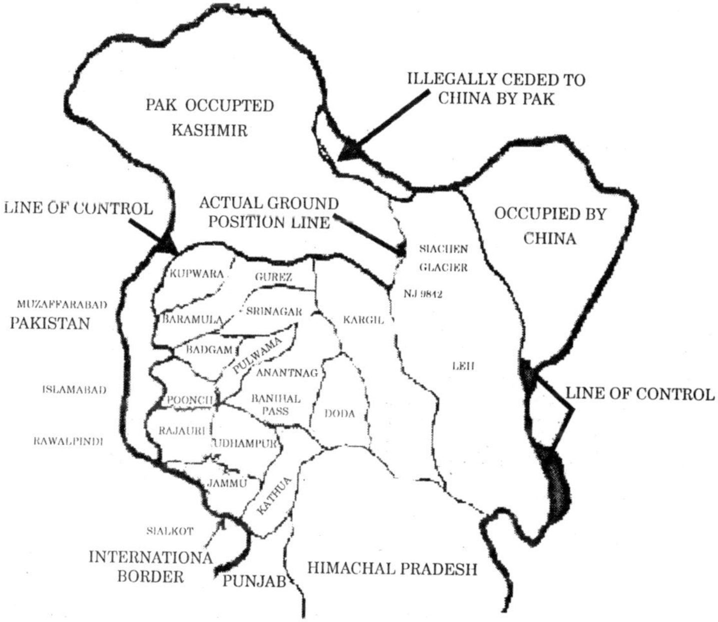

Not to Scale

Source: www.Kashmir-information.com

Annexure 2

Map of J&K Showing International Boundary

Map 1

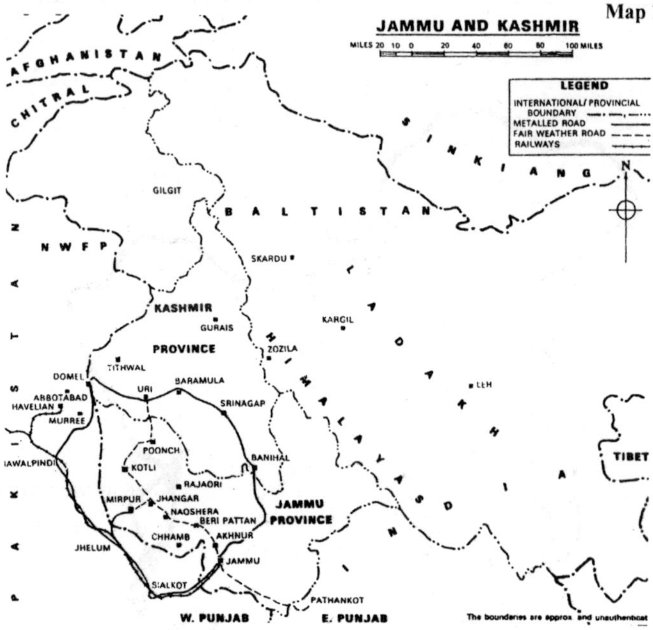

Source: Vas E.A., Without Baggage, Natraj Publishers, 1987, P.2.

Annexure 3

Communal Groupings in the State

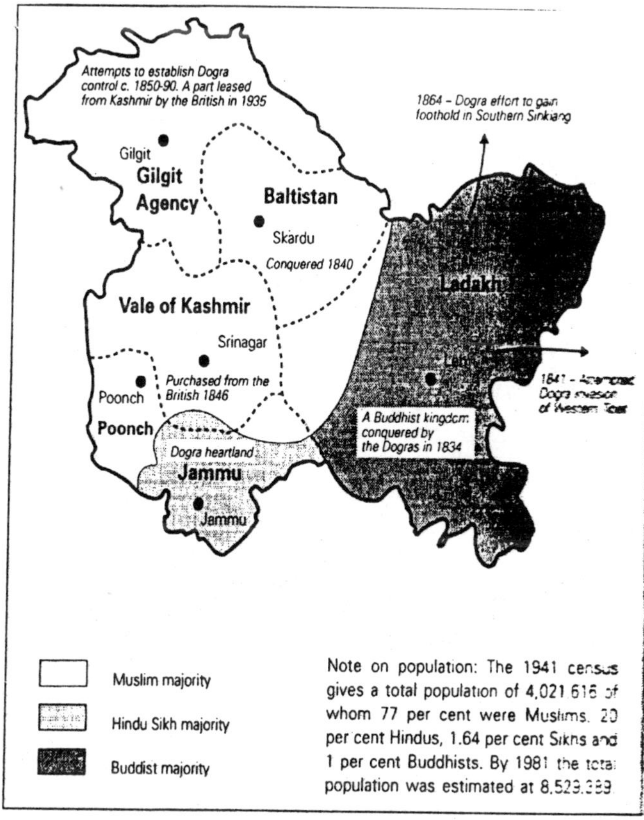

3. The Creation of the State of Jammu and Kashmir with Communal Groupings (Source: Alastair Lamb, *Crisis in Kashmir*, London 1966)

Annexure 4

An Independent State of J&K Sourced by JKLF

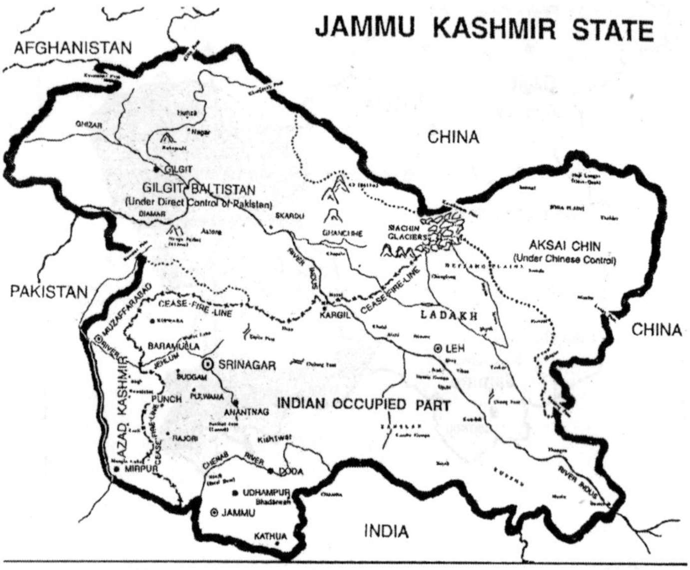

). An Independent State of Jammu and Kashmir? (Source: Jammu and Kashmir Liberation Front)

Source: Schofield Victoria, Kashmir in the Cross fire, Viva Books, 1997, P. 255.

Annexure 5

Map Showing Jammu Region

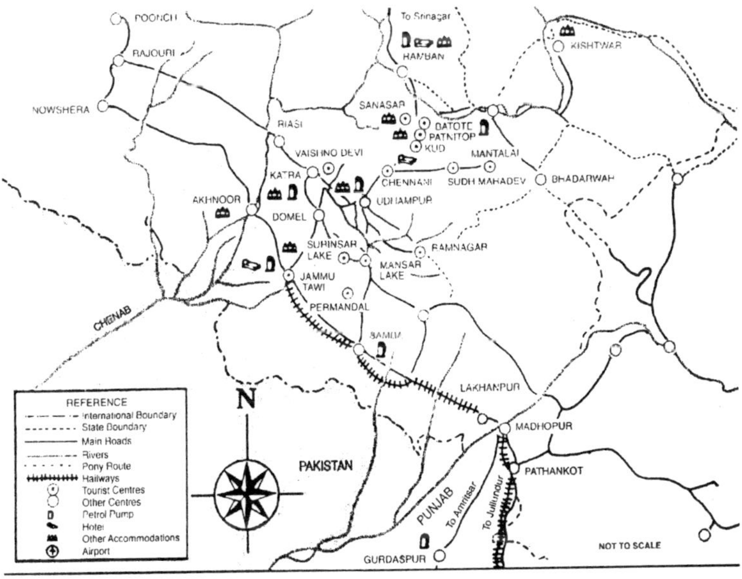

Annexure 6

Map Showing Kashmir Region

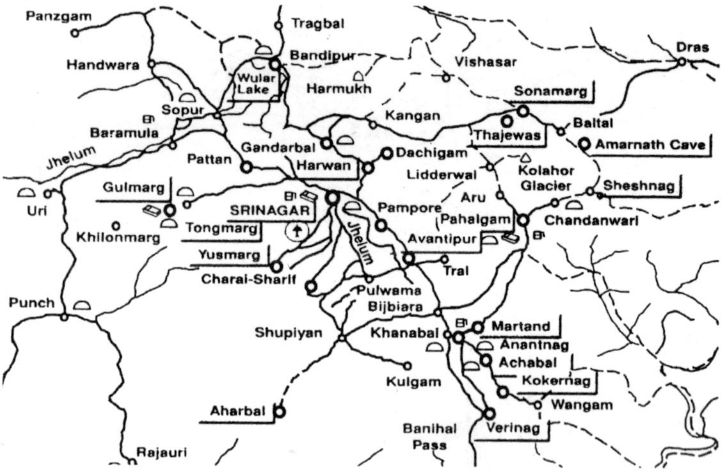

Annexure 7

Major Infiltration Routes

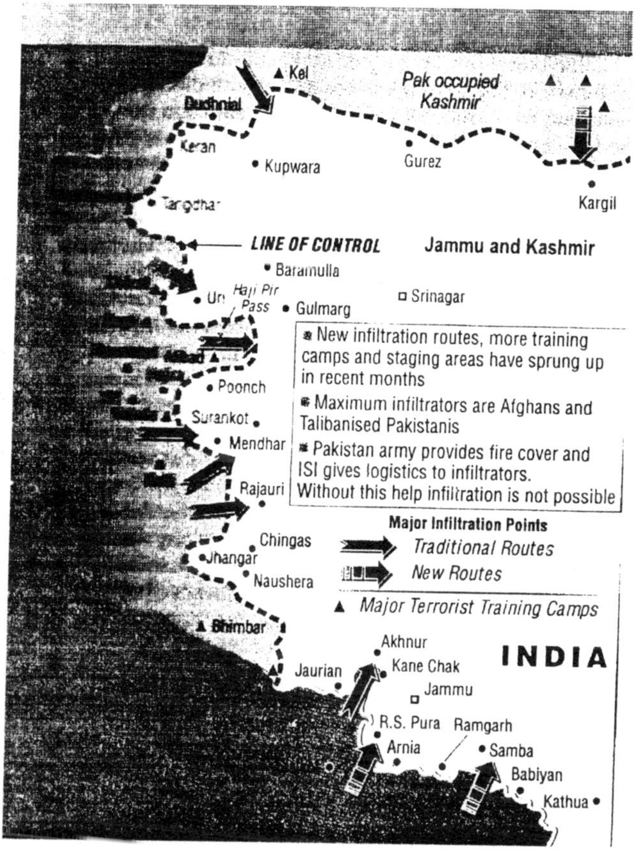

Source: Sood VK and Sawhney Pravin, *OPERATION PARAKRAM* The War Unfinished, SAGE Publications, 2003, P. 33.

Table 1.1

Area and Population

Jammu and Kashmir At a Glance

Area

i.	Area in sq kms	222236#
ii.	No. of Districts	14
iii.	No. of Tehsils	59
iv.	No. of C. D Blocks	621
v.	No. of Panchayats (provisional)	2661
vi.	No. of Villages	6652
vii.	No. of Urban Areas	68
viii.	No. of Urban Agglomeration	07

Population

			Persons	*Males*	*Females*
1.	Population				
		Total	10069917	5300574	4769343
		Rural	7564608	3925846	3638762
		Urban	2505309	1374728	1130581
2	Population Growth 1981-2001 Absolute.				
		Total	4082528	2135914	1946614
		Rural	2837622	1433433	1404189
		Urban	1244906	702481	542425

Contd.

3.	Percentage Growth				
		Total	68.19	67.49	68.96
		Rural	60.03	57.51	62.84
		Urban	98.77	104.50	92.22
4.	Percentage of Rural-Urban Population to Total population				
		Total	100.00	100.00	100.00
		Rural	75.12	74.06	76.29
		Urban	24.88	25.94	23.71
5.	Literates Absolute				
		Total	4704252	2999353	1704899
		Rural	3081972	2005936	1076036
		Urban	1622280	993417	628863
6.	Literacy Rate (Excluding 0-6 Population)				
		Total	54.46	65.75	41.82
		Rural	48.22	60.34	35.09
		Urban	72.17	80.30	62.22
7.	0-6 Population (Absolute)				
		Total	1431182	738839	692343
		Rural	1173672	601271	572401
		Urban	257510	137568	119942
8.	Percentage of Child Population to Total Population				
		Total	14.21	13.94	14.52
		Rural	15.52	15.32	15.73
		Urban	10.28	10.01	10.61
9.	Sex Ratio (0-6 Population) (Females per 1000 Males				
		Total	937		
		Rural	952		
		Urban	872		

Contd.

10. Density (Per Sq. Kms.)		
	Total	99
	Rural	75
	Urban	2637
11. Sex Ratio (Females per 1000 males)		
	Total	900
	Rural	927
	Urban	822

Source : Census 2001.

#(a) Includes 78114 Sq Kms under illegal occupation of Pakistan and 5180 Sq Kms illegally handed over by Pakistan to China and 37555 Sq Kms under illegal occupation of China in Leh (Ladakh) District.

#(b) The population figures exclude population of areas under unlawful occupation of Pakistan and China where Census could not be taken.

Table No 1.2

Yatries Visiting Vaishno Devi Ji and Amar Nath Ji Holy Caves

(Yatries in Lakh Numbers)

S/No	*Year*	*Amar Nath Ji Holy Cave*	*Vaishno Devi Ji*
1	2	3	4
1.	1950-51	NA	0.03
2.	1955-56	NA	0.06
3.	1960-61	0.04 (1963)	1.60
4.	1965	0.07	2.30
5.	1967	0.08	2.12
6.	1974	0.07	5.81
7.	1977	0.12	8.16

Contd.

8.	1978	0.14	8.82
9.	1980	0.20	12.13
10.	1985	0.42	14.85
11.	1986	0.51	13.95
12.	1987	0.52	18.57
13.	1988	0.96	19.92
14.	1989	0.95	23.12
15.	1990	0.05	21.69
16.	1991	0.16	31.15
17.	1992	0.55	35.16
18.	1993	0.56	33.68
19.	1994	0.47	37.04
20.	1995	0.60	40.12
21.	1996	1.20	43.35
22.	1997	0.79	44.34
23.	1998	1.50	46.22
24.	1999	1.14	46.70
25.	2000	1.73	52.17
26.	2001	1.19	50.57
27.	2002	1.11	44.32
28.	2003	1.53	54.00
29.	2004	4.00	61.10
30.	2005	4.00	(Till July) 35.68

Source: Director Tourism J&K

Table No 1.3

Tourists Visiting Kashmir Valley

(Tourists in Thousands)

Year	*Indian*	*Non-Indian*	*Total*
1	2	3	4
1951	9.33	1.25	10.58
1955	48.19	2.83	51.02
1960	63.37	11.19	74.56
1965	35.70	7.43	43.13
1969	129.75	19.95	149.70
1974	148.32	19.30	167.62
1978	443.34	59.32	502.66
1980	548.49	46.03	594.52
1985	465.60	32.02	503.62
1995	0.32	8.20	8.52
1996	0.37	9.59	9.96
1997	7.02	9.11	16.13
1998	99.64	10.25	109.89
1999	199.90	15.99	215.89
2000	104.34	7.58	111.92
2001	66.73	5.86	72.59
2002	24.67	2.68	27.35
2003	182.20	8.96	191.16
2004	358.10	18.63	376.73

Source : Director Tourism J&K

Table No 1.4

Country-wise Number of Foreign Tourists Visiting Kashmir Valley

(Tourists in Thousands)

S.No		*Country*										
		1971	*1978*	*1980*	*1985*	*1995*	*1996*	*1997*	*1998*	*1999*	*2000*	*2001*
1	*2*	*3*	*4*	*5*	*6*	*7*	*8*	*9*	*10*	*11*	*12*	*13*
1.	Canada	0.43	1.53	1.36	1.10	0.15	0.25	0.11	0.20	0.44	0.20	0.08
2.	U.S.A.	5.63	13.68	7.44	7.25	0.52	0.51	0.41	0.59	0.71	0.50	0.51
3.	France	1.45	4.43	5.35	3.63	0.47	0.36	0.32	0.71	1.00	0.26	0.18
4.	Germany	NA	4.62	4.28	2.92	0.52	0.43	0.42	0.55	0.98	0.46	0.29
5.	Italy	0.36	2.38	1.54	1.47	0.65	0.47	0.63	0.94	0.43	0.22	0.22
6.	Netherlands	0.37	1.45	0.82	0.76	0.11	0.06	0.03	0.02	0.43	0.11	0.04
7.	Spain	0.03	1.71	2.28	1.41	0.12	0.11	0.10	0.10	0.27	0.08	0.10
8.	Switzerland	0.42	2.63	0.93	0.80	0.35	0.20	0.04	0.05	0.35	0.11	0.29
9.	Russia	0.03	0.65	0.40	0.01	0.01	0.02	0.09	0.15	0.09	0.02	0.02
10.	SouthAfrica	0.36	0.64	1.14	1.15	0.11	0.09	0.12	0.14	0.66	0.13	0.09
11.	Malaysia	0.18	0.38	0.54	0.19	0.37	0.54	0.57	0.17	0.28	0.12	0.11
12.	Japan	0.68	0.97	1.26	1.03	0.36	0.38	0.35	0.35	0.53	0.37	0.29
13.	Australia	0.73	4.30	2.98	3.57	0.26	0.22	0.20	0.20	0.36	0.23	0.17
14.	New Zealand	0.08	1.27	0.79	0.46	0.08	0.14	0.05	0.05	0.50	0.06	0.02
15.	Iran	0.07	0.57	1.01	0.15	-	-	-	-	-	-	-
16.	Belgium	0.14	0.87	0.69	0.74	0.19	0.09	0.08	0.20	0.31	0.41	0.18
17.	U.K.	2.10	10.20	6.89	7.18	1.61	2.13	0.49	0.55	0.84	0.43	0.42
18.	Sweden	0.07	0.75	0.21	0.24	0.54	0.81	0.35	0.16	0.28	0.08	0.07
19.	Others	2.11	6.29	6.12	4.96	1.78	2.78	4.75	5.12	7.53	3.79	2.78
	Total	**15.24**	**59.32**	**46.06**	**38.02**	**8.20**	**9.59**	**9.11**	**10.25**	**15.99**	**7.58**	**5.86**

Source: Director Tourism J&K

Table No 1.5

No of Tourists Visiting Ladakh Region

Year	*Foreigners*	*Indian*	*Total No of Tourists*
1974	500	27	527
1975	650	128	778
1976	1798	253	2051
1977	7126	266	7392
1978	8748	873	9621
1979	9213	621	9831
1980	13104	1013	14117
1981	14000	-	14000
1982	12786	-	2786
1983	12833	-	12833
1984	11785	-	11785
1985	12245	6666	18911
1986	12828	3683	16511
1987	13668	4114	17802
1988	16256	8608	24864
1989	16079	6669	22748
1990	6342	396	6738
1991	8014	1041	9055
1992	3580	2438	16018
1993	12401	2000	14401
1994	15369	2080	17449
1995	12391	5594	17985
1996	13036	3537	16573
1997	12810	3991	16801
1998	15238	6792	22030
1999	9669	1905	11574
2000	11825	6217	18042
2001	15439	4260	19699
2002	5120	2959	8079
2003	15371	13031	28402
2004	21608	13483	35091
2005 (Till July)	10617	4000	14617

Graph No 1

Graphical Representation of Terrorist Incidents in J&K 1988-2004

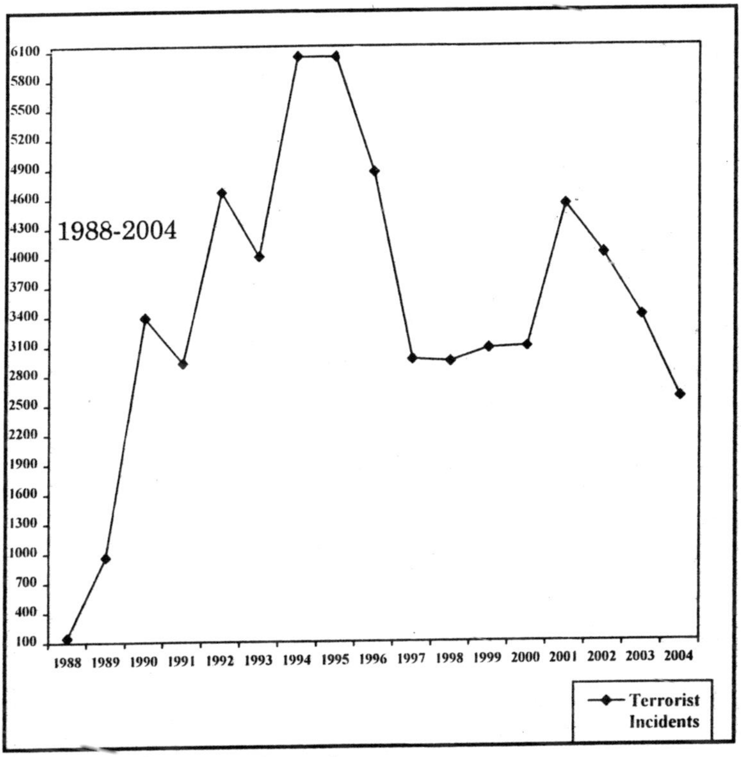

Source: CID Headquarters, Jammu

Graph No 2

Graphical Representation of Militants Killed in J&K 1990-2004

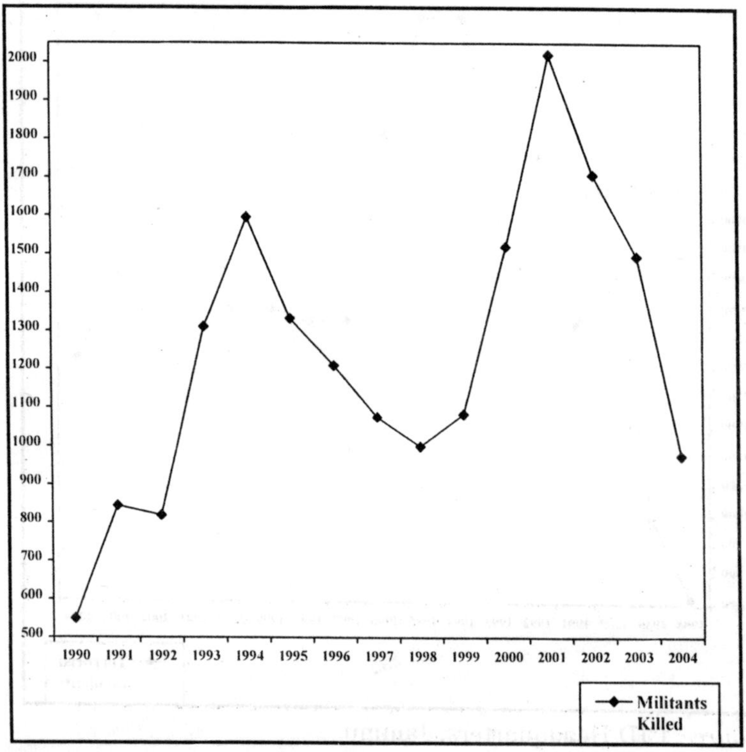

Source: CID Headquarters, Jammu

Graph No 3

Attacks on Security Forces

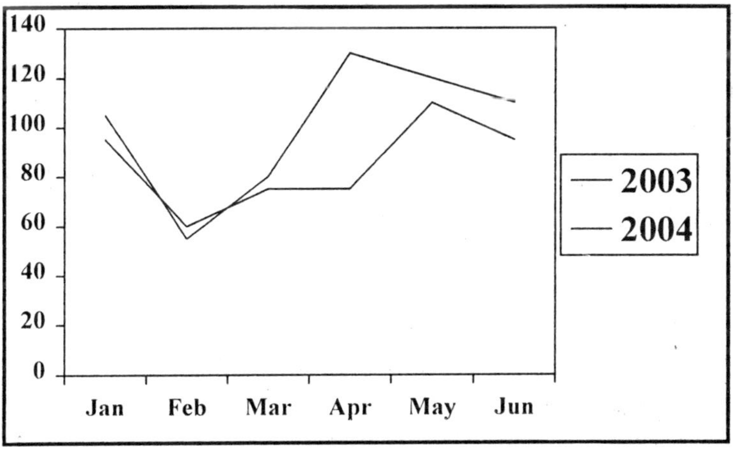

Source: Frontline 30 July 2004.

Graph No 4

Indian Forces Killed (Excluding SPOs)

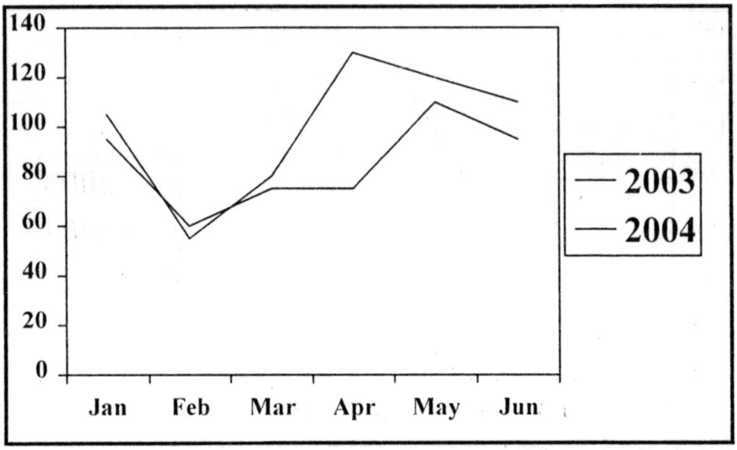

Source: Frontline 30 July 2004.

Graph No 5

Attacks on Civilians

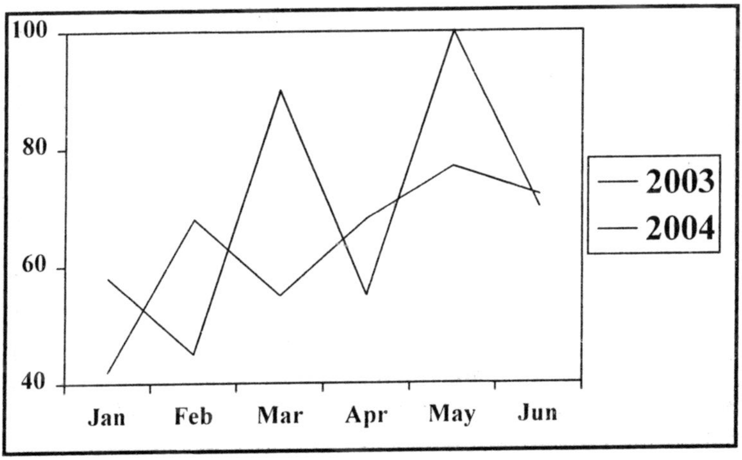

Source: Frontline 30 July 2004.

Graph No 6

Civilians Killed

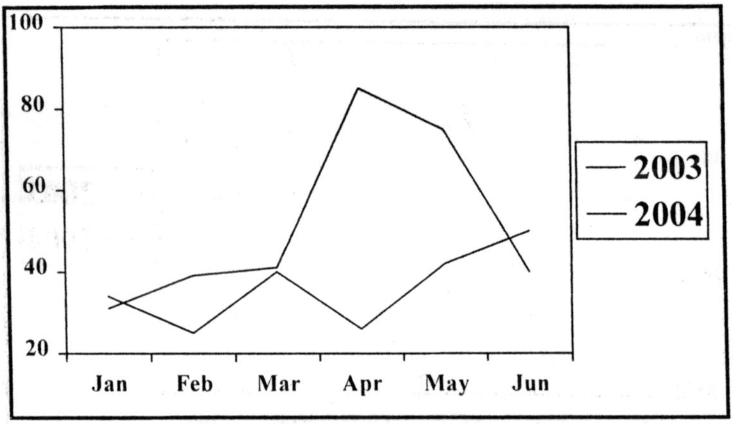

Source: Frontline 30 July 2004.

Graph No 7

Terrorists Killed

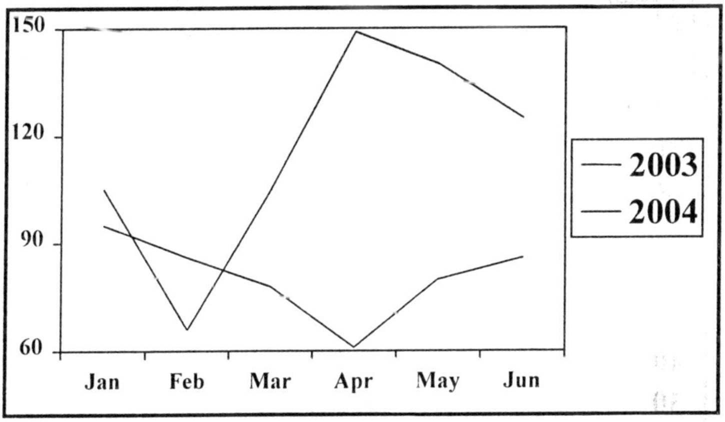

Source : Frontline 30 July 2004.

Graph No 8

Surge in Infiltration: 2004

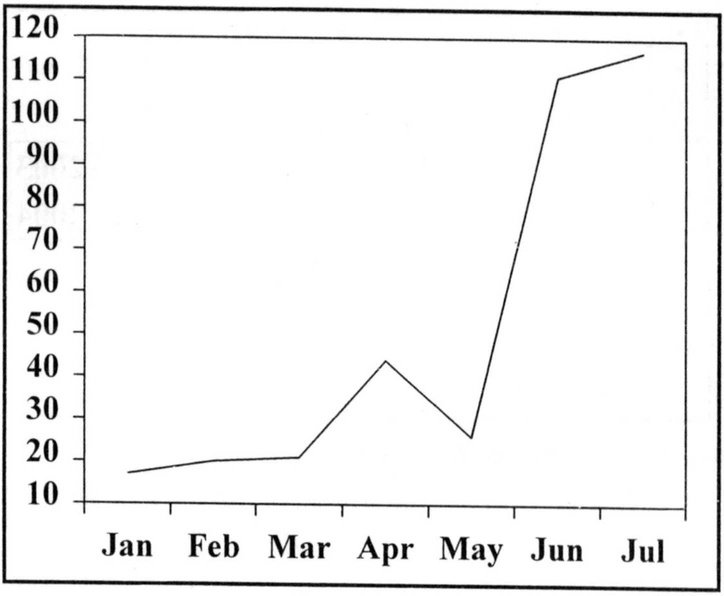

Source: India Today, 13 September 2004.

All figures are up to July 2004.

Note:

1. After the lull earlier this year, infiltration levels have sharply increased with more than 200 militants crossing the border in June and July.
2. A total of 1,587 incidents of violence till July 2004.
3. 479 civilians killed. 74 women and children were among the targets:

- Killed by firing -28
- Killed in blasts - 3
- By slitting throat - 7
- Injured in firing -21
- Tortured - 4
- Hurt in blasts -11

4. 48 moderate politicians killed. This includes 28 PDP activists, 11 NC activists and APHC leader Moulvi Mustaq who was killed on 29 May 2004.

Graph No 9

Graphical Representation of Tourists Visiting Jammu Region

Yatries Visiting Vaishno Devi Ji Holy Cave

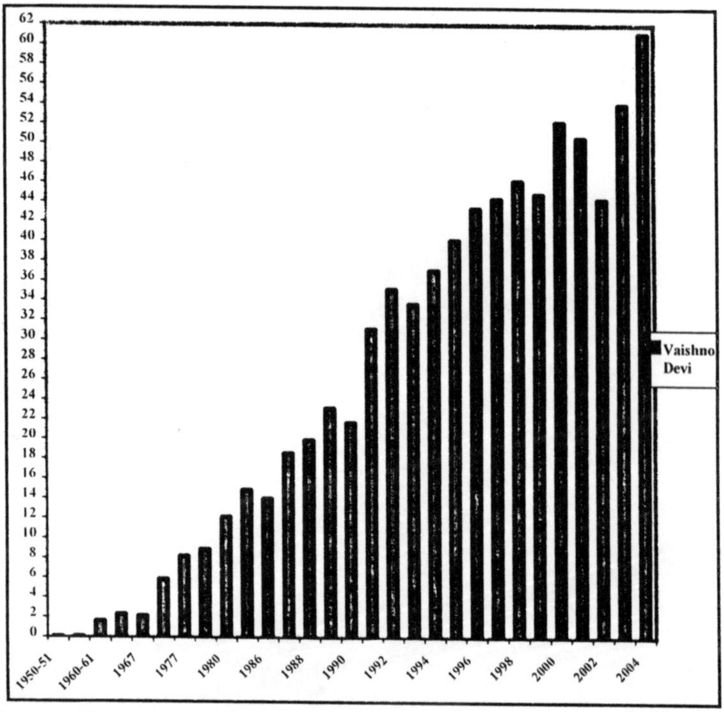

Source: Director Tourism, J&K.

Note: Y axis – No of pilgrims in Lakhs.

Graph No 10

Graphical Representation of Tourists Visiting Kashmir Valley

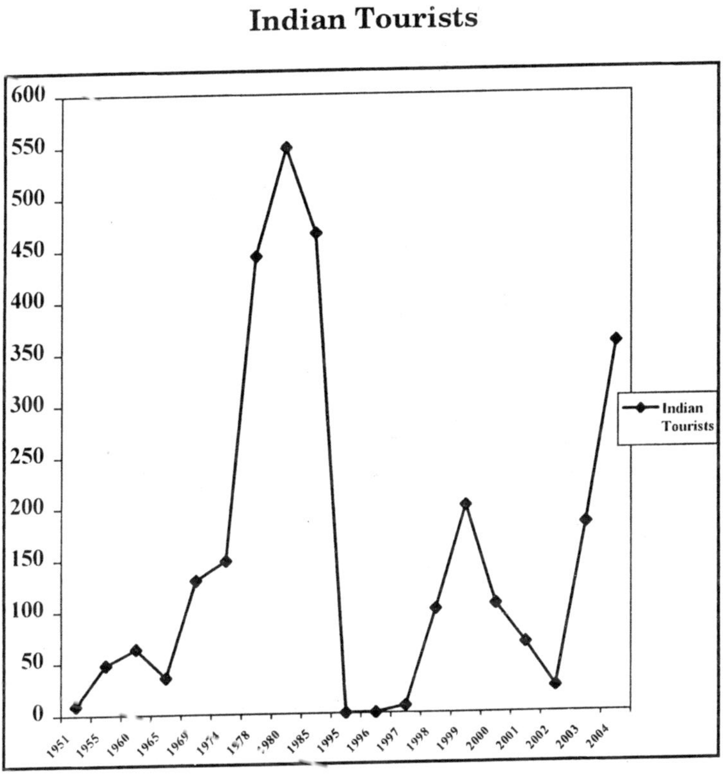

Source: Director Tourism J&K

Note: Y axis – No of tourists in thousands.

Graph No 11

Non Indian Tourists to Kashmir Valley

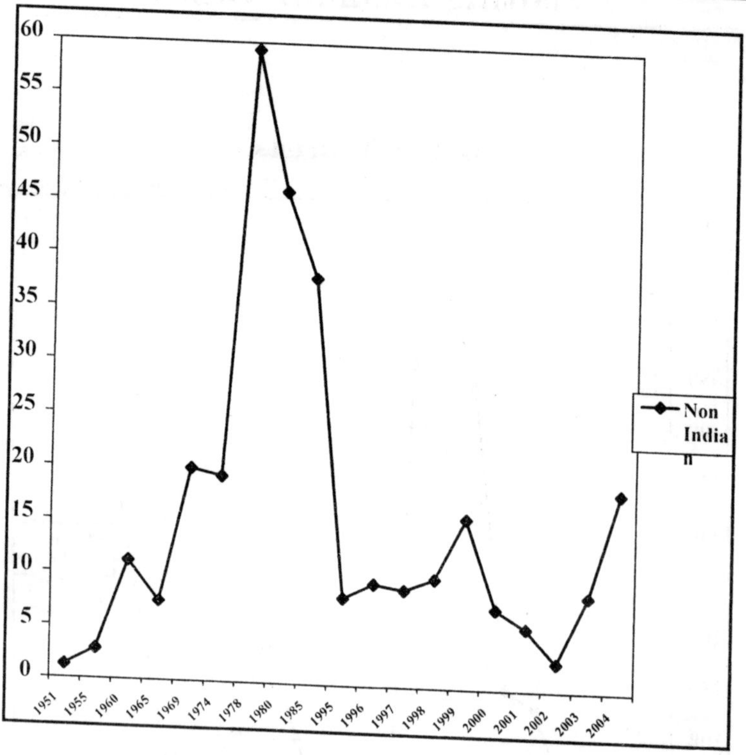

Source: Director Tourism J&K

Note: Y axis – No of tourists in thousands.

Graph No 12

Yatries Visiting Amar Nath Ji Holy Cave

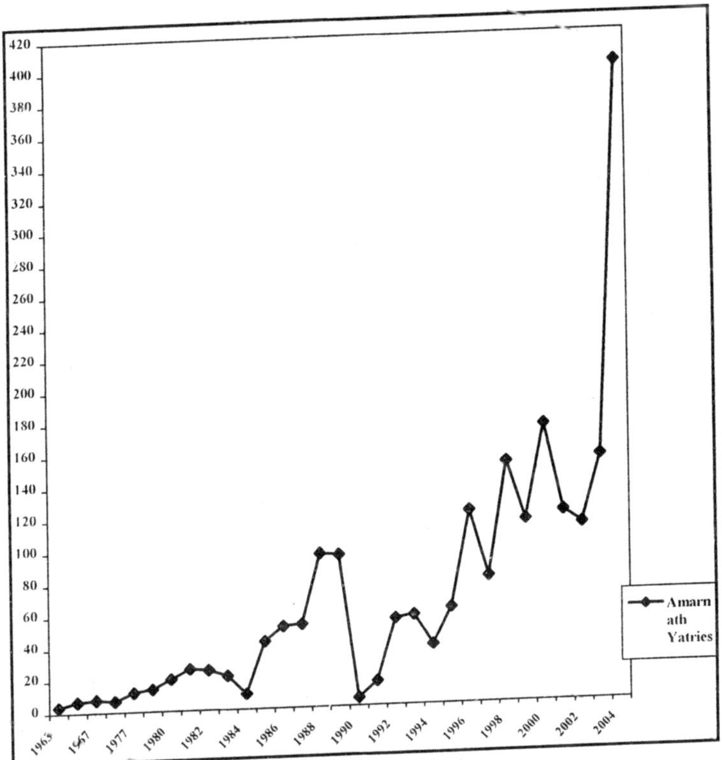

Source: Director Tourism J&K

Note: Y axis – No of pilgrims in thousands.

Graph No 13

Trends of the Tourists Inflow in Ladakh Region

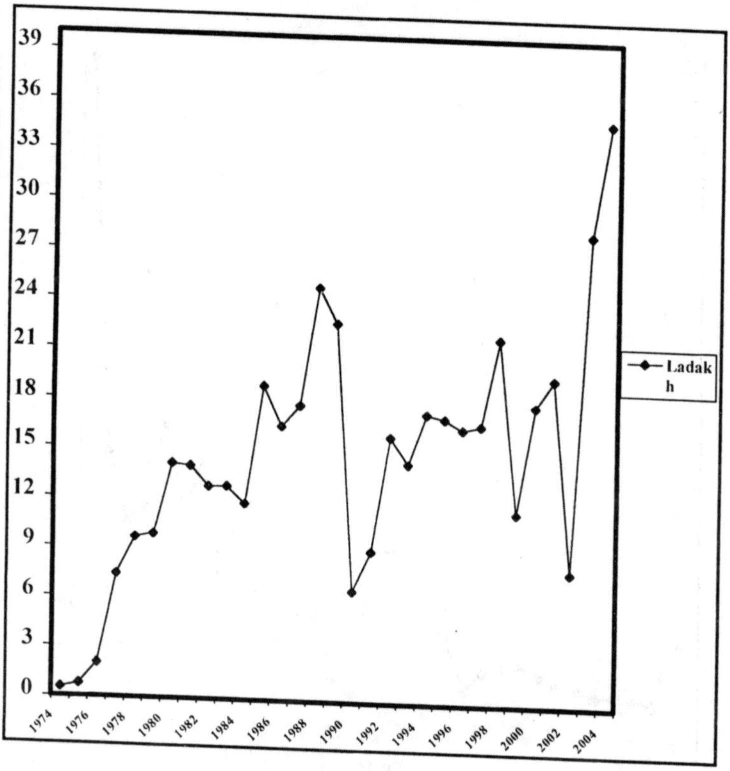

Source: Director Tourism J&K

Note: Y axis – No of tourists in thousands.

Bibliography

I Primary Sources

(a) Government Records

1. Army Liaison Cell, Army Headquarters, New Delhi, **Baatcheet,** September 2004 and November 2004.
2. Directorate of Information and Publications of Agriculture, September 2003, Government of India, **Hand Book of Agriculture**.
3. Govt of J&K, **Digest of Statistics 2001-2002**, Directorate of Economics and Statistics Planning and Development Department.
4. Institute of Defence Studies and Analyses, New Delhi , Vol 34, August 2004, The 9/11 Commission Report: Executive Summary, *Strategic Digest.*
5. J&K Tourism Department, **Kargil-Zanskar(Ladakh)**, January 2003.
6. J&K Tourism Department, **Jammu-You Won't Believe Your Eyes**, February 2003.
7. J&K Tourism Department, **For a True Jammu Experience**, 2003.
8. J&K Tourism Department, **Unforgettable Kashmir**, Feb 2003.
9. Ministry of Information and Broadcasting, Govt of India, Diary of National Events, **India-2003-A Reference Annual**, 2003
10. Publications Division, Ministry of I & B, " **Employment News 25 September-01 October 2004**", Vol 26, New Delhi.
11. Shri Mata Vaishno Devi Shrine Board, Govt of J&K, *Yatra- a Guide to the Holy Pilgrimage of Shri Mata Vaishno Devi Ji*, October 2003.

(b) News Papers/Magazines

1. **India Today**, 18 August 2003, 15 September 2003, 13 September 2004 and 29 November 2004.

2. **Frontline**, 17 January 2003, 18 July 2003 and 30 July 2004,
3. **J&K Reporter**, September 2003.
4. **The Week**, 24 October 2004 and 20 November 2004..
5. **The Indian** *Express(The Himalayan Mail),* Jammu.
6. **State Times**, Jammu.
7. **The Tribune**, Chandigarh.
8. **The Hindu**, New Delhi.
9. **The Times of India**, New Delhi.
10. **Daily Excelsior**, Jammu.
11. **The Kashmir Times**, Jammu/Srinagar.
12. **The Hindustan Times**, New Delhi.

II. Secondary Sources

1. Bakaya, N.L.
Holidaying and Trekking in Kashmir,
Navin Press, New Delhi, 1998.
2. Bakshi, S.R.
Kashmir Valley and its Culture,
Sarup and Sons, New Delhi, 1997.
3. Bakshi, S.R.
Kashmir: Tourism Monuments and Folklore,
Sarup and Sons, New Delhi, 1997.
4. Bansal, S.P. and Gupta Sunil
Tourism Towards 21st Century,
Deep and Deep Publications, Jammu, 1998.
5. Bloeria, Sudhir S.
Pakistan's Insurgency Vs India's Security,
Manas Publications, New Delhi, 2000.
6. Chomsky, Noam.
9/11, Natraj Publishers, Dehradun, 2002.
7. Crowther, Geoff.
India, a Travel Survival Kit,
Lonely Planet Publications, Australia, 1987.
8. Husain, Majid.
Geography of Jammu and Kashmir (Some Aspects),
Ariana Publishing House, New Delhi, 1985.

9. Karim, Afsir, Maj Gen
Counter Terrorism, The Pakistan Factor,
Lancer International, New Delhi, 1991.

10. Khurshid, Salman.
Beyond Terrorism: New Hope for Kashmir,
UBS Publications and Distributors, New Delhi, 1999.

11. Marwah, Ved.
Uncivil Wars- Pathology of Terrorism in India,
Harper Collins Publishers India, New Delhi, 1997.

12. Mehdi, Raza and Hanifa, Bano.
Declining Impact of Tourism Economy: A Case study of Dal Lake, Geography of Jammu and Kashmir: Some Aspects,
Compiled by Husain Majid, Ariana publishing House, New Delhi, 1985.

13. Nanda, K.K. Lt Gen
Conquering Kashmir–A Pakistani Obsession,
Lancers Books, New Delhi, 1996.

14. Nayar, V.K, Lt Gen
Threat from Within, India's Internal Security Environment,
Lancer Publishers, New Delhi, 1992.

15. Om Hari
Beyond the Kashmir Valley,
Har-Anand Publishers, New Delhi, 1998.

16. Padmanabhan, S. Gen,
The Writing on the Wall-India Checkmates America 2017,
Manas Publications, New Delhi, 2004.

17. Perera, Amrith Rohan.
International Terrorism,
Vikas Publishing House Pvt Ltd, New Delhi, 1997.

18. Prabhas Chandra
Global Eco Tourism, Codes, Protocols and Charters,
Kanishka Publishers and Distributors, New Delhi, 2003.

19. Rajiv, Rajendra.
World Famous Wars and Battles,
Kumar Family Books Pvt Ltd, New Delhi, 1982.

20. Ray, Arjun, Maj Gen.
Kashmir Diary –Psychology of Militancy,
Manas Publications, New Delhi, 1997.
21. Reddy, L.R.
The Worst of Global Terrorism,
APH Publishing Corporation, New Delhi, 2002.
22. Saharia, V.B.
Wildlife in India,
Natraj Publishers, Dehradun, 1982.
23. Saklani, D.D. Lt Gen
Kashmir Saga-A Bundle of Blunders,
Lancer Publishers-Spantech and Lancer, New Delhi/ London, 1999.
24. Schofield, Victoria.
Kashmir in the Crossfire,
Viva Books, New Delhi, 1997.
25. Sharma, D.P.
Countering Terrorism,
Lancers Books, New Delhi, 1992.
26. Sharma, Man Mohan.
Yatra. Pilgrimages in the Western Himalayas,
Trishul Publications, New Delhi, 1989.
27. Sharma, Suresh Kr and Usha.
History, Architecture and Tourism of Kashmir- Kashmir Through the Ages, Deep and Deep Publications, Jammu, 1996.
28. Sharma, Suresh Kr and Usha.
History, Architecture and Tourism of Kashmir- The Architectural Monuments of Kashmir,
Deep and Deep Publications, Jammu, 1996.
29. Singh, Harjeet, Col
Doda: An Insurgency in the Wilderness,
Lancer Publications, New Delhi, 1999.
30. Singh, Nagendra Kr.
Cultural Heritage of Jammu, Kashmir and Ladakh, Vol I, II and III,
Jay Kay Book House, Jammu, 1997.

31. Sood, V.K. Lt Gen and Sawhney Pravin
Operation Parakram : The War Unfinished,
SAGE Publications, New Delhi/London, 2003.

32. Vas, E.A. Lt Gen
Without Baggage-A Personal Account of the J&K Operations Oct 1947-Jan 1949,
Natraj Publishers, Dehradun, 1987.

33. Wright, Gillian.
Hill Stations of India,
Penguin Books, New Delhi, 1998.

III. Tertiary Sources

Web Sites

1. www.mastindia.com.
2. www.jktourism.org.
3. www.maavaishnodevi.org.
4. www.waragainstterror.com.
5. www.saag.com.
6. www.ipcs.com.

Index

A

Aby Nidal, 62
Achchbal—Symthan, 197
Adhoc Committee on International Terrorism, 72
Adkuwari, 130
Administration, 24, 88, 101, 108, 164, 169, 233
• Kashmir, 107
Advani, LK, 174
Afghan
• Mercenaries, 95
• Territory, 81
• War, 95
Afghanistan, 14, 51, 54, 63, 80-83, 87, 142
• Civil War in-, 82
• Mujahideen, 80
Africa and Middle East, 63
AGPL, 261, 263
Ahmad Omar Shaikh, 84
Ahmad Shah Masud, Tajik Commander, 81
Air India, 231-32
Airfields, 62
• Lod Airport, 62
• Rome, 62
• Tel Avives, 62
• Vienna, 62
Ajmer Sharif, 291
Akhnoor, 35, 118, 121
Al-Arifeen, 250
Al Jehad Militant Group, 87
Al Mansorian, 246
Al Nazreen, 174, 252
Al Omar, 84, 88
Al-Faran, 172
All India Hurriyat Conference (AIHC), 274
All India—Domestic Association, 299
All Jammu Hotels and Lodges Association, 182
All Party Hurriyat Conference, 172
Al-Mansuriyan, Militant Outfit, 174, see Al Mansorian also
Al-Qaida, 65, 84, 255-56
Amanullah Khan, 79
Amar Mahal Museum, 116
Amarnath (ji), 47, 132, 142-43, 197, 204
• Bhawan, 290
• Cave, 203
• Holy Cave, 139, 141, 143-44, 186
• Pilgrimage, 172-73, 206
• Shrine, 295
• Yatra, 139, 142, 176, 181, 195-96, 206, 210, 219, 229, 288-89
• Yatra Route, 315
• Yatri Bhavan, 290

America(ns), 50-52, 54, 64
American War Against Terrorism, 89
Amritsar—Lahore Bus Service, 269
Anantnag, 140, 172
Anantnag Dist., 197, 252
Annual Amarnath Yatra, 173
Ansar-ul-Islam, 76
Anti-Terrorist Operations, 65
Anti-US Attacks, 64
Architectural Monuments (Kashmir), 43
Armed Forces Special Powers Act, 169
Arms Act, 24
Arunachal Pradesh, 142
ASEAN (Association of South East Asian Nations), 72-73
Asghar Khan, Pak. Air Marshalls, 78
Asian Trade, 199
ASL Outer Hills, 35
Ateequllah Shah, 254
Attari, 271
Aul, AN, Maj. Gen., 216
Autonomous Kashmir, 276
Avantipur, 140
Awami League, 250
Ayodhya, 257
Ayodhya—Egypt, 255
Ayyengar, Gopalaswami, PM to Maharaja, 25
Azad Kashmir Resolution, 26

B

Baba Dhansar, 121
Baba Ghulam Shah Badshah Shrine, Jammu, 271
Babri Masjid, 80
Baghdad, 51, 255
Bagh-e-Bahu, 116, 118, 298
Bahadur Banda Bairagi, 121
Bahu Forest, 116, 118
Bahu Fort, 46, 185
Bah-ud-Din, 36
Bakshi, GD, Maj. Gen., 272
Bali, 255-56
Balidan Stambs, 290
Balkan State, 61
Baltal, 141
Baltal Route, 195
Baltistan, 34
Baltistan and Gilgit, 24
Baltistan Gilgit, 270
Banganga (Katra), 175-76, 203
Bangladesh, Formation of-, 31
Bangus, Dodhpathri and Mujpathri, 212
Bank of Japan, 66, 68
Baramulla, 39, 274, 282
Baramulla Dist., 29
Baramulla—Doda, 35
Bardan Monastery, 153
Bardhan, AB, 278
Barhanuddin Rabbani, 80-81
Barmullah and Uri, 292
Barsac and Medoc Type Wine, 39
Batote, 120
Bhat, Abdul Gani, 253, 279
Bhutto, Benazir, 79, 105
Bhutto, Zulfikar Ali, Pak PM, 31
Bihar and Andhra Pradesh, 14
Bijbehara, 254
Bodh Kherbu, 147
Bomb Blasts, 173, 253

British Indian Empire, 28
British Tourist, 204
BSF (Border Security Force), 94, 97, 99, 177, 246, 259
Buddha Amarnath, 123-24
Buddhism, 151
Buddhist(s), 33-34, 148, 200
- and Hindu Architecture, 43
- Culture, 35, 219
- Population, 146
- Temple, 149

Buddhists Saints, 149
Budhal, 35
Business Communities, 13

C

Cable Car, 191
Cable Car Project, 184
Camping, 146
Casablanca—Istanbul, 256
Ceasefire, 17, 29-30, 235, 245, 250, 273
Central Asia, 33, 44, 146
Centre for Environment Education, 299
Chechen Insurgency, 257
Chechen Rebels, 255
Chenab Basin, 119
Chenab Plan, 248
Cheshmashahi, 138, 143, 195, 198, 254
Chilas (Afghanistan Border), 34
China, 41, 103, 146, 154, 200
China and Pakistan, 30
Chinese, 33
- Aggression, 199
- Troops, 199

Chingus, 123-24
Choglamsar, Tibetan Refugee Camp, 156
Chopra, Vinod, Maj. Gen., 216
Chortens, 152
Christafeen, Oflore, Norweigian, 172
Christian Missionary School, 252
Civil Aviation Ministry, 195
Civil Liberties, 59
CMB (Confidence Building Measures), 249, 251
Convention Complex, 231-32
Conversions, 24
CPI(M), 278
CPI, 278
Cross-border Terrorism, 73
CRPF, 77, 97, 99, 178-79, 202, 226, 246, 253, 257
Cultural Pluralism, 73

D

Dal and Manasbal Lakes, 134
Dal and Nagin Lakes, 290
Dal Lake, 34, 39, 135-36, 138, 171, 178-79, 188, 193-94, 202-03, 218, 231-33 264, 283-84, 293-94, 300, 307
- Project, 300

Dardistan, 34
Dards and Buddhists Ladakhis, 144
Darhali, 35
Daughters of Nation, Women's Group, 88
Delhi Agreement, 181
Delhi—Kanniyakumari, 135
Delta, 99

Deobandism, 81
Developed Countries, 13
Dhanwantri Library of Univ. of Jammu, 20
Direct Action Resolution, 26
Dirges (Van), 43
Distance Education, 11
Distance of Towns from Jammu, 115
Districts of-, 98
- Anantnag, 98
- Badgam, 98

Della, 98
Doda, 98
- Pulwama, 98

Doda, 80, 95, 106
Dogra Art Gallery, 116
Dogra Art Museum, 46, 119
Dogra Rulers, 23, 46, 118
Donald, John Childs, 172
Dr. Sinha Gandhi, 27
Drang-Drung Glacier, 322
Dras, 149
Durand Line, 83
Dure Baha Banda, Hindu-Sikh Pilg. Centre, 171

E

Economic Development, 164
Economic Sanctions, 71
Economy, 112, 164
- American, 68
- India, 68
- World, 20, 66

Egypt and Iran, 283
Elections, 27, 31, 78, 92, 94-95
- In Kashmir, 31

Employment, 10
England and USA, 232
Ethnic Cleansing, 53
Europe Central Bank, 66, 68
European Economic Community (EEC), 72
Extradition Treaty, 268
Extremism, 114
Extremist Groups, 54

F

Farooq Abdullah, 31, 77-78, 255
Farooq, Mirwaiz Umar, 251, 275, 279
Fauna and Flora, 156-59
Federal Reserve Bank of New York, 66, 68
Federation of International Skiing Switzerland, 295
Fernandes, 93
Fidayeen, 84, 247, 254
Fidayeen Attack, 166
Fidayeen Suicide Attack, 175, 178
First World War, 61
Five-Year Plan (10 th), 306
Floriculture Centre, 198
Folk Tales of Kashmir, 41-42
Folk Tales, Dravidian—Kashmiri, 41
Forced Labour, 24
Foreign
- Mercenaries, 95, 99, 107, 251
- Terrorist Organization, 52-53
- Terrorists, 274
- Tourists, 219

Forex Market, 67
Forts of Reasi—Bashoti, 45

Forts of-, 45
France—Poland, 10
Frankfurt—Geneva, 232
Freedom-Fighters, 61
Fundamentalism, 91

G

Games and Sports, 192
Gandhi, Indira, 31
Gandhi, Mahatma, 28
Gandhi, Rajiv, 31
Gandhi, Sonia, 266, 281
Gangabal Lake, 45
Gas Pipeline, 268
Gauri Kund, 120
Geelani, Syed Ali Shah, 275
Geluks-Pa Sect, 153
Geneological Table of Dogra Rulers, 310
Gilgit, 34
Glancy Commission, 1931, 24, 26
Global
- Economy, 13
- Financial System, 67
- GDP, 10
- Labour Force, 10
- Tourism Agenda, 13

Golden Temple, 291
Golf Course, 135, 191
Gondola Cable Car, 296
Gon-Khang, 153
Govind Singh, 121
Great
- Himalaya Ranges, 142
- Himalayan Wall, 146, 149

Great Britain, 59
Greek Architecture, 43
Gujarat
- Border, 30
- Tourists, 298

Gulab Singh, Maharaja, 23, 25-29, 46, 118
Gulbagh Resort, 188
Gulf Tourists, 288
Gulmarg, 34, 134-35, 140, 187, 189, 191-94, 197, 207, 218, 286, 295-96
Gulmarg Cable Car, 163
Gulmarg Cabel Car Ropeway Project, 296
Gulmarg Development Authority (GDA), 191
Gulmarg-Gondola, 184

H

Hafiz Saeed, 90
Hafiz Syed Mohammad, 248
Handicrafts, 184
Harakat-ul-Ansar, Militant Group, 171-73
Haramukh, 132
Hari Parbat, 44
Hari Parbat Fort, 133
Hari Prasad, LG, 272-73
Hari Singh, Maharaja, 28-29, 77
Harkat-ul-Ansar, 63
Harkat-ul-Mujahideen, 83-84
Harvan, 44
Hazratbal, 17, 21, 206
Hazratbal Mosque, 233
Heli Skiing, 194
Hellslidt, D. Stockholm Convention Bureau, 231
Henaskut, 151
Highland Excursions, 194, 197

Hijackers, 65, 71
Hijacking, 69
Hikmatyar, Gulbuddin, 80-81
Himachal Pradesh, 211, 219
Himalayan Black Bear, 160
Hindu and Muslim Refugees, 28
Hindu Cave Shrine of Amarnath, 195
Hindu Population, 28, 112
Hindu Rajputs, 24
Hindus—Migration, 166
Hisbullah Islam Jamhooria, 76
Hizbul Mujahideen, 78-79, 85, 88, 95, 172, 235, 242, 250-51, 253
Holy Banganga, 122
Hostages, 69, 84
Hot Air Ballooning, 123, 194
Hotel and Restaurant Ass., 203
Hotel Chapter—Of India, 174
Hotel Corp. of India, 231
Human Rights, 9, 74, 103, 105
- Commission of Pakistan, 279
- Violations, 97, 102, 104

Hunzanagar, 34
Hurriyat, 274-76
- Conference, 279
- Leaders, 251, 275, 279

Hyderabad and Junagadh, 29

I

IC-814 Indian Airlines Hijack, 249
Immigration and Nationality Act (USA), 56
Immigration Check Post, 71
Imperialism, 61
IMRO (International Macedonian Revolutionary Organisastion), 61
India and Nepal, 14
India and Pakistan, 32, 102, 147, 215, 233, 235, 242, 245, 251, 261-62, 269, 276, 279, 326-27
- Border, 277
- Relations, 164
- Thaw, 291

India, Multi-Religious-, 28
India's Security, 18
Indian
- Aircraft IC-814, 84
- Airlines, 135, 154, 190, 288, 292
- Armed Forces, 33, 263
- Army, 29-30, 84, 90, 102, 154, 168-69, 216, 245, 272, 307

Independence Act, 28
- Kashmiri, 32
- Leadership, 86
- Mountaineering Foundation, 322-23
- National Congress, 25
- Security, 89
- Troops, 30
- Yogi Naropa, 152, 154

India-Pakistan
- Border, 205, 259
- Relations, 205, 260, 267, 278

Indira-Sheikh Accord, 181
Indo-European Round Table

Conference, 202
Indo-Iranian Culture, 36
Indo-Pakistan
- Dispute, 103
- Dialogue, 202
- Thaw, 208
- War, 1947-48, 17, 28
- War, 1965, 30
- War, 1971, 30-31

Infant Mortality Rate, 306
Infiltration, 32, 86, 90, 165, 169-70, 235, 242, 247, 251, 273, 277, 294, 358
Routes, 259, 343
Infrastructure Dev. Fin. Corp. (IDFC), 211
Instrument of Accession (IOA), 29, 77, 102-03
Insurgency, 9, 79, 91-92, 94, 96, 107, 213, 218, 248, 254
Intelligence Bureau Dept. of, 77
International
- Border, 31, 207, 258
- Boundaries, 9, 35
- Conventions, 70
- Golf Society Dubai, 289
- Pugwash Foundation, 215
- Security Operation, 93
- Terrorist Attacks, 61

Inter-State Council, 209, 232
Inter-Tanzeem Rivalry, 273
Intifada, 243-44
IOC, 103
Iran, Turkey and Saudi Arabia, 103
Iraq, 51, 255
ISI, 79-81, 83, 88, 91, 107
- Operation, 83

Islamabad, 91
Islamabad Council of World Affairs, 279
Islamic
- Monuments, 133-38
- Organization, 86

Israel, 51, 250
Israeli Tourists, 171
Israelis, 70

J

J&K, 9, 11, 14-19, 23-24, 30, 31, 33, 35, 38, 46, 69-70, 76, 79, 81, 85, 90-91, 106-09, 112-13, 118, 124-26, 132, 135, 163-65, 167-71, 177, 179-80, 185-86, 188, 192-93, 197, 201-06, 210, 212, 214, 216, 220-24, 229-34, 242-45, 247-49, 251, 253, 257, 259-60, 263, 265, 267, 273-76, 282, 286-88, 294, 298, 299-301, 306-309, 311, 337-38, 340
- Cultural Academy, 283
- Economy, 231
- Industries, 242
- Police, 77, 169
- Shri Mata Vaishnava Devi Shrine Act, 131
- State Division, 23
- Frontier Provinces (Dist. Ladakh, Gilgit), 23

Jammu Province, (Dist. Mirpur, Udh, Kathua), 23
- Kashmir Province (Dist. Anantnag, Bara, Muz), 23
- Terrorism, 15-18, 180
- Tourism, 11, 19, 156, 163, 201, 204, 206, 211-13, 217, 287

- Tourism Ministry, 307
- Tourist Development Corp., 117, 120
- Traders, 265
- Militancy in-, 76

Jaipur, 212
Jaish-e-Mohammad, 84, 86, 88
Jajjar Kotli,
- Amusement Park, 185, 186
- Tourist Camp, 121

Jalalabad Shura, 81
Jammu, 27, 33-34, 46, 80, 86, 99, 117-22, 174, 181-82, 196, 205, 231
- and Ladakh, 47, 105
- and Udhampur, 86
- Hotels and Lodges – Association, 297
- province, 45
- Region, 34, 106-07, 112-13, 164, 175, 181-82, 185-86, 217, 284, 298, 341, 360
- Tawi, 113, 177, 126
- Udhampur Rail Link, 286-87
- Udhampur, 184

Jammu, Kishtwar and Ladakh, 34
Jammu—Sialkot Road Highway, 261
Jammu-Udhampur Railway Line, 115
Januja, Asif Nawaz, Pak Army Chief, 93
Japan, 200
Japan Red Army, 70
Jaswant Singh, 84
Jawa, 41
Jawahar Tunnel, 285
Jehad, 18, 63, 89, 94, 248
Jehadi Groups, 276
Jehadis, 85-86, 88
JeM, 243, 249 see Jaish-e-Mohammad also
Jet Airlines, 135
Jews—Chinese, 36
Jinnah, Mohammad Ali, 28-29
JKCCCL (J&K Cable Car Corp. Ltd.), 209
JKLF (J&K Liberation Front), 32, 76, 78-79, 84-86, 93, 175, 189, 279, 340
- Activists, 171

JKTDC, 139, 189, 209, 295-97, 354
Joshi, BL, Gen., 94-96
Jugal Kishore, J&K Tourism Minister, 212
Jungal Gali, 122

K

Kabul, 63, 81
Kailas Mansarovar, 142
Kajik, 80
Kak, Ram Chandra, 44
Kaluchek Camp, 86
Kaman Bridge, 291
Kandahar, 84
Kanika Stupa, 152
Kanishka, 152
Kapur, Ashok, Lt. Gen., 235
Karachi Agreement, 262
Karakoram, 262
- Chain, 144
- Ranges, 35

Kargil, 33, 145-50, 152, 156, 200, 270
- and Leh, 199
- and Padum, 157
- Sector, 32, 83
- Skardu Road, 269
- War, 32, 83-84, 98, 149, 200, 219

Kargil-Zanskar Road, 322
Karn Damschen, 197
Karsh Monastery, 152-53
Kashmir Accession to
- India, 28
- Pakistan, 275

Kashmir, 23-29, 32-34, 36-41, 43-44, 46, 76-84, 85-92, 95-97, 103-07, 112-13, 132-35, 139, 141-42, 144-45, 155-56, 164, 177-79, 186-88, 192, 194-95, 208-13, 215, 219, 231, 234-35, 244-45, 247, 250, 253, 256, 259-60, 264-66, 276, 279-80, 288, 291, 295, 299, 306
- and Jammu, 34
- and Ladakh, 141, 148
- Arts and Crafts, 106
- Chamber of Commerce and Industry (KCCI), 297
- Cultural Festival, 287
- Delicacies, 117
- Folk Songs, 40
- Future, 26
- Handicrafts, 264
- Hotel Association, 297
- House Boat Owners Association, 174
- Jammu and Ladakh, 105
- Liberation Army (KLA), 89
- Militancy in-, 31, 170
- Movement, 88
- Present Status, 29
- Region, 112, 132-33, 164, 181, 186, 191, 217, 342
- Ruling Class-, 26
- Status, 31
- Tourism Industry, 202
- Tourism, 288
- Valley, Economy, 14
- Valley, Jammu and Ladakh, 163

Kashmir's Chief Languages, 36
- Dardi, 36
- Dogri, 36
- Kashmiri, 36
- Ladakhi, 36
- Pahari, 36
- Pakri, 36

Kashmir's Cultural Division, 36
- Baltistan, 36
- Dugar, 36
- Gilgit or Land of Dards, 36
- Ladakh, 36
- Mirpur, Poonch, Muzaffarabad, 36
- Valley of Kashmir, 36

Kashmir's
- Economy, 27
- Handicrafts, 141
- Silk, 142

Kashmiri
- Folk Songs, 42-43
- Broad Classification, 42
- Language, 40
- Militants, 87-88, 216
- Muslims, 96, 108
- Pandits Migrants, 215
- Pandits, 26, 78, 210, 253, 278

- Separatist Leader, 215
- Sharad, 36
- Women, 280

Kashmiris, 29-30, 36, 38, 43, 77, 84, 89, 90, 104-05, 108, 187-88, 215, 232-33, 249
- and Pakistan, 279
- Gulf Based, 187

Kasuri, Khurshid, Pak, 243
Kathmandu Conference, 215
Katra (Town), 197, 125-26, 129, 203, 217
Khalistan, 86
Khan Abdul Ghaffar Khan, 27
Khan, Ghulam Hassan, 281
Khan, Ghulam Rasool, 246
Kheer Bhawani Temple, 253
Khelsi, 147
Khir Bhawani Festival, 210
Khokhar, Riaz, 243
Khokrapar—Munebao Rail Link, 267-68, 270-71
Kidnapping of Foreign Tourists, 171
Kidnappings and Killings, 55, 62-63
King Lalithiadatiya, 282
King Partha, 45
Kogan, Mdm Claude, Swiss Climber, 322
Kolanor Glaciers, 139
Kongadour Slopes, 296
Korea, 200
Krimchi, 121
Krishna Ghati, 124
Krishna Rao, KV, Gen., 94-95, 100
Kud, 119, 122
Kulu-Manali (HP), 201, 204
Kupwara, 98-99
Kupwara and Tangdhar, 260
Kupwara Dist., 250
Kurdistan Workers Party, 63
Kushan Period, 44

L

Ladakh, 32-35, 112, 140, 146, 151, 155, 182, 198-99, 201, 205, 272, 286
Ladakh and Jammu, 181
Ladakh Region, 35, 112, 144-45, 201, 219, 231, 350
Ladakh's Wars, 155
Lahaul Spiti (HP), 35
Lahore, 30, 249, 271, 291
Lakes/Waterways Dev. Authority, 283-84, 294
Lakes/Waterways—, 300
Lal Mandi, 137
Lamayuru, 147
Language Riots, 30
Lashkar-e-Toiba, 63, 83-84, 86, 88, 174, 176, 243, 246, 249, 251
Latin American Guerrillas, 61
Lebanon, 70
Leh, 32, 98, 144-45, 148, 154, 199-00, 272, 286
- Airport, 144
- Gompa, 155
- Palace, 154-55

Liberation of Kashmir, 81
Libya, 70
Libya Plastic Expert, 70
Liddar River, 139, 143
Line of Control (LoC), 30, 32, 83, 90, 93, 97, 102, 109, 147,

149, 200, 207, 242-45, 251, 260, 262, 265-68, 275-76, 279
Literacy, 206
Lower Munda, 243

M

Madha Top, 122
Madhya Pradesh, 211
Madrasas, 82, 247
Madrid, 256
Madurai Kamraj University, 11
Mahabharata, 123
Mahajan, Mehar Chand, PM to Maharaja, 29
Mahamaya Temple, 118
Maitreya Sculpture, 146, 148
Majid Dar, 85
Makara—Half Bird, 41
Malaysia and Singapore, 213
Malik, Yaseen, 279
Manali, 205
Manasbal Lake, 140
Mangla Mala, 123
Manmohan Singh, PM India, 105, 179, 184, 234, 263-67, 275, 281, 283, 287, 328
Mansar Lake, 120
Mantatai, 120
Martand, 45
Masood Azhar, 90
Mass Communication System, 63
Mass Media, 19-20
Maulana Masood Azhar, 84, 249
Media Policy, 65
Mehbooba Mufti, 233, 297
Mendhar, 124
Middle East, 103, 190
Militancy, 9, 11, 18-19, 78, 86, 90, 93-96, 113, 169-74, 176-80, 187, 192-94, 198, 212, 217-18, 223, 234-35, 242, 248, 250-51, 254, 257, 291-94, 298, 300
- In Tourist Spots, 170

Militant Groups, 81, 164, 242
- Al Badr, 82
- Hizbul Mujahideen, 81-82

Markaz Dawa Al-Irshad, 82 (Lashkar-e-Toiba), 81
Militants Organization, 166
Militants, 18, 32, 60, 79, 87-88, 90, 93, 97, 99, 102, 104-07 165-66, 168-69, 202-05, 217-19, 233, 242, 244-46, 248, 250-51, 252-54, 258, 274, 280, 282
Mir, Ghulam Hasan, J&K Tourism Minister, 178, 183, 192, 196, 298-99
Mirpur—Kathua, 27
Mohammad Maqbool Shah, Freedom-Fighter, 245
Mohammad Yusuf Shah, 243
Mongolia, 41
Monuments in Srinagar, 312
Mountaineering, 146
Mountaineering in Ladakh, 322
Mountbatten, 29
Mubarak Mandi Palace, 46, 119, 298
Mufti Mohammad Sayeed, 32, 76, 196, 204, 213, 254, 265, 275, 288, 292, 300
Mughal Gardens, 208
Mujahids, 81, 83

Mulbek, 148
- Chhamba, 147-48
- Gompa, 148

Mulla Omar, 87, 89
Mumbai Bomb Blast, 86
Mumbai/Karachi Consulates, 268
Muney Monastery, 154
Mushtaq Zargar, 84, 88-89, 249
Muslim Conference, 25-27, 29, 103
Muslim League, 25, 28
Muslim Population, 35
Muslim United Front (MUF), 31
Muzaffar Hussain Baig, 282
Mystics of Kashmir, 37

N

Nagbal, 44
Nagin Lake, 138
Najibullah, Soviet Backed Pres. Afghanistan, 80
Nalanda and Taxila, 36
Nanga Parbat, 34
Nangali School, 124
Nankana Saheb, 291
Narasimha Rao, PV, PM, 94
Narendraditya, King, 44
Naro-Nasjal Festival, 153
Nation States, 9
National
- Conference, 25-27, 31, 244-45, 250, 274
- Liberation Movement, 64
- Winter Games, 193

Natural Calamities, 11
Naushera, 123
Nawab Sharif, 83
NCC, 96
Nehru Park, 136
Nehru, Jawaharlal, PM of India, 28-29, 77
Netherlands, 59
Niharika Yatri Niwas, 126
Nimmu, 147
Nishat Bagh, 138
Noori Chhumb, 123-24
North East, 14
North East and Jammu and Kashmir, 234
Notified Area Committee, 130
Nuclear
- Hot Line, 268
- Weapons, 57, 91, 103

Number of Militants Killed, 168
Nun-Kun, 322
Nunwan, 196
Nur Jahan, 140
Nurla, 147
Nusra, 286

O

Omasi-La, 154
Operation
- Badr, 83
- Enduring Freedom, 86
- Prakaram, 18, 168
- Rakshak, 169
- Sadbhavana, 216, 272, 301
- Vijay, 32

Organization of American State (OAS), 72-73

Orthodox Church Groups, 63
Osama Bin Laden, 54, 85, 87, 89, 256

P

Padmasambhava, 149
Padum, 152-53
Padum-Kishtwar Trekking Trail, 154
Pahalgam, 133, 142, 171-72, 174, 181, 184, 188, 190, 197, 203, 218-19, 286
  and Baltal, 288
  and Chandanwari, 173
  to Bisaran and Tulian, 184
  Tourist Traffic Movement, 188
Pakistan, 9, 18, 23, 25-33, 63, 70, 77-81, 83-91, 93, 95, 97-98, 102-05, 107-09, 163-65, 170, 172, 206-07, 214, 232-33, 235, 243, 245, 247, 248, 250, 257, 260-61, 263-64, 266, 268-69, 270-71, 274-76, 279, 291, 293
- Accession to-, 27
- and Afghanistan Border, 83
- and Terrorism, 47
- Army, 83, 168, 245
- Day, 27
- Diplomacy, 93
- Economy, 91
- Foreign Policy, 82
- Government, 69
- Muslim Majority-, 28
- Occupied Kashmir (PoK), 79-81, 87, 89-91, 93, 97, 107, 248-49, 265, 274, 276

Peace Coalition, 279
Pilgrims, 214
- Raiders, 78
- Sponsored Militancy, 164
- Sponsored
- Terrorism, 9, 164, 167
- Terrorist Incidents, 168
- Western, 23

Pakistan's
- Frontier Tribesmen, 29
- Military Movement, 32

Pakistani
- Currency, 96
- Intruders, 33
- Leadership, 27, 93
- Madrasas, 80, 81
- Nationals, 89, 171

Pashtun Population, 83
Policy, 89
- Troops, 30

Pakistani—Samiti, 270
Pakistan—Saudi Arabia, 81
Palanquin Services, 130
Palestinians, 51, 63
Palestinians Group, 72
Pampore, Centre of Kashmir's Saffron Industry, 139
Pan-Am-103, 64
Panchari, Hill Resort, 121
Panchtarni, 143, 196,
Pandrathan Temple, 45, 139
Pan-Islamic Nationalism, 31
Punjab and Haryana, 63
Para Gliding, 194
Para Military Force, 99-100, 234, 307
Parasailing, 122
Pari Mahal, 138
Parihasporo, 282

Parkachik Glacier, 322
Parks/Sanctuaries, 160
Partition, 278
Pasdaran-i-Inquilaabi Islam, 171
Pashtuns, 82-83
Patel, Sardar Vallabhbhai, 29
Pathankot, 121
Patni Top Hill Resort, 119, 286
Patni Top Mountains, 120, 122-123
Patni Top, 197
Patni Top—Mntalai, 184
Pawar, Sharad, 93
Payech, 44
PDP (People's Democratic Party), 212, 233, 244-46, 297
Peace Mission J&K, 214
Peaks, 323
Pearl Harbour, 52
Peer Baba, 118
Peer Khoh, 117
Penzila, 148, 150-51, 322
Pervez Musharraf, 83-86, 88, 90, 105, 109, 243, 264-67, 269, 275-76
Phugthet, 154
Pilot, Rajesh, 94
Pir Panjal, 132, 134
Pir Panjal Range, 34-35
Plebiscite, 30
Poma Glaski, French Firm, 191
Poonch, 23, 28, 216, 265, 267
- and Rajouri Dist., 281
- Revolt, 28
- Town, 124
Potala (Lhasa), 155
Princely States, 28
- Hyderabad, 28
- Junagadh, 28
- Kashmir, 28
Proxy War, 107
Pulwama, 253
Punjab, 93
Punjab State, 23, 69-70
Purmandal, 121
Purmandal Temple, 121

Q

Qatar Airways, 210
Quit Kashmir, 26

R

Raghunath Temple, 46, 116, 118, 123, 174-75
Raja Bahulochan, 46, 118
Rajan, Maj. P., 11
Rajasthan's Economy, 270
Rajiv-Farooq Accord, 181
Rajouri, 86, 98-99
Rajouri and Poonch Dist., 35
Rajouri-Poonch, 123
Rajput and Gujjars, 35
Ram Kund, 124
Ranbir Canal, 118
Ranbir Singh, Maharaja, 46, 117-18
Ranbireshwar Temple, 46, 116-118
Rangdum, 148, 150
Rann of Kutch (Gujarat), 30
Rashtriya Rifle (RR), 94-99
Rawalpindi-Srinagar, 45
Red Gompa, 155
Religious

- Extremism and Fanaticism, 53
- Extremists, 18
- Fanaticism, 18, 73
- Fundamentalism, 101
- Minorities, 79
- Shrines, 19

Resort System, 195
Rice Cultivation, 38
River
- Chenab, 118, 121, 245, 267
- Devak, 121
- Gambhir, 115
- Indus, 144, 155
- Jhelum, 133, 135-36, 140, 307
- Lingti-Tsarap, 154

Rafting, 146
- Stod, 153

Suru, 150
- Tawi, 46, 231, 298

Rodrigues, SF, Gen., 93-94
Rohtang Pass (HP), 219
Romeo Force, 271-72
RSS, 27
Rubaiya Sayeed Kidnapping, 76
Rusi-La, 149

S

SAARC, 72-73
- Convention, 70
- Nations, 295

Salal Dam and Lake, 121
Saltoro Ridge, 262-63
Samdari and Munebao, 271
Sanasar, 119
Sangram, 139
Sanjichhat Helepad, 130
Sankaracharya Hill, 137
Sanskar Gompa, 155
Sanskrit Inscriptions, 36
Saraswati Dham, 126
SARS, 210
Saspul, 147
Saudi Arabia, 51, 257
Saudi Exports, 188
Saudi Wahabism, 81-82
Sayed Bashir Ahmad, 281
Scott, Sir Henry (MG), 28
Second World War, 28, 52
Security Agencies, 71
Security
- Forces, 101, 113, 180, 214, 216, 218-19, 225-30, 233, 244, 249, 255, 353
- Measures, 14

Sen, Sushmita, 293
Separatist Movement, 79
Sha Baltes, 144
Shahdra Sharief Shrine, Rajouri, 123, 271
Shaivites, 121
Shakti Bhavan, 126-27
Shalimar Bagh, 138
Shankaracharya, 44
Sheikh Makhdom Hamza, Muslim Saint, 36
Sheikh Mohammad Abdullah, 25-29, 31, 78, 245
Sheikh Tahir, Kashmir Militant, 216
Shergol, 148
Sheshnag, 139, 143, 196
Shey, Summer Palace, 156
Shikara Owners Association, 174

Shiv Hori, 120
Shivaliks, 142
Shri Amarnath Shrine Board (SASB), 288-89
Shri Partap Singh Museum, 137
Shrine Board, 125-27, 130-31, 286
Siachen, 267
Siachen Glacier, 261
Siachen—Saltoro Ridge Region, 263
Sikh Agitation in Punjab, 30
Silk Factory, 290
Silk Route to China, 144
Silver/Golden Islands, 136
Simla, 31
Simla Agreement, 102-03
Sindh, 270
Singh, Ajai Vikram, 261
Sinha, SK, 164, 202, 211, 260, 288-89, 309
Skiing, 193
Society, 14, 17, 60, 101
Sodha, Hindu Singh, 270
Solar Steam Generation (Ladakh), 272
Sonamarg, 141, 145, 184, 197, 218, 286
Sonamarg—Gulmarg, 197
Soviet Missile, 70
Soviet Troops (Army), 80
Soviet Union, 30, 64
Special Award for Tourism, 212
Special National Tourism Award, 113, 164, 309
Spitok Gompa, 154-55
Sri Lanka, 10
Srinagar and Nagrota, 98
Srinagar Leh Route, 316
Srinagar—Khansbal Road, 44
Srinagar—Muzaffarabad, 188
Srinagar-Muzaffarabad Bus Service, 249-50, 267, 270
Stand Still Agreement, 28
State Academy of Arts and Culture, 36
State Forest Corporation, 166
Stone Temples at Avantipur and Martand, 44
Straw, Jack, 85
Sub-Sahara Africa, 103
Suchetgarh, 258
Sudh Mahadev, 120
Sufi Culture, 247
Sufi Music Festival, 282
Sufi Saints, 248
Sufis, 77
Sufism, 78, 247-48, 282
Suicide Bombers, 86, 255
Suicide Bombs, 58
Sulla Mohammad Shah, 36
Sundarbani—Sansar Route, 122
Super Powers, 9
Surankote, 257
Surinsar Lake, 120
Surjeet, Harkishan Singh, 278
Suru and Zanskar Valley, 322
Swiss National Bank, 66
Switzerland, 191, 197
Syed Salahuddin, 78, 85, 248, 250-51
Syria, 63

T

Takht-i-Sulaiman, 44
Taliban, 54, 81-84, 89
- and Pakistan, 82
- Resurgence, 51
- Talibanized
- Jash-e-Mohammad, 85
- Jehadis, 87, 99
- Outfits, 84

Tamil Nadu, 212
Tanda Army Camp, 203
Tangdhar, Kishtwar, Uri and Kargil, 195
Tariq Waseem Ghazi, 261
Tashkent, 30
Temples of Babore—Budhawar, 45
Territorial Army, 96, 216
Terrorism, 9, 11, 13-14, 16-18, 32, 50-51, 53-55, 58-66, 69-70, 72-74, 86, 95, 104, 163, 165, 179-80, 185, 204-05, 210, 224, 230, 233-35, 243, 255, 257, 274, 277, 300-01, 306, 309
- and Fanaticism, 54
- Combat, 72, 73
- Combating, 69
- Defence, 55-56
- Global, 17-18, 20, 50, 55, 168
- In Jammu and Kashmir, 17, 180
- International, 9, 13-14, 18, 20, 51, 54, 60-61, 63, 72-73
- Japanese, 62
- Nuclear, 65
- Political, 56
- Sikh, 62
- State-, 56
- Suppression of-, 70

Turkish, 62
- Unconventional, 62-63

Terrorist
- Activity, 56-57, 76
- Combat, 63
- Groups, 63, 65-66, 69, 72, 74
- Baader-Meinhof, 72
- Basque, 72
- Red Brigade, 72
- Incidents, 19, 63-64, 69, 167, 294, 351
- Movement, 86, 101
- Organization, 57, 60, 63
- Outfits, 9, 78

Tactics, 61, 53, 164
Training Camps, 248
Terrotists Bases, 97
Thakur, DD, 232
Thar Desert, 271
Tibet, 35
Tibetan
- Border, 34
- Buddhism, 149
- Clans, 219
- Plateau, 33
- Refugees, 112

Tirupati Balaji Shrine, 183, 217
Tiske Gompa, 156
Totalitarian Countries, 58
Tour Operators—India, 299
Tour Promoters, 14
Tourism, 9-11, 13, 16, 19, 106, 112-13, 156, 163-64, 179, 198-202, 204-07, 211, 217-18, 224, 226, 231-32, 234, 249, 271,

284, 287, 291, 298, 325
- Adventure, 122, 156, 190, 197
- Aerosports, 123
- and Travel Industry in India, 10
- Convention, 231-32
- Corporation of-, 212
- Domestic, 187
- Eco-Friendly, 195
- Economy in India, 10

Tourism, Industry, 10, 11, 13-14, 164, 230, 235, 284, 292
Tourism, Infrastructure, 197, 242
- International, 199
- Industry, 10-11, 13-14, 164, 230, 235, 284, 292
- Infrastructure, 197, 242
- International, 199
- J&K, 187
- Kashmir, 212
- Maharashtra, 212
- Punjab, 212
- Planners, 15
- Promotion, 113
- Religious, 271-72
- Sector, 282
- Skiing, 122

Trekking, 122, 141
- Winter, 192

Tourist
- Spots, 228-30
- Spot's Security, 227
- Statistics, 348

Traffic, 15
Travel Agents Association of Ladakh, 199
Travel Agents Society of Kashmir, 174
Travel and Tourism, 308
Travel Operators, 11
Trekking Routes, 317, 321
Trekking, 146, 172
Tribals, 28
Trikuta Hills, 119, 130, 175, 286
Tripura, 142
Tsa-Zar Monastery, 153
Tsunami, 11
Tungri, 153

U

Udhampur, 99, 106, 290
Udhampur and Doda Dist., 259
UK, 10, 103, 109, 279
UK and Australia, 204
Ulster, 70
UN (United Nations), 51-52, 72, 103, 109, 279
- Ceasefire, 29
- Commission for India and Pakistan (UNCIP), 29
- Mediation on Kashmir, 104
- Mission, 51
- Peacekeeping Force, 109
- Resolutions, 64, 103
- Security Assembly, 29

Union Tourism Ministry, 11
UPA Government, 243, 281
Uranium and Plutonium, 65
Urgyan-Dzong, Meditation Retreat, 149
Uri, Karnali and Baramullah, 282-83
US, 13, 51, 53-54, 56, 63, 65, 67-68, 80, 86, 102, 168, 172,

253, 257
- Attacks 9/11, 13
- Banking System, 66
- Citizens/Property, 58
- Embassies in Africa, 52
- Marines, 58
- Markets, 66

US, Great Britain, Germany, 172
USA/UK, 51
Uttar Pradesh, 211

V

Vaishnava Devi(ji), 19, 118-19, 124, 182, 217, 283, 286, 295, 299
- Cave Shrine, 183
- Pilgrims, 176-77, 203
- Shrine, 203
- Yatra, 175

Vaishnavi Dham, 126
Vajpayee Peace Initiative, 243
Vajpayee, Atal Behari, PM India, 265, 326
Valley, 146-47
- Batalik—Mushkoh, 32
- Chiktan, 146-47
- Dras, 146-47
- Himalayan, 33
- Kanji, 151
- Kashmir, 11, 14, 16, 33, 35, 45, 47, 101, 109, 112, 121, 133, 160, 174, 177, 180-81, 183, 186-87, 193-94, 197, 205, 214, 217, 219, 245-46, 278, 286, 293
- Liddar, 44
- Mushkoo, 146, 149
- Suru and Zanskar, 145-46
- Suru, 146, 149-50
- Tiger Hill, 146
- Toto-ling , 146
- Wakha River Valley, 148
- Wakha-Mulbek, 146-47
- Zanskar, 146, 148, 156

VDC Arms Training Camps, 258
Verinag, 136
Vienna and Milan, 61
Village Defence Committee (VDC), 107, 257-58, 259
- Arms Training Camps, 258

W

Wagah-Attari Route, 267
Wakha Rgyal, 148
Wall Street, 68
War Council, 27
Wazi, Abdul Aziz, 214
West Asia, 51, 53-55
West Germany and Italy, 59
Western Europe, 63
Wildlife Sanctuary, 159
Winter Games Federation of India, 295
Working Groups, 72
- Sweden, 72
- UK, 72
- Uruguay, 72
- USA, 72

World
- Bank, 245, 267
- Tourism Mart London, 213

- Tourists Organization, 179
- Trade Centre, 50-51, 64, 68
- Bombings, 64
- Travel and Tourism Summit, (WTTC), 210

World War II, 66
Wular Lake, 136, 140

Y

Yatra Registration, 129
Yugoslavia, 63

Z

Zabarwam
- Hills, 195
- Range, 188, 195

Zangla, 153
Zanskar, 33, 151-55, 286
- Group, 323
- Region, 200

Ziarat Chhotey Shah, 124
Zoji La, 141, 145
Zongkpul Monastery, 154